DR. MARY WALKER'S

CIVIL WAR

DR. MARY WALKER'S

CIVIL WAR

ONE WOMAN'S JOURNEY
to the MEDAL *of* HONOR *and the*
FIGHT *for* WOMEN'S RIGHTS

THERESA KAMINSKI

LYONS
PRESS

Guilford, Connecticut

For Charles,
for everything

An imprint of The Rowman & Littlefield Publishing Group, Inc.
4501 Forbes Blvd., Ste. 200
Lanham, MD 20706
www.rowman.com

Distributed by NATIONAL BOOK NETWORK

British Library Cataloguing in Publication Information available

Library of Congress Cataloging-in-Publication Data available

ISBN 978-1-4930-3609-7 (cloth : alk. paper)
ISBN 978-1-4930-3610-3 (electronic)

∞™ The paper used in this publication meets the minimum requirements of American National Standard for Information Sciences—Permanence of Paper for Printed Library Materials, ANSI/NISO Z39.48-1992.

CONTENTS

Not until this "cruel war" has ceased, and peace shall again be ours, and a dozen histories be written containing all the facts and events that each historian shall have collected, and the noble women from all be compiled, not, I say, until then shall the world know how much women have done.

—Dr. Mary Edwards Walker, 1863

INTRODUCTION:
"I WILL ALWAYS BE SOMEBODY"

ON APRIL 10, 1864, DR. MARY WALKER CLIMBED UP INTO THE FRONT of her horse-drawn wagon. She snapped the reins and started back to the Union encampment at Lee and Gordon's Mills in northern Georgia, near the Tennessee border. Spring had broken cold in this part of the country, and she was tired from a long day of treating civilians, whose medical care had been interrupted by the scattered warfare in the area. Before Walker reached the safety of the Federal stronghold, though, she saw Confederate soldiers heading toward her, weapons drawn.

The short and slender thirty-one-year-old native of Oswego, New York, was a Yankee in enemy territory. Raised to value independent thinking and liberty, Mary Edwards Walker had always been a radical. From childhood, she had embraced abolition, the most important political and social reform movement of the antebellum years—and the most controversial. She believed in women's equality, too, and had pursued an occupation in a male-dominated profession. Walker enrolled in the Syracuse Medical College in 1853, one of the few institutions that accepted women, and graduated two years later. She opened a private practice, mostly treating women and children, but her career took a different turn after the Civil War started in 1861.

Now, in the early spring of 1864, the doctor realized she had been taking a big risk. The area of northern Georgia in which she worked was unstable; after three years of warfare, the Union controlled only a small sliver. Georgia, joining with other states in the Deep South, had seceded in January 1861. Tennesseans, however, had been riven over secession since the firing on Fort Sumter three months later. It became the last state to join the Confederacy, and Unionist sympathy remained strong in many places, often provoking violence among its citizens. In late November 1863, Tennessee came under Union control, yet pro-Confederate guerrillas continued terrorizing anyone with Northern leanings. Though not in an active battle zone, nearby Lee and Gordon's Mills was a front-line location where some 580 Northern soldiers spent their days drilling and patrolling the camp's perimeter, on the lookout for any enemy movement.

Mary Walker arrived in this area during the fall of 1863, when it had been engulfed by the Battle of Chickamauga, one of the bloodiest clashes between Union and Confederate forces in the Western Theater. The battle was a key component of the Union Army's attempt to control strategic railroad lines and push into Georgia from Tennessee. It did not work. Major General William Rosecrans got his men back to Union-occupied Chattanooga, about fifteen miles north, but suffered significant losses. Of the 60,000 Union troops engaged, over 16,000 were killed, wounded, and missing or captured. Confederate general Braxton Bragg's 65,000 soldiers suffered more than 18,000 casualties, making immediate pursuit of Rosecrans impossible.

Despite Confederate efforts to retake Chattanooga in October and November of 1863, the city remained under Union control, thanks to the well-timed arrival of reinforcements and the strategies of generals Ulysses S. Grant and George H. Thomas. Though Thomas was an accomplished officer, he never became as well-known as Grant. Born to a slaveholding family in Virginia, the future general graduated from West Point in 1840 and became an army artillery officer. He saw action in the Seminole Wars and in the Mexican-American War, where he served with Braxton Bragg. Thomas returned as an instructor to West Point, then under the command of fellow Virginian, Robert E. Lee.

At the start of the Civil War, George Thomas chose country over state and remained with the Union Army, receiving rapid promotions throughout 1861. After commanding a brigade at the First Battle of Bull Run, he transferred to the Western Theater, where he participated in campaigns in Kentucky, Ohio, and Tennessee. Following the North's painful rout at Chickamauga, Thomas gained the nickname "the Rock of Chickamauga" for standing in the face of an overwhelming enemy, and succeeded Rosecrans as the head of the Army of the Cumberland.

Mary Walker met General Thomas at a battlefield hospital in Chattanooga during the fall of 1863. As casualties from Chickamauga streamed in, he observed her professionalism and efficiency as she juggled her duties: monitoring several wards, supervising assistant surgeons, and assisting in surgeries. Walker made a memorable impression, and not only because of her skills. She was attractive, with mahogany curls framing an open, lovely face. And she wore trousers. Of all the sights General Thomas had seen during the war, this would have been one of the strangest.

After Chickamauga, Thomas remained in the Tennessee-Georgia area with 60,000 men, laying the groundwork for General William Tecumseh Sherman's assault on Atlanta. When Thomas learned that the 52nd Ohio Volunteers' physician, Dr. J. A. Rosa, died in January 1864, he decided Mary Walker would make an ideal replacement. In March, Thomas signed her on as a contract surgeon, with a salary equivalent to a lieutenant: eighty dollars a month. She was the only woman to receive such a position during the Civil War. It had taken her two and a half years of hard work to get it.

Contract signed, Dr. Mary Walker reported to Colonel Daniel McCook Jr., stationed at Lee and Gordon's Mills. They were already acquainted. Like General Thomas, McCook first met Walker at the Chattanooga hospital, and he, too, noted her abilities. An Ohio native two years younger than Walker, McCook had worked in a Leavenworth, Kansas, law firm with William Tecumseh Sherman until the beginning of the war. McCook served with the 1st Division of the Army of the Ohio at the Battle of Shiloh in April 1862 before joining the 52nd Ohio Volunteers in July.

While McCook welcomed the new doctor to Lee and Gordon's Mills, his men proved less than enthusiastic. From their experiences, "woman" and "doctor" did not go together, and Mary Walker's arrival in the spring of 1864 shocked them. Not only did the soldiers believe a military camp was no place for a woman, they balked at the sight of one who walked around in public wearing the dark blue uniform of a Union officer, complete with trousers and a long coat. Only her long curls, visible beneath a serviceable hat, confirmed her gender.

The troops also griped that Dr. Walker spent too little time tending their needs, though in truth most who required attention suffered from illnesses rather than life-threatening wounds. At Colonel McCook's suggestion, the doctor started treating civilians in her spare time, even though this meant traveling into enemy-held territory. Cautious but undeterred, she packed two pistols along with her medical supplies and rode out with two orderlies. McCook frequently sent armed soldiers to accompany Walker, but he could not always spare the men.

Mary Walker preferred traveling alone. She was not oblivious to the risks; as a woman out on her own in isolated areas, she faced assault and/or murder. But she worried that the sight of uniformed Union soldiers flanking her wagon might frighten some people into refusing medical care. That concern did not extend to her own self-styled uniform. She was too proud to stop wearing it, even though its blue color advertised her association with the Union. Out on one of her escort-less trips, a couple of Confederate soldiers stopped her wagon, interrogated her, and then directed her to take the wagon into a nearby barn. Walker looked over at the structure and the stout fence surrounding it and knew that whatever the soldiers had in mind, it was not good. She refused to move the wagon, telling the two men she had a patient waiting for her, and, after conferring between themselves, they let her go on her way.

Dr. Walker reported the incident to Colonel McCook when she returned to Lee and Gordon's Mills. He and his officers listened carefully to her story, especially her description of the Confederate who seemed to be the leader. The men believed Walker had encountered Champ Ferguson, the most feared guerrilla fighter in the area. At the beginning of the war, Ferguson lived with his wife and daughter in the Cumberland Mountains in Tennessee, a place divided over the question of secession. Ferguson, a staunch supporter of the South, organized a pro-Confederate group of men and began attacking anyone who favored the Union. Though he did not officially belong to the Confederate Army, Ferguson operated with its approval, adopting the rank of captain.

The Union considered him an outlaw and a murderer. In December 1862, Major General Rosecrans had issued an order to the 1st Kentucky Cavalry to capture Ferguson, yet the guerrilla leader remained at large. Colonel McCook did not doubt Mary Walker's story, but he was skeptical of Champ Ferguson's. Ferguson vowed to kill every Union sympathizer he encountered, and McCook did not believe he would spare Walker simply because she was a woman. Moreover, Ferguson was known to be operating in Fentress County, Tennessee, about 138 miles north of Lee and Gordon's Mills. Still, any suspicion that Ferguson might be in the area was a piece of information worth passing up the chain of command.

That was the other reason Mary Walker took the risk to venture alone into Confederate territory. Colonel McCook had selected her as a contract surgeon because he knew she was willing to spy for the Union Army while she was out among the enemy. Walker's role as a physician provided a solid—but not foolproof—cover. Soon after her arrival at Lee and Gordon's Mills, the men of the 52nd Ohio Volunteers had figured out she was a spy.

Back in 1862, Mary Walker had offered to observe and report on Southern activities for the Union. She had already worked as a doctor in and around Washington, DC, which bordered the Confederate state of Virginia. Walker realized her profession could get her back and forth across enemy lines with ease. In September she wrote to the secretary of war, Edwin Stanton, saying that she would travel to Richmond under a white flag to treat wounded and sick Union prisoners. Using her own method of secret handwriting, she would then "give you information as [to] their forces and plans and any important information." The doctor also volunteered to undertake whatever "secret service" Stanton needed. That phrase signaled she knew about Allan Pinkerton's creation, at the direction of President Abraham Lincoln, of the Secret Service that gathered intelligence on the Confederate military.

Now, in 1864, with preparations under way for General Sherman's Atlanta Campaign, General Thomas knew Mary Walker could obtain useful information for the Union Army. She proved willing and fearless in the field, but she had a finite amount of luck. On April 10, some picket guards with Confederate general Daniel Harvey Hill's command stopped Mary Walker as she traveled back to Lee and Gordon's Mills from one of her medical missions. Hill and his men had participated in the Battle of Chickamauga and remained in the vicinity with the Army of Tennessee, looking for any opportunity to force out the Union Army. When the guards saw Mary Walker's uniform, they questioned her about her activities. Nothing she said convinced them that she did not have an ulterior motive for being in Confederate territory. At gunpoint, they took her prisoner.

⌒⌒

"I will always be somebody."

During a time when women were expected to be deferential and domestic, Mary Edwards Walker fashioned herself into a well-known, important person. This is the story of how she accomplished that through her involvement in two major events of the nineteenth century: the Civil War, and the women's rights movement. It is also the story of how and why, because of her radical ideas, she has been written out of history.

The great wave of reform that engulfed central and western New York State in the first half of the nineteenth century deeply affected Mary Walker as she came of age. Especially intrigued by the link she saw between women's health and women's rights, she promoted dress reform and enrolled in medical school. Because of her commitment to abolition and the preservation of the Union, she worked as a doctor for the military during the Civil War. That job sometimes put her in dangerous situations, and she spent time as a Confederate prisoner of war. Mary Walker's astonishing wartime exploits earned her the Congressional Medal of Honor, the only woman ever to receive the award.

Though this book spans Mary Walker's entire life, it is not a traditional cradle-to-grave biography. It is, instead, a way to delve into the histories of the Civil War and the campaign for women's rights, especially suffrage, in a fresh way. Through Mary Walker, we see the Civil War through the actions of a woman as involved in the war as a woman could be. Though it is true that perhaps a few hundred women disguised themselves as men to fight as soldiers, Walker never intended to hide who she was. She believed that as a woman, she was entitled to perform the work she chose, and that while engaged in that labor, she was entitled to the same treatment as a man. This belief fueled her pursuit throughout the war for a military commission—an officer's rank with commensurate pay and authority.

Since the United States military denied Mary Walker a commission because she was a woman, her experiences during the Civil War are those of an "inside outsider." Initially, she volunteered her services to work within the male bastion of military medicine, and she persisted long enough to receive a paid position with the army as a civilian doctor. As a woman and a civilian, Dr. Walker remained an outsider even when she worked alongside military physicians.

Mary Walker had a similar inside outsider status with the women's rights movement. She worked tirelessly to promote gender equality, but her ideology and methods marginalized her from the mainstream movement and earned her a reputation as a radical. Elizabeth Cady Stanton and Susan B. Anthony, Walker's contemporaries—and, on occasion, colleagues—tried to control the movement's message and public image. Anyone who did not conform was marginalized. Mary Walker did not fit, and she refused to compromise or back down.

What made Mary Walker a radical in the eyes of women like Stanton and Anthony was her prioritization of dress reform as the key to women's rights. The doctor believed contemporary female fashions—layers of restricting undergarments and floor-sweeping skirts—harmed women's health and physically prevented them from keeping up with men. As long as women could not or would not change what they wore, they would never achieve equality with men. While in her twenties, Walker began wearing some version of what was known as the "Bloomer costume." (Editor and publisher Amelia Jenks Bloomer was so devoted to dress reform that its most well-known style—a shortened dress over a pair of trousers—was named for her.) Mary Walker refused to give it up even after Stanton and Anthony decided it was not a primary objective of the women's rights movement.

Mary Walker also clashed with movement regulars over women's suffrage. They all supported women's voting rights, but sharply differed on how to achieve them. Stanton and Anthony began their suffrage work by attempting to convince individual state legislatures to grant women the right to vote, then put their efforts behind securing a constitutional amendment. Walker believed that since women were citizens of the

United States, the Constitution already guaranteed their suffrage. All women had to do was show up at the polls and vote, a tactic the suffrage movement called the New Departure. She persisted in this belief despite the Supreme Court's 1875 decision in *Minor v. Happersett* that rejected this interpretation.

"She persisted." That is a familiar phrase today, a rallying cry for women struggling for gender equality. Throughout her life, Mary Walker persisted, never compromising her beliefs simply to fit in. And she made those beliefs public. For years, Walker's writing on women's rights appeared in a reform journal, *The Sibyl*. In 1871, she published a book titled *Hit: Essays on Women's Rights*, covering topics ranging from love and marriage to temperance. An 1873 petition the doctor made to Congress, called the "Crowning Constitutional Argument," presented her legal reasonings over women's suffrage, and was later published as a pamphlet, in 1907. Her second book, *Unmasked, or the Science of Immorality*, came out in 1878.

These sources, coupled with extensive newspaper coverage of Mary Walker's activities and government documents, make it easy to track the public side of her life. Less clear is the personal side. She did not keep a journal or diary. Like her contemporaries, she wrote letters, but most of those have not survived. She kept correspondence from others, which provides one-sided glimpses of her conversations with friends, family members, patients, and fellow reformers. Consequently, the gaps in her story have been filled in with the narratives of other women in similar circumstances. This helps to create a more nuanced interpretation of Mary Walker's life and a more richly textured history of her times. Above all, the life of this radical, persistent doctor shows women's place in the historical record, and proves that all history is women's history.

CHAPTER ONE

Getting to Washington

IN THE EARLY FALL OF 1861, DR. MARY WALKER, A TWENTY-NINE-
year-old dedicated reformer and passionate supporter of the Union, went
to Washington, DC. The Civil War, which had begun because of white
Southerners' fears about the election of Abraham Lincoln in November
1860, was five months old. Lincoln, an Illinois Republican, was a committed Free-Soiler—an opponent of the expansion of slavery into the
Western territories of the United States. White Southerners worried he
was also an abolitionist, and despite Lincoln's reassurances during the
tumultuous 1860 campaign season, they remained convinced that if he
became president, he would end slavery throughout the United States.

Determined to protect their peculiar institution, Southern states
began withdrawing from the Union in December 1860. In early 1861,
the secessionist states formed the Confederate States of America, wrote a
constitution, and raised an army. Nothing Lincoln said could get them to
change their minds. The first military confrontation came five weeks after
Lincoln's inauguration. Confederate forces fired on the Union installa-
tion at Fort Sumter, South Carolina, on April 12, 1861. The fort quickly
surrendered. The president called up 75,000 militiamen for ninety days of
Federal service; the Confederacy had already signed up 60,000. Each side
figured they could whip the other in a matter of days, but now, as Mary
Walker headed to Washington, DC, nearly half a year had gone by with
no resolution.

Like most Americans, North and South, the doctor paid close attention to these developments. It was an astonishing thing, this unraveling
of the Union. But for Walker, raised in west central New York State by

parents deeply involved in a variety of antebellum reform causes, including abolition, the war offered possibilities for significant changes in the United States. And as she also understood, a person's ability to contribute to that effort was based on gender and race. White men could demonstrate their patriotic loyalty by putting on uniforms and picking up weapons. Their claim to citizenship was that clear: They could vote; they could fight in a war.

Black men experienced more difficulties. Lincoln's Union government proved ambivalent about signing them for active military service. African Americans who tried to volunteer after Fort Sumter found themselves turned away from recruitment offices. In Cincinnati, a white man bluntly informed a black man, "This is a white man's war." It was not, though, and black men knew it. As much as the Northern government promoted its goal of preserving the Union, African Americans understood from the beginning that the war would end slavery. Still, not until mid-1862, when it took the first steps toward abolition, did the Union government overturn a 1792 law forbidding black men from bearing arms in the US military.

The war also propelled women into action. In addition to raising troops, the Union had to make sure they were outfitted and supplied, a massive undertaking for which it was unprepared. But Northern women were. For generations, black and white women had organized themselves in their communities, often through churches, to address a variety of charitable concerns, ranging from providing food and shelter for widows and orphans to "rescuing" prostitutes from their way of life. After Fort Sumter, women applied this expertise to the war effort. Author Louisa May Alcott captured this spirit with the main character in her book, *Hospital Sketches*, who declared, "I *want* something to do."

The women of Bridgeport, Connecticut, felt the same, and on April 15, 1861, they created the first recorded ladies' aid society to benefit Union soldiers. Within weeks, hundreds of these groups, staffed by thousands of women who wanted to do something, sprang up in Northern cities and towns. Also known as soldiers' aid or relief societies, the local groups consisted of women of all ages who used their family and social connections to collect a variety of supplies—including food, clothing, bedding, and hospital items—and deliver them to soldiers from their communities. Over the four years of the war, hundreds of thousands of women, both black and white, participated.

The Union could not afford to pay women for this work. Instead, their donated labor was encouraged and portrayed as a selfless extension of their domestic duties. It was also promoted as temporary. Once the war ended, women would return to their traditional roles in the home. This understanding served as a barrier to anyone who tried to use the war to disrupt gender boundaries. Louisa May Alcott demonstrated her acceptance of this dynamic when she wrote in her diary, "I long to be a man; but as I can't fight, I will content myself with working for those who can."

Dr. Mary Walker embraced part of this sentiment. She never wanted to be a man and fight in the war, but she intended to help those, both men and women, who did. Like the women who organized the soldiers' aid societies, Walker believed she had a duty to contribute to the war effort. Unlike most of those women, she had a specialized skill to offer, and she had her own ideas about how to make the best use of it. But she needed to make one big change in her life before she could head to Washington to do it.

———

At the start of the war, Mary Walker lived in Rome, New York, a prosperous canal town of about 3,600 people located over two hundred miles northwest of New York City. She practiced medicine there, initially along with her husband, Albert E. Miller. The two met in medical school in Syracuse. They were nearly the same age, and like Walker, Miller had grown up on a farm—first in Covert, New York, then in Virgil, about forty miles south of Syracuse. He was smart and charming and had interest in the many reforms that swept the antebellum United States. Walker believed she had found a kindred spirit. They married in November 1855, nine months after receiving their medical degrees.

The minister Mary Walker selected to preside over her marriage ceremony shared her dedication to abolition and women's rights. Samuel J. May, an 1820 graduate of the Harvard Divinity School and the uncle of Louisa May Alcott, was a prominent minister in the Unitarian Church.

Emphasizing the moral teachings of Jesus Christ and committed to putting this ideology into action, Unitarians were among the most devoted participants in social reform. In the 1830s, May joined the abolitionist movement, serving as a lecturer for the New England Anti-Slavery Society. He eventually accepted a position at the Unitarian Church of the Messiah in Syracuse, New York, about forty miles south of Mary Walker's hometown of Oswego. There, May's abolition work expanded to assisting the Underground Railroad, which moved enslaved people from the South to freedom in the North.

The Reverend Samuel May started promoting women's rights with his November 1845 sermon, "The Rights and Condition of Women," which was subsequently printed and widely circulated. Beginning with quotes from Genesis ("In the day that God created man, in the likeness of God made he him; male and female created he them; and blessed them, and called their name Adam") and Galatians ("There is neither male nor female, for ye are all one in Christ Jesus"), he called for gender equality and women's suffrage.

Mary Walker's parents had lived in Syracuse for ten years before she was born, and she later attended medical school there, so it is not surprising she knew Samuel May. Since she likely had read and admired his sermon about women's rights, she asked him to perform the wedding ceremony on November 16, 1855, in her family home in Oswego. Knowing the young woman as they did, the guests would not have been surprised to find Samuel May officiating. Nor would they have been startled to see the bride and groom wearing similar attire. Walker donned an elegant version of the Bloomer costume for the occasion.

What may have caused a few murmurs was the Reverend Mr. May's omission of the word "obey" from the marriage vows, done at Mary Walker's request. Within this circle of abolitionists and women's rights advocates, the alteration was unusual but not unheard of. Elizabeth Cady—the cousin of Oswego's most prominent citizen, well-known abolitionist, Gerrit Smith—also left the word out during her wedding to Henry Stanton in 1840. The exclusion may have originally been Stanton's idea. In 1838, he attended the nuptials of two abolitionists, Theodore Weld and Angelina Grimké, who had declined to use the word. Given Elizabeth

Cady's interest in women's rights issues, it is likely that Stanton described those vows to her and suggested they do the same.

Six months before the Walker–Miller wedding, a leading women's rights and abolitionist lecturer named Lucy Stone also left out all references to obedience during her wedding to Henry Blackwell. The details of that ceremony had been widely publicized, including coverage by the influential abolitionist paper, *The Liberator*. Mary Walker already knew about Blackwell and his older sister. Just a few years earlier, Elizabeth Blackwell had become the first woman to earn a medical degree in the United States, and went on to found the New York Dispensary for Poor Women and Children in 1853.

Mary Walker drew inspiration from these women, especially those in the Stone-Blackwell family. Like Lucy Stone, Walker kept her maiden name, though she sometimes preceded it, unhyphenated, with her husband's last name. Like Elizabeth Blackwell, she focused her career on medical care for women and children. Mary Walker and Albert Miller approached marriage as a personal and professional partnership. When Walker joined Miller's medical practice in Rome, the couple put up a new sign—Miller and Walker, Physicians—but they worked out of separate offices. Deeply concerned about women's health issues, in 1859 Walker urged the state of New York to set up a foundling hospital to care for unmarried women and their children. Such a facility, Walker argued, would drastically cut the number of abortions that these women sought.

This could have been part of Mary Walker's strategy for furthering her own career. An institution catering to women and children, she may have assumed, would need a person with her qualifications and experiences to run it. The doctor found the cause so compelling that she chose to write about it. In the mid-nineteenth century, this was a daring topic for public discussion. Unwed motherhood raised the specter of illicit sex. Victorians believed that intimate relations belonged within the sanctity of marriage, mostly for the purpose of procreation. Birth control was unreliable and generally considered disreputable. But Dr. Walker understood how pregnancy and childbearing affected women's health, and believed that continued ignorance about them imperiled women.

The Sibyl: A Review of the Tastes, Errors and Fashions of Society published her article about the foundling hospital in its August 1859 issue. The doctor crafted the piece as "a hastily written whisper to every woman," and described the proposed institution as a "necessary evil." From such a place, "innocent" babies could be adopted, and their mothers "could go out and sin no more" once they had recovered from childbirth. Mary Walker signed off with a dramatic, "Yours in every woman's cause."

This article represented another facet of Dr. Walker's career: writing. She wrote because she considered it the best way to circulate her ideas and ensure that she would become well known enough to become a somebody. Many of her writings promoted her views on health, medicine, and women's rights. The crucial link between them was dress reform. In 1856 the doctor joined the Dress Reform Association (DRA) that organized in central New York to promote "reform in women's dress, especially in regard to long skirts, tight waists and all other styles and modes which are incompatible with good health, refined taste, simplicity, economy and beauty." The following year, she began writing for the DRA's official publication, *The Sibyl*.

The periodical had been launched by John Whitbeck Hasbrouck, editor of the *Middletown Whig Press*, and his wife, Dr. Lydia Sayer Hasbrouck, an avid dress reformer. Five years older than Mary Walker, Lydia Sayer was born to a farming family in Warwick, New York. In her early twenties, she became interested in health issues and began wearing reform dress. Determined to prepare for medical school, Sayer tried to enroll in the Seward Seminary in Florida, New York, about sixty miles north of her hometown. The school refused to admit her unless she resumed wearing a dress, and she declined to give up her bloomers. Sayer's treatment by the Seward faculty, she later recalled, "anchored me in the ranks of women's rights advocates, and as I left that house I registered a vow that I would stand or fall in the battle for women's physical, political and educational freedom and equality."

Lydia Sayer instead attended the Elmira Collegiate Seminary, an academically rigorous institution that offered a curriculum equal to those at men's colleges. Around 1853, Sayer moved to New York City and enrolled in Dr. Russell Trall's new Hygeio-Therapeutic College, located at

15 Laight Street. Originally an allopath—a nineteenth-century term for a physician who practiced evidence-based or "modern" medicine—Trall had come to embrace hygiene as the most effective method for treating patients. His college's program, which admitted about an equal number of men and women, awarded an MD upon completion. Its curriculum centered on what was known as "eclectic" medicine, emphasizing hydrotherapy, hygiene, exercise, and diet to promote health and treat illness. The school's students also participated in clinics at Bellevue Hospital. When Lydia Sayer finished her degree, she opened a medical practice in Washington, DC, and began lecturing and writing about hydrotherapy and health issues.

In 1856, John Hasbrouck invited Lydia Sayer to give a series of lectures in Orange County, New York. Her arrival coincided with the creation of the DRA, which she joined. Impressed with Sayer's commitment to health and dress reform as well as with her writing talent, Hasbrouck helped her start *The Sibyl* in July 1856. Hasbrouck and Sayer married a few weeks later, with the bride decked out in a white Bloomer costume.

Lydia Hasbrouck and Mary Walker developed a close friendship based on common interests. During the first year of *The Sibyl*'s publication, Hasbrouck wrote most of its articles, but she soon decided Walker would make an excellent contributor. Other female doctors regularly wrote for the magazine, including Fidelia Harris, Ellen Beard, and Harriet Austin. Mary Walker's first piece, in which she was identified as "a lady physician from Rome [New York]," appeared as a letter to the editor in January 1857. She described an upcoming dress reform convention in Canastota, New York: "We expect there will be a good attendance of those who are richly provided with common sense, intelligence, and decision of character." Walker herself planned to be among the attendees, accompanied by "several very liberal persons in this place."

In the next issue, Lydia Hasbrouck gave Mary Walker her "warmest thanks for her promptness and kindness" in delivering a timely account on the Canastota convention. In her recap, Walker reported on the reading of a letter from Elizabeth Cady Stanton, Gerrit Smith's participation in the business committee, and her own presentation. "Dr. Miller Walker of Rome later spoke to the advantages of short dress," and closed her speech by pointing out the women at the conference who wore model outfits. Walker's participation in the DRA and her writings for *The Sibyl* placed her in the orbit of other well-known reformers of the day: Samuel May, Gerrit Smith, Elizabeth Cady Stanton, and Angelina Grimké. Walker also took to the lecture circuit to convince women to adopt reform dress.

For four years, Mary Walker and Albert Miller appeared to be a devoted, hardworking couple. They tended their medical practice in Rome, and they each promoted reform through writing and speaking. Miller's physiology lecture engagements frequently took him as far as the East Coast. Lyman Worden, who boarded with Walker and Miller for a time, observed the couple at close quarters. He noted Mary Walker had the "*entire charge* of the directing of the housekeeping," while keeping the same medical practice hours as her husband. Worden considered Walker an "affectionate wife," and many times saw her take "more pains to please him [Miller], & assist him, than I have witnessed in wives who had been married as long as she had been."

Since no babies arrived within the first couple of years of the marriage, Mary Walker and her husband may have used some form of birth control. Fertility rates among white, native-born, middle-class Northerners dropped during the 1800s, from just over seven children per couple in 1800 to 5.42 children in 1850. Limiting the number of offspring allowed couples to better preserve their middle-class status and helped protect women's health. Family limitation was also believed to result in stronger marriages and children. As doctors, Walker and Miller understood the biology and physiology of contraception, and books about it aimed at nonmedical experts were readily available at the time. Utopian socialist Robert Dale Owen's *Moral Physiology*, published in 1831, remained in print until the 1870s. The next year, Dr. Charles Knowlton's *Fruits of Philosophy; or the Private Companion of Young Married People* became available and remained popular through ten editions. These books and others provided information about postcoital douching, vaginal sponges, and withdrawal.

Many authors recommended married couples abstain from sex as the most foolproof method of contraception. Since that was not always possible, or desirable, women often shared information with family members and close friends about what worked for them, including homemade recipes for birth control and methods for abortion. A range of advice for dealing with what was euphemistically referred to as "obstructed menses" circulated: special teas and elixirs, vigorous exercise, hot baths, douching, sharp instruments inserted into the vagina. Mary Walker would have been aware of all these, but it is not clear she ever used any.

Not all the advice for married couples focused on birth control. A satisfying sexual relationship was considered a necessary component of a successful marriage. Men were expected to control their sexual urges and women were considered to have less sexual desire than men, but not *no* sexual desire. *Young Married Lady's Private Medical Guide*, a French publication translated for American readers and made available in 1853, explained the role of the clitoris in female sexual pleasure. Since Mary Walker did not leave any personal letters describing the intimate details of her marriage to Albert Miller, this part of her life remains inaccessible.

During the mid-1850s, national events likely absorbed as much of Mary Walker's attention as her domestic and professional life. As an ardent abolitionist, she would have kept up with all the news about slavery, which was driving deeper divisions into American society and politics. National attention turned to the Kansas Territory, where proslavery and antislavery factions battled for dominance in local government to determine whether Kansas would enter the Union as a free state. When proslavery supporters attacked the free-soil town of Lawrence in May 1856, a messianic abolitionist named John Brown led a group of supporters to murder five proslavery settlers at Pottawatomie Creek.

The events in what many people referred to as Bleeding Kansas affected the presidential election that fall. The Democratic Party felt compelled to turn away from its most well-liked candidate, Illinois senator Stephen Douglas. As the architect of the 1854 Kansas–Nebraska Act that promoted popular sovereignty as the preferred method for deciding the slavery question in territories that sought admission to the Union, Douglas carried the taint of the violence in Kansas. The Democrats turned instead to James Buchanan, a longtime Party loyalist from Pennsylvania.

The new Republican Party squared off against the Democrats that year. Founded in 1854 as a reaction to the Kansas–Nebraska Act, it brought together former members of the Whig Party, antislavery Democrats, and proponents of free soil who wanted the Western territories open for free laborers: "Free Soil, Free Labor, Free Men." In 1856, Republicans chose John C. Frémont, the famed explorer of the West, veteran of the Mexican-American War, and former senator from California, as its candidate. Though Frémont had little political experience, he was widely respected for his exploits in the West, and he promoted free soil. Democrats warned that a Republican victory would encourage Southern states to leave the Union to protect slavery. Buchanan won the election.

With popular sovereignty corrupted by the violence in Kansas as residents physically fought and engaged in rigged elections, and Southern states threatening secession if they did not get their way, Americans looked to the Supreme Court for a definitive ruling on the legality of slavery. The Court's decision on the *Dred Scott* case in March 1857 made white Southerners happy. Scott sued for his freedom because his owner had taken him into a free state and a free territory. The Court found that this did not make him free. Moreover, the Court determined that no person of African descent could be a citizen of the United States, and that Congress had exceeded its authority in restricting slavery in the territories. Republicans and other abolitionists and Free-Soilers were appalled, and vowed to continue their attempts to end slavery.

In October 1859, John Brown carried out another violent attack against slavery, this time in the state of Virginia. His plan involved sparking an all-out revolution against slavery, during which more and more enslaved people would rise against their masters. Six prominent abolitionists, including businessman and philanthropist Gerrit Smith, provided Brown with money to finance the scheme. Brown and a group of about twenty armed men seized the Federal arsenal at Harpers Ferry, intending to collect enough weapons to supply everyone who would join the revolt. Word quickly spread, and local militias and a company of US Marines surrounded the building and attacked the revolutionaries. Ten of Brown's foot soldiers died, and Brown was arrested and charged with treason and murder. Found guilty, the state of Virginia executed him in December.

Against this backdrop of national upheaval, Mary Walker's private life unraveled. In late 1859, she learned Albert Miller had been repeatedly unfaithful. The information shattered her belief in her egalitarian marriage and killed her love for her husband. Walker rejected the sexual double standard that excused men's premarital or extramarital sexual activity while condemning women's. She did not excuse Miller's behavior. When she confronted him about his extramarital affairs and he admitted to them, she demanded a divorce.

At the time, most Americans considered divorce more scandalous than marital infidelity. Wives were expected to quietly accept their husbands' affairs, to understand they were part of men's nature. The principles of coverture, rooted in English common law, governed women's lives. As married women, their legal identities became covered by their husbands'. Therefore, women had few rights of their own, including the ability to own property, enter into a contract, and claim custody of their children. Divorces were difficult to obtain in the United States. Each state made its own divorce laws, and New York had one of the strictest in the country. Fault-based, it required either the husband or the wife to prove that the other had committed an offense egregious enough to warrant divorce. For New York, which established its divorce law in 1787, only adultery qualified.

Divorce cases were heard in open court, where the press eagerly covered the most high-profile ones. An avid reader with an interest in legal issues, Mary Walker likely knew about Catherine Walker (no relation), who sued her husband Wildes Walker for divorce and for custody of their three children in 1854. Reporters flocked to cover the trial because Catherine Walker, who came from a wealthy family in Maine, had married a man with minimal prospects. She could afford to pay an entire team of lawyers to prove her husband had conducted adulterous relationships with several women, including prostitutes, while serving time in a debtors' prison in New York. Wildes Walker lodged counterclaims of infidelities on his wife's part. It did not take long for the jury to find in Mrs. Walker's favor, granting her the divorce and custody of the children, but not before the details of their marriage and her husband's liaisons became public.

Albert Miller seemed stunned by his wife's request for a divorce. But after four years of marriage he should have known that Mary Walker would not ignore his behavior. He also apparently did not understand how hurt and betrayed she felt by his affairs. Instead of apologies or denials, Miller suggested "if she would not get a bill of divorce from him she might have the same *privileges*." He may have been alluding to some version of free love, a radical reform of traditional marriage that established a tenuous foothold in the United States in the mid-1800s. Touted as a way to balance the need for sexual freedom inherent in ideas about individualism with the restraint necessary to preserve social order, free lovers promoted monogamous, heterosexual unions based on love and mutual desire. Marriage was optional.

Though Mary Walker embraced many radical ideas throughout her life, free love was not one of them. She expected her husband to remain faithful to her out of love and respect. For his adultery, Walker threw Albert Miller out of their house and started to think about how to secure a divorce. She wept when she told boarder Lyman Worden what Miller had said to her, vowing she "would never live with a man that was so *vile* as to make such a proposition to a *wife*, and that people who thought her *so happy* knew little of her *wretchedness*."

New York law stipulated that Mary Walker had to prove Albert Miller's adultery, but finding evidence could be difficult and time-consuming. The longer it dragged on, the more likely she would become a subject of gossip. Moreover, New York mandated a five-year waiting period between the time the divorce was granted and the date it would become final. The doctor wanted the whole thing over as quickly as possible. With some research she learned that in 1843, while a territory, Iowa had instituted liberal divorce laws. Unlike New York, Iowa identified several justifications for ending a marriage, including impotence, bigamy, desertion, drunkenness, and cruelty. Iowa's divorce statute also included this elastic catchall: "When either party shall offer such indignities to the person of the other as shall render his or her situation intolerable."

To Mary Walker, this seemed an easy point to prove. Since the Iowa law required a six-month-long residency prior to filing for divorce, she arranged to lodge with Albert Emerson House and his wife Louisa in Delhi, a town of fewer than four hundred people in western Iowa. A thirty-one-year-old lawyer, House had been born in Granby, New York, about sixteen miles south of Walker's hometown of Oswego. At some point, the House family had moved to Oswego and become acquainted with the Walkers. Dr. Walker felt a close-enough connection to Albert House to turn to him for advice and assistance. He likely helped Walker with interpreting Iowa law and may have offered her a discount on legal services.

When Mary Walker arrived in Delhi in the summer of 1860, she planned to stay at least six months. She had suspended her medical practice in Rome, leaving her with only her savings. In return for her room and board, she may have offered free medical care to Louisa House and her baby boy, born in 1859. Dr. Walker also tried to earn a bit of money by writing for the Delhi newspaper, but the editor rejected her first submission as too outlandish. He refused to believe that such a young woman had already accomplished so much with her life.

Waiting was never Mary Walker's strong suit. She decided to further her education by attending the Bowen Collegiate Institute, a new Presbyterian school located in Hopkinton, about eight miles south of Delhi. She was one of ninety-eight young men and women who enrolled in the fall of 1860. The doctor had been learning German on her own, and when she saw it listed among the subjects taught at Bowen, she decided to embark on a formal study of the language. After paying the tuition, though, school officials told her they did not have a faculty member to teach German. During the previous winter term, the college had hired one of its students to teach the course, but he was no longer available.

Mary Walker objected to the unfairness of the situation—that a promise made had been broken—not an unreasonable reaction, given what she had endured with her husband. She threatened to sue if Bowen failed to offer the German class. The college's president, the Reverend Jerome Allen, PhD, believed his hands were tied. As a new institution, Bowen lacked the financial resources to add another course. While Walker waited to see what would happen, she decided that rhetoric classes would be useful for the parallel career she had been developing in public lecturing. These "rhetorical exercises" were only available to male students, so she quickly garnered their support for her participation.

The campaign did not escape the notice of Lucy Cooley, Bowen's director of women students, who disapproved of Mary Walker taking part in rhetoric. When she learned that the doctor had also attended a meeting at the Hopkinton debating society and was scheduled to speak at its next event, Cooley forbade her to do so. This set up a contest of wills between two women who had much in common. Both were the same age and shared a strong commitment to women's education. Yet Walker had no intention of obeying Cooley's edict. For the doctor, the issue of a woman's right to her choice of education was compounded by a matter of jurisdiction. The debating society was a town organization, not a campus one, and Walker attended its events in the evening, on her own time. Therefore, Cooley, a school official, could not tell her what to do.

To make her point, Mary Walker engaged in the next debate. To make hers, Lucy Cooley suspended the upstart student from Bowen. The men of the debating society, most of whom were enrolled at the college, showed their support for Walker by walking out of the school with her and marching in protest through the streets of Hopkinton. School administrators immediately suspended the male students. They asked for reinstatement, but only if Mary Walker could return. Cooley would not budge; she did not want Walker allowed back. The young men dropped that demand and returned to their classes. Dr. Walker remained banned.

Later in life, she claimed that her membership in the debating society was not the only thing that caused her expulsion from Bowen. Offended that the school divided its chapel into separate sections for men and women, Mary Walker refused to sit on the women's side. She wrote articles for the Bowen newspaper, all of them about women's rights issues. And she wore her Bloomer costume everywhere. That, she believed, was what bothered school administrators the most. Bowen's president, the Reverend Mr. Allen, allegedly said to her, "Miss Walker, we like you very much. We have no objection whatever to your character or conduct, but only to your clothes."

The matter of her divorce soon overshadowed the struggle at Bowen. While in Iowa, Mary Walker wrote regularly to B. F. Chapman, a lawyer in Rome. At some point during their correspondence, she told him she had moved to Iowa to get a divorce. He wrote back with unexpected news. New York State did not recognize out-of-state divorces. Normally a careful researcher, it is unclear how Walker missed this, but her shock over her husband's behavior may have been a factor. It is also not clear why Albert House, an Iowa attorney, had not mentioned this. With no legitimate reason to remain in Delhi, Mary Walker returned to Rome, where she resumed her medical practice and hired Chapman as her divorce attorney.

The divorce dragged on through the rest of 1860 and into 1861. Abraham Lincoln was elected president, South Carolina became the first state to secede from the Union, and the Civil War started. Meanwhile, a court-appointed neutral referee, D. D. Walrath, investigated Mary Walker's claim that Albert Miller had committed adultery. Walrath found evidence that Miller had several affairs while on a lecture tour of New England and had fathered at least one child. On September 16, 1861, the New York State supreme court granted Mary Walker a divorce, which would be final in five years. After that, she would be free to remarry. But Miller, the guilty spouse, could not remarry while his ex-wife was alive.

With her marriage ended, Mary Walker closed her medical practice in Rome and boarded a train for Washington, DC. The trip probably took more than a day, especially if she changed lines in New York City, and perhaps even Philadelphia. Traveling through Maryland would have been unnerving. The slave state remained with the Union after Fort Sumter, but Confederate sympathies there ran deep. When Abraham Lincoln made his way to Washington by train from Springfield, Illinois, for his March 1861 inauguration, extraordinary measures had to be taken to ensure his safety. Allan Pinkerton, the private detective who went on to organize the Secret Service, had uncovered credible evidence of an assassination conspiracy, the so-called Baltimore Plot. Within a year, Mary Walker would propose putting her role as a doctor to work for Pinkerton's organization.

As her train chugged into Washington from the north, she would have viewed a city prepared for a siege. General George B. McClellan, recently appointed to lead the Union's Army of the Potomac, ordered the construction of thirty-three miles of entrenchments and fortifications to protect the capital from Confederate attacks. The biggest threat came from the neighboring state of Virginia, which had seceded in May, about a month after the start of the Civil War.

During the spring and into the summer of 1861, both sides struggled to gain a clear-enough advantage to force the conflict to a conclusion.

Early engagements at Sewell's Point and Aquia Creek in Virginia ended in draws. Confederates prevailed at Big Bethel and Blackburn's Ford in Virginia and in Carthage, Missouri. The Union acquitted itself at Philippi and Rich Mountain, Virginia, but lost a major engagement in July at Manassas.

Located about twenty-seven miles west of Washington, DC, in northern Virginia, Manassas boasted an important railroad junction. In Union hands, it would give Federal troops a direct path to the new Confederate capital of Richmond. In mid-July, General Irvin McDowell, a former staff officer, gathered some 35,000 troops in Washington and marched them west. They made it as far as Centreville, near a creek called Bull Run, where Confederate general Pierre G. T. Beauregard had already deployed 20,000 men. After a couple of days of scouting and a few minor skirmishes, on July 21 McDowell ordered his troops to attack.

By that time, Beauregard had received significant reinforcements, including General Joseph E. Johnston's 10,000-strong force and the "stone wall" of General Thomas J. Jackson's men. McDowell's green recruits pushed forward as commanded, but they were hungry, thirsty, and weakened from the effects of heatstroke. In the face of increasing enemy numbers, McDowell could not field reinforcements quickly enough. By late that afternoon, the battle ended in a decisive Confederate victory. Southern troops took over 1,200 prisoners, about 600 Union soldiers died, and another 950 were wounded. In the South, this confrontation was known as the Battle of Manassas, and in the North, as the Battle of Bull Run.

When Mary Walker arrived in Washington two months after that big battle, the city was still reeling from the aftereffects. Troop movements in and out of the capital swelled Washington's population, which at the time of the 1860 election numbered a bit above 75,000. It was the biggest city she had ever encountered, its streets bursting with soldiers and their families, refugees, government workers, businessmen, and laborers. She would not have taken the time to gawk at her surroundings. She had come to Washington on important business. After arriving at the Italian-style depot on New Jersey Avenue and C Street, the doctor might have walked the two miles to her destination at 17th Street and Pennsylvania

Avenue NW, or perhaps she took a horse-drawn omnibus. There, a stately two-story brick structure, the Northwest Executive Building, housed the War Department. Once inside, she made her way to the office of the head man, Secretary of War Simon Cameron.

Mary Walker's decision to present herself to the War Department was not unusual. In the nineteenth century, people who wanted to speak to federal officials, even the president, and could bear the expense of the journey, expected they would be seen. Several days after the attack on Fort Sumter, fifty-nine-year-old Dorothea Dix, the internationally recognized expert on the reform of hospitals for the mentally ill, had made such a trip. After she heard that Confederate sympathizers in Baltimore had set upon the 6th Massachusetts Volunteers, killing four and wounding several others as they traveled by train to Washington, DC, she headed to the capital to monitor the soldiers' welfare.

Concerned about the availability of quality medical care for the troops, Dorothea Dix went straight to the Executive Mansion to talk to President Lincoln about the military's needs. Only thirty surgeons belonged to the army at this point, though civilian doctors and even medical students had already begun to enlist. Lincoln soon required that every time a new volunteer regiment of soldiers organized in any state, its governor had to appoint it a surgeon and assistant surgeon. Only one general hospital, the City Infirmary, existed in Washington, and even at the beginning of the war its facilities could not be stretched to meet the military's needs. The army took over the Capitol building and established the city's first military hospital. Throughout the remainder of the year, the military opened about one additional hospital in the city per month.

Dorothea Dix offered to manage the military hospitals and keep them supplied with everything they needed to operate efficiently, including female nurses. President Lincoln's secretary, John Hay, wrote of the meeting, "She makes the most munificent and generous offers." Secretary of War Simon Cameron made a written acceptance of these offers on April 23. The War Department scored a tremendous coup, mostly because of the considerable savings to the military. Dix made it clear she was volunteering; she required no salary. She planned to solicit private donations and to efficiently manage government supplies to keep the hospitals stocked with needed materials. The female nurses Dix envisioned recruiting for duty—from respectable white middle-class families—would also offer to serve, but would receive a salary of forty cents a day plus rations.

Well pleased with this bargain, on June 10 Simon Cameron issued Dorothea Dix a military commission, without rank but with the title of Superintendent of Women Nurses for the Union Army. He did not intend this as a precedent-setting appointment to encourage women to seek official positions with the military. The War Department set clear parameters for Dix's duties: While she took charge of the hospitals in and near Washington, her authority over personnel was limited to the women she recruited as nurses. The army's medical department, likewise, had no intention of parceling out any more-senior positions to women. While male doctors may have respected Dix's administrative skills, they did not consider her an equal. She was a woman, and she was not a physician.

As a health-care reformer, Dorothea Dix believed that women were naturally suited to nursing, but she understood public perceptions about the tender sensibilities of women. Most people considered young single women too innocent for exposure to the harsh masculine realities of military life. They worried that frivolous young women might use nursing as a cover for flirting with young men as they searched for a husband. There were also concerns about married women. It was one thing for them to take care of their husbands and children, even some extended family members. It was quite another for them to handle the unclothed bodies of strangers.

Dorothea Dix believed the public would accept the "right" kind of women, married or single, as nurses. According to Dix, training or experience came second to character and appearance. For her nurse corps, she selected women over the age of thirty, preferring those between thirty-five and fifty, who were healthy and strong, neat and plain. She instructed them to wear dark colors—brown or black—and forbade adornments such as hoops, bows, and jewelry. The women had to provide at least two written references of their good character and sober work ethic.

Those Dorothea Dix chose for this military "service" were not accorded equal rank or equal pay with soldiers. The women volunteered and paid all or part of their own expenses. Though they received a nominal salary, this reinforced their image as selfless helpers, and it kept the men at ease, reassuring them that the women would not challenge their authority or lay claim to their jobs. In all, a few thousand women made their way to Washington, DC, during the war to work for Dorothea Dix's nursing staff.

Most American women, like Dorothea Dix, Louisa May Alcott, and the thousands who joined ladies' aid societies, were content to make their contributions to the war effort without challenging their traditional roles in society. They pushed at the boundaries a bit to accommodate the kind of work the war required, but they never imagined the lines would not hold. When Dr. Mary Walker presented herself to the secretary of war in late September 1861, she was prepared to upend those gender conventions.

CHAPTER TWO

Commission Seeker

Dr. Mary Walker met with sixty-two-year-old Simon Cameron, a tall, clean-shaven man with an abundance of white hair. Any optimism that she would get what she wanted from him was likely tempered by what she knew of his background. Cameron, a native Pennsylvanian, had spent decades first carving out a business career, then a political one. During the 1820s and 1830s, he accumulated a tidy fortune from printing and publishing, railroads, and banking. Then, in the 1840s, he entered the United States Senate as a Democrat. Abolitionist sentiments led him to the Republican Party in 1856, and he returned to the Senate again in 1857. Though the Pennsylvanian remained committed to antislavery, he was not associated with the other reforms Mary Walker embraced, particularly women's rights.

Additionally, rumors of scandal dogged Simon Cameron. He had never shook allegations of corruption leveled at him in the late 1830s. While serving as commissioner for the Winnebago tribe, Cameron was caught adjusting their land claims through notes paid by his own bank, and later lost the post. In 1857, the Senate Judiciary Committee investigated charges that he had won his Senate seat through "corrupt and unlawful means." Though quickly cleared of any wrongdoing, the taint to Cameron's reputation remained. Yet he hung on to enough power in the Republican Party that President Lincoln selected him to serve as secretary of war.

From this, Mary Walker understood that, although they were contemporaries, Simon Cameron was a man very unlike her father. Born in 1798, Alvah Walker grew up in Greenwich, Massachusetts, west of

Plymouth Colony, where his ancestors first settled in the 1600s. Four family members from his maternal side had signed the Mayflower Compact. Walker became a carpenter, and in 1821 he married twenty-year-old Vesta Whitcomb, also from Greenwich. The newlyweds left Massachusetts for central New York, settling in Syracuse, where they stayed for ten years, raising four daughters. Then the family moved thirty-five miles northwest to a farm in Oswego Town, the small west-side neighbor of the larger city of Oswego, both on the shore of Lake Ontario. Mary Edwards Walker was born there on November 26, 1832. The last of the Walker children, the longed-for son, Alvah Jr., arrived two years later.

The Walkers lived in the quiet rural setting of Oswego Town, only five miles away from the vibrant, bustling city. There they conducted their commercial transactions, selling what they raised on their farm, and buying whatever else they needed. The city of Oswego grew rapidly and prospered in the antebellum period, thanks to its connection first with the Erie Canal, in 1829, and then with the railroad, in 1848. Iron, lumber, flour, grain, salt, and starch became the backbones of manufacture and trade. Social and cultural opportunities abounded, and churches of various denominations sprang up.

Oswego, both town and city, sat in New York's "burned-over district," so called because the religious revivalism of the Second Great Awakening had engulfed this central part of the state. Alvah and Vesta Walker, however, had not been drawn into it, and they did not encourage their children to participate. As freethinkers, they disliked the evangelicalism of the revival, which they found too conservative, and they urged their children to approach all religions with their minds rather than their hearts. The family alternated Sunday worship between the Methodists and the Baptists.

As a teenager, Mary Walker's intellectual curiosity about religion led her to the Spiritualism movement. The belief that humans could communicate with the dead can be traced back at least to the eighteenth century, when the ideas of Franz Anton Mesmer in Austria and Emanuel Swedenborg in Sweden gained large followings. They caught on in the United States in 1848, when the three Fox sisters of Hydesville, New York, claimed the dead spoke through them through a series of rapping or knocking sounds. Spiritualism offered hope and consolation to the living—that they had some control over their salvation. It also presented women with unprecedented opportunities for religious leadership.

The popularity of Spiritualism intersected with the abolitionist movement, which the Walker family supported. Two ardent spiritualists, Amy and Isaac Post of Rochester, were also antislavery Quakers. They used their home as a stop on the Underground Railroad, that moved escaped slaves to safety in the North, and as a meeting place for abolitionists. William Lloyd Garrison, head of the American Anti-Slavery Society, Frederick Douglass, a former slave and now publisher of the abolitionist *North Star*, and Susan B. Anthony, the temperance and abolitionist activist who would soon go on to greater fame, all visited the Posts' home and delivered talks on the evils of slavery.

Linked into this Rochester group was a man whose ideas about gender and race reform influenced Mary Walker. The wealthy New York philanthropist Gerrit Smith was born in Utica in 1797, making him a contemporary of both Simon Cameron and Alvah Walker. Though Smith lived in Peterboro, his business interests, including land holdings, banking, and railroads, took him throughout the state of New York. He spent a lot of time in Oswego, where he owned most of the city's land, and purchased shares in the commercial bank and the canal company. Smith used a portion of his fortune to support a variety of causes—he bankrolled Oswego's first public library—but his primary commitment was to abolition. By 1847, he had developed close ties to Frederick Douglass.

Slavery, now illegal in New York, had been integral to the state's growth and prosperity. Enslaved people made up about 20 percent of its inhabitants during the colonial period, when just over 40 percent of its households had slaves. Trade and commerce abounded in the large port city of New York, a hefty portion of which involved the slave trade. Enslaved people worked in this urban area, sometimes on the docks, loading and unloading vessels, and sometimes in households, performing a variety of domestic tasks. Farmers throughout the state, including Gerrit Smith's father, purchased the enslaved to work their land. It took more than a decade after the end of the American Revolution for New York to implement a plan for emancipation, one that gradually, rather than immediately, freed enslaved people. According to the 1830 census, taken two years before Mary Walker was born, seventy-five slaves still lived in New York. The 1840 census was the first to list no slaves.

When New Yorkers like Gerrit Smith began working for abolition, they knew very well the institution's history in their home state, and many had encountered an enslaved person in their own lifetime. In 1831, Smith helped organize an antislavery meeting at the Syracuse Baptist Church, one of the places where Alvah and Vesta Walker worshipped before they moved to Oswego. As progressives and freethinkers, the Walkers supported abolition. The Underground Railroad stopped at their house, and they attended many antislavery lectures in Oswego. Sarah and Angelina Grimké, Maria Stewart, and Fanny Wright, all popular abolitionist speakers, traveled through the area in the 1830s, and Frederick Douglass made an appearance in Oswego in 1849.

As she grew up in Oswego, Mary Walker learned from these accomplished people, whether she read their essays or listened to their lectures. Most importantly, she had female role models who showed her that women belonged in public spaces as much as they belonged in the home. They inspired her to do something extraordinary with her life, to be somebody. In 1859, as tensions over slavery heightened, Dr. Walker wrote an article for *The Sibyl* entitled "Women Soldiers." She rejected the "conservative argument" that since women did not fight in wars they were not entitled to vote. Walker argued that women in the past had fought, and in some of those instances, like the American Revolution, they had helped men attain the political rights they now enjoyed. This, she pointed out, was unfair. Moreover, she believed men prevented women from fighting out of fear that they would acquit themselves in battle better than men. Walker predicted that "if war should break out," many of the current eight hundred bloomer-wearing women in the North would serve in the military.

Now, in Simon Cameron's office in September 1861, Mary Walker made her proposal for service. She told the secretary of war she wanted a commission as a physician in the US Army. This would provide her with recognized authority over men in the lower ranks and would give her an officer's status and pay. Cameron did not hedge his response. He refused, explaining that the military did not commission women, nor did it hire them to work as doctors. He did not mention the appointment he had made a few months earlier, naming Dorothea Dix as superintendent of army nurses. She held no rank, though, and supervised women who fulfilled their nurturing roles by taking care of wounded and sick soldiers under the daily direction of male doctors.

Hiring Dorothea Dix was as far as the War Department would go in bending traditional gender roles. Even Elizabeth Blackwell, who held the medical credentials that Dix lacked, could not make inroads. Born in England in 1821 and raised in Cincinnati, Ohio, Blackwell may have been the first woman to graduate from an accredited American medical college. After working for several years as a schoolteacher, she had secured admission to the Geneva Medical College in upstate New York, graduating first in her class in 1849.

Blackwell traveled overseas to continue her training at hospitals in London and Paris. Though interested in hygiene and preventive care, her professors tried to restrict her studies to women's health issues. Faced with limited options, Blackwell, who never married, opened a clinic for poor women in New York City in 1851. The facility also supplied jobs to other female physicians. By the time the Civil War started a decade later, she was a seasoned doctor, well-known, well-connected, and well-respected in the nation's largest city.

Within two weeks of the start of the war, the forty-year-old physician decided the Union military needed all the help it could get. On April 26, 1861, she and Louisa Lee Schuyler, great-granddaughter of Alexander Hamilton, held a large public meeting at the Cooper Institute and founded the Women's Central Relief Association (WCRA) to accomplish two main goals. First, the WCRA would organize the hundreds of ladies' aid societies that had sprung up across the North, like the one in Bridgeport, Connecticut. These local groups were made up of women of all ages who used their family and social connections to collect a variety of materials—including food, clothing, bedding, and hospital supplies—and deliver them to soldiers from their communities.

Blackwell planned for the WCRA to enhance the efficiency of the ladies' aid societies and encourage women to think more expansively about the needs of the nation.

Second, and of equal importance, Dr. Blackwell intended the WCRA to liaise with the army's medical department to recruit and train women to serve as nurses. As a credentialed physician, Blackwell considered herself the most qualified person to take on this task. Formal training did not exist for female nurses, so she designed a curriculum to prepare women to handle military patients. Professionalism, the doctor believed, was key to her nurses gaining acceptance from the American public and from male doctors.

But Elizabeth Blackwell's plans ran afoul of influential men unwilling to cede that much power to women. Within two months of the WCRA's founding, prominent New York City men—including some who had helped to organize the WCRA—decided they wanted to head an organization to centralize war-relief efforts. In June 1861, the federal government authorized the United States Sanitary Commission (USSC) to work with the War Department and the army's medical bureau to oversee all aspects of care for the troops, including the hiring and training of women who wanted to care for the troops did not want to sign up with Dorothea Dix's army nurses. Three months later, Dr. Blackwell conceded she had been outmaneuvered, and agreed to turn the WCRA into a branch of the USSC.

Secretary of War Cameron's rejection of Dr. Walker's request reflected this kind of gendered power structure. His refusal was likely compounded by his distaste for the way Walker presented herself in his office. She wore a skirt that fell to just below her knees over a pair of men's-style trousers, topped with a close-fitting jacket. Only her hat and hairstyle, both of current fashion, could be labeled feminine. Most nineteenth-century Americans considered the Bloomer costume a shocking aberration of women's traditional attire. Fashion and custom dictated that women's apparel cover them from head to foot. Proper dresses had high necks, long sleeves, layers of petticoats, and hems that swept the floor. Lace-up, calf-high boots prohibited a flash of ankles, and a hat topped off the modesty whenever a woman ventured outside her home.

By the early 1860s, bloomers—well-known because of mostly derisive newspaper and magazine coverage—rarely appeared on a woman out in public. But Mary Walker had been dressing in this fashion since before the outfit got its name. As progressives and freethinkers, her parents, Alvah and Vesta Walker, believed in equality between men and women. No men's work or women's work existed in their household, only work. Vesta and her daughters performed domestic chores *and* toiled in the fields. As a girl living on the farm, Mary Walker partially based her decision to wear trousers on practicality: This outfit enabled her to move more easily to accomplish her work.

The education she received from her parents also influenced her fashion choice. In the late 1830s, Alvah and Vesta Walker built a school on their property and allowed boys and girls from the area to attend free of charge. There, Mary Walker first learned the basics of history, geography, mathematics, and physiology from her parents, who served as the school's first teachers. Education extended into their home, where the Walkers instructed their offspring on the latest ideas in health care, with an emphasis on the importance of personal hygiene.

Over the years, Alvah Walker had amassed a large collection of medical books, mostly to help his wife through the various illnesses that plagued her throughout her several pregnancies. He embraced eclectic medicine, the approach that relied on physical therapy, diet, exercise, and natural or botanical remedies. Many practitioners were self-taught, but by the 1830s, eclectic medical schools had started to open on the East Coast and in the Midwest. Through the rest of the nineteenth century, eclectic medicine vied with allopathic (or regular) medicine for dominance in treating American patients.

Women figured prominently in the eclectic community, drawing from their traditional roles as midwives, and as a result of the recent emphasis on girls' education. Yet, their presence attracted controversy because they violated traditional gender roles by encroaching on a masculine profession, and by publicly talking about matters that alluded to sexuality. In Massachusetts during the 1830s, schoolteacher Mary Gove began reading medical books to figure out the source of her own chronic ill health and the cause of her four miscarriages. She believed many of women's medical problems could be traced to ignorance about their own bodies, so she began offering lectures to women on anatomy and physiology, considered shocking at the time.

Mary Gove recommended showers with cold water, avoiding meat and tobacco, wearing corsets as infrequently as possible, and taking regular exercise—preferably outdoors. After divorcing her abusive husband, Gove published a book, *Lectures to Ladies on Anatomy and Physiology*, and opened a water-cure clinic in New York City. With her second husband, Thomas Low Nichols, she established the American Hydropathic Institute in New York City in 1851. Thomas and Mary Nichols promoted hydrotherapy over drug-based medical treatments, which put them squarely in the orbit of eclectic medical practitioners.

New Yorker Paulina Kellogg came to her medical studies through a more-circuitous route. Thwarted from religious missionary work because she was a woman, she married Francis Wright, a wealthy merchant. Together, they joined an antislavery society in Utica, New York, and, in the late 1830s, supported the efforts of Ernestine Rose to get the New York legislature to pass the Married Women's Property Act. After she was widowed in 1845, Wright studied women's anatomy and physiology and began lecturing on those topics.

By the time Mary Walker began reading her father's medical texts, eclectic medicine was widespread. She absorbed its principles, putting into lifelong practice the habits of bodily cleanliness, including abstention from alcohol and tobacco, and wearing nonrestrictive clothing. At sixteen, the young woman knew she wanted to be a doctor and planned to pursue a medical degree. Three years later, in 1851, after she'd learned everything she could at her parents' free school, she followed in her older sisters' footsteps and left home for the next phase of her education. Walker enrolled in Falley Seminary, in Fulton, New York, a coeducational institution located about ten miles south of Oswego. Like most students who attended, she completed a yearlong three-term course.

Falley's curriculum neatly dovetailed with the eclectic medicine movement and the education and values Mary Walker had received back home in Oswego. The Falley campus, where she continued her studies in the natural sciences, algebra, and grammar, banned tobacco and alcohol.

Temperance gained large numbers of supporters through the antebellum period, but the school's science course offerings were rather daring for the time. Thanks to the pioneering efforts of Mary Gove Nichols and Paulina Wright, female students attended lectures on physiology and hygiene, normally considered inappropriate topics for women.

There is no evidence that Mary Walker donned trousers while she attended Falley, but popularization of the Bloomer outfit, as limited as it turned out to be, coincided with her time there. Even before the nineteenth century, women wore pants on occasion, as Walker had done on the farm, to make certain tasks easier. The dress reform movement that developed about midway through the nineteenth century moved beyond expediency to embrace a women's rights ideology. Fashion, some women's rights advocates believed, served as the visual, external indicator of gender, reinforcing its power dynamics. Men wore the pants, figuratively and literally.

Gerrit Smith, the prominent Oswego businessman and philanthropist, recognized the link between women's subordinate status and their clothing. Long dresses and layers of undergarments hampered women's mobility. Women would not achieve equality with men until they could physically keep up with them. In 1851, Gerrit Smith's daughter, Elizabeth Smith Miller, designed and began wearing an outfit that featured a pair of trousers, or "Turkish" pantaloons, worn under a shortened dress. The attire not only challenged prevailing beliefs about gender, but also promoted women's health by taking pressure off their internal organs, as it eliminated the stays and other restrictive devices that were part of their traditional dress. It encouraged women to exercise, which eclectic medical practitioners promoted as essential to good health. Amelia Bloomer used her women's rights newspaper, *The Lily*, to so vigorously promote the style that the costume soon bore her name.

The Smiths' cousin, Elizabeth Cady Stanton, joined them in promoting dress reform by wearing bloomers. By the beginning of the 1850s, Stanton's reputation as a reformer was spreading across the Northeast and the Midwest. As a teenager living in Johnstown, New York, Elizabeth Cady had excelled at mathematics and languages at the local academy. After graduating, she moved fifty miles away to attend the Troy Female Seminary, where she received one of the finest educations available to girls at the time. She frequently visited the Smith family home in Peterboro, where she learned about the reform movements of the day, including married women's property rights and abolition. Cady also met the antislavery speaker and journalist Henry Stanton there. Shortly after their wedding in 1840—during which they omitted the word "obey" from the ceremony—Stanton introduced his bride to the recently married Theodore and Angelina Weld, major figures in the abolition movement.

During the late 1830s, Angelina Grimké Weld and her older sister, Sarah Grimké, originally from a slaveholding family in South Carolina, began exploring the similarities between the lack of rights for enslaved people and for women. These ideas intrigued Elizabeth Cady Stanton, as did the commitment of Weld's family to the health reforms of Sylvester Graham. Like eclectic medical practitioners, Graham advised his followers to give up alcohol and meat, wear loose clothing, take cold baths, and get regular exercise. Stanton became a lifelong devotee.

During her honeymoon in 1840, while she and Henry Stanton attended the World Anti-Slavery Convention in London, Elizabeth Cady Stanton met the Philadelphia Quaker and seasoned abolitionist, Lucretia Mott. Since the 1830s, Mott promoted biracial activist groups, helping to found the integrated Pennsylvania Anti-Slavery Society and the Philadelphia Female Anti-Slavery Society. In her long association with the abolitionist movement, Mott experienced the routine segregation of women, who were usually relegated to their own, gender-specific organizations. She was not surprised to find female delegates to the London conference seated in a section separate from the men. It upset Elizabeth Cady Stanton, though, and she and Mott talked about it as they forged a friendship. After returning stateside, the two women occasionally corresponded.

Busy raising children and moving households while her husband struggled to provide for them all, Elizabeth Cady Stanton lacked time for active involvement with causes. But when momentum picked up for New York's Married Women's Property Act, she circulated petitions and lobbied members of the legislature. Finally enacted in 1848, the law gave married women the right to control their own personal property and real estate.

Not long after the Stantons had settled in Seneca Falls, New York, Elizabeth Cady Stanton met again with Lucretia Mott, who was visiting relatives and friends nearby. In the rush of conversations about women's roles in society, family, and religion, the small group of women planned a women's rights convention. Held at the Wesleyan Chapel in Seneca Falls on July 19 and 20, 1848, the meeting attracted about three hundred attendees, both men and women. Amelia Bloomer was among the crowd that listened to a reading of, discussed, and voted on Stanton's "A Declaration of Rights and Sentiments," which included a demand for women's voting rights. The passage of this controversial measure—Lucretia Mott had not approved—was largely due to the eloquent support of Frederick Douglass, the abolitionist and former slave closely associated with Gerrit Smith.

State newspapers covered the Seneca Falls Convention, which stirred some debate about the place and status of women. Mary Walker, fifteen years old and living fifty miles north, in Oswego, probably read the stories. Given all the connections among the various reformers in New York, especially through Gerrit Smith, it is difficult to believe she heard nothing about it, and impossible to believe that she would not have agreed with Elizabeth Cady Stanton's declaration. More women's rights meetings followed Seneca Falls, stretching beyond New York, to Ohio and Indiana. In 1850, activists decided there was enough interest in the topic for a national women's rights convention, which became an annual event until the Civil War. Elizabeth Cady Stanton emerged as a prominent participant, along with her political partner, the temperance advocate Susan B. Anthony, whom she met in 1851. Lucy Stone also played an important part in the movement.

When Elizabeth Cady Stanton began wearing the Bloomer costume in 1851, it became a symbol of women's rights. Once the outfit moved from practicality to ideology, a public backlash ensued, with many newspapers and magazines publishing scathing articles about the outfit and the women who wore it. Most women's rights activists quickly abandoned bloomers. According to Stanton, one of the first to return to her floor-length dresses, "the physical freedom enjoyed did not compensate for the persistent persecution and petty annoyances suffered at every turn."

Given her early interest in social and political reforms, Mary Walker probably followed the news of the dramatic rise and fall of the Bloomer costume during her year at the Falley Seminary. The school's health and science curriculum also would have helped her refine her ideas about appropriate dress for women. Walker's first job after graduating in 1852—as a schoolteacher in nearby Minetto—provided economic independence and allowed her the intellectual space to devise practical applications for those beliefs. She introduced her students to innovative theories about health and science, including dress reform.

Taking inspiration from the celebrated opera singer Jenny Lind, Mary Walker designed and wore her own version of the Bloomer costume. Known as the Swedish Nightingale, Lind arrived in the United States in 1850, just before her thirtieth birthday, for an eighteen-month tour, arranged by P. T. Barnum, the popular showman. Barnum knew that few people stateside had heard of Jenny Lind, so he began promoting her shows before she set foot on American soil. "A visit from such a woman who regards her artistic powers as a gift from Heaven and who helps the afflicted and distressed will be a blessing to America," he proclaimed.

Though it is unlikely that Mary Walker was one of the tens of thousands who saw Jenny Lind in person, she did not miss the rampant "Lind mania" that spread throughout the country. Lind's performances received extensive media coverage, and enterprising marketers attached her name to almost every commercial product available, from shirts and hats to sausages. Mary Walker would have been intrigued by reports that Jenny Lind intended to use the profits from her tour to benefit a variety of charities, including establishing free schools in Sweden. Through Lind's wild popularity, Walker glimpsed another way in which dedication to causes could make a woman a somebody.

The young schoolteacher also found Jenny Lind's clothing choices interesting. During her American tour, Lind performed either in a tasteful, fashionable evening gown or a simple, loose-fitting white dress. The top portion of that white dress came to be known as the "Jenny Lind waist." Mary Walker copied this style and sewed the waist into a skirt, which she shortened to mid-calf length. She then put on a pair of trousers beneath the new construction.

This may have been the first time that Mary Walker appeared in public, away from home, in reform dress. The first version of the outfit likely raised eyebrows, but criticisms did not surface until she shortened the skirted portion to her knees. A local farmer saw her walking along a country road and took exception to her costume. He rallied a gaggle of boys who threw eggs and other items at Walker as they chased her. By wearing her Bloomer outfit, she publicly declared her radical beliefs about women's equality. She learned right away that not only did people disagree with her, they would also try to intimidate her out of her beliefs. Walker remained resolute; no one could convince her she was wrong.

Despite this incident, and although she enjoyed her time in Minetto, Mary Walker never considered teaching the pinnacle of her wage-earning career. Rather, it was a means to an end. After about two years, she had saved enough money to pay for her medical school tuition. However, despite her educational background, it would be a challenge to find a medical school that would admit a woman.

The most prestigious medical schools in the United States barred women. Their curricula embraced regular medicine, or allopathy, which relied on prescribing drugs or surgery to remedy medical ailments based on diagnoses and courses of treatment that had already been proven. During the antebellum period, these medical schools declined to admit women, arguing that they lacked the intellectual capacity to handle the academic rigors of a regular medical education. The Geneva Medical College in western New York made an exception in the late 1840s and admitted Elizabeth Blackwell, who graduated in 1849, after which they refused to admit any more female students.

Given Mary Walker's education and her commitment to reform, it is unlikely she would have been a good philosophical fit with a regular medical school. Instead, she preferred an eclectic approach that emphasized homeopathy, herbal treatments, and exercise. These schools had fewer qualms about accepting women, but were not bastions of equality. To prove they were as intellectually rigorous as the allopathy colleges, some excluded women or restricted their access to certain courses.

Mary Walker did not need to look far for a place that would be a good fit. Thirty-six miles south of Minetto sat Syracuse Medical College. In the late 1840s, Dr. Stephen H. Potter, graduate of the Reformed Medical College in Worthington, Ohio, began planning an eclectic medical school in New York. He chose the city of Syracuse because of its residents' deep commitment to social and political reform, particularly abolition. In that spirit of reform, Central Medical College of New York opened its admissions to women. However, the school's faculty and administration divided over the meaning and practice of eclectic medicine. Potter—forceful, imposing, and eloquent—refused to compromise his vision. A group of dissenters left to set up another institution in Rochester. Potter reorganized Central and incorporated it in 1850 as the Syracuse Medical College. Certified by the State of New York, it opened in early 1851. Like its predecessor, the college admitted women and pledged to treat them equally with the male students. Its first class of eighty students contained four women.

In 1853, Alvah Walker accompanied his daughter to Syracuse for a visit to the four-story rectangular building that housed the medical college. They learned that its two-year program, on par with allopathic medical schools, consisted of two or three thirteen-week terms and included classes in anatomy, chemistry and botany, therapeutics and pharmacy, physiology, obstetrics, and pathology. Each faculty member, in addition to teaching responsibilities, served as a preceptor to a new student, providing individual, personalized guidance and instruction. A term cost fifty-five dollars, and students paid an additional $1.50 a week for room and board. In today's money, this would equal about $3,300 per term for tuition, plus $640 in living expenses, or about $12,000 for the three-term program.

Mary Walker began her medical studies at Syracuse in December 1853. The school's founder, Dr. Stephen Potter, who taught the principles and practice of surgery and obstetrics, and edited *The American Medical and Surgical Journal*, became Walker's preceptor. She and the other students attended a series of classes and devoted time outside of the classroom to additional training. Walker usually spent hers with Potter. She opted to remain for three terms, between which she interned with a licensed doctor to get hands-on training. To earn some money, she worked as a subscription agent for Dr. Potter's medical journal.

Those medical school years also coincided with an international event that would later inspire Mary Walker to make her trip to Washington, DC. The Crimean War broke out in October 1853, about two months before she enrolled at Syracuse. An alliance made up of France, Britain, Sardinia, and the Ottoman Empire fought against Imperial Russia, ostensibly over the rights of Christian minorities in the Holy Land, but deeply rooted in the determination of France and Britain to prevent the Russian empire from spreading. It lasted until the allied nations defeated Russia in March 1856.

Because of the telegraph and advances in photography, stories and pictures from the war regularly appeared in newspapers and magazines. Mary Walker immersed herself in reports about the illnesses and wounds the British soldiers suffered and the efforts of Florence Nightingale to alleviate their pain. Born to an upper-class British family in 1820, Nightingale was drawn to nursing through her religious faith. She left her post in London as superintendent of the Institute for the Care of Sick Gentlewomen in October 1854 and led a team of volunteer nurses to the Crimea to tend to the soldiers.

Florence Nightingale's dispatches from the Front, highlighting its desperate conditions, forced the British government to focus more on medical care for its troops. Nicknamed "The Lady of the Lamp," she also improved sanitary conditions at the field hospital, which helped prevent thousands of needless deaths. Mary Walker felt a connection with Nightingale, and she wanted to aid the British soldiers. Not long before her graduation from medical school, Walker wrote to the United States secretary of war, Jefferson Davis, and asked about the possibility of working as a doctor for the British military. Nothing came from her request, but it was a clear indication of her adventuresome spirit and her assumption that she possessed skills valuable to the military.

It is no wonder that in September 1861 Mary Walker ended up in the office of another secretary of war to offer her services as a physician. But Simon Cameron turned her down. The US military did not, and would not, commission a woman as a doctor. Mary Walker remained undeterred. If Cameron would not give her what she wanted, she would get it some other way.

CHAPTER THREE

Volunteer Surgeon

DISMISSED BY THE SECRETARY OF WAR, DR. MARY WALKER SEARCHED Washington, DC, for a position at one of the new military hospitals. During the Civil War, "new" meant repurposed. Many of the city's public buildings underwent conversions to meet wartime needs, including the Capitol, where the basement now contained a bakery to produce soldiers' bread rations. By 1865, Washington would have dozens of new facilities that never quite managed to meet the military's vast medical needs.

On 7th Street between P and G Streets in northwestern DC, Mary Walker found the Indiana Hospital. Sprawled across the second floor of the US Patent Office Building, it was one of the city's early conversions. The hospital's founders were federal employees from Indiana looking for a place to primarily treat wounded soldiers from their own state. They took advantage of the recent departure of the 1st Rhode Island Regiment from the upper levels of the Patent building, and staked claim to the second floor. Like the other converted medical facilities in the capital, the Indiana Hospital, sometimes referred to as the Patent Office Hospital, suffered from poor ventilation, overcrowding, and understaffing.

Mary Walker selected this facility because she heard that its head surgeon, Dr. J. N. Green, lacked an assistant and was chronically overworked. He treated members of the 19th Indiana Volunteers, organized in Indianapolis at the end of July 1861. Later that summer the regiment headed to the nation's capital and joined the Army of the Potomac, part of the 3rd Brigade, McDowell's Division. In September, the 19th Indiana engaged in actions in northern Virginia, including a skirmish at Lewinsville and the occupation of Falls Church.

By the end of that month, J. N. Green was the lone doctor on staff at the Indiana Hospital, aided by several nurses. Green, who had come to Washington from New York, knew how all-consuming the tasks were—his predecessor had worked himself to death. Now, due to a shortage of trained medical personnel, Green failed to replace the assistant physician who had briefly worked for him. These circumstances led Mary Walker to believe she had a good chance of stepping into that position. After meeting the female doctor and learning about her qualifications, fully understanding her background in eclectic medicine, Green wanted to hire her. Unfortunately, he lacked the authority to do so. That permission, Green told Walker, must come from the man in charge of the US Army's medical department, surgeon general Clement Finley.

The sixty-four-year-old native Pennsylvanian was the tenth surgeon general to serve the US Army. Finley received his medical degree from the University of Pennsylvania School of Medicine in 1818, the same year he accepted a commission as a surgeon's mate in the 1st Infantry. During the Black Hawk War of the early 1830s, Dr. Finley took an appointment as chief medical officer for the duration of the conflict. He held a similar position in the Mexican-American War in the 1840s, serving General Zachary Taylor in Texas and General Winfield Scott in Mexico City. Through Finley's decades of conscientious service, officers and enlisted men held him in high regard.

Weeks after the start of the Civil War, President Lincoln named Clement Finley surgeon general of the army. Building on his previous wartime experiences, the physician moved quickly to recruit additional doctors and open more hospitals. Mary Walker may have assumed that Finley's single-minded focus on medical matters would make him more amenable to giving her a commission than the secretary of war had been. She presented him with a written request from Dr. Green, along with a recommendation letter from Dr. E. H. Stockwell, a professor at the Physopathic Medical College of Ohio, which confirmed her medical education and described her as a "lady of many virtues." Still, Finley turned her down. As far as he was concerned, the fact that she was a woman overrode all other considerations.

Now that both the secretary of war and the surgeon general had denied Mary Walker a commission, she moved down the chain of command to the assistant surgeon general, Robert C. Wood. A contemporary of Finley's, Wood hailed from Rhode Island, graduated from New York City's College of Physicians and Surgeons in 1821, and entered military service four years later as an assistant surgeon. During the Mexican-American War, he ran the general hospital at Point Isabel during the Rio Grande Campaign. In 1848, Wood returned to the East Coast to take the position of post surgeon at Fort McHenry in Maryland. After his brother-in-law, Jefferson Davis, became the secretary of war under Franklin Pierce's administration, Wood received an appointment to the surgeon general's office in Washington.

A couple of months after the start of the war, Major Wood also accepted a seat on the board of managers of the United States Sanitary Commission (USSC), the organization that had usurped Dr. Elizabeth Blackwell's Women's Central Relief Association (WCRA). Henry Whitney Bellows, a Unitarian minister from New York City, helped Blackwell set up the WCRA, then decided a male-run group would more appropriately liaise with the army. In June 1861, he created the USSC as a predominantly civilian advisory board to the Army Medical Bureau, designed to assist the military in providing the best medical treatment for Union soldiers. However, the USSC's twelve regional branches, encompassing 7,000 soldiers' aid societies, were run by women, an acknowledgment of their indispensable labor and organizational expertise.

Robert Wood's involvement with the USSC marked him as more progressive than his surgeon general boss, Clement Finley. Finley supported the USSC, but grudgingly. He disapproved of its plan to hire female nurses, and was skeptical of its emphasis on improving hygiene and sanitation. It was no wonder he turned down Mary Walker's request for a commission. Wood proved more amenable; he was aware of the impressive work women had been doing to provide efficient medical care for military personnel. Wood raised Walker's hopes when he told her he had no objection to issuing her a commission, but he quickly dashed them when he declined to go over Finley's head.

Commission-less, Mary Walker returned to the Indiana Hospital and volunteered her services to Dr. Green. He was so grateful that he offered to pay her out of his own salary. "I replied that he needed all that he [had] for his wife and children, and that I should not accept of any, but I would be his assistant surgeon just the same as though I had been appointed." The recognition and the money that accompanied a commission were important to Walker, but so was the work. As a patriot, she intended to contribute to the war effort, and she would do that with her medical skills, even if that put her in potentially dangerous situations.

To cut down on expenses and maximize medical care, Dr. Walker took up residence in the Patent Office Building along with Dr. Green, three female nurses, and a few male nurses. The hours were long, and the Indiana Hospital remained understaffed. Its patient population fluctuated, sometimes with as few as eighty beds filled, at other times, with around one hundred men crowding the facility. One of Walker's primary responsibilities was to perform pre-admittance examinations of patients to make sure they did not have smallpox. "Patients were daily brought in ambulances to the west sidewalk of the Patent Office Building," she later wrote. Dr. Green would send for her "to come down and examine the cases so that no cases of possible smallpox might be taken up there" to the hospital ward.

Illness ran rampant during the Civil War. About 620,000 soldiers died altogether, with disease causing two-thirds of those fatalities. The close quarters of military life allowed the rapid spread of measles, scarlet fever, and smallpox, which army doctors referred to as eruptive fevers. Men who showed signs of any of these were shunted into "pest houses" for containment. Though more men contracted measles, the higher death rate from smallpox made it more feared. A viral infection, smallpox spread through face-to-face contact via coughing and sneezing. Fever and body aches were followed by a red rash in the mouth and on the tongue, culminating in a pustule rash on the rest of the body.

Smallpox had plagued humans for thousands of years, typically killing three out of every ten people who caught it. Those who survived bore telltale scars. A successful vaccination had been developed, but it was not widely used in the early 1800s. During the Civil War, desperate soldiers fashioned their own vaccine, taking pus from an afflicted compatriot and scratching it into their skin. Their limited medical knowledge made this a high-risk proposition. As it turned out, not all the pus originated from smallpox. Health consequences ranged from failing to develop an immunity to contracting another dangerous disease, like syphilis. These attempts at self-inoculation also left thousands of soldiers incapacitated for weeks at a time, interfering with the army's readiness for battle.

Doctors like Mary Walker managed to contain smallpox during the war. Pure, unadulterated vaccines reached enough soldiers to prevent an epidemic, but not enough to eradicate the disease. Quarantine, the primary method Walker relied on, also helped to stem the contagion. Since she had already been inoculated, she did not worry about contracting the disease. She had to act immediately, though, examining patients upon their arrival at the Patent Office Building, no matter the time of day or night. Soldiers exhibiting symptoms were sent on to Washington's eruptive fever hospital, located in a two-story brick home at 23rd and S Streets, which became the Kalorama Hospital.

Not long after joining the staff at the Indiana Hospital, Dr. Mary Walker took over the night shift. "As soon as the soldiers learned of my being a physician they were very much pleased, and whenever they felt worse in the night so that they wished to have a surgeon called I was the one that was sent for." This gave Dr. Green a much-needed break, and Walker believed her assistance "no doubt prevented him also from passing away from over work as did his predecessor." Yet "night shift" proved a misnomer. Because of the patient load, at least during those first weeks, the female doctor typically worked both day and night.

The hospital patients looked forward to seeing Dr. Walker at any time. "The soldiers would say that they had rather see me than have anything brought to them because they knew that I knew so much, and they would consult me regarding their cases." The men relied on her to tell them the truth about their health, though Walker took care not to tread on Dr. Green's authority and contradict his diagnoses. She understood that he risked his own reputation by taking her on, even as a volunteer, and she wanted to do her job so well that someone in the government would change his mind and offer her a commission.

The soldiers Mary Walker treated were probably unaware of her official position at the hospital, but they liked her because she took care of them, talked to them, and even wrote letters for them. She considered this kind of compassion essential to the healing process. The men also liked Walker because she was young and pretty. One day, as she made her way through the hospital ward, aware that the patients felt particularly gloomy, she made a point of smiling at each of them, trying to engage in light conversation. On a stand next to one man's bed, Dr. Walker saw a small photograph case. Assuming it contained a picture of his girlfriend or wife, she said, "I suppose the sweetest face in the world is in that case." The soldier replied, "Yes, you open it and you will see the sweetest face that I ever saw." She opened it and found a mirror. The sight of her surprised look kept him cheered up for several days.

Mary Walker was not oblivious to her attractiveness and its effect on men. Dorothea Dix, superintendent of the army nurses, toured the Indiana Hospital, and Walker found herself "somewhat amused" at Dix's behavior that day in the fall of 1861. "She seemed in such a troubled mood about something when she first saw me," Walker later remembered. Then she found out about Dix's dedication to keeping "young and good looking women out of the hospital." Walker assumed Dix was unhappy about finding one of those women not only working in the hospital, but working with the title of "doctor." That Mary Walker wore trousers no doubt added to Dix's disapproval. Perhaps worst of all for this professional administrator, Dix held no authority over Walker, and both women knew it.

Everything about Dorothea Dix's conduct during that visit irritated Mary Walker more than it amused her. She criticized the superintendent's disdainful reaction to the sight of a soldier's uncovered foot as he lay in bed. "She turned her head the other way," Walker observed, "seeming not to see the condition, while I was so disgusted with such sham modesty that I hastened to arrange the soldier's bedclothing." The doctor believed that small actions like straightening sheets for a wounded soldier represented the true spirit of service in promoting the Union's cause. She expressed limited admiration for Dorothea Dix, describing her as a "good hearted woman" who had performed a "great service in insane asylums." She had no similar words of praise for Dix's work with the army.

That true spirit of service imbued Mary Walker's work at the Indiana Hospital. Although other doctors eventually joined the staff, her workload shifted but did not lessen. Because she had treated so many patients, she witnessed the rapid depletion of supplies. Dr. Walker considered it part of her duties to make sure they were replenished, yet she knew it was not as easy as filing a requisition. Into the fall of 1861, the US Army's Medical Department struggled to supply all its hospitals, mostly because it had to rely on coordinating transportation with the Quartermaster Corps, which had its own priorities. The US Sanitary Commission, the civilian agency founded to help the military meet those medical needs, was in the early months of operation, developing what would become—but was not yet—an efficient supply network.

Dr. Mary Walker opted to bypass these large organizations and rely on what she knew best: local networks of volunteers. Soldiers' aid (or relief) societies had sprung up throughout the North after Fort Sumter, and Walker wrote to as many as she could, asking for supplies. Even this system experienced glitches. Around November 1861, the doctor contacted Edwin Stone, pastor of the North Congregational Church and head of the Relief Society in Providence, Rhode Island. Stone replied that his organization would be happy to send supplies, noting that he had once lived in Indiana, so he felt an affinity for the namesake hospital. Walker waited through December for the promised items, then followed up with Stone. His letter was apologetic. The Relief Society had indeed packed up a box of supplies, but it had "mistakenly not been sent."

A few of Dr. Walker's extra duties took her away from Washington, sometimes for days at a stretch. As she wrote to her sister and brother-in-law that November, "I suppose you all expected me to go to war, and I thought it would be too cruel to disappoint you, and have accordingly made my way to 'Dixie Land.'" Walker occasionally traveled to Virginia, a Confederate state with portions in Union control, to help newly discharged patients get settled at home. Steamboats departed Washington every half-hour for the thirty-minute voyage along the Potomac River to Alexandria. This city, "built of bricks . . . looks quite desolate, as nearly all of the wealthy people have gone farther South since the trouble commenced." From Alexandria, the doctor periodically made the two-and-a-half-mile journey to Camp Williams, a vast tent city that stretched along the banks of the Potomac, to see if she could be of assistance.

These trips into Dixie did not take Mary Walker too far south, but they served as a sobering reminder of how close the Confederacy was to Union territory, even its capital. Though located in a seceded state, Alexandria had been occupied by Union troops since late May 1861. About eight miles south of Washington on the Potomac River, Alexandria held too much strategic value for the Union to leave it in Confederate hands. After Virginia left the Union on May 23, President Lincoln ordered Northern troops to take both Alexandria and Arlington. In advance of their arrival, declining to engage the North at this point, Confederate general Robert E. Lee sent his men off to Manassas Junction. Only one Union soldier lost his life during the otherwise peaceful occupation. Twenty-four-year-old Colonel Elmer Ellsworth, until recently a law clerk working for Lincoln, was shot dead by an irate Confederate sympathizer when Ellsworth removed the secessionist flag that flew over his hotel.

The Union occupation held, and Alexandria swiftly transformed into a war town. President Lincoln imposed martial law. Movement in and out of the city required a pass, and its population swelled to 17,000 by the end of the war. As additional troops moved in, more restaurants, saloons, and brothels opened, their owners swearing allegiance to the United States government. Abandoned homes and public buildings turned into supply depots, military offices, prisons, and hospitals—more than thirty of them, with beds for over 6,500 men. Because of the huge Union presence and its proximity to the Union's capital, Alexandria also attracted Confederate spies and saboteurs. This may have given Dr. Mary Walker an idea about another way she could contribute to the war effort, which, three years later, put her at the mercy of enemy soldiers in Georgia.

When Mary Walker arrived in Washington in late September 1861, the city buzzed with stories about Rose O'Neal Greenhow, currently under house arrest for spying for the South. Born to a slaveholding family in Maryland, Greenhow moved to DC around 1830 to live with an aunt who ran a popular boardinghouse at the Old Capitol. She met a lot of important and influential people—Whigs, Democrats, and, later, Republicans—who sparked her interest in politics. In 1835 the dark-haired beauty married Robert Greenhow Jr., a lawyer from Virginia who worked for the State Department. After she was widowed in 1854, Greenhow became a prominent socialite, hosting a fashionable salon at her home at 398 16th Street NW that attracted the sharpest political minds of the time.

During the election of 1860, Rose Greenhow did not hide her dislike of Abraham Lincoln, and she supported the right of Southern states to secede from the Union. Yet, Northern politicians and military officers continued to attend her social functions, where they spoke freely about unfolding events, unaware that Greenhow might pose a threat to them. Even before Fort Sumter, she funneled information to Southern secessionists, and Captain Thomas Jordan recruited Rose Greenhow as a spy. A native Virginian, Jordan was a West Point graduate who had fought in the Seminole Wars and the Mexican-American War. Before 1860 ended, he supported secession—he resigned his commission to join the Confederate Army in May 1861—and started an espionage ring with Greenhow at the center of his DC operation.

Men liked to talk to the personable and attractive Rose Greenhow. Though they knew of her Southern sympathies, it took some time, and a costly lesson, before they accepted that she was capable of treachery. For months, Greenhow engaged her guests in conversation; sometimes she would expertly manipulate them to talk about things she wanted to know, and then she would code the information and send it on to Confederate leaders through Captain Jordan's network. At the beginning of July, Greenhow learned the details of Brigadier General Irvin McDowell's plan to attack Confederate forces at Manassas, Virginia.

On July 9, Rose Greenhow coded a message, rolled it in a piece of silk, and gave it to her courier, sixteen-year-old Bettie Duvall. The young woman wrapped the small bundle up in the bun at the back of her head, got into a milk cart, and drove across the Chain Bridge to Confederate brigadier general Pierre Gustave Toutant Beauregard's headquarters at the Fairfax County Courthouse. Duvall met first with General Milledge Bonham and told him she carried an urgent message for Beauregard. When Bonham promised to pass it along, he watched as "she took out her tucking comb and let fall the longest and most beautiful roll of hair I have ever seen. She took then from the back of her head, where it had been safely tied, a small package, not larger than a silver dollar, sewed up in silk."

Though Beauregard received similar information from other sources, he gave special credit to Rose Greenhow for helping the Confederacy secure its victory at the First Battle of Bull Run. Northerners expressed shock over this unexpected event, and rumors began circulating in Washington that Greenhow was a spy. Aware of the gossip, she nevertheless continued her work. For about six weeks, Allan Pinkerton, head of the Union's new secret service, surveilled the activities at Greenhow's home. In the late-morning heat of August 23, as Greenhow returned home from running errands, Pinkerton arrested her and ordered the house searched. While the search was in progress, Greenhow asked permission to change her clothes. Pinkerton obliged, and as soon as she was alone, she destroyed some incriminating documents she had been carrying.

Allan Pinkerton's men found more than enough evidence in the rest of the house to prove Rose Greenhow's involvement in espionage. He declined to imprison her, perhaps as part of a strategy to catch her compatriots. Over the next week or so, other women in Washington were discovered to be corresponding with Confederates. They also were not imprisoned, but instead brought to Greenhow's home to serve their house arrest with her. Every day, Greenhow underwent an interrogation. Almost every day, she managed to get some information from her jailers or her visitors and pass it along. Pinkerton observed, "She has not ceased to lay plans, to attempt the bribery of officers having her in charge, to make use of signs from the windows of her house to her friends on the street, to communicate with such friends and through them . . . to the rebels."

When Mary Walker began her work with the Indiana Hospital in the fall of 1861, Rose Greenhow remained in her 16th Street home under the watchful eyes of Pinkerton and his men. Learning about Greenhow's activities, Walker thought about how women could use their gender to their advantage as spies. The doctor would have also realized that no cover, no matter how brilliantly conceived, was foolproof. She kept these ideas in the back of her mind. But not too far back. She anticipated it might not be long before she could make a similar contribution to the Union.

Dr. Mary Walker soon became a familiar figure in Washington, DC, and many people considered her an oddity. There had been no female medical doctor in the capital since Lydia Hasbrouck had practiced there in the 1850s. Walker's physical appearance made her even more unusual than Hasbrouck. The physician from Oswego continued to wear her own version of reform dress: a knee-length frock over trousers. Even decades later, one young woman remembered catching sight of Mary Walker in the city.

Julia Taft was also well known in the capital city. As a teenager, she had arrived there from Lyons, New York, with her family after her father, a longtime member of the Democratic Party, accepted a position in the late 1850s as an examiner with the US Patent Office. Horatio Nelson Taft rented a home at 15th and L Streets near Franklin Square, and he leased two enslaved workers from a Virginia owner to ease his wife's housekeeping burdens. Taft earned enough from the Patent Office to keep his family comfortable. Though not part of the Washington elite, the Tafts frequently socialized with a variety of politicians and federal government employees.

Julia Taft enrolled in Madame Smith's French School, not far from the White House. The institution specialized in teaching the French language, as well as its literature and history. In true "finishing" fashion, the young women learned deportment and the proper curtsy for presentation at court. All of this came in handy when the eighteen-year-old Prince of Wales—later, Edward VII of England—visited Washington in October 1860 and toured the school. Taft conversed with the prince in French, and she was one of three students selected to play a game of tenpins in the school gymnasium with the royal visitor.

The results of the November elections ended Julia Taft's studies at the French School. Though she later explained that the place closed that fall because of "unsettled conditions" in Washington, in fact, Madame Smith was a secessionist who could not bear the thought of Abraham Lincoln as president. Smith shuttered her school and moved on to Richmond. Horatio Taft did not believe his daughter's education was complete, so he sent Julia back to New York, to the Elmira Collegiate Seminary, the same institution Mary Walker's friend, Lydia Sayer, had attended a few years earlier.

Within a few months, politics again interfered with Julia Taft's education. All the talk of secession, especially the likelihood that Virginia would leave the Union, prompted Horatio Taft to gather his children under one roof. When he learned that the local county sheriff in New York planned to travel to Washington for Lincoln's inauguration, he arranged for Julia to accompany him. Charles Sabin Taft, Julia's older half-brother, also arrived that spring of 1861, as a doctor with the recently organized US Signal Corps.

Between Lincoln's inauguration and the beginning of the war, Julia Taft, now sixteen years old, spent much of her time shuttling her little brothers between their home and the Executive Mansion to play with Tad and Willie Lincoln. The boys' mothers, who met at one of the city's many social events, orchestrated the friendships. Julia Taft, pretty and personable, became a favorite of both Abraham and Mary Lincoln, easily engaging them in conversation, sometimes spending hours at the president's home.

When the war started, Julia Taft decided she had to do something to support the Union war effort. Between her half-brother's profession and her father's place of work—part of the Patent Office Building had been converted into the Indiana Hospital—it is hardly surprising she chose nursing. "I wanted to be a regular nurse but Miss Dix, who was head of the nurses, told me she never took any under thirty years of age." At the Washington Infirmary, Dr. Charles Taft refused to employ women of any age as nurses. He let male medical students perform those duties, but he allowed his sister to volunteer. "I went there often to read to the soldiers, write letters for them or play cards with them."

Julia Taft wanted to do more. In July 1861, Dr. Norman Barnes, a surgeon with the 27th New York Volunteers and a friend of Horatio Taft, offered her a position as his "assistant surgeon." With youthful naiveté, Taft thought she would help the doctor with "complicated surgeries," and that she would be "sent to staunch the wounds of handsome soldiers." Instead, she worked as Barnes's secretary, handling correspondence from friends and family members looking for soldiers from the unit. The next time Julia Taft delivered her younger brothers to the president's house, she told the Lincolns about the job. Abe Lincoln ruffled Taft's dark curls and said, "Well, well. Little Julie an assistant surgeon. When McClellan hears that, he'll advance on Richmond at once."

Writing letters for Dr. Barnes did not seem much different than what Julia Taft had been doing at her brother's hospital. But with Barnes, she had a title—misleading as it was—and then an incredible opportunity. When the 27th moved out toward Manassas to participate in the First Battle of Bull Run, Taft was tasked with visiting the sick and wounded from the regiment who were left behind in the hospital and reporting on their condition to the doctor twice a week. Two of the soldiers needed to be invalided out, but the officers who had to sign the discharge papers were away with the 27th in Virginia. Taft and her father secured travel passes to cross into Virginia and go to the encampment, where Taft got the signatures she needed.

By the fall of 1861, as the number of sick and wounded soldiers in Washington, DC, increased, Julia Taft undertook more duties at her brother's hospital. In addition to reading, she brought food and coffee to the patients, and she learned how to clean a wound without fainting at the sight of blood. Still, Charles Taft remained resolute: No woman doctor would work in his hospital. As his sister remembered, "Dr. Mary Walker wanted to be taken on his staff but he had a horror of her because she wore men's clothes. I knew her quite well, though her natty men's suits always gave me a pain." Walker likely crossed paths often with Julia Taft. The physician worked at the Indiana Hospital, in the same building as Horatio Taft. She also stopped in at other area hospitals to lend a hand whenever she could, and to inquire about a permanent position.

Neither of the Taft siblings approved of Mary Walker's sartorial choices. Dr. Walker understood how her appearance affected some people, yet she refused to give up reform dress. In early December 1861, she wrote to Lydia Hasbrouck at *The Sibyl*, "Do not think because I have been silent thus long, that I have been returned to dressical chains, and am consequently unfit for the battles of life—for such is not the fact." The doctor insisted that "any person of substance" judges others only on character, not on what they wear. And she practiced judicious conversation on the topic. "It is my motto to live my principles, and not say much about them to those who will be made bitter and unhappy," she explained to Hasbrouck. "I intend to speak my sentiments when I do speak, but I think that silences [are] sometimes better than parlances."

Other women in the medical profession also rejected "dressical chains." Dr. Fidelia Rachel Harris Reid, an 1857 graduate of the Eclectic Medical Institute of Cincinnati, received approval in May 1861 from the Wisconsin governor to establish the Florence Nightingale Union, a training program for female nurses. She set up a branch in Berlin, Wisconsin, where she lived with her husband, the Reverend Harris Reid, formerly a practicing physician, now a Unitarian minister.

From the early days of the Florence Nightingale Union, Dr. Reid had expressed concern over Dorothea Dix's vision of a female nurse corps. Reid wrote an article for *The Sibyl* on "Short Dresses in the Army," published in June 1861, as the Union scrambled to meet the medical needs of its military. Reid pointed out that she had been very busy since the start of the war, treating patients who failed to thrive under allopathic care. She lauded the women who offered their services to the Union. "But what cannot we women do, in cases of emergencies?" Reid asked, assuming readers of *The Sibyl* knew the answer. And she took the opportunity to promote dress reform. "Every day I bless the short dress. How could I do what I do without them?" Bloomer costumes afforded practicality and ease of movement. Reid could not understand why Dorothea Dix advised her that any woman working in a hospital should abandon them.

Fidelia Reid refused to give up the "short dress," as did Mary Walker. Both women knew their fashion choice alienated some people, but as Walker pointed out, she intended to "live my principles." Though men like Dr. Charles Taft had a "horror" of Mary Walker, others, like J. M. Mackenzie, appreciated her talents. In October 1861, Walker met Mackenzie, a doctor who traveled from Sacramento, California, to treat Union soldiers. Whether they worked together in one of the Washington hospitals or had conversed at a social occasion, Mackenzie thought so highly of Walker's abilities that he wrote her a letter of support, which she used in her continued quest to secure a commission. Yet even coupled with Dr. Green's repeated recommendations to the surgeon general, she remained unsuccessful.

As 1861 drew to a close, Mary Walker realized she must take another tack. No matter how hard she worked in Washington, no matter how many people she knew, she could not get the official position she wanted. Her decision to enroll in the Hygeio-Therapeutic College in New York City—the same one her friend Lydia Hasbrouck had attended in the 1850s—may seem an odd choice given that she wanted to improve her chances of receiving a commission. The school based its curriculum on eclectic methods, which the army medical establishment considered hardly better than quackery. Mary Walker's association with this kind of program would not enhance her credentials in their eyes.

From her perspective, based on what she had experienced during those few months at the Indiana Hospital, wounded soldiers would benefit from the treatments emphasized at the Hygeio-Therapeutic. Dr. Walker had a low opinion of the most current method of dealing with battle wounds—amputation—which she often found unwarranted. It was also the treatment her patients feared the most. Those who had been wounded in the arm or leg would ask Walker "in the most pitiful manner" if the amputation recommended by one of the other ward surgeons was really necessary. They told Walker they would rather die than live without a limb. These cases affected her the most, making it "very difficult for me to suppress my emotions."

The amputation diagnoses presented Mary Walker with a dilemma, because she "did not wish to be unprofessional and say anything to other medical officers' patients that would seem like giving advice outside of a council [sic]." She worried that if she clashed too often with other doctors about amputation, she would find herself blacklisted from all the military hospitals in Washington. It was a tough position. The doctor wanted to continue her medical work, wanted to observe "medical etiquette," but when she witnessed what she believed was an unnecessary amputation, she concluded that she had a "higher duty" to her patients.

Once, Dr. Walker had been brought in to assist in an operation "where it was no more necessary than to amputate anybody's arm that had never been injured." The soldier had suffered from what she assessed as a "slight flesh wound," yet two doctors decided the arm had to come off. Walker suspected the surgeons really wanted practice. She considered the whole episode distasteful and vowed to figure out a way to cut down on needless amputations without losing her job.

Normally a direct person, in this situation Mary Walker opted for discretion. As she made her rounds at city hospitals, "whenever I found that there were more contemplated operations, and a complaint from a soldier that a decision had been made to remove a limb, I casually asked to see it, and in almost every instance saw amputation was not only unnecessary, but to me it seemed wickedly cruel." Instead of confronting the surgeon, she spoke to the patient, first securing a promise he would not tell anyone about their conversation. Then Walker let him know that "no one was obliged to submit to an amputation unless he chose to do so, that his limbs belonged to himself." If the doctor insisted, the patient should "kick up a fuss and swear at the doctor, and declare that if they forced him to have an operation that he would never rest after his recovery until he had shot them dead."

Surgeons performed an estimated 60,000 amputations during the war, which accounted for three-quarters of all operations. Mary Walker was not the only doctor concerned about the high frequency of this surgery, but especially in battlefield hospitals, physicians believed this was the best way to save a wounded soldier's life. The Minié ball, a new style of bullet created by a French army officer in the 1840s, did more damage to the human body than the old musket ball. When a Minié ball crashed into a limb, it shattered bone and pulped muscles and ligaments. The most sophisticated treatment method—the one most likely to save the patient's life—was amputation. The doctors who performed the surgery were trained for the procedure, and contrary to persistent myths, patients routinely received a chloroform anesthesia. But due to limited understanding about germs, surgeons operated without clean hands or sterilized equipment. Patients who survived the amputation ran the risk of dying from postoperative infection.

Mary Walker's roundabout intervention saved the limbs of some patients, but she may not have always been correct with her counsel. Wounded soldiers who refused amputation often suffered lifelong pain and mobility problems. Walker and other physicians of the eclectic school were on the right track with their emphasis on hygiene and cleanliness, though. Dr. Walker wanted to make sure she was current with the latest theories and practices, so in early 1862 she enrolled in the Hygeio-Therapeutic College in New York City.

The decision to expand her credentials at this institution is another example of Mary Walker's uncompromising attitude toward the practice of medicine. She might have gained more acceptance from male military doctors had she signed up for an allopathic medical program. But because of her background in health reform, she did not believe in that method—and not even the war could change her mind. Besides, continued discrimination against female students would have made it difficult for her to find an allopathic school to accept her.

In addition to the intellectual stimulation of returning to a classroom environment, Dr. Walker probably experienced a psychological boost from getting back to the familiarity of eclectic medicine and its reform-minded practitioners. Walker's time at the Hygeio-Therapeutic College may have overlapped with that of Dr. Lydia Folger Fowler, who had attended the Central Medical College of Syracuse, the forerunner of Walker's alma mater, the Syracuse Medical College. A decade older than Mary Walker, Fowler had been born and raised in Massachusetts. The Folger family could trace its lineage to Benjamin Franklin, and Lydia Fowler claimed as cousin to both Lucretia Mott, who had organized the Seneca Falls Convention, and Maria Mitchell, the noted astronomer.

As a teenager, Lydia Folger attended the Wheaton Female Seminary in Massachusetts, where she later taught for a couple of years. In 1844 she married Lorenzo Fowler, a phrenologist, and frequently accompanied him on the lecture circuit. While he talked to male audiences about the relationship between the size and shape of a person's skull to his character and intellect, she lectured to women about child care and hygiene. The couple built a profitable business from lecturing and publishing on the topics of physiology, phrenology, and astronomy. During the 1840s, Lorenzo Fowler began editing both the *American Phrenological Journal* and the *Water-Cure Journal*, both important within the eclectic medical community.

In 1849, the Central Medical College in Syracuse accepted Lydia Fowler as one of eight female students in that year's coeducational class.

By the time she enrolled in her second term, Fowler was serving as the principal of the school's Female Department. She received her medical degree in 1850, and the following year Central Medical College hired her as a professor of midwifery and diseases of women and children. Fowler was the first American-born woman to earn this degree and the first woman to receive a professorship at a medical school.

After Central closed in 1852, Dr. Fowler went into private practice in New York City, where she primarily treated women and children. She continued writing and lecturing as well, sometimes accompanying her husband on his speaking tours. As one of the few women in the medical profession, Fowler became interested in the broader cause of women's rights. She joined the burgeoning movement in the 1850s, attending several women's rights conventions, and sometimes serving as secretary of those meetings. In 1860 the Fowlers moved to England. When they returned in 1862, Dr. Fowler accepted a position as the clinical midwifery instructor at the Hygeio-Therapeutic College, where she may have met Mary Walker.

Even if Walker's time there had not overlapped with Dr. Fowler's, she was not the only woman in the program. During the winter of 1862, Dr. Huldah Page served as professor at the college, and the sixteen students enrolled that term were split evenly—eight men and eight women. Because Mary Walker already had an MD, she took a shortened course, spending three months taking classes rather than five. She also attended clinics at Bellevue Hospital, and she wrote a thesis called "The Secessionists." The Hygeio-Therapeutic College held a graduation ceremony and party on April 1, 1862, which included remarks by the professors, reform songs written for the occasion, and recognition of women physicians as "living protests against injustice, and noble examples of energy, capability, and usefulness."

Armed with these enhanced credentials, Mary Walker set off to figure out another way to secure a military commission.

CHAPTER FOUR

Field Surgeon

Dr. Mary Walker still could not secure a commission. She speculated that bolstering her medical credentials would convince military authorities to offer her one, but that failed to happen. The doctor returned to Washington in early April 1862, eventually renting in the northwest part of the city, at 52 Morton Street. She resumed volunteer work at the military hospitals, probably supporting herself by treating private patients.

There was no shortage of sick and wounded who needed care that spring and summer. In early 1862, while Mary Walker advanced her medical education in New York, the war ground on through its first year, dashing hopes on both sides for a quick victory. In the west, Brigadier General Ulysses S. Grant and Flag Officer Andrew H. Foote coordinated an attack on the Confederate Fort Henry, on the Tennessee River near the Tennessee–Kentucky border. The fort surrendered on February 6. Ten days later, nearby Fort Donelson capitulated as well, putting both the Tennessee and Cumberland Rivers under Union control, forcing the Confederates out of western Kentucky and earning Grant a promotion to major general.

The Henry and Donelson victories paved the way for a larger one downriver at Shiloh, in southwestern Tennessee, near Confederate general Albert Sidney Johnston's encampment at Corinth, Mississippi. Grant's Army of Western Tennessee and Major General Don Carlos Buell's Army of the Ohio, a combined force of some 63,000, squared off against 40,000 Confederates on April 6 and 7. Though Southern troops appeared on the brink of victory after the first day of fighting, they suffered a decisive reversal the next. The 20,000 killed and wounded there—unprecedented casualties—proved that neither side intended to give up. After Shiloh, General Grant understood that only a "complete conquest" of the South would end the war.

Confederate Major General Stonewall Jackson kept after the Federals. His spring Valley Campaign, which stretched from March into June, successfully pitted 17,000 Southerners against the Union's far superior forces in the Shenandoah Valley, about 131 miles west of Washington, DC. Meanwhile, Union general George McClellan launched his Peninsula Campaign in April, not long after Mary Walker returned to the capital. McClellan planned to use the James and York Rivers in Virginia to facilitate his troops' capture of Richmond. It took over four hundred vessels to move more than 110,000 troops and supplies to the Peninsula. Although the Yankees reached the outskirts of the Confederate capital by the end of May, heavy rains slowed their advance. Robert E. Lee took command of Southern forces around Richmond at the beginning of June, after the inconclusive battle at Seven Pines. At the end of the month, the Seven Days Battles pushed McClellan's men away from the Confederate capital and back down the Virginia Peninsula.

These battles meant Washington hospitals overflowed with patients, keeping Dr. Mary Walker busy. At the beginning of the Peninsula Campaign, Frederick Law Olmsted, executive secretary of the US Sanitary Commission, convinced Secretary of War Edwin Stanton to authorize the creation of a fleet of hospital ships to transport the sick and wounded to the capital for treatment. A variety of government-owned ships were converted into floating hospitals. The new Hospital Transport Service (HTS) improved treatment of soldiers, but did not perfect it. Passage from battlefield to DC hospitals often took as long as four days, with many patients left unattended for hours at a time because of a lack of medical personnel.

Northern white women stepped in to fill this shortage with the HTS, taking on nursing jobs. At the outbreak of war, thirty-one-year-old Katherine Prescott Wormeley first joined the Newport Ladies' Aid Society in Rhode Island, and she received a Union contract to sew 50,000 uniform shirts for soldiers. In late April 1862, she learned about the Sanitary Commission's hospital ships and decided on nursing as her next contribution to the war effort. Wormeley traveled to New York in May to board the repurposed steamer, the *Daniel Webster*, and later served on the *Wilson Small*. She and three other women were assigned duties as matrons, which seemed to Wormeley more like housekeeping than nursing. "We attend to the beds, the linen, the clothing of the patients. We have a pantry and store-room, and are required to do all the cooking for the sick, and see that it is properly distributed according to the surgeons' orders. We are also to have a general superintendence over the condition of the wards and over the nurses, who are all men."

An outbreak of typhoid fever expanded Katherine Wormeley's duties. Soon, she and the other white women took on nursing tasks such as bandaging wounds to meet all the patients' critical care needs. Wormeley had no kind words for civilian doctors who ignored ill men in favor of the wounded because, she believed, the physicians preferred to spend time in surgery. She also disparaged contraband workers, freed African Americans who she thought did not pay close enough attention to their tasks. By the end of the summer, the army's upgraded ambulance service absorbed most of the HTS's transportation responsibilities, freeing up Katherine Wormeley and the other matrons to transfer to positions in regular military hospitals in Washington, DC, and other points north.

The capital city struggled with the rapid changes brought on by the war. Journalist Mary Clemmer Ames described Washington in 1862 as a "third rate Southern city." Its mansions lacked modern conveniences, its buildings were "low, small and shabby in the extreme," and most of its public buildings stood unfinished. The war only contributed to this lack-luster air. "Forts bristled above every hill-top. Soldiers were entrenched at every gate-way. Shed hospitals covered acres on acres in every suburb. Churches, art-halls and private mansions were filled with the wounded and dying of the American armies."

Mary Ames had arrived in Washington at the beginning of the war, joining her once-estranged husband, Daniel Ames, a Methodist minister who felt the call to provide spiritual guidance for the troops. Mary Ames immediately volunteered as a nurse at a variety of hospitals. In the streets she saw "soldiers foot-sore, sun-burned, and weary, their clothes begrimed, their banners torn, their hearts sick with hope deferred, ready to die with the anguish of long defeat."

With so many people moving in and out of the capital, security tightened. This helped protect the military, but it choked the residents' civil liberties. In July 1861, General George McClellan appointed a provost marshal for the city. Colonel Andrew Porter, a West Point graduate and veteran of the Mexican-American War, commanded 1,000 infantrymen plus a cavalry squadron and artillery battery to keep order in Washington. Porter controlled public drunkenness, made sure army officers reported to their assigned posts, issued passes for civilians who wanted to travel to Virginia, and surveilled residents suspected of disloyalty.

By the fall of 1861, the provost marshal was ordering the arrests of people who appeared to be working against the Union. President Lincoln informed his secretary of state, William Seward, in October that he had suspended habeas corpus in Washington. In February 1862, Provost Marshal Porter labeled the city a military encampment and placed it under the jurisdiction of military laws. The local police force expanded to assist the provost marshal.

Concerned about loyalty to the Union, President Lincoln required all army officers and federal employees to swear an oath of allegiance. In July 1861, Congress created a committee, which met in secret, to investigate federal workers suspected of disloyalty and who refused to take the oath. The following summer, Congress expanded the oath to the Ironclad Test Oath, requiring it of all federal officials, including members of their own body.

The administration's obsession with loyalty targeted men. Despite the high-profile arrest and detention of Rose Greenhow and several other secessionist women in August 1861, Union officials remained largely unconcerned about the political views and attendant behavior of women. Yet during the spring and summer of 1862, newspapers reported on the actions of another Confederate woman caught spying.

Isabella Maria Boyd, known as Belle, was born into a prosperous merchant family in Martinsburg, Virginia, in 1844. After Virginia seceded from the Union in 1861, Boyd's father joined the Confederate Army and was away from home in July when Union troops led by General Robert

Patterson occupied the town. Boyd first came to the attention of Union authorities when she shot and killed a Union soldier for verbally abusing her and her mother while attempting to raise the Stars and Stripes over their family home.

Because of Belle Boyd's youth and because she was a woman, she did not suffer any legal consequences. Over the next several months, she busied herself with nursing duties and keeping company with soldiers. As General Stonewall Jackson began his campaign in the Shenandoah Valley in the early spring of 1862, Boyd realized that her social and family connections could help her obtain information beneficial to the Confederate cause. She chatted and flirted with Union soldiers who willingly talked about Federal deployments and troop strengths. Boyd passed this information to the other side.

In mid-May of 1862, when Belle Boyd turned up in Union-occupied Front Royal, ostensibly to visit relatives, her reputation had preceded her. One newspaper correspondent described her as "an accomplished prostitute who has figured largely in the rebel cause," and reported that Federal authorities had been advised to arrest her. No one heeded the warning. When Stonewall Jackson launched a successful surprise attack on Front Royal on May 23, Belle Boyd waved a handkerchief at Confederate forces, directing their fire to Union lines.

Though the town once again reverted to Union control by June, Belle Boyd remained, carrying on her activities without sanction. A Union surgeon finally wrote to Secretary of War Stanton, apprising him of the dangers the young woman posed. After an investigation by the Secret Service, Stanton issued an arrest warrant in mid-July. Boyd was deposited in the Old Capitol Prison in Washington, DC, missing Rose Greenhow, recently released, by about a month. She spent fifteen months there, after which she gained her freedom through a prisoner exchange. Like Greenhow, Boyd headed to England to solicit help for the Confederate cause.

North and South, newspapers ran stories about Belle Boyd, usually referring to her as "notorious." One referred to her as a "betrayer . . . insanely devoted to the rebel cause." This journalist was preoccupied with Belle Boyd's looks, bemused at how she could attract so many men. "She is merely a brusque, talkative woman, red haired with keen, courageous grey eyes. . . . Her teeth are prominent, and she is meagre in person."

Mary Walker would not have felt any sympathy for Belle Boyd because of the young woman's Confederate loyalties. But the doctor would have been sensitive to the ways in which newspaper articles focused on Boyd's personal relationships and her physical appearance. While Walker approached dress reform as a political, women's rights issue, she understood its connection to women's private lives. People in the nineteenth century invested a lot of gendered meaning into clothing items. Those who violated the norms risked public and private ridicule and found themselves subjected to speculation about their own gender.

Few people in Washington, if any, knew about Mary Walker's personal life. No one would have known about her marriage to Albert Miller unless she had told them. As a private person, it is unlikely she would have raised the subject in conversation. If Dr. Walker dressed like other women, she would have blended in with the throngs of wives, sweethearts, mothers, and sisters who crowded the capital. But she wore trousers, which marked her, in the eyes of the public, as an "abnormal" woman.

Therefore, Mary Walker's continued dedication to dress reform was radical. In July 1862, *The Sibyl* published a letter from Walker that reiterated this. "I still report myself at the call of the dress reform roll," she wrote after an absence in the periodical of more than six months, and she insisted that the "principle involved is still valid." She criticized activists like Elizabeth Cady Stanton and Lucy Stone, who had abandoned the Bloomer costume. For them, fashion was a consequence of women's oppression rather than a cause, so they chose to concentrate their campaign for women's rights elsewhere.

According to Dr. Walker, these women lacked the fortitude to handle public criticism, and she decried their insufficient commitment: "It is literally impossible for one with any force of character and humanity to remain 'in the background,' when convinced by knowledge and reason, that their mission is evidently one that will result in great good to those whose necessities demand what they have not the power to gain for themselves."

The doctor's clashes with the military establishment had not diminished her force of character. They only made her more determined. The

Union's progress in the war also strengthened her commitment to be part of its positive changes. Like other abolitionists, Mary Walker believed the sectional conflict would ultimately unite the country and end the practice of slavery. She went home to Oswego in October 1862 and delivered several lectures on her experiences in Washington, DC. In some, Walker emphasized her work at the Indiana Hospital, and she probably took the opportunity to solicit donations for military hospitals. When she talked about the capital city, she focused on abolition there, underscoring how the Union's war aim had shifted to emancipation. Her Oswego audiences, with their long heritage of reform, would have been abuzz with the latest news.

President Lincoln signed the Compensated Emancipation Act in April 1862, and ended slavery in Washington, DC. Slave owners loyal to the Union had until July 15 to apply for up to $300 for each liberated slave. Any newly freed slave, who was willing, would be sent to Africa. Slavery had existed in Washington since 1790 when the city was first carved out from territory belonging to the slaveholding states of Maryland and Virginia. Within a decade, Washington had developed into a slave-trading center, a convenient location for transporting enslaved people between the upper and lower South. This made slavery highly visible in the capital city of a country that prided itself on freedom and liberty.

Though the practice of slavery hung on in DC, it did not thrive. Increasingly, owners granted freedom to enslaved people. Between 1820 and 1860 slave numbers dropped by more than half, from 6,400 to 3,100, and free blacks outnumbered the enslaved population by more than three to one. The Compromise of 1850, a complicated piece of federal legislation that, among other things, brought California into the Union as a free state, also abolished the slave trade in Washington. The 1862 Compensated Emancipation Act signaled that the federal government did not want to wait for voluntary manumissions; it intended to end slavery wherever it existed.

Politicians debated how to accomplish that goal. President Lincoln, a staunch Free-Soiler, always believed that Congress lacked the authority to abolish slavery where it already existed. Lincoln supported the Compensated Emancipation Act because it functioned like a state law—Washington was a discreet federal district over which Congress had direct jurisdiction. Radical Republicans, strongly committed to abolition, continued to push the president to do more. For them, the war provided the perfect opportunity because it was about slavery. As Indiana congressman George Julian commented in a speech to the House of Representatives in January 1862, "When I say that this rebellion has its source and life in slavery, I only repeat a simple truism."

For other white Northerners, that truism did not register so quickly. Since Fort Sumter, for them the war had been about the preservation of the Union. That was worth fighting and dying for. But most white Northerners were not abolitionists. If they felt any concern about the inhumanity of slavery, that did not mean they believed in racial equality. President Lincoln worried that an immediate universal emancipation of enslaved people would alienate the Northern whites who now supported the war. He believed it would enrage whites in the slaveholding border states that had remained with the Union, so he proceeded with caution.

Union military officials could not afford to be overly prudent. From their perspective, the work of enslaved people supported the Confederacy. Without that assistance, Southern troops would be deprived of many of their necessities, including food and clothing. During the first month of the war, General Benjamin Butler laid the foundation for turning military concerns into abolitionist policy. Before the war, he had been a Massachusetts lawyer and politician, and a brigadier general in the state militia. Although a member of the Democratic Party and an anti-abolitionist, he did not support secession.

After Fort Sumter, Butler joined the 8th Massachusetts Volunteers as brigadier general and, by late April 1861, led his troops to secure Annapolis, Maryland. He did the same in Baltimore; then, Butler, now a major general, received orders to take Fort Monroe, situated at the mouth of the James River near Norfolk, Virginia. Three enslaved men belonging to a Confederate officer fled to the fort on May 23, just as the state of Virginia ratified secession. One of his fellow officers arrived at Fort Monroe under a flag of truce and asked for the return of the men. General Butler refused. He pointed out that since Virginia had seceded, US laws regarding runaway slaves no longer applied. The three men, while not technically freed, remained at the Union fort as contraband of war.

Secretary of War Simon Cameron approved Butler's actions, and over the next weeks hundreds of enslaved people turned up at Fort Monroe, seeking sanctuary from their masters. This action of self-emancipation became common throughout slaveholding states and territories. Whenever enslaved people saw the opportunity, they secured their own freedom. They did not wait for a government or a military to do it for them. But in 1861, as far as the Union was concerned, "contraband" did not necessarily mean free. Congress passed the first Confiscation Act in early August, which allowed the Union to "confiscate Property used for Insurrectionary Purposes," but it only affected those enslaved people forced to work directly for the Confederacy. When General John C. Frémont, commander of the Western Department, issued a proclamation at the end of the month, freeing all enslaved people in Missouri, Lincoln ordered him to bring it in line with the Confiscation Act.

The president was not yet ready for a large-scale emancipation, so the cause moved along incrementally. In March 1862, about a month before slavery ended in Washington, DC, Congress passed an Act Prohibiting the Return of Slaves, an article of war that made it a court-martial offense for a soldier to relinquish a runaway enslaved person to their master. Three months later, Congress outlawed slavery in the US territories. Meanwhile, President Lincoln's discussions with politicians from the slaveholding border states about gradual, compensated emancipation went nowhere. During the summer of 1862, Lincoln talked to his Cabinet members about the possibility of issuing an emancipation proclamation, and he drafted one before the end of July.

That month, Congress passed another Confiscation Act, this time giving the military the power to free enslaved people from disloyal owners. As the Union military made progress into Confederate territory, it liberated more and more people. Finally, the institution of slavery no longer seemed sustainable. Though Lincoln had his proclamation ready, his secretary of state, William Seward, advised him to postpone issuing it until the Union won a battle. That finally happened—sort of—in Sharpsburg, Maryland, on September 17, 1862, along the Antietam Creek.

As the war entered its second year, the Union struggled for a major military victory. That spring, Stonewall Jackson's Valley Campaign prevented Federal troops from securing the Shenandoah Valley. The Seven Days Battles, at the end of June, succeeded in protecting the Confederate capital of Richmond, Virginia. A rematch at Manassas in late August gave General Robert E. Lee a decisive offensive victory that encouraged him to take the fight farther north, into Union territory.

Though outnumbered nearly two to one, Lee's forces held fast on that long day in September, from the Hagerstown Pike through a twenty-four-acre cornfield, and across a sunken road near the Dunker Church. Five hours of fighting in the morning produced 12,000 casualties, and the conflict raged into the afternoon. At dark, the number of the dead and wounded had jumped to more than 22,000, the single bloodiest day of the war. It took ten days to bury the dead. The two shattered, exhausted armies remained in place the following day, each willing to fight only if the other made the first move. Neither did. When Lee took his troops back to Virginia on September 19, General McClellan let the Confederates slip away. The Union general claimed it as a victory.

Antietam brought Clara Barton into the field once more. As bullets flew, the forty-year-old Patent Office employee arrived around noon with a wagonload of medical supplies at the northern edge of the cornfield. McClellan's troops had moved to Sharpsburg so quickly that the quartermaster could not keep up, hardly an uncommon occurrence during the early years of the war. Barton had been keenly aware of this supply problem since the previous April.

Like Dorothea Dix, the superintendent of army nurses, Clara Barton was alarmed when she heard of the attack on Union soldiers as they traveled through Baltimore right after Fort Sumter in April 1861. Some of the injured soldiers hailed from Barton's home state of Massachusetts, so she went to the DC train station to see what she could do to help. Throughout her life, Barton never hesitated to assist others. As a child in North Oxford in the 1830s, she had nursed her brother back to health after he had suffered a serious head injury from a fall.

Clara Barton felt the sting of gender discrimination as she pursued a teaching career. The young single women who went into classrooms in the early 1800s were often assigned summer sessions, which paid less than the winter terms dominated by male instructors, and they were shut out of administrative positions. Barton wanted the sessions that paid the highest salaries; she wanted to be the principal. Burned out after a few years, she moved to Washington, DC, in early 1854. A Massachusetts congressman helped the former schoolteacher secure a job as a clerk in the Patent Office, an unusual position for a woman, for which she received the same annual salary as the male clerks. The men resented her presence and found ways to harass her every day.

Schooled in patriotism since childhood, Clara Barton enthusiastically supported a Northern victory when the Civil War broke out. On April 19, 1861, she braved a rowdy crowd at the Washington train station to see what assistance she could offer the men of the 6th Massachusetts Regiment—dozens of them her former students—who had been attacked by secessionists in Baltimore. Barton found them lodging, fresh clothing, toiletries, and food. As tens of thousands of soldiers crowded into the capital, she visited, especially those from Massachusetts and New Jersey, collecting and distributing supplies to them. After the First Battle of Bull Run in July 1861, Barton became involved with DC hospitals, including the one set up in the Patent Office Building, bringing in a variety of items and spending time with the patients.

Working primarily with local ladies' aid societies, Clara Barton's cache of goods quickly filled three warehouses. During that summer and fall, she continued her employment at the Patent Office, likely encountering Dr. Mary Walker, who volunteered at the Indiana Hospital headquartered there. Barton was often out and about in Washington, delivering items directly to soldiers as they arrived at the train station and on hospital transport ships. She wanted to meet the needs of the young men wherever they were. In early August 1862, with the support of Massachusetts senator Henry Wilson, Massachusetts governor John Andrew, and quartermaster Colonel Daniel H. Rucker, Barton headed to the Virginia front with wagonloads of supplies.

After making deliveries to Union encampments around Fredericksburg, Clara Barton arrived at Culpeper on August 13, four days after John Pope's forces lost to Robert E. Lee, resulting in about 2,000 federal casualties. Many of the wounded were still there, medical personnel stretched thin trying to treat them all. Over two days and nights, Barton distributed what she brought and assisted doctors the best she could. On August 31, she made her way to Manassas to do the same, one of the first relief workers to reach the site of the Second Battle of Bull Run. Confederates continued to skirmish in the area, their snipers taking potshots at anyone in a blue uniform. In September, Clara Barton and her supply wagons were absorbed into the army's ten-mile train as it made its way through Maryland, headed for Sharpsburg.

Confronted with so many wounded along Antietam Creek, she took the initiative in administering medical care. She used her pocketknife to remove a bullet from a soldier's face. As she helped another to a drink of water, a bullet passed through her sleeve and struck the young man. One Yankee resisted Clara Barton's efforts to change the bandages that wound down around his chest. She insisted, and uncovered the identity of Mary Galloway, a teenager from Frederick, Maryland, who had joined the army to find her fiancé. Harry Barnard, an officer with the 3rd Wisconsin, had met Galloway in the fall of 1861 when his unit was part of the Union occupying force of Frederick. The two fell in love, and Galloway felt the sting of separation after Barnard moved on to his next posting. When his regiment passed through the town on its way to Antietam, Galloway decided to follow him. She found a uniform and posed as a hospital steward.

Confederate fire hit Mary Galloway as she neared Hagerstown Pike. For thirty-six hours she lay unattended, inexpertly self-bandaged and bleeding from a bullet wound in her neck. Dr. F. H. Harwood, a Wisconsin surgeon, found the soldier and grew suspicious when Galloway refused treatment. Harwood had already seen Clara Barton out among the fallen and called her over. Once Barton had convinced Galloway to admit who she was, the young woman allowed Harwood to remove the bullet, whose odd trajectory prevented it from killing her. Barton arranged to have Mary Galloway moved to Frederick, where she eventually reunited with Harry Barnard, who had also been wounded in battle.

Seven women were with the Union Army at Antietam, maybe more. In the case of Sarah Emma Edmonds, one of the most famous women who assumed the identity of a man to serve in the military, the claim of being at Antietam proved false. Born in Canada in 1841, Edmonds left home as a teenager to escape her abusive father. She adopted the name Franklin Thompson, dressed in men's clothing to make sure that her father could not track her down, and moved across the border. In May 1861, Edmonds gave up her job as a traveling bookseller to enlist with the 2nd Michigan Infantry, which mustered quickly enough to be in the East in time to cover the Union retreat from the First Battle of Bull Run. She then spent several months in Washington, DC, as a hospital attendant, where she may have encountered Mary Walker.

While working at a regimental hospital south of Alexandria, Virginia, Sarah Edmonds forged a strong friendship with another soldier, Jerome Robbins. She revealed her identity to him, perhaps because she found herself falling in love. Robbins did not reciprocate, but he kept her secret, which allowed her to remain with the 2nd Michigan. In early 1862, Edmonds received new orders to serve as the mail carrier for the regiment. She then marched off for the Peninsula Campaign, during which she engaged in some spying missions and sustained three serious injuries over several months. Edmonds refused medical treatment because she did not want anyone to find out she was a woman.

The 2nd Michigan Infantry saw action at a variety of places, but for part of September 1862, it was bivouacked near Fairfax Station, Virginia, and was not sent to Antietam. Yet in the memoir of her military service, Sarah Edmonds placed herself at Sharpsburg and included an account that echoed Clara Barton's experience with Mary Galloway. As Edmonds related the story, she found a soldier suffering with a neck wound. When a surgeon confirmed that the private would not live, the young man confessed to Edmonds that he really was a woman. An orphan, she had enlisted with her brother, who died earlier in the day. Edmonds carried out the soldier's dying wish—to be buried on the field—without anyone else knowing what she had done.

Sarah Edmonds published the first edition of her wartime memoir in 1864. Malaria and emotional exhaustion cut her military service short, forcing her to leave in 1863, before the end of her enlistment period, to seek treatment. After she recovered, she worked as a female nurse with the United States Christian Commission, a charitable organization founded by the Young Men's Christian Association (YMCA), to provide material and spiritual support for Union soldiers. The next year Edmonds revealed her exploits in the book eventually titled *Nurse and Spy in the Union Army*. She never identified her regiment or the man's name she had adopted. She freely borrowed stories she had heard, including that of Mary Galloway. Edmonds understood its dramatic impact and reinforced what Americans already knew: Women were taking extraordinary steps to contribute to the war effort.

The book did extremely well, selling about 175,000 copies to readers who found Sarah Edmonds's life both thrilling and appalling. The publisher's note to the 1865 edition advised, "Should any of her readers object to some of her disguises, it may be sufficient to remind them it was from the purest motives and most praiseworthy patriotism, that she laid aside, for a time, her own costume, and assumed that of the opposite sex, enduring hardships, suffering untold privations, and hazarding her life for her adopted country, in its trying hour of need." Sarah Edmonds directed her royalties to the Christian Commission, where she continued to work. In 1867 she married a carpenter and raised a family. In the 1880s, Sarah Edmonds Seelye successfully applied for a veteran's pension. She may be the only woman to have received this benefit because of her service as a soldier.

Sarah Edmonds's fictionalized memoir was not the first time Americans read about women in the military. Such stories stretched back to the Revolution, the most well-known that of Deborah Sampson, from Plympton, Massachusetts. After serving as an indentured servant and working as a teacher, looking for adventure and a better salary, Sampson decided to join the Continental Army. In May 1782, she donned male attire, took the name Robert Shurtliff, and signed up forty miles away from her hometown. Sampson served with the Light Infantry Company of the Fourth Massachusetts Regiment and saw action at Tarrytown, New York. Published accounts of her exploits, mostly laudatory, first appeared in 1797, and were still available in the antebellum years.

Romanticized stories of women like Deborah Sampson cropped up at the beginning of the Civil War. In the early spring of 1861, Susan Jones, a waitress in Columbus, Ohio, fell in love with Second Lieutenant Edward McGill. After the war started, McGill was ordered to Camp Dennison in Cincinnati. Determined to stay with him, Jones disguised herself as a man, adopted the name Robert Wilson, and enlisted in Company G of the 3rd Ohio Volunteer Infantry Regiment. She trained alongside the other soldiers and helped build the barracks at Camp Dennison.

As Robert Wilson, Jones fit in easily with the regiment. But when she approached Colonel Isaac Morrow for permission to switch to a different work crew, he became suspicious about her identity and ordered a physical examination. Even though Morrow issued an honorable discharge for Susan Jones, soldiers escorted her from the camp to the city jail in Columbus. It is unclear how long she remained there, though public opinion may have been responsible for a quick release. Reporters published positive depictions of her actions. One referred to her as brave and virtuous. Another remarked that though Jones "does unsex herself and takes up arms in defence of her country," it was unfair to punish her with jail time.

The political outcome of the bloody battle at Antietam caused a public stir. President Lincoln met with his Cabinet five days after hostilities ceased in Sharpsburg and told them he had made an agreement with God. If the Confederates were forced from Maryland, he would issue an emancipation proclamation. Lincoln wished the Union's victory had been more decisive, but it was enough. The time had come to change the direction of the war. The Emancipation Proclamation gave the seceded states until January 1, 1863, to return to the Union. If not, their enslaved population would be considered free.

When Dr. Mary Walker went home to Oswego in October 1862, the proclamation was still new and, for many white Northerners, controversial. White men had proved more than willing to fight for the Union, but convincing them to fight a war for emancipation was trickier. Racism existed in the North, where free blacks lived and worked in communities separate from whites. Black men could not vote in Illinois, Pennsylvania, New Jersey, and Ohio. In the late 1830s, the Pennsylvania state supreme court decreed in the case of *Hobbs v. Fogg*, "a free negro or mulatto is not a citizen within the meaning of the constitution and laws of the United

States, and of the state of Pennsylvania, and, therefore, is not entitled to the right of suffrage." Ending racial discrimination throughout the North would become a divisive, ongoing process.

Given the strong reform impulse in Oswego, the speech Mary Walker gave there about Washington, DC, likely reached a sympathetic audience. Walker's lecture, probably part of a fund-raising series, blended patriotism with a call for women's rights and abolition. Much of her talk centered on a verbal tour of the city's important government buildings, and she included details about the president's home, and meeting Mr. and Mrs. Lincoln. Walker's description of the collections of the Smithsonian segued into an account of the institution's antislavery lecture series. It attracted the "best, & most radical" speakers who "received the most deafening applause."

Dr. Walker also schooled her audience about the city's hospitals. She highlighted the work of the "pure, true, *noble* women" who risked their lives among contagious patients because of the dire need for medical personnel. She pointed out that these women, motivated by "pure benevolence & the highest of patriotism," were "slandered by those who have not the moral courage to step outside of time honored customs when our nation is in such peril." Walker predicted that the brave female hospital workers would receive justice in the end, "knowing that *right* is always the majority."

There is little doubt that Mary Walker considered herself one of those pure, true, noble women who endured slander for her determination to serve the war effort. Despite her best efforts, she had been unable to secure a commission by proving her worth in one of the Washington hospitals. Walker concluded that she would do the same as Clara Barton and other women—go to the Front. That was where the troops needed her the most. It is not clear why the doctor waited so long, though her fund-raising in Oswego indicates money was an issue. She needed some means of support while she donated her services to the Union.

In early November 1862, not long after returning to Washington from Oswego, Mary Walker assisted New York soldiers in obtaining furloughs so they could return home to vote. The midterm elections were particularly important, especially because of the preliminary Emancipation

Proclamation. The Republican Party needed to maintain congressional control in order to carry out its wartime agenda. Dr. Walker understood what was at stake at both the national and state levels, and the gubernatorial race in New York underscored the Republicans' precarious position. New York's incumbent Republican governor, Edwin D. Morgan, declined nomination for a second term. The state party ran General James Wadsworth against Democrat and former New York governor Horatio Seymour. Though a Unionist, Seymour criticized President Lincoln's wartime policies, which Walker would have found worrisome.

One day the doctor happened past a building in Washington that had been turned into a military transportation office. A large group of soldiers had gathered, impatient to secure the documents necessary so they could return home to vote. Walker heard some of the men complain that only about half of them would be able to do so. She pushed her way through the crowd, "amidst the cheers of the men," and offered to stay until midnight to help with the paperwork. The officer in charge replied that the office had to close at four o'clock. His staff was so overwhelmed with the travel requests that even with the extra help, not everyone would get out on time. Dr. Walker sat down and started filling out the forms. The last men departed on the 3:00 a.m. train. "I helped others to vote if not allowed to myself," she pointed out. Women's suffrage was never out of her thoughts. Though the soldiers voted, the outcome was not what Walker had hoped. Seymour scored a narrow victory over his Republican rival.

After the election, Mary Walker headed west of DC to Virginia, where Major General Ambrose Burnside was devising his strategy to defeat the Confederates. Though George McClellan had led Union troops to enough of a victory at Antietam that President Lincoln issued the preliminary Emancipation Proclamation, the general had failed to pursue Robert E. Lee from the battlefield. Even after Lincoln ordered him to go after the enemy, McClellan claimed he lacked the resources to successfully confront the Army of Northern Virginia. On November 7, Lincoln named Burnside the new leader of the Army of the Potomac.

A West Point graduate, Burnside served in the Mexican-American War as an artillery officer. One of the jobs he held after he left the army in 1853 was as treasurer for the Illinois Central Railroad, run by George McClellan, a former classmate at West Point. When the Civil War started, Burnside raised a regiment of volunteers from Rhode Island, which fought at the First Battle of Bull Run in 1861. Despite the Union defeat there, Burnside received rapid promotion to brigadier general of the volunteer forces. He led an expeditionary force into the coastal area of North Carolina, which ended with enough success to earn him another promotion—this time, to major general. In 1862 Burnside and his men were back with McClellan's Army of the Potomac, and they fought, undistinguished, at Antietam.

Unlike George McClellan, Ambrose Burnside took quick action. Within a week of his appointment, he began moving about 120,000 soldiers closer to Richmond, planning to capture the Confederate capital. Mary Walker joined his forces at Warrenton, a thriving market town originally of about six hundred people located twenty-one miles west of Manassas. Union and Confederate troops had been skirmishing in Fauquier County since the second Bull Run battle at the end of August 1862. Despite recent advances in ambulance services and the number of makeshift hospitals that had sprung up in Warrenton, many of the sick and wounded remained unattended as Burnside prepared to leave the town.

Carrying with her a blank book for keeping track of the names of patients, Dr. Walker found some men on the floor of an old house, many suffering the effects of typhoid. When she approached the officer in charge, he confessed that he was worn out from trying to treat all the patients while preparing the able-bodied men to head toward Richmond. "For God's sake, do something for them if you can," he told her. She could. Taking stock of the available supplies, the doctor found only a bucket of water and a cup. She hurried to the surrounding homes and asked for donations, but soon learned the Confederates had taken everything of value for their own hospital shortly before the Northerners had arrived.

Repeatedly told that nothing was left that could be used to bathe patients' faces, Mary Walker finally saw a two-quart basin in one woman's home and asked for it. "She said she would gladly give it to me but that the Confederate hospital had removed from there but a brief time previously, and had taken away every dish that could be used in dressing the wounded, and had finally come and asked for her last vegetable dish." The woman had resisted until the Confederate gave her a dollar for it and told her she could have it back when they had to move on. "I took the cue," Walker later remembered, and she offered the woman the same arrangement, giving up one of her own silver dollars.

With one problem solved, Mary Walker confronted another. She needed to find a way to make towels, because basin water alone could not wash the patients who were incapable of doing it themselves. Walker returned to her hotel room, which cost her three dollars a night, and went through her belongings. "As brilliant ideas had commenced to rush through my mind, the next one was to tear up a long night-dress I had with me into pieces about a foot square."

Dr. Walker delegated the task of washing patients' faces and hands to a soldier, instructing him that each one must receive clean water. Then she sat down to rest, keeping an eye on the man as he carried out his duties. Even when she went for lunch at her hotel, she did not forget her patients. "I did not have as much as I wished for myself, but I saved the greater part of the corn-bread and carried it to the sick, who had only hard-tack and coffee."

Now that Mary Walker had accomplished what she could for the patients in the short term, she set about securing their future care. Since General Burnside was still at the encampment, the doctor took her normal track. She went to the man at the top. "I soon went to headquarters, reported the condition of the sick, and asked that they be immediately [sent] to Washington where they could be properly cared for." Burnside did not question Mary Walker's expertise. He did not wave her away or denigrate her gender or her clothing choices. This may have been a matter of expediency. "The condition of the army at this time was such that raids from the opposing forces were expected at any time," Walker recalled. Burnside needed as many fit men as possible for his planned assault on Richmond. Those unable to travel with the army were entitled to quality medical attention, which the doctor was willing to facilitate.

General Burnside dictated an order for his aide-de-camp, Major William Cutting, which authorized Dr. Mary Walker to accompany the patients to Washington, DC. "All persons should afford her every facility in caring for" the men along the way. On November 15, the day the Union Army marched off toward Richmond via Falmouth, the doctor boarded a train for Washington with her patients. Of the seven train cars designated for patient transfer, only one was a passenger car. "Some of the not very sick were placed upon the tops of the cars, as there was not enough room in the freight cars for them all."

Most of the people in the passenger car were visiting dignitaries who were not required to give up their seats to the patients. Mary Walker may have intended an insult when she later described those passengers as "some brave persons" who had gone to Warrenton on a variety of military-related business and were now "especially anxious to get out of danger." One of the important passengers was Massachusetts senator Henry Wilson, a future vice president of the United States. Walker also noted, not happily, that no one told her those people would be on the train.

They had not traveled far before the train reached Warrenton Junction. It stopped there while one engine and two cars were detached, going on to Alexandria. The remaining engine and cars sat on the tracks. Acutely aware of the suffering of her patients, especially those on top of the train in the brisk November cold, Mary Walker checked on them. She found the men "as comfortable as they could expect, as they expressed themselves, with the exception of two. As I approached one I saw that he was near the other shore." She managed to write down the names of both men before they died so their families could be notified. After her rounds, she realized the train remained at the junction. The engineer was waiting for orders, but there was not a single officer on board. Using the authority General Burnside conveyed, Dr. Walker told the engineer to proceed to Washington. "I could not help suppressing a smile at the thought of his stating that he was waiting for orders, and that in reality I was then military conductor of the train that bore one of the law-makers of the nation not only, but its citizens and its helpless defenders."

A group of men and women bearing baskets full of sandwiches was on hand at the station when the train pulled in. Private citizens and charitable organizations had been feeding transient soldiers in this way since the beginning of the war. Mary Walker, tired and hungry from her long day, asked for a bit of food only to be told that the sandwiches were reserved for the sick. She explained, "I had just alighted from the train where I had been down to the front, but it was with reluctance that they [let] me have one of these." This probably felt like a humiliation to her. All the work she donated to the cause still went unrecognized by others.

Arrangements had already been made to transport the patients to area hospitals. Mary Walker had discharged the duty General Burnside had assigned to her, yet still felt an obligation to the two men who had died on the train. She passed on their names to an official with the War Department so the families could be notified. Walker sent her own letter to one of the families. "I gave to them a history of the brave life and the death of the soldier, signing my full name."

Families cherished this type of personal condolence. The staggering fatalities of the Civil War—some 620,000—kept the minds of Americans focused on death. Frederick Law Olmsted, executive secretary of the Sanitary Commission, described the country as a "republic of suffering." Survivors sought the solace of knowing that their loved ones experienced a "Good Death," a belief rooted in religious faith and expressed through middle-class rituals. According to believers, a good death consisted of the final, willing surrender to God, ideally witnessed by family members. The way in which a person passed away set the tone for their eternal existence in the afterlife. Since most soldiers died far from home, families took great comfort in the letters they received from fellow soldiers, commanding officers, ministers, or doctors who witnessed their loved one's demise and could attest it had been a good death.

As a doctor and a middle-class woman, Mary Walker understood the importance of these death rituals and took the appropriate action. She was nonplussed, however, when she received a thank-you note from this soldier's parents. It opened with the salutation "Dear Sir." Walker knew it had to do with assumptions about gender. Since she had used her title of "Doctor" in the correspondence, the family assumed she was a man. "They must have supposed that Mary was a boy's name as well as Marion."

Mary Walker remained out of the field for about a month after her return from Warrenton. Because her work attracted positive attention from General Burnside, she now had a powerful supporter who could secure her access to other battlefields, especially where the general was involved. Burnside had planned a quick move from Warrenton, getting his troops over the Rappahannock River before the Confederates could amass a large-enough force to prevent the Union from moving on toward Richmond. But a delay in the delivery of the pontoons the general needed to build a crossing bridge wrecked that plan. Robert E. Lee positioned about 75,000 men in the hills south of the river and waited.

Confederate sharpshooters harassed the Union engineers as they built three pontoon bridges at Fredericksburg on December 11, 1862. Once a bustling commercial area, the city had suffered since the beginning of the war, shrinking from a population of 5,000 to 4,000, and losing much of its business. Three Union regiments crossed the river safely and dispensed with the snipers, smoothing the way for the remainder of Burnside's men. The battle of Fredericksburg commenced on December 13, and despite its superior number of forces, the Union suffered a crushing defeat. However, unlike with previous major engagements, sufficient medical facilities, supplies, and personnel had been planned in advance and were ready to care for the 13,000 casualties.

Dr. Jonathan Letterman, who joined the army in 1849 as an assistant surgeon, had struggled with speed and logistics since he was named medical director of the Army of the Potomac in June 1862. He pushed for an expanded ambulance corps independent of the quartermasters, staffed by medical specialists capable of delivering frontline care and rapid transportation to behind-the-lines hospitals. General McClellan approved the plan in August, but implementation did not prove as easy as Letterman had hoped. The system was not set up in time to make a difference at the Second Battle of Bull Run at the end of the month.

In September at Antietam, Dr. Letterman's planned provisions got tangled up with the Quartermaster Corps and disruptions in railroad service, which had made Clara Barton's contributions so valuable. Transportation of the sick and injured proceeded more smoothly. Letterman had two hundred new ambulances at the ready, and though their crews were not thoroughly trained, fifty ambulance caravans efficiently delivered patients to hospitals in Frederick, Maryland. During the late fall,

Letterman fine-tuned the supply system, the ambulance service, and the management of the field hospitals.

With plenty of time to prepare for Fredericksburg, Jonathan Letterman ordered medical supplies, food, and clothing from New York and Washington, and he had them stored at Aquia Creek and Falmouth. Nearly one thousand ambulances were made ready, their officers well-practiced in all aspects of the service. On December 12, Letterman and his medical staff went into Fredericksburg to find buildings to serve as field hospitals. As casualties piled up the next day, the cases were handled more efficiently than ever.

Dr. Mary Walker volunteered at Lacy House in Falmouth, a behind-the-lines station where soldiers received treatment before being sent on to Washington. Lacy House was an almost-century-old Georgian-style home that overlooked the Rappahannock River. The plantation had originally been owned by William Fitzhugh, a delegate to the Second Continental Congress, who called the residence Chatham House, after William Pitt, the Earl of Chatham. In the late 1850s, James Horace Lacy purchased the plantation, which operated on the labor of about forty enslaved people.

At the start of the war, the thirty-seven-year-old Lacy enlisted with the Confederacy, leaving his wife Betty to run the plantation and take care of their children. Union general Irvin McDowell moved into Fredericksburg in April 1862 with 30,000 men. He chose Chatham, which he and his officers referred to as Lacy House in their correspondence and reports, for his headquarters, forcing Betty Lacy and the children to move out. McDowell oversaw railroad repairs and bridge building over the Rappahannock, all in preparation for an attack on Richmond. President Lincoln even traveled to Lacy House to discuss these plans with the general, which did not come to fruition.

General Burnside left Warrenton seven months later and brought his men to Falmouth as he planned his Richmond assault. Though the general set up at the nearby Phillips House, his soldiers pitched their white tents around Lacy House, and Major General Edwin Sumner claimed the mansion for his field headquarters. Clara Barton arrived there before Mary Walker. After Antietam, Barton had been laid low with typhoid fever. It was not until after the first week of October 1862 that she felt well enough to resume work, aiding the sick and wounded at Camp Misery in Alexandria, Virginia. A couple of weeks later Barton rejoined the Army of the Potomac, and she traveled with Burnside's Ninth Corps in her ambulance wagon. By the time she reached Warrenton in November, winter weather covered the area, bringing freezing temperatures and snow. Barton likely crossed paths with Mary Walker, since both women treated patients at Warrenton before boarding a train to escort them back to Washington.

Clara Barton remained in the capital until December, recuperating from a variety of illnesses that had plagued her in the field. When she received a message from one of her assistants that she was needed in Falmouth, she gathered up supplies and went. By December 8, Barton was settled in a room at Lacy House, which she shared with another female volunteer. Over the next few days, she met with soldiers bivouacked in the area, conferred with Sanitary Commission agents, and toured Jonathan Letterman's new medical facilities. On December 11, as Barton watched the bridge construction on the Rappahannock River from the Lacy House veranda, she dodged Confederate sniper fire.

While Clara Barton tended to those wounded in this action, she received a summons from a brigade surgeon working at a dressing station in Fredericksburg who needed her. She and her assistants braved enemy fire to get into the city—she lost part of her skirt to an exploding shell fragment—and they set up a soup kitchen at the aid station. Barton spent the next day back at Lacy House, now the designated branch hospital for the Second Corps, taking care of the ever-increasing number of patients arriving as Burnside prepared for all-out battle. Like Dr. Mary Walker at Warrenton, Clara Barton wrote down the names of the men who died at Lacy House, detailing the causes and circumstances of the deaths and noting the burial sites.

In the early morning of December 13, the day of the Battle of Fredericksburg, Clara Barton made her rounds in Lacy House amid a Confederate bombardment. A few hours later, as the fighting continued, the nurse insisted on going into the city to work at a dressing station. Thousands of Union soldiers fell under the withering fire of the Confederates.

She stayed through the night, after the slaughter finally ended, lighting fires to keep the patients warm until surgeons could tend their wounds in the morning.

Clara Barton returned to Lacy House two days later, probably around the time Mary Walker arrived from Washington. Casualties from the battle were high for the Union—close to 13,000—and nearly 500 wounded men would undergo amputations. Hundreds of patients crowded inside Lacy House, some tucked under table legs on the floors, others jammed into the shelves of china cupboards. Those who had been evacuated later from Fredericksburg had to settle for space on its grounds. Barton gave up her room in the house, moving into a tent next to her supply wagon. She set up another soup kitchen, provided heated bricks and blankets to the shivering soldiers, and offered comfort to those scheduled for surgery.

Dr. Walker plunged into the grim work at the mansion. None of the military doctors questioned her right to be there. She may have implied that she had General Burnside's permission, or it may have been because so many men needed medical attention, but no one tried to send her away. "I was directed by the managing surgeons to take any cases I chose and dress them preparitory [*sic*] to sending them to Washington." One man remained alive and "perfectly sensible" even though a shell had blown a hole the size of a silver dollar in his skull. The doctor watched his brain pulse as he talked. She had never seen such a thing and was astonished to learn that the patient, quickly transferred to Washington, lived for several days before succumbing to his injuries.

Walt Whitman arrived at Lacy House about a week after the battle ended, looking for his younger brother George. The forty-three-year-old poet, already becoming well-known from his 1855 volume *Leaves of Grass*, had been living in Brooklyn, New York, with his mother. A few days after the battle of Fredericksburg, the *New-York Tribune* published a casualty list for the 51st New York, which included First Lieutenant G. W. Whitmore. Concerned that perhaps his brother George's name had been misspelled, and worried about the extent of his injuries, Walt traveled to Washington.

The trip took three days. Whitman competed for space on both ferry and train with thousands of others also on their way to the capital. He spent two days stopping in at each of the city's dozens of hospitals, but failed to locate George Whitman. A couple of acquaintances helped Whitman to secure a pass to board an army train headed for Falmouth. The poet arrived at Lacy House on December 19, and his first look at the grounds inspired little hope about the fate of his brother. Whitman saw "a heap of feet, legs, arms, and human fragments, cut, bloody, black and blue, swelled and sickening," plus dead bodies lined up in the garden, "each covered with its brown woollen blanket."

Late in the afternoon, with a great deal of relief, Walt Whitman found George alive and unbothered by the superficial facial wound he had sustained at Fredericksburg. The younger Whitman's good spirits had been further buoyed by his recent promotion to captain. Walt Whitman stayed in Falmouth for two weeks, an experience that changed his life. He visited with the soldiers, marveling at their camaraderie and ingenuity. The observations he noted in his journal became the basis for poems and essays.

On Sunday, December 21, Whitman went inside Lacy House for the first time. Clara Barton was there, and Mary Walker likely was, too, but Whitman only noticed the wounded. "Some of the men were dying. I had nothing to give at that visit, but wrote a few letters to folks home, mothers, &c. Talk'd to three or four, who seem'd most susceptible to it, and needing it." The poet also noted how the patients had been crowded into the home, and he did not see any system to their treatment. "I have no doubt the best that can be done; all the wounds pretty bad."

Although Dr. Jonathan Letterman's innovations had done much to improve the process of treating wounded soldiers, they could not conjure enough trained medical professionals to care for the injured. No matter how hard Clara Barton worked, she often found herself overwhelmed at the tasks yet to be completed. She tended so many that at one point, she recalled, "I wrung the blood from the bottom of my clothing, before I could step, for the weight about my feet." Lacy House, despite all the nurses' efforts, ran ineffectively, and patients suffered for it.

Through the last half of December, Lacy House gradually lost occupants. The more-fortunate patients were either released or transferred to a Washington hospital. The less fortunate died, their bodies added to the graveyard on the grounds, close to one hundred in all. Within days after Christmas—Clara Barton's birthday—both she and Walt Whitman separately left Falmouth and returned to Washington, accompanying wounded soldiers along the way. Both kept careful lists of the men's names and other identifying information so their families could be notified.

Though their time in Falmouth and at Lacy House overlapped, there is no evidence that Walt Whitman and Clara Barton met. He had likely seen her at work, and the soldiers knew her by name. Whitman became so deeply impressed with the hospital volunteers' work that he spent the rest of the war in Washington doing the same. He made hundreds of hospital visits in and around DC, reading to thousands of patients, writing letters home for them, bringing food and clothing, and even dressing wounds. From her rooms in the city, Clara Barton, exhausted and near penniless, began planning for her next trip into the field.

Even as more patients were transferred, Dr. Mary Walker continued to work at Lacy House, though it is unclear for how long. Fredericksburg had proved such a devastating battle that President Lincoln ordered General Burnside's troops to remain in Falmouth through the winter to recuperate. Walker tended to their illnesses, most of them probably exacerbated by the weather. Though the army did not pay her, she was entitled to draw rations and received a tent assignment. This inspired the doctor to add the green surgeon's sash to her outfit, a visual indicator of her role in camp. "I had not then any government authority to do so," Walker admitted, but she knew she could not wait for others to give her what she wanted.

CHAPTER FIVE

In the Field, In the City

On January 1, 1863, President Lincoln held a reception at the Executive Mansion. For three hours, he shook hands with hundreds of people who had come to celebrate this special New Year's Day. After greeting his visitors, Lincoln proceeded to the main event: signing the Emancipation Proclamation. A few changes had been made to the preliminary version he had issued the previous September. Lincoln asked enslaved people not to rise up in violence, unless it was a matter of self-defense; stressed that the newly freed would have the opportunity to work for "reasonable wages"; and expanded the Militia Act to bring formerly enslaved men into the Union Army. At the end, the president clarified he relied on the authority of the Constitution, military necessity, and the "considerate judgment of mankind" as the justification for emancipation.

Happy crowds of black and white citizens congregated at various places in Washington, including the Israel Bethel AME Church, waiting for copies of the document. People broke into song, and guns and cannons were fired in salute. Dr. Mary Walker may not have been in Washington, DC, for the day's celebrations, but in February she attended the Twenty-Ninth Annual Subscription Anniversary. Held every year at the Church of the Puritans in New York City, the event raised money for the *National Anti-Slavery Standard*, the official publication of the American Anti-Slavery Society. That year, it also celebrated the Emancipation Proclamation.

During 1863, Mary Walker split her time between the city and the field; one set of activities intertwined with the other. She probably continued to support herself by seeing private patients, taking donations, and accepting money from her father. Walker's work in the field with the army in 1862, first at Warrenton, then at Fredericksburg, made it easier for her to secure the necessary travel passes to move through Virginia and other forward locations. Since General Ambrose Burnside had given his tacit approval, other officers and officials proved willing to do the same. The doctor also affiliated with the Sanitary Commission from time to time, which facilitated her ability to get into the field.

While the military more readily accepted Mary Walker's presence with the troops, it held fast in its refusal to offer her any kind of official status that would include a rank and a steady salary. Preston King, a Republican senator from her home state of New York, tried to intervene on her behalf by writing to Secretary of War Edwin Stanton in early January 1863. He explained that Walker performed as a "physician and surgeon in the Hospitals and in attendance upon the sick and wounded of the volunteers." King wrote about the expenses Walker incurred, especially the personal donations she made for patient care. There would be "justice & propriety" in providing her with compensation. Stanton's office replied that no "authority of law" existed for doing so.

Around the time Preston King wrote this letter, Mary Walker tended patients at a convalescence camp near Fort Barnard in Virginia. The fort had been built in late 1861 in Arlington County, part of a ring of defensive fortifications on the Virginia side of the Potomac River erected to protect Washington, DC. She found among the wounded a group of men from her hometown of Oswego, New York. As she had done at Falmouth, Walker took the time to talk to the soldiers, recording their names, their illness or injury, and which Washington hospital they would be transferred to. She compiled this information and sent it on for publication in the Oswego newspaper so the men's families would know what had happened to them.

Like Mary Walker, other women went into the field that winter. After a brief respite in Washington, Clara Barton returned to Falmouth during the latter half of January 1863. Barton witnessed what came to be known as the Mud March—General Burnside's final, futile attempt to get his men across the Rappahannock River. Unseasonably mild temperatures and driving rains foiled his plan, leaving his troops dispirited and exhausted. Barton took care of the men, most of whom suffered from illnesses, and offered moral support, but she was not the only female nurse in the area. Dorothea Dix's army nurses had spread out into forward locations, along with Sanitary Commission nurses and relief workers. Worried about her ability to maintain authority over her own work, Clara Barton requested and received permission from the War Department in March to travel to Port Royal, South Carolina, to continue nursing there.

The repeated defeats and humiliating debacles like the Mud March affected Northern morale to the point that military enlistments in state volunteer regiments declined and desertions rose. Congress stepped in to nationalize conscription, hoping the threat of a draft would encourage men to sign up. The Enrollment Act of 1863, passed on March 3, required all male citizens and male immigrants who applied for citizenship and were between the ages of twenty and forty-five to enroll for military service. The act included African Americans, who had been trying to join since the beginning of the war. Each congressional district received a quota of soldiers to provide within fifty days. If that could not get accomplished through volunteers, then a lottery was held—drawing names from the list of enrollees—to make up the difference.

Through the subsequent four draft calls, not all of the 776,000 men whose names were drawn went into the military. About one-fifth fled their jurisdiction to evade service, one-eighth who reported for duty were released because enough volunteers had signed up, and three-fifths of the remaining received a medical or personal hardship exemption. This left 207,000 men drafted, but not all of them served, either. The Enrollment Act allowed draftees the option of providing a substitute—young men between the ages of eighteen and nineteen or immigrants who had yet to apply for citizenship—and 74,000 did so. An additional 87,000 paid a $300 fee for an exemption. Draftees and substitutes made up only 13 percent of Union soldiers. The act had been successful in encouraging volunteers.

Mary Walker had been trying to volunteer since 1861, and she traveled throughout Virginia offering medical care in hopes of receiving a commission. A military pass dated May 8, 1863, put her at Aquia Creek, where wounded soldiers awaited transport to Washington hospitals. Located forty-four miles south of Washington, DC, Aquia Creek was regarded as a strategic location by both the Union and the Confederacy because of its access to the Potomac River, and because of its railroad terminus. A naval battle in late May 1861 failed to rout the Rebels, who remained there until the early spring of 1862, when they blew up the wharves and decamped to defend Richmond.

The Union military settled in that spring, rebuilding wharves and storage facilities to facilitate the movement of its troops and supplies. With no direct railroad service between Washington and Fredericksburg, Aquia Creek remained a valuable location, as sick and wounded soldiers headed for hospitals in the capital still transferred trains there. Mary Walker likely spent considerable time at Aquia, but this May date was particularly important: It was two days after the Battle of Chancellorsville, which had concluded in a stunning Union defeat.

Following January's Mud March debacle, President Lincoln had replaced General Burnside with Major General Joseph Hooker, to lead the Army of the Potomac. The career army officer proved popular with the men. He reorganized his fighting force, got rid of dishonest quartermasters, brought in better-quality food, and improved conditions in the hospitals. While his troops wintered in the Fredericksburg area, Hooker planned his attack on Richmond, certain he could accomplish what his predecessors had failed to do.

At the end of April, he was ready. He divided his 120,000-man army into three parts to more efficiently outflank Robert E. Lee's far less numerous entrenched forces. On the final day of the month, 70,000 infantry of the Army of the Potomac approached Chancellorsville, a small crossroads nine miles west of Fredericksburg. Lee and Stonewall Jackson came up with an ingenious dual counter-maneuver that, over the next few days, handed the South one of its biggest victories. By the time Hooker and his men had crossed back over the Rappahannock on May 6, the Union had suffered over 17,000 casualties, and the Confederacy, about 13,000, including the death of Jackson.

At the start of the battle, about 28,000 Northern soldiers of the Sixth Corps, under the leadership of Major General John Sedgwick, had proceeded to Fredericksburg to challenge the Confederates. Sedgwick, grandson of a Revolutionary War general, had been shot three times during the Battle of Antietam in September 1862. His lengthy recuperation prevented him from fighting at the Battle of Fredericksburg in December, depriving him of his first opportunity to see Mary Walker at work. But this may have happened the second time around. According to a newspaper account, Walker was "more recently at Sedgwich's [*sic*] crossing below Fredericksburg," a reference to the general's role in the Chancellorsville campaign.

When Dr. Walker received a military pass for Aquia Creek on May 8, it is likely she traveled there from the Fredericksburg area, where she must have been treating the wounded of Sixth Corps. She recalled that day in May at Aquia as "oppressively hot, the banks high from the boat, and the plank leading thereto was necessarily much inclined." As stretcher bearers hurried to place the patients on board the ship, the doctor noticed they were carried headfirst, which she worried might cause brain injury. Making sure her surgeon's sash was visible, she "ordered every one to take them feet first, thus preventing congestion of the brain, which must have been produced, but for constant directions from her."

The outcome of Chancellorsville shocked the Union. Two years into the war, the human toll continued to mount, with no end in sight. Walt Whitman, now living in Washington, DC, felt depressed at the sight of the wounded arriving at the 6th Street Wharf, about a thousand each day. Two boatloads of soldiers were brought in early one evening when Whitman was present. Offloaded on the dock and the surrounding area, they laid there while a rainstorm hit. "The men are lying on blankets, old quilts, &c., with bloody rags bound round heads, arms, and legs," the poet wrote. "The men generally make little or no ado, whatever their sufferings. A few groans that cannot be suppress'd, and occasionally a scream of pain as they lift a man into the ambulance."

Mary Walker was at the same location when the Confederate prisoners of war arrived. President Lincoln stood close enough to her that she could see his "care-worn cheeks." She also noted the bedraggled appearance of the POWs. Many of them lacked basic clothing: hats, jackets, shoes. Those items worn by the soldiers "looked as though they had served them since 1860." Despite these deprivations, Southerners were decided to fight on. Northerners' morale plummeted.

Dr. Walker did not acknowledge these sinking sentiments. She continued to write for *The Sibyl*, though not as often as she would have liked. In July, while Americans were caught up in the news of yet another great battle, Walker published an article called "Soldiers' Appreciation of Noble Women." She emphasized the important work women contributed to the war effort, noting that soldiers were "highly appreciative." The doctor insisted only "low and ignorant men look upon women as dolls or drudges . . . but the truly noble appreciate worth wherever it is found." She praised a few women by name—Mrs. Mary Husband, Miss Gilson, Miss McKay—whom she met at various corps hospitals. "I have met a number of others and heard of still more," she said, and she thought highly of their work.

This affirmation of women's competence may have brought some comfort to those reading about Gettysburg. Flush with his decisive victory at Chancellorsville, General Lee convinced Confederate president Jefferson Davis and Secretary of War James Seddon that the time was right for a major offensive. To relieve the beleaguered state of Virginia and provide Southern troops the opportunity to forage for food in Northern territory, Lee proposed to attack the Union on its own soil in Pennsylvania. He believed this maneuver would also yield political benefits by disgracing the Union's Republican Party and giving more power to the Peace Democrats, who wanted a negotiated settlement to the war. Moreover, a significant Southern victory at this point might sway some foreign governments to recognize the legitimacy of the Confederate government.

In June 1863, Lee began moving 75,000 men of the Army of Northern Virginia into Pennsylvania. They seized what they needed along the way, often but not always leaving Confederate IOUs for food, clothing, and horses. In a stunning reminder of why the war was being fought, some soldiers kidnapped free black citizens of Pennsylvania and sold them south into slavery.

Union general Joseph Hooker, still smarting from Chancellorsville, moved too slowly in pursuit. Before the month ended, President Lincoln replaced him with General George Meade. Mostly known for his prewar topographical work in the army, in 1861 Meade received a promotion to brigadier general and took command of a group of Pennsylvania volunteers. He served at the Second Battle of Bull Run, Antietam, Fredericksburg, and Chancellorsville before heading the Army of the Potomac.

At the beginning of July, the two armies found themselves at Gettysburg, a town of about 2,400 people just over the Maryland border in southern Pennsylvania. Meade had not expected to engage the Confederates there. The army's medical and quartermaster departments did not have quite enough time to move the necessary amount of supplies to the area, but the Sanitary Commission did. Its agents followed the movements of Meade's army to decide where to set up supply depots, allowing its provisions to reach the troops at the start of the battle.

The fight at Gettysburg lasted three days, and it brought the victory Northerners had been waiting for. It cost 3,100 Union lives, with another 14,000 wounded. A total of six million pounds of dead bodies, both human and animal, lay on the battlefield. Meade failed to press the advantage—"We have done well enough," he told an officer—and allowed Lee's men to slip back into Virginia. The Confederate general lost more than a third of his army. Of the 18,000 Confederate wounded, 7,000 were left behind. The Army of Northern Virginia lacked the means to remove them south for treatment, leaving them to the good graces of Union doctors and nurses.

Soldiers benefited from the Sanitary Commission's largesse. Tons of bread, butter, eggs, milk, fish, poultry, red meat, and vegetables—plus thousands of clothing items—were made available. Field hospitals received enough beds, kitchens, and tents to feed 16,000 men and shelter 1,200. The Sanitary Commission also set up a lodge and food service at the railroad station to care for the patients being transferred to hospitals for additional treatment.

Sophronia Bucklin was one of the first female nurses to arrive at Gettysburg. Born in 1828 or 1830, probably in Ohio, she had been living with relatives in Ithaca, New York, working as a tailoress, before the start of the Civil War. In 1862, Bucklin had either moved nearly forty miles north to Auburn or she was visiting there when the matron of the Orphan Asylum,

Sarah Strong Reed, suggested she meet with the board of directors for the local Soldiers' Aid Society. The two women had been watching a group of soldiers, likely members of the 75th New York Infantry, playing ball on a field near the orphanage, Bucklin remarked, "I wish I knew of some way to get into the military service to take care of just such boys as those, when they shall need it."

Patriotism motivated Sophronia Bucklin. Like the young men inspired to give up their jobs and their education to join the military, Bucklin believed young women felt a loyalty to country that "lent also to our hearts its thrilling measure, and sent us out to do and dare for those whose strong arms were to retrieve the honor of our insulted flag." Women could not put on uniforms and fight (at least, not officially), but they could choose "our silent journeys into hospitals and camps" to take care of those who did. Still, it took Bucklin more than a year to secure a nursing position.

Sophronia Bucklin was "led by Providence into the right channel"—her conversation with Sarah Reed, who likely put in a good word with the board of the Soldiers' Aid Society. After the meeting, the men agreed to sponsor Bucklin as a nurse, subject to the approval of Dorothea Dix, the army's superintendent of nurses. In July 1862, Bucklin received official notice. William Hammond, the surgeon general, confirmed her appointment and instructed her to apply to Dix for a position. Dix's list of instructions for women who wanted to nurse in army hospitals arrived at the same time. Bucklin would receive forty cents a day plus rations for her service. By the time she had put together the requisite items, the Battle of Antietam had already taken place. She arrived soon after in the capital and reported directly to Dix.

The nurse superintendent was still at Antietam, but she had left orders for Sophronia Bucklin to report for duty at the Judiciary Square Hospital, where she was tasked with bringing food to patients and keeping them clean. The former tailoress learned the work quickly as she moved through successive hospital appointments, gaining confidence along the way. But Bucklin clashed with the many doctors who disapproved of female nurses. After a few weeks at the Wolfe-street Hospital in Alexandria, Virginia, in the spring of 1863, the surgeon in charge pronounced Bucklin inefficient and dismissed her. Bucklin helped out the Sanitary Commission as she kept up with the news of Meade's army. She asked Dorothea Dix to send her to Pennsylvania, only to be told she was too young for field work. Frederick Knapp, director of the Sanitary Commission's Special Relief Department, disagreed, and asked Bucklin to continue her work for the organization at Gettysburg.

On her way to the battlefield, Sophronia Bucklin crossed paths with Dix in Maryland. The superintendent was on her way back from Pennsylvania, and when she realized Bucklin's determination to serve at the Front, she told the young woman to report to the hospital on the grounds of the Lutheran Theological Seminary. Bucklin arrived in Gettysburg on Saturday and saw everywhere "evidence of mortal combat, everywhere wounded men were lying in the streets on heaps of blood-stained straw, everywhere there was hurry and confusion, while soldiers were groaning and suffering."

Bucklin spent her time in the tents set up in the field outside of the hospital. "I washed agonized faces, combed out matted hair, bandaged slight wounds, and administered drinks of raspberry vinegar and lemon syrup." She observed firsthand how much the work of the Sanitary Commission mattered. "Without its generous supplies, untold suffering would have visited us, for Government stores could not be obtained, and in view of the host of wounded the ordinary hospital supplies were as a drop of water in the depths of the cool, silent well."

Soon, forty women toiled in the hospital tents, including seven army nurses. Sophronia Bucklin was assigned a tent, originally outfitted only with an iron bed with wooden slats. She slept without sheets and a pillow; she believed the patients needed them more. She worked hours without a break. "Hunger gnawed at my vitals; swollen feet almost refused to support me; wearied limbs found but little rest upon the bare slats of my bedstead." Yet one doctor tried to have her dismissed over a disagreement about serving milk to her patients. Sophronia Bucklin remained at Gettysburg for four months, until the hospital was dismantled.

Mary Walker arrived in the area after the battle concluded, "while on march to overtake General Lee on his Pennsylvania return trip." The July weather was so hot that soldiers died of sunstroke. Walker managed to save the lives of some men by insisting they ride in the ambulance, overriding the orders of the driver not to take on passengers. She gave up her place in the wagon "and let some soldiers ride for a little distance who were nearly exhausted, or carried a musket for them while she was riding."

Accompanying the doctor on part of this journey was an army quartermaster with the New Jersey infantry, Joseph H. Painter, and his wife, Dr. Esther "Hettie" Kersey Painter. Both were Quakers from Pennsylvania who supported temperance, abolition, and suffrage. After their two sons grew up, Hettie Painter enrolled in the Pennsylvania Medical College and graduated in 1860. The forty-year-old doctor volunteered her medical services at the start of the war. Despite her degree, she was relegated to nursing duties and addressed as Mrs. Painter. For three months, she stayed in Washington treating soldiers wounded at the First Battle of Bull Run. Painter returned home to Camden, New Jersey, after she somehow lost the use of her right hand.

Brigadier General Philip Kearney, commander of the First New Jersey Brigade, asked Dr. Painter to return to work for the Union. It is not clear why such a high-ranking officer made this individual appeal. Hettie Painter's husband, Joseph, may have been related to the influential Painter family of West Chester, Pennsylvania, which included Lieutenant Colonel (later Brigadier General) William F. Painter, a member of the Quartermaster Department. Dr. Painter, presumably recovered from her injury, complied with the general's request. She established a hospital south of the Potomac River and Kearney assigned forty men to work as her assistants. With the facility up and running, Painter went back to New Jersey.

After the Second Battle of Bull Run in August 1862, fellow Philadelphia native Major Joseph Barnes sent Dr. Painter a telegram, requesting her services in Washington. Barnes had arrived in the city in May, attached to the surgeon general's office, and was named attending surgeon. Under Barnes's authority, Painter "took charge" of the Georgetown College Hospital before moving on to the Armory Square Hospital. At some point, the New Jersey and Pennsylvania governors commissioned Painter to work with the Army of the Potomac, to follow the troops and provide them with medical care.

After Gettysburg, Dr. Painter spent considerable time in the field. Her quartermaster husband accompanied her along the way, likely providing the necessary supplies as well as additional security if they strayed too far from the army. When Mary Walker joined the couple, she would have found them congenial. They all shared a deep commitment to reform, and Walker likely enjoyed the opportunity to talk to another female doctor.

The trio stopped in Piedmont, Virginia, about fifty miles west of Washington, DC, which boasted a strategic railroad station. In 1861, Stonewall Jackson used the depot to move his troops to Manassas for the First Battle of Bull Run. During the war, both Union and Confederate troops passed through Piedmont, taking to the village's churches for shelter. In the late 1850s, both the Episcopalians and the Methodists had put up new buildings, and at least one of them served as a hospital. Doctors Walker and Painter learned that one of the hospitals lacked a medical officer, so they decided to check on the facility's current patients.

They were in poor condition, suffering from fevers and malnutrition, with nothing but hardtack, that ubiquitous flour-and-water biscuit, on hand for meals. Mary Walker traveled into the village to look for more nutritious food. To the locals, weary from the constant skirmishes in the area, food had become too valuable to sell for money. When she finally found a quarter bushel of cornmeal, she parted with a pair of her boots to get it. A servant in a home about a mile away from the church agreed to cook the cornmeal into gruel. The two doctors transported buckets of food to the patients via horseback and saved the men from starvation.

As the soldiers recuperated, they grew rambunctious. They caught and killed a pig and hid it in the church until they could figure out a way to cook it. Mary Walker found their treasure "and made a speech, explaining the injury which would result from eating an animal that had been run down and dressed in such an oppressively hot day." She told the men they must bury the animal, and they followed her order.

The disappearance of such a valuable farm animal would not have gone unnoticed by the locals and would have increased their resentment toward the Union occupiers. Civilians had little recourse in such matters, which were often explained as necessary "requisitions" or "confiscations." In another incident, two Piedmont women stood up to Union soldiers and demanded the return of their property. The men took a sidesaddle from the Shacklett sisters with the intention of making a present of it to Mary Walker. It was the third such instance of attempted gift-giving since Gettysburg. The doctor was important to the men, and they considered the thefts a sign of appreciation for her services, gratitude that she had sacrificed her own comfort and security to take care of them. It may also have been an attempt to curry romantic favor. Each time the situation arose, Walker insisted the confiscated item go back to its original owner. Now, the Shackletts insisted as well.

Susan Shacklett, about thirty years old, and her younger sister Roberta had spent their entire lives on their family's prosperous farm on the outskirts of Piedmont. Before the war, the family's real estate was valued at $5,250, with an additional $2,500 of personal property. Factored in there were about ten enslaved workers. The townspeople admired Susan and Roberta Shacklett for their culture, refinement, piety, and civic-mindedness. When their father Chapman Shacklett died in 1858, the sisters had likely been raising funds for the new Cool Spring Methodist Church. As women living without male protection, they became accustomed to standing up for themselves.

After the Union soldiers took the saddle, the Shacklett siblings "used their only weapon in defense . . . which was such earnest English that the soldiers had determined to burn up all their buildings." The confrontation was set. The Shackletts wanted their saddle back, Mary Walker refused it as a gift, and the men insisted she have it. They told Walker that if she did not take it, they would destroy it. And because they were affronted that the sisters had used such unladylike language to express their displeasure, they decided to burn down the farmhouse and other buildings.

"When arguments of justice utterly failed," Mary Walker later remembered, she "touched their avarice, and induced them to sell the saddle to its owner for $5." The soldiers may have agreed to this—though Susan and Roberta Shacklett likely did not—but they refused to reconsider their plan to torch the property. Walker promised to spend every night sleeping in the Shackletts' home and "be burnt up with those women, as they had no more made the war than she had herself, and were no more indignant at wrongs." Walker and the Painters stayed with the two local women until the men gave up and returned the saddle and "other things . . . that were of no use to soldiers."

Traveling in the field had its dangers, even in places where there were no active battles. Dr. Walker particularly worried about snakes. For three nights she shared a tent with the Painters, "where she was obliged to stay, being so far from habitations that there was nothing she could do but to stay" in the Virginia countryside. One morning a captain woke up to find a large snake coiled on the blanket at his feet. "It was so heavy that the captain supposed it was a dog, and paid no attention to it, until it began to move away at sunrise." Soldiers in the encampment searched for the snake for several days before they found it and killed it. Dr. Walker suffered "agonizing fears" each night until the snake was found. She remembered a soldier who had been bitten on the mouth and "died too horrible a death for contemplation." For the doctor, this was terrifying. "The United States Treasury has never contained enough money to compensate her for three nights of such an experience," she later wrote.

Despite her fears, Mary Walker remained with the Army of the Potomac. She became such a fixture that several local newspapers ran complimentary stories about her. Reporters considered her a somebody; one described her as a camp follower of "noteworthy personage." While the article erroneously reported that Walker had "received a regular medical education," it also made clear her commitment to women's equality: "[She] believes her sex ought not to disqualify her from the performance of deeds of mercy to the suffering heroes of the Republic." Considering Dr. Walker's professional skills, the reporter found it strange that she had "never been formally assigned to any particular duty."

This kind of publicity helped the doctor's various endeavors to assist Union soldiers, whether in the field or in Washington, DC. She had become so well-known in the capital by 1863 that her name was added to the guest list for the annual spring reception at the Executive Mansion. Walker proved such a delightful guest that she received an invitation every year for the rest of her life. She mingled with government officials and other influential people at the party that year and likely talked to them about her work. She met Abraham Lincoln and Mary Todd Lincoln, finding the president "cordial," and his wife, "lively and pleasing."

Whenever Mary Walker returned from the field, she found plenty to do in Washington. She wrote about women's rights issues. In March 1863, she penned a piece for *The Sibyl*, focusing on dress reform. The early spring in Washington had been rainy, turning its mostly dirt streets into thoroughfares of muck. The proliferation of streetcars added a new dimension to the problem of women wearing long hoop skirts—they tracked mud onto the public conveyances, causing problems for all passengers. For the doctor, this illustrated another justification for the superiority of the Bloomer costume. Yet she acknowledged the slow pace of reform. "It is far better to feel that we are meeting and enduring in a cause that will benefit our suffering sex," she asserted, "than to feel that we have lived to no purpose."

Lydia Hasbrouck, editor of *The Sibyl*, considered Mary Walker one of the magazine's most important contributors. Hasbrouck addressed Walker in that March 1863 issue, calling on the doctor to provide information "concerning the progress of our cause at the Nation's Capital." It is likely Hasbrouck referred to reform in general: "Much of good to woman ought to come of the present upheaval of things, and it behooves the wide-awake, working ones among them to continue active, vigilant, and unwearying in the good cause."

In response, Mary Walker wrote "Woman's Mind," a long piece that ran in the next issue, revealing ongoing frustrations with perceptions of women's intellectual inferiority. "How often we hear men underrating a woman's mind when they are not capable of comprehending the women occupying their immediate circle." Indeed, many women had "minds vastly superior to their male friends" that were "capable of the profoundest reasoning." She concluded with a tinge of acerbity, "Woman's mind is an emanation from deity, and man's mind very probably emanated from the same source."

Time in the city also provided Mary Walker with abundant opportunities to help soldiers. She tended patients in city hospitals, and she raised money to keep the hospitals staffed and supplied. In late February 1863, Walker participated in the Grand Fair fund-raiser at Odd Fellows Hall on 7th Street NW. The event boasted "new and original attractions" to encourage donations from people who had been giving for almost two years. The "popular philanthropist" Dr. Mary Walker appeared at the fair to "render her favorite ode in costume": "For the Dear Old Flag."

The Independent Order of Odd Fellows, founded at the beginning of the century as a fraternal organization devoted to a variety of charitable endeavors, was one of many groups that encouraged donations to the war effort. In October 1863, the Sanitary Commission put on a spectacular fair in Chicago that became a model for future fund-raising events. A three-mile parade with nine marching troop divisions, thousands of children singing "John Brown's Body," and hundreds of wagons laden with produce headed to the army kicked off the festivities. Buildings exhibited a variety of wares for sale, the proceeds going to the Sanitary Commission. President Lincoln donated an original draft of the Emancipation Proclamation, which sold for $3,000. That first Sanitary Commission fair raised close to $80,000 ($1,600,000 in 2019 money), an astonishing amount of money.

Dr. Walker assisted soldiers with legal matters, especially with charges of desertion. Her interest in the law stemmed from her devotion to women's rights issues, and throughout her life she exhibited an active interest in lawful justice. During the war, desertions happened regularly, and penalties were rarely consistent. Though a capital offense, the Union could not afford to execute the nearly one-quarter of a million men who abandoned the military. Whenever possible, they were encouraged to return, often with little or no punishment. President Lincoln favored leniency except in situations where the deserters had provided information to the enemy.

Desertions had always been a problem in Washington, where secessionist sympathizers encouraged Union soldiers to walk away from their service. Soldiers had an easier time in the capital city finding civilian clothes to swap out their uniforms—until the Provost Guard began arresting shopkeepers who facilitated the purchases. Still, desertions only increased in 1863 after the Emancipation Proclamation made the war about abolition, and the Enrollment Act targeted young men who lacked a willingness to serve.

In September 1862, Forrest Hall, a tall Greek revival building on Wisconsin Avenue in Georgetown, was converted into a military prison. The once-elegant home that hosted meetings for organizations like the

Masons and the Woman's Christian Temperance Union now held several hundred deserters, serving sentences that ranged from sixty days to five years of hard labor. In February 1863, Stone Hospital was designated a facility for sick and wounded deserters, a temporary shelter for patients on the way to Forrest Hall.

The Bureau of Deserters, staffed by the provost marshal, arrested six thousand men in July 1863. Zealous in their pursuit, one innocent soldier was arrested for every two true deserters. This raised concerns about the entire process.

One day, Mary Walker stopped at the post office and someone handed her a stack of papers addressed to "Lady Dr. Walker, the soldiers' true friend." They were from men at the Forrest Hall prison who claimed they had been unjustly detained for desertion and begged her to come see them. One, William Lawyer, a soldier from New York who had been taken prisoner at Fredericksburg, was paroled from a Confederate jail in Richmond, ending up in Washington with the 16th New York Battery. Lawyer had contracted an illness that required a two-month convalescence. While on the way back to his regiment, the provost marshal arrested him and took him to Forrest Hall. Lawyer's illness flared, so he was taken to Stone Hospital, where he awaited transfer back to Forrest. He implored Dr. Walker to take his case, though it is not clear what happened to him.

Dr. Walker promptly went to Forrest Hall, where for six hours she wrote down dozens of men's statements to present to the War Department. She argued that the soldiers were not deserters but rather victims of overzealous detectives, presumably working for the provost marshal, out for the bounty paid for bringing in men who had left their units. Walker advised the secretary of war to stop the practice of paying incentives, and requested transportation for the men to be returned to their regiments. Stanton agreed.

Union soldiers requested Mary Walker's help again in 1863, after several of them had been held in a "common jail" without trial for five months. Again, the doctor took their statements and "went to the War Department and insisted on immediate trials." A Colonel Alexander presided over the court-martial, with Walker representing the soldiers, "the first time that a woman had acted as attorney" in this kind of a case in Washington. When one of the soldiers was convicted, Walker wrote to Colonel Joseph Holt, the judge advocate general, pointing out that a key piece of testimony had been omitted. Holt reversed the conviction.

Mary Walker also helped create the Invalid Corps. As she treated patients, she realized the army "had no regulation to keep any soldiers who were partially disabled for duty." Many of those men told her how much they hated the idea of being sent home when they were still capable of performing some kind of valuable work, such as "wait[ing] on the boys in hospital, and [. . . doing] guard duty, where they did not have to stand up all the time." Walker discussed the manpower issue with Colonel Edward Townsend, acting adjutant general of the army. She pointed out that "partially disabled" men could free up hundreds of the "able-bodied" by protecting public buildings and fortifications around Washington, "as all that was needed was a show of a soldier holding a musket."

Townsend concurred. He asked Dr. Walker "if she suggested a different uniform to distinguish them," which she thought was a good idea. At the end of April 1863, the War Department issued General Orders No. 105. It allowed sick or wounded soldiers the opportunity to take on light duty along the lines of Mary Walker's suggestions. Sporting distinctive sky blue uniforms with dark blue trim, the sturdiest carried muskets on duty, while the others made do with pistols and sabers. By December, the Invalid Corps in Washington numbered 12,000, providing additional security for the city while freeing up other soldiers to fight.

These kinds of activities increased Mary Walker's visibility in the capital. The Union League of Washington thought so highly of her work that its officers invited her to address its members in August, about her experiences with the Army of the Potomac. The organization had been founded in early 1863, one of several of its kind that had popped up in the North during the war. Headquartered on the second floor of a building on 9th Street, the league identified as its primary purpose "to bind together ALL loyal men in a common union to maintain the power, glory, and integrity of the [U]nion."

The following month, *The Sibyl* reprinted a *New-York Tribune* article that praised "Women in the Army," particularly Mary Walker. It opened with the story of nineteen-year-old Miss Jones, "somewhat masculine" but with "comely features," who left her home in Cambridge, Massachusetts, to become a vivandière for a New York regiment. Inspired by French women who served in the Crimean War by traveling with the troops and selling consumer items to soldiers and providing medical care, some American regiments allowed women to do the same. A vivandière was often the wife or daughter of someone serving in the regiment, and she usually wore a uniform.

Jones may have been encouraged by reports of Marie Brose Tepe, who joined the 27th Pennsylvania Volunteer Infantry Regiment with her husband in the spring of 1861. Tepe had immigrated to the United States from France as a teenager, so she was well acquainted with the vivandière tradition. The Tepes served at the First Battle of Bull Run, with Marie tending the wounded as bullets flew. After a falling-out with her husband, Marie Tepe signed up with the 114th Pennsylvania Volunteers, a Zouave regiment. She received a salary and dressed in the unit's distinctive red-and-blue uniform, complete with a holstered revolver. In action at Fredericksburg, Tepe sustained a bullet wound to the ankle, but took to the field again at Chancellorsville, for which she earned the Kearny Cross, and again, at Gettysburg.

Miss Jones, however, was not content with the traditional vivandière duties. To improve her chances of receiving a commission, she read up on "military studies," hoping to convince her commanding officer to put her to work as a scout or spy. No commission was forthcoming, so Jones decided to go out on her own and gather intelligence. The provost marshal arrested her and had her jailed in Washington. Authorities informed Jones she would be released only if she ceased her activities. According to the report, Jones "lingers in prison, with the hope of one day being understood and employed." The author of the article remarked that the behavior of Jones's commanding officer and the provost marshal was "of a piece with the stupidity that opposed the use of colored soldiers" in the military.

After this laudatory description of Miss Jones, the author turned to their next subject. "I would mention another who refuses to unsex herself, and demands recognition, without the deception of male attire." The article detailed Dr. Mary Walker's contributions to the army's medical care of its soldiers, both in various Washington hospitals and in the field with the Army of the Potomac, all without receiving a salary. "Her competence was tested and approved," yet her petitions to the surgeon general were denied.

The article also asserted that the doctor "has been anxious for employment as a spy," a public acknowledgment that would make her goal more difficult to achieve. According to the report, Walker applied to General Marsena R. Patrick for this work. A native New Yorker and West Point graduate, in 1862 Patrick received an appointment as brigadier general of volunteers. After a stint as military governor of Fredericksburg, Virginia, and as a division commander under General McClellan, in October 1862 he became provost marshal of the Army of the Potomac. Patrick had a hand in creating the Bureau of Military Information in early 1863, which employed a network of field intelligence agents.

Dr. Walker believed her profession made her a perfect candidate for this organization, but General Patrick did not agree. Even though Mary Walker secured endorsements from generals Winfield Scott Hancock and Darius Couch, "Gen. Meade gives her no encouragement." In summation, the reporter asked, "Do the Army Regulations anywhere FORBID it? Alas! What 'ism' is more absurd than Conservatism? If a woman is proved competent for a duty, and anxious to perform it, why restrain her?"

Lydia Hasbrouck, editor of *The Sibyl*, followed up for her readers. "We believe her [Mary Walker] to be one of the bravest, noblest, and truest of women." Hasbrouck, "indignant" that the military did not give official recognition to Walker's accomplishments, encouraged people to send donations to the doctor so she could continue tending to the troops.

During the early fall of 1863, Mary Walker extended her field work beyond Virginia and into Tennessee. When she heard about the fighting at Chickamauga in northern Georgia, she traveled to one of the several volunteer hospitals that had been established in Chattanooga, Tennessee, about fifteen miles north of the fighting. From September 18 to 20, 1863, Major General William Rosecrans tried—and failed—to push his Army of the Cumberland into Georgia from Tennessee. Of the 60,000 Union troops engaged, over 16,000 were killed, wounded, and missing or captured. Confederate general Braxton Bragg's 65,000-strong Army of Tennessee suffered more than 18,000 casualties, making immediate pursuit of Rosecrans impossible.

The area remained dangerous. The Confederate victory at Chickamauga was good for the South, of course, but Bragg viewed Chattanooga as the real prize. If he could not get the Northerners out through battle, he would starve them out. Between Confederate hilltop artillery to the south and infantry on the roads to the east and west, the Union could only bring in supplies to the city from the mountainous north. By mid-October, the Yankees were down to half rations.

The Confederate chokehold on Chattanooga ended by late October. In the wake of General Rosecrans's failure at Chickamauga, Union divisions from other locales were dispatched to Tennessee to shore up the Army of the Cumberland. President Lincoln created the Division of the Mississippi in mid-October, putting Ulysses S. Grant in command. Under Grant's leadership, Union troops sent the enemy's infantry on the road west of Chattanooga scattering, and supplies flowed into the city.

Mary Walker stayed on through this. She probably met General George Thomas, dubbed the "Rock of Chickamauga," through her hospital work. He liked what he saw and would remember her. On November 2, 1863, the doctor wrote to Edwin Stanton, the secretary of war, with a bold proposal. "Will you give me authority to get up a regiment of men, to be called *Walker's U.S. Patriots*, subject to all general orders, in Vol. Regts?" she inquired. She planned to enlist volunteers from any of the loyal states, with the understanding that she would serve as the regiment's first assistant surgeon. Walker signed off, "Hoping to hear from you soon & to receive the *order* solicited." She underscored her signature with a bold flourish.

Not surprisingly, Stanton declined Mary Walker's offer. Although the army still thrived on volunteer enlistments, having a woman organize a regiment was unheard of. Even Walker's assurances that she could get men to reenlist and could get paroled prisoners to sign up was not enough to convince the secretary of war to approve the unconventional plan. Another year was drawing to a close, with the doctor without a commission. But she had cause to hope. In November, General Grant replaced Rosecrans with Thomas at the head of the Army of the Cumberland.

Walker knew how highly Thomas thought of her. He might be inclined to secure an official position for her.

Meanwhile, the woman doctor's reputation for helping soldiers continued to spread. In mid-November Mary Walker received a letter from twenty-one-year-old Captain Alexander Springsteen of Schodack, New York. Springsteen had enlisted a year earlier with Company G of the 12th New York Volunteer Infantry Regiment. After the War Department created the Bureau of Colored Troops in May 1863, to bring more black men into the service, many men from the 12th New York were tapped for officer duty in those new units. Springsteen, regarded as "modest and gentlemanly" by his colleagues, was one. As the regiment's chaplain explained, "They had passed a rigid examination, for only men of special fitness were deemed qualified to lead in a service demanding not only intelligence and skill and patience, but unusual daring."

In October 1863 Springsteen received a promotion to captain of Company K of the 2nd US Colored Infantry Regiment. His new assignment put him at Camp Casey in Arlington, Virginia, near Washington. The facility housed about 1,800 soldiers, most of them from the 23rd US Colored Troops, but other African-American units bivouacked and trained there, including Springsteen's. He wrote to Mary Walker, addressing her as "Kind Friend"; in fact, the entire tone of the letter suggested a prior acquaintance. (The 12th New York had been at Warrenton in 1862, so it is possible the young soldier had met her there.)

"I have no doubt but that you will be surprised on receiving a letter from me," Alexander Springsteen wrote. "But I must look to the comfort of my men." In the cold of the late fall, they needed mittens, "100 prs. with forefinger on them" to keep their hands warm while shooting their weapons. "I know of no one except you on whom to make a *special requisition* and expect [it] to be filled." Springsteen knew he was asking for something out of the ordinary, and he trusted Mary Walker could arrange it. He added a more personal line about his own recent exploits, then corrected himself. "But this is a business letter."

Dr. Walker may have been a bit delayed in orchestrating the delivery of Springsteen's mittens. During the third week of November 1863, she was away from Washington, in Pittsburgh for some unspecified reason.

Her appearance on the city streets caused a stir. According to a newspaper report, Walker, "a patriotic lady, who had conferred innumerable blessings upon the sick and wounded in the Army of the Potomac," was "subjected to considerable annoyance" because of the "singularity" of her outfit. She was dressed in her usual wartime attire: below-the-knee tunic with a white collar and necktie over pants, topped with a military overcoat and cape. A lady's hat completed the ensemble.

The "considerable annoyance" Walker contended with consisted of flagrant staring and rude comments that she must be a Rebel spy. But word quickly spread about her work with the Union Army, and the people in Pittsburgh calmed down, realizing that Dr. Walker's clothing "better suited the noble work in which she is engaged." For the remainder of her time in that city, she was "treated with all the courtesy and respect which were due to a person of her character and mission."

Perhaps reflecting on this incident, Mary Walker penned her final article for *The Sibyl*, which ran in December. Ironically, in that same issue the magazine published an excerpt from a letter Walker wrote to Lydia Hasbrouck. The doctor lamented she had intended to write an article, and to write more often, "but you have no idea how hard I labor in a thousand directions, and positively have not had time when I have not been so WEARY." Yet Walker managed to finish a piece called "Positions that Women Ought of Right to Occupy," in which she linked women's wartime contributions to the cause of women's rights.

"Much good to women is sure to result from this war, for her true worth will be seen in a thousand ways," Mary Walker began. She made subtle references to the cherished heritage of the American Revolution. "We are a people that right all wrongs when subjects are agitated sufficiently to prove to the public that wrongs have an existence." She warned men that when they tried to define women's place and keep them there, "you not only show that you have perverted the principles of our dear republican country ... but you show a tyranic [*sic*] spirit that is a disgrace to anyone born under the Stars and Stripes."

Addressing the current war, Mary Walker wrote that she could not understand why the army hired women as laundresses but not as doctors. "This war would have closed long since if women had been properly employed." Again, she blamed men. "Mr. Men, if you will not do it now, and give noble, patriotic women positions of trust and usefulness, if you withhold them simply because they are women, you will protract this war until so many men will be killed that women will be in power, and will have their God-given rights to fill every sphere they wish to; for woman aspires to nothing that she is not capable of doing." She concluded the piece by describing herself as "an agitator of the wrong everywhere."

At the end of 1863, Mary Walker found another wrong to be put right. Since the beginning of the war, many unaccompanied women like herself traveled to Washington, DC. Most came to take care of loved ones as they recuperated in city hospitals, or for visits with family members when their regiments passed through. But women on their own were suspect; often they were assumed to be prostitutes. Even before the war, prostitution flourished in the capital. Its most famous and fashionable brothel—located on Maryland Avenue in the southwest part of the city, and run by Mary Ann Hall—employed around seventeen women. About five hundred other "bawdy houses" abounded. During the war, between 5,000 and 7,500 women engaged in the sex trade in Washington.

Unless visiting women already had friends or family in the city, they could not find a reputable place to spend the night. Dr. Walker confronted this reality one day as she walked along the east side of the Treasury Building and observed the sidewalk and street in a "sanguinary condition." Thinking she could help, she asked a policeman if he knew who had been injured. He told her that the wife of a Union soldier fell down. He called for a carriage and found a soldier to escort the woman to the train station, "for instructions." Walker asked why the woman was not taken to a hospital, and the policeman replied, "There was no city hospital to take her to."

The young woman was pregnant with her first child. Her husband had been away with the army for a few months, and she had not received a single letter from him. Worried that he was sick or wounded, she came to Washington to check the hospitals, assuming she could find him in a day, then go home. Her futile search took a long time, and she spent even more trying to find a hotel room. Turned away at every one, she "made efforts and pleaded to be taken into some private house where she had money enough to pay her expenses." No one allowed her in because her "prospective condition was so evident." The people she encountered assumed she was a woman of loose morals. Exhausted, she had collapsed on the street. The "sanguinary condition" indicated she likely miscarried.

Mary Walker asked the policeman "if there was no woman's home in the city" that provided shelter for soldiers' wives, mothers, and sisters. He said no, though policemen who worked at the Baltimore and Ohio train station "had impoverished themselves helping women who came to Washington in various conditions of distress because they could not see women suffer." The policeman told her a similar story about a respectable middle-aged woman with "plenty of money for her expenses in her pocket, [who] stayed all night under one of the evergreens in Jackson Square, opposite the President's House." No hotel would accept her because she did not carry enough baggage, which raised suspicions that she was a prostitute.

Outraged at the treatment of these women, Mary Walker "immediately began to study up ways and means to remedy this defect." She turned to women's groups first. At public lectures on women's suffrage at the Odd Fellows Hall and at the Union League Hall, she received a few minutes to solicit funds on "behalf of a respectable woman's home." With that seed money, she rented a house on 10th Street across from Ford's Theatre, for forty dollars a month. She approached the assistant adjutant general, Edward Canby, for cots, blankets, sheets, and pillowcases, "those things that for any reason were condemned as not being fit for soldiers' hospitals." Canby obliged, and with the house furnished, Walker hired a matron to run it. The city's police superintendent, William Webb, agreed to instruct his officers to direct women to the doctor's establishment.

When Mary Walker found a couple of rooms at City Hall she thought would be perfect "for the purpose of taking women in there in case they were in trouble from any cause," city officials donated them. Walker rose early each morning and "repaired to these rooms to see who were there and what their necessities were so that they could be removed in a perfect manner" to an appropriate accommodation. Major General Daniel Rucker of the Quartermaster Department agreed to send an ambulance and driver to the doctor every morning "for the purpose of going with these women to find their sick or wounded relatives." Walker appreciated Rucker's generosity. "This was given me much to the relief of distressed women and of their soldier-relatives."

To ensure the visiting unaccompanied women knew about this service, Mary Walker placed notices in Washington newspapers describing the accommodations. Addressing "females who are homeless," she announced she had "secured respectable rooms where they can remain overnight, *free of charge*." She offered a place for "prospective mothers who are without homes and means . . . and who will *endeavor to lead better lives*" at a temporary foundling hospital until the permanent one was ready. Walker requested that those in need of lodging should come to her home at 374 9th Street before seven o'clock in the evening. She may have been flooded with visitors, because she placed an ad a few days later directing "all women in distress" to see her at City Hall between eleven a.m. and noon. "Her duties are such that she cannot see any such at any other hour or any other place."

Reaction to the establishment of the residence for homeless women was generally positive. One Washington newspaper referred to it as "a new and benevolent idea," specifying that the "object is intended to relieve only as are worthy." Charitable programs in the nineteenth century focused on helping the "worthy poor," and Dr. Walker's assistance to the unaccompanied women followed this practice. To keep the shelter going, she understood she needed help soliciting funds, so at the beginning of 1864 she recruited volunteers for the Women's Relief Association.

By mid-January, Mary Walker had assembled a team of well-known Washington women that included three doctors' wives and the wife of a judge. Mrs. Mary Hay served as the association's president, with Walker taking on the position of secretary and member of the business committee. Sensitive to propriety, the members debated attaching a sign, "Destitute Women's Home," to the building on 10th Street. Some thought it would be helpful to women searching for an overnight accommodation, while others believed it might attract the "wrong" kind of woman. Walker preferred to forego the sign, claiming it was "better to receive and discriminate women at the City Hall building."

Over the course of six weeks, the Women's Relief Association had secured several hundred lodgings and meals for women and children who arrived from New York, Massachusetts, New Jersey, Pennsylvania, and Maryland, "all of whom were perfect strangers to every member." Of these, eight were found "unworthy" and sent home, and two were situated in industrial homes for long-term lodging and work. In mid-February 1864, Walker reported the association had received $127 in donations, plus forty beds and blankets from the War Department. Kate Chase Sprague, daughter of Lincoln's treasury secretary, wife of the governor of Rhode Island, and perhaps the most socially prominent woman in DC, pledged fifty dollars.

In addition to conducting the intake interviews at City Hall, Dr. Walker also donated her medical services to the women and children who stayed at the 10th Street house. She stretched herself to her limits. Because she was overworked—and because the association now stood on solid footing—she resigned her position as secretary at the February 15 meeting. The members present "expressed satisfaction" with her services and gave her a unanimous vote of thanks.

Five days later, Mary Walker published a letter in Washington's *National Republican*, correcting the details about the supplies donated by the War Department to the Women's Relief Association. She specifically thanked General Canby for his "humane" generosity. The doctor then addressed the criticisms that arose over her departure from the group. Reiterating the point she had made at the February 15 meeting, she explained she gave two months professional services to the association. Now, feeling "that I cannot afford to donate any more at present," she concluded, "My heart is still with the cause, but my energies must be in another direction."

CHAPTER SIX

Union Spy

AT THE BEGINNING OF 1864, DR. MARY WALKER IMMERSED HERSELF IN women-led organizations. She made the Women's Relief Association successful, and she also worked with the Women's Loyal National League. The latter was founded in New York City in May 1863 by Elizabeth Cady Stanton and Susan B. Anthony, women's rights activists Walker would come to know well. The Loyal League sought to add constitutional authority to President Lincoln's Emancipation Proclamation by securing an amendment outlawing slavery. From their office in the Cooper Institute, Stanton and Anthony launched a massive petition drive in support of a proposed amendment. The league successfully presented over 400,000 signatures to Congress by the time it dissolved in August 1864.

One of the most controversial aspects of the Loyal League was the insistence of Stanton and Anthony on linking emancipation and women's rights. A resolution debated at the organizational meeting stated, "There can never be true peace in this republic until the civil and political rights of all citizens of African descent and all Women are practically established." It was a bold claim to citizenship for two groups long denied equal standing as citizens. Though both women supported abolition, their priority was women's rights, and the resolution highlighted their determination to work for these dual freedoms. Despite the controversy the resolution generated—some women worried the pairing would dilute support for emancipation—league members adopted it.

Mary Walker believed in universal equality as much as she favored emancipation. She approved of the Loyal League because of its stance on female medical professionals. One of the adopted resolutions read, "[W] omen now acting as nurses in our hospitals, who are regular graduates of medicine, should be recognized as physicians and surgeons, and receive the same remuneration for their services as men." Dr. Walker traveled to New York City in January 1864 to lecture at the Cooper Institute, where the league had been holding weekly lectures since its founding. She concluded her presentation with the recitation of a poem written by Episcopalian minister A. Cleveland Coxe in 1840, which now had an added significance:

> We are living, we are dwelling,
> in a grand and awful time,
> in an age on ages telling,
> to be living is sublime.
> Hark! The waking up of nations,
> hosts advancing to the fray.

The comfort Dr. Walker may have drawn from supportive women likely helped to soften the blow of the next two disappointments from men who held the power to grant her commission. When she learned Secretary of War Stanton had rejected her offer to raise a volunteer regiment and serve as its surgeon, she went over his head. On January 11, she wrote to President Lincoln that she had "rendered much of valuable service in her efforts to promote the cause of the Union." She explained that she had been doing the work of an assistant surgeon, both in hospitals and in the field, without pay. Walker also cited "several measures that are of great importance to Government," particularly the creation of the Invalid Corps.

The doctor asserted she had been "denied a commission, solely on the ground of her sex." She told Lincoln she believed "had a man been as useful to our country as she modestly claims to have been, a star would have been taken from the National Heavens and placed upon his shoulder." Walker wanted a commission that would allow her "to go whenever and wherever there is a battle that she may render aid in the field hospitals." She emphasized not only her bravery and patriotism, but also her willingness to compromise. Walker asked Lincoln to assign her to the women's ward at Douglas Hospital, where "there cannot possibly be any objection urged on account of sex."

Housed in a row of three brick residences at the corner of 2nd and I Streets NW, known as "Douglas Row" or "Minnesota Row," the hospital was named in honor of Stephen Douglas. The well-known Democratic senator from Illinois, who had challenged Abraham Lincoln for the presidency in 1860, had lived in one of those mansions until his death in June 1861. The government leased the expanse of property, converting it into a well-appointed three-hundred-bed hospital that opened in January 1862. Mary Walker may have chosen Douglas Hospital because it utilized a contingent of female nurses, the Catholic Sisters of Mercy. She probably encountered them in Chattanooga, where the nuns cared for the wounded on the battlefield. For Dr. Walker, Douglas Hospital would have been the ideal destination for the unaccompanied women who needed medical care that she assisted through the Women's Relief Association.

President Lincoln took the time to reply to Mary Walker's request—a recognition of her valuable contributions to the war effort, and perhaps, to their earlier meeting at a White House reception. But it was not the reply the doctor wanted. Though she later claimed Lincoln endorsed her request with a simple, "I am willing," his response was more qualified, and less in her favor. The War Department held jurisdiction over such appointments, Lincoln wrote. He described it as an "organized system in the hands of men supposed to be learned in that profession," and he believed it would "injure the service for me, with strong hand, to thrust among them anyone, male or female, against their consent." If the War Department wanted to give Walker a position, Lincoln was willing for her to have it.

Rebuffed by both the secretary of war and the president, Mary Walker once again resorted to traveling on her own authority. In February 1864, she returned to Chattanooga, where her work had been appreciated. While tending patients in General Hospital No. 2, she encountered a soldier with such an unusual story that she notified reporters. The young man with the 90th Illinois Infantry Regiment, using the name Frank Miller, had been taken prisoner in October 1863 by Confederate forces in Florence, Alabama, and transferred to Atlanta. Guards had shot Miller in the leg when he tried to escape. While undergoing treatment for his wound, prison doctors found that Miller was a woman.

In mid-February 1864, Frank Miller—who initially refused to disclose her real name—was part of a prisoner exchange. She ended up in Chattanooga, where she met Mary Walker, who convinced her to talk to reporters. The doctor considered Miller's story "a singular case of female martial spirit and patriotic devotion to the flag." The young woman and her brother, both orphans, had enlisted in the 65th Illinois Home Guards in the spring of 1861, and he was killed the following year, at Shiloh. Miller continued her service with the 90th Illinois until her capture. She claimed that once Confederate president Jefferson Davis found out she was a woman, he offered her a commission if she defected to the South. Miller, a staunch Unionist, declined.

Reporters shared Mary Walker's high opinion of Frank Miller. One wrote, "Whether it was love of adventure, or love of country, or some less worthy motive, that led her to don her soldier's uniform, she belongs clearly to the class of heroines thought worthy to wear wreaths." Miller finally admitted her real name was Frances Hook, and she allowed a photographer to take her picture. Dr. Mary Walker believed that instead of sending Hook home, the army should make her military service official by granting her a lieutenant's commission thereby setting a precedent for other women. "Congress should assign women to duty in the army, with compensation, as well as colored men, averring that patriotism has no sex."

A reporter stressed that Mary Walker was serious about her proposal. "We are certain that the 'Doctor' is thoroughly in earnest." Equality was always at the forefront of Walker's mind. The commission she pursued was not only for herself; she believed all women were entitled to serve with the army, according to their abilities, and they were entitled to be paid for their work. Dr. Walker made a case for this at every opportunity.

Her progress toward that goal was assisted by acquaintances she cultivated during the war. General George Thomas had never forgotten Mary Walker's work in Tennessee, and he thought about her when he found out that Dr. J. A. Rosa, assistant surgeon to the 52nd Ohio Volunteers, had died near the beginning of 1864. Thomas decided that Dr. Walker should replace Rosa, and he began the process of securing her appointment. It was not exactly what Walker wanted, but it came close. Thomas planned to hire her as a civilian contract surgeon, complete with a lieutenant-level salary of eighty dollars a month.

Illinois congressman John Franklin Farnsworth pushed the process along by sending a letter to Robert Wood, the assistant surgeon general who had been sympathetic to Mary Walker's quest for a commission. At the end of his congressional term in 1861, the forty-year-old Farnsworth organized the 8th Illinois Volunteer Cavalry at the behest of his friend, Abraham Lincoln. Farnsworth likely met Mary Walker during 1862 while the 8th Illinois was with the Army of the Potomac in Virginia.

Colonel Farnsworth received a promotion to brigadier general in December 1862, but he had already been elected to Congress again, and resigned his commission in March 1863. His political and military backgrounds meant he wielded a lot of influence, and he used it on Mary Walker's behalf. At the end of February 1864, Farnsworth wrote to Wood, "Mrs. Dr. Walker is desirous of doing some good in your department." The congressman pointed out that for more than two years she had been "active, efficient, and very useful in her administrations to the sick and wounded soldiers." Emphasizing Walker's unblemished character, Farnsworth encouraged Wood to find her "some good position, where she can properly support herself—and at the same time be most useful."

In early March 1864, General Wood instructed Dr. Mary Walker to proceed to Chattanooga to undergo the army's pre-contract medical board evaluation. This had nothing to do with her gender and everything to do with her profession. Most of the 5,500 male civilian doctors who became army surgeons faced an examination. Back in the fall of 1861, individual states had begun setting up examination boards to assess the doctors who would be treating the volunteer forces. After William Hammond became surgeon general the following spring, he brought order and standardization to what had originally been a disorganized system. Candidates for commission or promotion were tested over several days. A written autobiography assessed literacy skills, followed by brief essays on medical topics including surgery, anatomy, and pharmacology. The candidate then endured verbal quizzing on a variety of technical issues, followed by observations while treating patients.

Though Hammond strove for objectivity through the evaluation system, it was subject to political and personal influences. Secretary of War Stanton exerted pressure in certain individual cases. The allopathic or "regular" doctors who dominated the examination boards denigrated practitioners of homeopathic and eclectic medicine. Dr. Mary Walker had the influence of General Thomas and Congressman Farnsworth in her favor, which might have been enough to counter her eclectic training and her gender. But she had incurred the disfavor of doctors associated with the Army of the Cumberland, so it was with a great sense of unease that she traveled to Chattanooga to face the medical board they controlled.

Ohio native Glover S. Perin enlisted as an assistant surgeon with the army in 1847, at the age of twenty-four, and in May 1861 was promoted to major and surgeon. He joined the Army of the Cumberland as its medical director in February 1863. From Murfreesboro, Tennessee, he set about reorganizing its ambulance system, which General Rosecrans had also found inefficient. Perin admired the work of Jonathan Letterman, his counterpart with the Army of the Potomac, and began implementing his field hospital and medical supply systems, a process that took about a year.

At Chickamauga in September 1863, Perin's careful planning was overwhelmed by a fast-moving battle that put ambulances and field hospitals farther from the wounded than he had intended. On the last day of the battle, Confederate forces overran seven of the hospitals on the heels of a rapid Union withdrawal. Thousands of the wounded flooded into behind-the-lines hospitals, especially in Chattanooga, where Dr. Mary Walker had gone when she heard about the battle. The Sanitary Commission helped find shelter for overflow patients and brought in much-needed supplies. Food was so scarce in the area that many of the sick and wounded had not eaten for two days. Perin's desperation for doctors did not mean he welcomed Walker. It is likely he knew of her arrival, and it is possible they met, but he did not approve of female doctors, especially ones with eclectic training.

Dr. Roberts Bartholow agreed with Perin. An 1852 graduate of the University of Maryland's medical school, Bartholow worked as a physician in Baltimore before joining the army in 1857. As an assistant surgeon during the war, Bartholow served as medical purveyor for the Army of the Potomac, acquiring medical supplies and performing physicals on recruits. Bartholow published *A Manual of Instructions for Enlisting and Discharging Soldiers* to evaluate the physical and mental health of recruits. He also headed up military hospitals in several different cities, which was how he first encountered Dr. Mary Walker at Washington's Lincoln General Hospital in 1863.

The largest military medical facility in the city, located about a mile from the Capitol building, the Lincoln Hospital had opened in December 1862. Its twenty pavilions and twenty-five tent wards housed over 2,500 patients and teemed with staff, including Catholic nursing sisters. Mary Walker donated some of her time to that hospital, and she caught Dr. Bartholow's attention sometime in 1863. He was not impressed. Bartholow later remembered Walker in the hospital "in some pretended inspectorial capacity," operating under the authority of the secretary of war, like a "spy and informer." He watched as she "pretended to have power to obtain redress of grievances, and industriously sat about hearing and contriving them."

Dr. Bartholow did not regard Mary Walker as a physician. He considered her, incorrectly, an agent of the War Department, sent to root out inefficiencies and incompetencies of his medical staff, something he clearly did not appreciate, especially from a woman. Bartholow took note that Walker "was dressed in that hybrid costume which has since become so notorious" when she came to the hospital in Washington. The way she acted when she arrived in Chattanooga also concerned him. She had orders from Surgeon General Wood to report to Glover Perin and demanded he employ her as a medical officer.

According to Roberts Bartholow, Glover Perin "was not a little astonished at the apparition" that was Dr. Walker, and he was "indignant that the lives of the sick and wounded men should be intrusted [*sic*] to such a medical monstrosity." Bartholow admitted that even before Walker's medical board examination, Perin had decided she should not receive a position. As a member of the board, Perin expected to have his way.

Though Perin was medical director of the Army of the Cumberland, Dr. George E. Cooper, who would soon take up that position, sat at the head of the board that examined Mary Walker in March 1864. Like Perin, Cooper had joined the army as an assistant surgeon in 1847. During the first year of the war Cooper worked as a medical purveyor in Philadelphia. He shared his colleagues' disapproval of female doctors, and before the examination began, he told Dr. Walker he did not "want any female surgeons." The likelihood that she would receive a fair evaluation was zero.

According to Dr. Bartholow, Mary Walker acted both flustered and flirtatious in front of the medical board. She arrived "with a little feminine tremor and confusion" and attempted to "propitiate us and secure a favorable report, so that we might take it for granted she possessed the requisite knowledge." During the proceedings, she "betrayed such utter ignorance of any subject in the whole range of medical science, that we found it a difficult matter to conduct an examination." The board unanimously concluded that she "had no more medical knowledge than any housewife," and the only suitable position for her was as a nurse. Bartholow claimed his fellow doctors were sympathetic to the young female doctor, and "we treated her with the utmost delicacy and consideration."

Courtesy was not what Mary Walker had experienced, or expected, but she had assumed everyone would behave professionally. When she arrived in Chattanooga in March, she presented her documentation to Dr. Cooper, who was acting in Dr. Perin's place. Cooper responded to Surgeon General Wood's order with anger, telling Walker that Wood had "*no business*" sending her to Chattanooga, because he "would not have a woman surgeon in his department." Cooper went on with comments that the woman doctor found "*harsh*, unpatriotic, and unkind." She warned him she would notify General Thomas if he ignored Wood's order. Cooper said he would call the medical board together for an examination the following day, probably assuming she would feel too intimidated to appear. But Mary Walker replied that she "was ready for one, & wished one."

Convinced that Dr. Cooper had already made up his mind that he "would not have the 'dignity of the profession' so trampled upon as to have a *female* invasion in the *Military* Department," Dr. Walker went to see the "*noble*" General Thomas anyway. She told him she thought the examination would be unfair, and that she didn't know if she should bother showing up for it. Thomas replied that she should keep the appointment to "see what Cooper would do," and to report back to him.

Mary Walker felt buoyed by Thomas's continuing support, so she appeared before the medical board. Neither Cooper nor Perin sat with the three examiners, "all young men, two of whom were younger both in years and practice" than she. "I had scarcely entered the room before I felt the *Cooper influence* and was almost *dumb*," she remembered. "I felt that the examination was intended to be a *farce, & more than half* the time was consumed in questions regarding subjects that were *exclusively feminine* & had no sort of relation to the diseases & wounds of *soldiers*."

After answering questions about obstetrics, Mary Walker faced "trivial" ones that were more matters of opinion than real medical issues facing the enlisted, all of which "could be decided according to whether the applicant was desired to win or fail." Though she knew she had performed poorly, at the end of the examination, she asked the board to forward a favorable report to General Thomas. The final judgment, far from positive, equated the doctor's medical knowledge with that of a housewife or nurse. George Cooper offered to hire her on as a nurse, but Dr. Walker refused.

She went to Dr. Francis Salter, head surgeon of Chattanooga Hospital No. 1, and asked for a position as an assistant surgeon. He put her in charge of the measles ward, where all sixty patients made a full recovery under her care. Salter also appointed Dr. Walker as inspector of several other wards, "to relieve himself of the duty," giving her "an opportunity to openly direct the assistant surgeons in such wards in all cases." She intervened in the case of Private Theobald Bramsby of Company K of the 11th Ohio Infantry Regiment, who had sustained such a severe hand wound that a surgeon had prescribed amputation. She ordered the operation delayed for two weeks, and later learned that Bramsby's hand had healed well enough for him to return to active duty.

Dr. Salter had no concerns about Mary Walker's qualifications. He explained that while she could continue the work, the medical board's finding prevented him from paying her a salary. This arrangement, however, would not improve her situation. She must have felt a hefty dose of relief and justification when General Thomas set aside the medical board's recommendation. On March 10, 1864, his chief of staff, William D. Whipple, sent an order to medical director Glover Perin: "The Major General Commanding directs that you will instruct the Doctress, who reported to you a day or two since, to report to Col. Danl. McCook" at Lee and Gordon's Mills, in northern Georgia.

Dr. Perin resisted. He replied the next day in a letter to General Whipple that he had received the communication about "Miss Mary E. Walker, the reputed doctress, and in reply would respectfully call your attention to the enclosed order, with copy of the proceedings of the Board of Medical Examiners in reference to her qualifications for the practice of medicine."

But General Thomas already knew about the report, and the subsequent response from his office was so swift that on the same day, Perin wrote to Mary Walker. Addressing her as "Miss" rather than "Dr.," he made it clear the appointment was not his idea. "In compliance with the directions of the General Commanding," she was to proceed to Lee and Gordon's Mills. Penning the customary "Very Respectfully" and "Your obt. Servant" above his signature must have been painful.

Mary Walker knew about the assignment even as Dr. Perin chafed over ordering it. General Thomas had called Walker into his office while her hospital patients convalesced and told her that Colonel Daniel McCook Jr. "had his headquarters in a house with a family at the front, where surgical work would be expected soon, and that he would direct Dr. Cooper to give me an order to report to him." That duty ultimately ended up with Perin. Dr. Walker let Dr. Salter, her boss at the hospital, know about the change in her status. He was reluctant to let her go. He offered to talk to Thomas and insist he needed her in Chattanooga, but Walker explained that she preferred the more-forward assignment. Roberts Bartholow, one of the examining board doctors, expressed shock that Mary Walker was headed "to the extreme front!"

On March 14, 1864, Colonel McCook issued Special Orders No. 8, which verified that "Dr. Mary E. Walker, having reported to this Brigade by order of Genl. Thomas, is hereby assigned for duty to the 52d Ohio

Vol. Infantry." This was the closest she ever came to securing a commission. Instead of military status, Walker became a contract civilian assistant surgeon, roughly equal to the rank of lieutenant. She earned eighty dollars a month, and the army provided her with a horse and saddle. She wore a uniform of her own design, a modified Bloomer costume in navy, with a green sash identifying her as a surgeon. *The Sibyl* notified its readers of Walker's accomplishment: "The young lady is said to be very pretty, and to thoroughly understand her profession."

Colonel McCook had set up his headquarters in the home of the town's miller. Mary Walker arrived in an ambulance and was shown to her quarters—the kitchen, which she shared with the miller's family. Even in a forward location, propriety mattered. This sleeping arrangement was considered respectable for a single woman living in an area dominated by men. McCook welcomed the doctor to the encampment. They had already met in Chattanooga, and like General Thomas, McCook admired Walker's abilities and believed she would be an asset to the regiment. Perhaps sensitive to his troops' feelings about a female doctor, McCook treated her "with every consideration, never for once being in my company alone."

Despite this precaution, Colonel McCook's men talked. Levi A. Ross, a twenty-nine-year-old captain of Company K, 86th Illinois Infantry, stationed at Lee and Gordon's Mills, admitted his fellow soldiers mostly laughed at the doctor and gossiped that her relationship with McCook went beyond the professional. Nixon B. Stewart, a corporal or sergeant with Company E of the 52nd Ohio, documented the misinformation and unease surrounding her arrival. The men believed Mary Walker was a first lieutenant, though "how she got her commission no one seemed to know," perhaps hinting at a romantic connection. Stewart claimed that the "men seemed to hate her, and she did little or nothing for the sick of the regiment."

Dr. Walker believed her job as contract surgeon made her one of Colonel McCook's staff officers. He entrusted her with a great deal of authority. One day when a general review was held several miles from Lee and Gordon's Mills, the colonel and his men needed to leave early in the morning to arrive in time. In his absence, McCook ordered Dr. Walker to replace her green surgeon's sash with a red one, for officer of the day, and to hold a review for the remaining pickets in camp. "I did so, having the orderly ride by my side," and the guards turned out like it was a typical inspection. "This is the only instance in the war, as far as I am aware," the doctor later remembered, "where a woman made a revue [sic]."

Although General Thomas had told Dr. Walker that the 52nd would soon need a surgeon, its current medical needs were not critical. Colonel McCook's men were wintering, and patients with serious wounds had already been transferred to hospitals. When the locals, experiencing "great distress outside of the Union lines," learned of the female doctor's presence at Lee and Gordon's Mills, they came to her and "begged for medical attendance." McCook encouraged Walker to treat the civilians, "which was the polite way of giving an order." She responded to calls for medical, surgical, obstetrical, and even dental treatment, frequently traveling into Confederate territory to do so. "It was dangerous going out there," she remembered. "[T]he two officers and two orderlies that accompanied me were armed, and I had two revolvers in my saddle as well."

One mother sent for the doctor because her sixteen-year-old son had contracted typhoid. He and some of his friends were hiding out in a forest, staying away from the Confederate soldiers trying to press them into service. The mother and her daughters took food out to the young men, hiding it under their dresses to avoid attracting attention. The soldiers caught up with them and took the boys away, but left the son because he was too weak to march. Dr. Walker brought him enough medicine "to last some little time, perhaps until his recovery." When she saw how thin he was, she also gave him the one rare food item she had brought along for her own meal: an orange.

Even with armed escorts, travels away from the encampment could be dangerous. A request came in late one afternoon for Dr. Walker to treat a sick child who lived several miles from Lee and Gordon's Mills. The timing and location meant that the doctor would be out in enemy territory after dark. Colonel McCook did not want her to go; he considered the area particularly hazardous, even for his men. Walker insisted, telling the colonel she would travel alone if necessary. McCook relented, sending a couple of officers and orderlies with her. The group rode through a forest so dense they "had to manage not to have the branches get into the eyes of our horses."

The officers remained outside the house while Mary Walker tended the patient, "a beautiful child" about a year or two old, suffering from tetanus. The youngster's mother was there, along with several men, which made Walker uneasy. She knew her patient stood a slim chance of recovery even if she remained for several days to provide round-the-clock treatment. "I felt a little afraid to stay," the doctor admitted. She gave the mother detailed instructions and said she would try to return the next day to see if the little one improved. She left the house and quietly told her escorts about the men inside. "We went away very leisurely, but we had not proceeded but a short distance before we hastened as rapidly as possible towards our headquarters." The next morning, Walker decided she had been overly cautious and planned to go back and check on the child. McCook refused permission. The latest intelligence from the area deemed it too dangerous. Dr. Walker probably never learned the patient's fate.

Many of the locals were intrigued that the new physician with the Union forces was a woman, and they likely expected sympathy—or at least empathy—from her. One day at dusk, "a poor woman rode up with two children on her horse, and a bag, hoping to beg some meal." Dr. Walker was in fact sympathetic. She convinced Colonel McCook to give the woman what she needed, "with the promise that she would not come again, nor tell where she got it." Walker also gave up her bed so the woman and her children had a safe place to sleep instead of riding out in the dark. She concluded, "There is no doubt that General McCook's kindness to this woman, and my professional duties to these people, caused a great many of them to abandon their allegiance to the [C]onfederacy."

Because of her style of dress, the locals regarded Mary Walker with some curiosity and confusion. The mother of the child with tetanus had addressed her as "Sir." She had declined to spend the night with that family because, as a Union doctor, she felt unsafe. In another case, Walker concluded she needed an overnight stay. She had no worries about the family, but "the house had a wing upon its rear side, while attached to the house there was no communicating door." She did not want to sleep alone in an outside room. She asked the mother if the daughter could sleep with her, and the older woman consented.

Communal sleeping arrangements, though on the decline in middle-class urban homes, were still common in rural households. Family members, including servants, often shared the same bed. In winter, it was the easiest way to keep warm, and year-round it provided siblings and spouses the opportunity for private conversations. Due to a lack of guest rooms, it was not unusual for visitors like Mary Walker to bunk in with the host family. The bed was also a recognized site of sexual activity, which, in the nineteenth century, was supposed to be restricted to men and women who were married to each other.

On her next visit to that family, Mary Walker was surprised by what happened when she requested the same arrangement. "[T]he mother said that I could sleep in the same place, but that I would have to sleep alone." The doctor again explained her concern about sleeping in a detached room, and asked why the daughter could not stay with her, as she had done before.

The mother hesitated before admitting that "the people all around there said [Walker] was a man." Walker asked why they believed that, and the woman answered, "Because no woman could know as much as I knew" about medical treatment. Walker pointed out that her daughter "has said nothing against me, since she could have nothing to say." The woman allowed that this was true, "but still, as everybody said I was a man, she did not wish her daughter to sleep with me."

The women struck a compromise. Mother and daughter accompanied Mary Walker to the room where the doctor unbraided her own hair. "You can take hold of it and pull my hair as much as you like," Walker told the mother, "and you will see that my hair is long like other women's." The woman yanked on the tresses and told Walker she had heard about "false hair" cleverly attached to a person's head. Finally, the mother was convinced Mary Walker was a woman, and allowed her daughter to sleep in the same bed with her.

The family was reassured enough about the doctor's gender that a married daughter who lived a bit farther away asked Mary Walker to spend the next night with her, "to have the honor of having a woman physician stay in her house." The windowless log home consisted of one large room that contained two beds, "both made up clean and with good [bed]clothes." Before the two women were ready to turn in for the evening, they heard a whistle from outside. "My husband has come home," the woman said to Mary Walker. He was a Confederate soldier on a twenty-four-hour leave. He had seen a horse outside, with its fine saddle, and wondered why a Union soldier would be inside his house. "When [he] found it was myself he shook hands and seemed delighted to see me," Walker remembered. "[He] told me that he had been impressed in the service, that none of the men around there wanted to fight the Yankees."

Nevertheless, the man took his Confederate service seriously. If he were not on leave, he said to Dr. Walker, "you have a good horse and a good bridle and saddle, and I should take them all away from you." Since he was not on duty, he promised all those things would be there in the morning.

The man went back outside for a few minutes while she got ready for bed. "And of course I turned my face to the wall when he came in to retire in the other bed," Walker later wrote, without mentioning any awkwardness of sharing a room with a young married couple just reunited after a forced separation. She left the next morning, riding her own horse.

Mary Walker became a familiar figure in the area. Even if people did not quite understand that a woman could be a doctor, they did not hesitate to utilize her expertise. She did not charge for her services. "The people in that country were in a pitiable condition" because of the activity of both the Union and Confederate armies. Northern troops moved through the area in small squads, cautious not to venture too far from camp. Southern soldiers "had been all through there pressing every man into service," leaving the women to fend for themselves, or, as they told Dr. Walker, "to root hog or die." The chickens and pigs the women managed to raise "were so small and so poor from insufficient food" that they provided few nutrients to those who ate them. The women went to great lengths to hide the animals from soldiers searching for provisions, but almost always invited the doctor to share a meal.

Locals relied on Mary Walker for more than medical treatment. Women, especially, asked for help with other things related to their domestic duties. A woman with a "young lady daughter" wanted the doctor to take one of them with her horse and their wagon to purchase some cotton thread from a mill in Ringgold, Georgia, about thirteen miles northeast of Lee and Gordon's Mills. Many women in that area still wove their own cloth, which they used for sewing their own dresses.

Although Dr. Walker wanted to help, she told the mother, "I was afraid to go down there with my blue uniform on, for fear that they would take my horse away and take me prisoner." The woman offered one of her daughter's dresses along with a bonnet. Mary Walker swapped out most of her clothing, but she could not part with her trousers—she worried she would catch cold without them. She rolled up the bottoms a couple of times to keep them hidden under the long skirt, and she and the daughter traveled to the cotton mill.

The pair looked like any two women come to purchase thread, at least until the daughter handed over a five-dollar greenback in payment. Shocked to see Northern currency, the man conducting the sale, possibly the mill owner, asked where the money had come from. The young woman admitted she sold butter and eggs to Union troops. As the man held on to the bill, he said he did not like Yankee money, and that it was against the law to accept it. Mary Walker understood his dilemma. Everyone in the area was "deplorably poor," with Confederate paper money rapidly dropping in value. The man needed the greenback as much as the young woman needed the thread.

Dressed as a Georgia woman should be, Dr. Walker knew once she opened her mouth, the man would peg her for a Yankee. "I then tried to help the girl out and tried to talk just as she talked and told me to talk it, that 'we would say nothin' about it, that we had come so far, and had not got no Confederate money.'" Reassured, the man completed the transaction and the two women went on their way. As they drove their wagon up a steep, secluded hill, they saw a couple of Confederate soldiers in rapid pursuit. Walker reached over to take hold of the reins and the whip, intent on outrunning them, but the whip dropped out of her hands. Now they had no chance of getting away. The doctor did not think it was safe for her companion to get out of the wagon to look for the lost item. Once on the ground, it would be too easy for the soldiers to grab her, and both women would have been worried about sexual assault.

Mary Walker "feared that if I attempted to alight for the purpose of getting the whip I could not do so without having my pants seen." She worried about being taken prisoner less than an attack by the soldiers. "I cannot tell how great my fears were that I would be suspected of being some other person than my dress indicated." She kept her face obscured by the bonnet and once again affected a local accent. Walker said, "Go 'lang" to the horse, "just as some people down there did speak to a horse, hoping that this Confederate officer would think that I was one of the young women residing near there."

The Confederates had only wanted to come to the women's rescue. They saw the wagon struggle up the hill and now positioned their horses at the back of the vehicle to give it a boost. With the wagon easily rolling, one of the officers pulled up alongside it, trying to get a look at Mary Walker. Aware that "my face was fresher than those brought up in the South in the country," she dipped it again under the bonnet, as if in modesty. He asked what they were carrying, and the women's reply about the thread satisfied him. He and his partner rode off.

Time and again, Dr. Walker ventured into enemy territory to help civilians. "The people expressed so much gratitude that I lost all fear of anything being done to myself." Yet Walker kept her wits about her. On her way to care for patients, two Confederate soldiers stopped her as she passed by a barn about three miles from Lee and Gordon's Mills. A high fence covered three sides of the barn, cutting off the sightline from the road. The doctor explained her mission, and one of the Confederates "recognized that I was from the Union army by my dress and speech." He told her to drive into the barn.

"In the coolest manner," Mary Walker asked why he wanted her in the barn. She told him she was in a hurry to get to her patients. The soldier wanted to know if she carried any revolvers with her. Walker replied with an honest no; she had left her firearms at camp. One of her patients suffered from a bad tooth that needed pulling, Walker told him, and offered to show her medical equipment. As she shifted the reins to reach for her bag, he called, "Stop. I do not want to see your instruments." She knew he thought she was reaching for a gun. She wanted access to her equipment because it included a surgeon's lancet, which she intended to use "on a jugular vein of her own if unable to defend herself with it." The Confederate conferred with his colleague for a few long minutes, then told Dr. Walker to go on her way.

The doctor took these risks not only to help people in need, but to assist the Union military as well. As a woman and a physician, her ability to easily travel back and forth behind enemy lines provided good opportunities for intelligence gathering. In September 1862, Walker had written a letter to the secretary of war, offering to use a code she had invented to pass information about Confederate troop movements to Allan Pinkerton's Secret Service. "Any 'secret service' that your Hon. Body may wish performed, will find me one eminently fitted to do it."

This request was passed on to Major General Henry Halleck, general in chief of the army, who did not respond. During the summer of 1863, Mary Walker again raised the possibility with generals Patrick, Hancock, and Couch. Patrick turned her down, but Hancock and Couch were receptive, until General George Meade, commander of the Army of the Potomac, quashed the idea. But according to General George Thomas, when he met with Walker later that year, she requested assignment to the 52nd Ohio, "in order that she might get through the lines & obtain information from the enemy." Thomas approved, understanding that Dr. Walker would rely on her persona as the "woman doctor" to make her way through Confederate territory. For some, however, this was not her best disguise. At Colonel McCook's headquarters, according to soldier Nixon Stewart, "all this time many of the boys believed her to be a spy."

Intelligence was of vital importance in the spring of 1864 as General William Tecumseh Sherman prepared his Atlanta Campaign. He needed information about Confederate activities throughout Georgia. Every time Mary Walker traveled to enemy territory, she kept her eyes and ears open. Anything she gleaned about the Confederate military and Southern civilians could help Sherman. While Walker's patients may have suspected this, Southern soldiers certainly did.

On her way back to Lee and Gordon's Mills on April 10, 1864, a few of Confederate general Daniel Harvey Hill's soldiers, weapons drawn, detained Dr. Mary Walker. Hill and his men, veterans of the Battle of Chickamauga, had remained in the vicinity with the Army of Tennessee, looking for any opportunity to force out the Union Army. The details of her capture, as with most things related to espionage, are murky. The doctor claimed, "I was taken prisoner while acting in the capacity of acting assistant surgeon," implying she was on a medical call when captured. A Richmond, Virginia, newspaper reported, "She is quite sprightly, converses fluently, says she only wished to deliver letters and had no idea of being arrested."

Confederate major James Wylie Ratchford, a twenty-four-year-old assistant adjutant general assigned to Major General Thomas Hindman at the Army of Tennessee's headquarters at Dalton, Georgia, clarified the circumstances. "Presuming on her connection with the medical fraternity and her sex, [she] rode boldly up to our picket and asked if he would take some letters which she wished delivered within our lines." Mary Walker may have intentionally provoked capture, gambling that she could secure particularly valuable information from inside the Confederate military prison system and get released in time for it to be useful to Sherman. That explains why, instead of evading enemy soldiers, she approached them.

One of the guards informed Dr. Walker he would take her, along with the letters. Major Ratchford remembered she was "indignant, and protested vigorously against being taken prisoner." He believed the Southern military ended up with "a white elephant on their hands." General Hill concurred, though he was "very much amused" by Walker's outrage over her capture. He told her "she was probably giving him as much inconvenience as he was giving her, as he could neither keep her nor turn her loose." Benedict J. Semmes, a captain in the depot commissary at Dalton, witnessed the doctor's arrival. He was less complimentary than Ratchford. "We were all amused and disgusted too at the sight of a *thing* that nothing but the debased and the depraved Yankee nation could produce—'a female doctor.'" Semmes noted her uniform and pronounced her "fair, but not good looking, and of course had tongue enough for a regiment of men."

Captain Semmes hoped that General Joseph Johnston would order Mary Walker "dressed in a homespun frock and bonnet and sent back to the Yankee lines, or put in a lunatic asylum." Instead, she remained at Dalton for a few days, until her presence annoyed Johnston so much that he ordered her transferred to Richmond. The ride took several days by horseback. One of the guards accompanying Dr. Walker feigned illness in futile hope of forcing her to misdiagnose him so he and his compatriots could ridicule her. When she refused their offers of wine, she gained their respect, but little was shown for her when she arrived in the Confederate capital. People in the streets called out "Fresh fish," indicating a new prisoner had arrived.

Mary Walker was taken to the provost marshal's office on 10th Street, between Capitol and Broad Streets. Major Isaac H. Carrington, a lawyer in civilian life, had taken charge of it a few weeks earlier. As provost marshal, he had the authority to issue passes to anyone who wanted to leave Richmond, and he had oversight of stragglers, deserters, and suspected spies. Despite later claims that his "administration was a pure one," Carrington came to the posting under a cloud. As commissioner of prisoners in Richmond, he had been criticized for ignoring the health of those incarcerated, leading to a high prison death rate. In fact, military prisoners, North and South, had a higher mortality rate than soldiers in the field.

Major Carrington may have been the one who ordered Dr. Mary Walker to Castle Thunder Prison, but Brigadier General William M. Gardner, commander of all military prisons in the East, took charge of her case. Gardner considered Walker "the most personable and gentlemanly looking young woman" he had ever seen, who exhibited "good birth and refinement as well as superior intellect." Nevertheless, he lectured her about her clothing, pointing out that "feminine garb" may have helped her get away with her spying. Besides, as a woman, she had "no place" in the war at all. Gardner berated her until "her composure finally gave way, and she got to crying, just as an ordinary woman might have done."

General Gardner informed Dr. Walker of his intention to exchange her for a Confederate prisoner as soon as possible, because none of the Richmond jails were suitable for female prisoners. Not suitable, perhaps, but Richmond jails did indeed hold women, including Castle Thunder Prison, where Mary Walker ended up. Even before the horror stories of Andersonville circulated, word of the substandard Confederate prison facilities in Richmond had spread. General John Winder set up Castle Thunder in August 1862, taking over three buildings on Cary Street: two factories and a warehouse. Designed to hold 1,400 prisoners, its population—men and women, Unionists and Confederates—swelled to more than 3,000 within five months. Inmates had little access to medicine, food, and clean clothing. Its commandant, Captain George W. Alexander, was investigated by the Confederate Congress for the reported violence and cruelty at the prison, but it failed to condemn the practices.

At Castle Thunder, Mary Walker joined about one hundred women incarcerated in the tobacco warehouse. Female offenders included prostitutes, spies, wives of Union soldiers, and women caught wearing Confederate uniforms. Until the doctor's arrival, the prison's most famous female inhabitant was Cuban-born Loreta Velazquez, incarcerated in the summer of 1863 after her arrest for wearing a Confederate uniform. It was not the first time Velazquez had appeared before the provost marshal to answer this charge. In the fall of 1861, she had used the name Mary Anne Keith in Lynchburg, Virginia, introducing herself as Lieutenant Harry Buford when out in public, in uniform. Arrested and sent to Richmond, Velazquez appeared before General Winder, who questioned and released her.

Over the next eighteen months, Loreta Velazquez claimed participation in the battles of Fort Donelson, Shiloh, and Pittsburg Landing. She worked as a Confederate spy in New Orleans, and probably other places as well. Throughout the war, she alternated between male and female attire and personae as circumstances dictated. In June of 1863, she wrote to the Confederate War Department detailing her accomplishments and requesting a commission. Instead, Velazquez was arrested in Mobile, Alabama, and brought to Richmond, where General Winder questioned her again and ordered her to Castle Thunder. She remained for a few days as the provost marshal's office concluded its investigation, and the press eagerly reported the escapades of the "female lieutenant."

Local reporters did not cover the female Yankee doctor as kindly. One Richmond paper described Mary Walker's 1864 arrival in the city: "Her appearance on the street in full male costume, with the exception of a gipsey [*sic*] hat, created quite an excitement," but not in a good way. It concluded with the observation that she was "ugly and skinny, and apparently above thirty years of age." The doctor, who read the newspapers, could not let a published mistake go. She always insisted she did not dress like a man, and she wanted everyone in Richmond to know that.

On April 21, 1864, Mary Walker sent a letter to the *Richmond Dispatch* and asked the editor to correct a similar mistake it had made. "Simple *justice* demands correction," she wrote. "I am attired in what is usually called the 'bloomer' or 'reform dress,' which is similar to other ladies', with the exception of its being shorter and more physiological than long dresses." The editor poked fun at Walker's concern: "The utter ignorance of our reporter . . . must be urged as his excuse for the grave mistake." The tone of this coverage was noted by *The Sibyl* in an update about Mary Walker published in its final issue: "The Richmond papers make merry over her short dress, for she still adheres to the 'Bloomer.'"

The city reporters continued their negative portrayals. In May 1864, the *Richmond Examiner* put her physician's title in quotation marks, casting doubt on its validity. The story reported that the "strong-minded" Mary Walker was "angry for a horse and anxious for a ride" through the streets. "As horse-flesh is growing scarce under the influence of the impressment act, it is not probable that she will be accommodated." Though this went unmentioned, as a prisoner, it was unlikely authorities would provide her with the means for her escape.

Newspapers in the North and South ran an excerpt from a letter Mary Walker wrote to her mother from Castle Thunder. The *National Republican*, which had covered many of the doctor's activities in Washington, DC, during the war, prefaced the selection with the observation, "[I]t appears that the little surgeoness bears her imprisonment lightly." Mary Walker told her mother not to grieve about her circumstances. "I am living in a three-story brick castle, with plenty to eat and a clean bed to sleep in." She roomed with, twenty-year-old Martha Manus from nearby Corinth, Mississippi, a pleasant woman arrested for spying. The "officers are gentlemanly and kind, and it will not be long before I am exchanged."

That took much longer than Mary Walker expected. Although General Gardner's decision to exchange her was sincere, the process dragged on because the treatment of prisoners generated controversy between the

North and the South. During the first year or so of the war, the few people captured had been housed in existing buildings until informal exchanges could be arranged. Field commanders usually preferred to do this as quickly as possible, often right after an engagement. The Confederacy soon lacked the resources to feed prisoners, and, chronically undermanned, they needed their soldiers back, so they pushed for a formal program to facilitate exchanges. Northern civilians were also in favor, but President Lincoln hesitated to enter into any arrangement that might appear to confer legitimacy on the Confederate government.

As a compromise, the opposing armies rather than governments had agreed to the Dix-Hill Cartel in July 1862. The Hill of the cartel was Confederate general Daniel Hill, whose men had captured Mary Walker. The prisoner exchange system established a list of equivalents, stipulating ratios between captured officers and enlisted men. It also provided for agents who could handle the logistics of the exchanges at the designated locations of Aiken's Landing, Virginia, and Vicksburg, Mississippi. It made allowances for parole after ten days of capture, in which a freed prisoner promised not to fight until a formal exchange was arranged. There were also provisions for the exchange of noncombatants, the category under which Mary Walker fell.

The cartel proceeded for about a year, until the Confederate government announced that captured black Union soldiers and their officers would either be enslaved or executed. In response, on July 30, 1863, President Lincoln signed General Orders No. 252, which stated: "If the enemy shall sell or enslave any one because of his color, the offence shall be punished by retaliation upon the enemy's prisoners in our possession." Some informal exchanges took place, but in the second half of the year, prison populations swelled, with thousands of captives.

On April 17, 1864, seven days after Confederate pickets had arrested Dr. Mary Walker, Lieutenant General Ulysses S. Grant, now commanding the Union armies, put a stop to all exchanges between the two sides until the South had agreed that "no distinction will be made in the exchange between white and colored prisoners." He also ordered all women to leave battlefield areas, unwilling to let them languish indefinitely in Confederate prisons if captured. Many ignored the order.

Grant's concern about how female prisoners would be treated was borne out by Mary Walker's experiences in Castle Thunder. The letter she wrote to her mother was designed to soothe the older woman's fears, not to document reality. Food, which may have started out plentiful, quickly became less abundant and less appetizing. Bread was made with water, worms infiltrated the peas, vermin thrived in the rice, and all the bacon was rotten. When the doctor realized her lack of protein had reached a critical level, she schemed with a commissary clerk to bring in some fresh eggs, which were not allowed to the general prison population. She believed those eggs saved her life.

Mary Walker described how "in the warm nights bed vermin came out to feast on her, and they were of all sizes, and she was employed in exterminating them until the small hours [of] the morning." Three times in four months the walls were whitewashed in unsuccessful attempts to kill the bugs. Prison regulations kept gaslights burning through the night. "It injured her eyes, although she would not have felt safe without it." Walker's cell could not protect her. One day, as she rested on her cot because she felt faint, a musket ball crashed through the floor where she had been standing just moments earlier.

With the rest of the prisoners, the doctor went hungry, and her health suffered from it. She lost weight and strength, and eye problems plagued her for the rest of her life. In some respects, she was treated better than others. This was not unusual. Military prison camps normally provided superior accommodations and food to officers. According to J. L. Burrows, a clergyman who ministered to those in the nearby Libby Prison, Mary Walker "sometimes was permitted to stroll into the streets, where her display of Bloomer costume, blouse, trowsers [sic] and boots secured her a following of astonished and admiring boys." Imprisonment had not broken her spirit. "She was quite chatty, and seemed rather to enjoy the notoriety of her position." Her semiprivate room, access to newspapers, and outside privileges under escort marked her as a special prisoner.

The Yankee doctor did not remain idle through her imprisonment. She volunteered to care for patients in Castle Thunder's hospital, but prison officials, likely dubious of her medical credentials, declined her offer. Still, Mary Walker managed to use her medical training. A man "connected with the prison" asked for her help in avoiding service in the Confederate Army. She concocted a mixture of apple and red pepper, instructing the man to eat it and then run several blocks before reporting for his medical examination. A diagnosis of the "worst disease of the heart" earned him an exemption from military service. Walker also put considerable thought and experimentation into finding the cause and prevention of rabies. She later mistakenly claimed she had succeeded.

With her talent for prose, Mary Walker wrote letters for prisoners, making important requests. A Confederate soldier found guilty of desertion and sentenced to death appealed to President Jefferson Davis with a letter penned by the doctor, which the soldier then copied in his own hand. She asked that Davis issue a pardon and send the young man back to his regiment. Otherwise, his execution "would make one less to sustain the Confederacy." The soldier was dubious the letter would do any good; everyone knew he opposed the war. But Walker encouraged him, reminding him to copy the letter exactly, with proper capitalizations and punctuation. "Then the President would think him worth saving." Two days later, the soldier's pardon arrived.

After the departure of that soldier, a middle-aged couple who had been arrested for allowing Union soldiers to occupy their plantation moved into the room next to Mary Walker's. The woman "groaned and cried," beside herself with worry for their children, who had been left behind. She feared her sixteen-year-old daughter, without anyone to protect her, "would be carried off." The woman told Dr. Walker that neither she nor her husband supported the war in any way. Walker wrote a letter for the man to copy, "stating the injustice of such [an] arrest, the helpless little family left at the mercy of both armies, and the impossibility of one lone man to prevent a squad of Yanks from landing." The couple was released.

When Mary Walker found out that Timothy McKean of the 33rd Massachusetts Infantry was due to be executed as a spy, she sent him some peanuts and the last bill of Confederate money she had. The doctor may have known McKean from Falmouth, where he had wintered after fighting at Fredericksburg. McKean sent a note of acknowledgment to the doctor and insisted he was a deserter, not a spy. He had left his unit after Gettysburg. She might have encouraged him to emphasize this with his captors. The Confederates either concluded McKean had only walked away from his regiment or decided any spying he had done was not harmful, and released him in a prisoner exchange.

At the end of June, one report circulated about Mary Walker's alleged bad behavior. The *Richmond Examiner* referred to her as "Miss Doctress, Miscegenation, Philosophical Walker," and described an altercation she had instigated. "She got mad, pitched into several of her room-mates in long clothes, and tore out handsfuls [*sic*] of auburn hair from the head of one of them." Walker then yelled about secession and stalked off into another room, "where she is now lady and lioness of all she surveys." The piece also claimed she sang loudly whenever she heard cannon fire and that she had a lover in Libby Prison, who she communicated with via signals. Allowing for hyperbole and for bias against the doctor as an unconventional woman and a Yankee, the article may have documented the stress she felt from her circumstances. "She thinks it hard, very hard, that she is not allowed to go home," the article concluded.

Mary Walker wanted to go home. Throughout her imprisonment, she had regularly requested an exchange. On the last Saturday of April, two detectives had escorted the doctor to General Winder's office. Her appearance on the Richmond streets caused "some excitement among the juveniles and negroes" because she wore her "*outré* costume, of men's pants, boots and short cloak and broad brimmed beaver hat." Winder listened to Walker's appeal, then turned her down, allegedly saying, "I believe you are a spy, Sir, and shall keep you here till it is ascertained—You can't go, Sir."

Failing with Winder, Dr. Walker tried another avenue. If Confederate officials would not give her what she wanted, perhaps some pressure from someone high up in the Union government could move things along. One of the Union prisoners she met at Castle Thunder, West Virginia lawyer R. Finn, was slated for exchange on June 26. She asked him to contact Edwin Stanton, the secretary of war, on her behalf. Neither Walker nor Finn ever elaborated about how they met or the extent of their relationship, but Finn carried out her wish. He let Stanton know that the doctor "requested me to write to inform you that she is incarcerated in Castle

Thunder, Richmond, [Virginia], and that she wishes you to procure her release."

That did not work, either. In late July, Dr. Walker met with General Gardner and asked him for her freedom. According to a story in the *Richmond Whig*, she "would have been sent North long ago but for the fact that since she has been incarcerated, she has been detected in some ilicit [*sic*]correspondence." To improve her chances, she handed Gardner a thirty-page manuscript she wrote about the upcoming presidential election in the United States. From her time in the Confederacy, the doctor had learned Southerners wanted General George McClellan, who favored a negotiated peace, to be the choice of the Democratic Party to challenge Abraham Lincoln. She believed she could turn that desire to her advantage.

Lincoln's reelection in November 1864 was not a foregone conclusion. Many Northerners were still unhappy about the draft and about the Emancipation Proclamation. During the spring and summer campaigns, the Union had suffered heavy casualties at the Battle of the Wilderness, Spotsylvania, Petersburg, and Kennesaw Mountain. Fresh from victories over the Union at Lynchburg, Virginia, and Frederick, Maryland, Confederate forces under General Jubal Early came within five miles of Washington, DC, in July. General Grant redeployed about 18,000 trained soldiers who were guarding the capital to Petersburg, attempting to crush the Confederate Army. Only 4,000 members of the Home Guard and local militia remained. But Early's men had been marching for weeks in blistering heat and could not muster the energy for a strong attack before Grant's reinforcements arrived. All the heavy losses and incremental gains led Northerners to question Lincoln's fitness as commander in chief.

In light of these events, Mary Walker "concocted a ruse." She wrote a paper "purporting to be a Democratic electioneering document, highly laudatory of McClellan, and giving the rebels to understand that its delivery in the Northern States would materially assist the [McClellan supporters, known as] Little Macs." Gardner may have believed Walker was sincere. Shortly after he accepted her treatise, she learned a prisoner exchange had been arranged.

On August 9, 1864, a ship carrying Confederate prisoners arrived at Aiken's Landing, one of the designated exchange locations under the Dix-Hill Cartel. The next day, Robert Ould, the Confederacy's official agent of exchange, struck an agreement with his Union counterpart for a prisoner swap. On the list from Castle Thunder was "the notorious Miss Dr. Mary E. Walker, Surgeoness of the 52nd Ohio Regulars," plus two male doctors and a captain. As Walker exited the prison on August 12, she gave a loud "Huzzah!," doffed her plumed hat, and bowed to the officials. She boarded the steamer *John Brooks*, headed for City Point, Virginia, the headquarters for General Grant's Richmond–Petersburg campaign.

Mary Walker was free.

CHAPTER SEVEN

Surgeon in Charge

THE NEWLY RELEASED PRISONER RETURNED TO WASHINGTON, DC, with only a set of well-worn clothes on her back. Mary Walker's contract with the army would end on August 23, 1864, and once again she needed to find a way to support herself. She had not been at Lee and Gordon's Mills long enough to receive any pay before her arrest, and was not clear about how much salary the army owed her. The doctor contacted General Thomas and Adjutant General E. D. Townsend for clarification, and the two men corresponded about her situation via telegram. In a rare acknowledgment of Dr. Walker's spying duties, Townsend asked, "Is there anything due the woman, and if so what amount for secret service or other services." Neither man wanted her to end up with nothing. The army sent Dr. Walker five months' back pay, for her time at Lee and Gordon's Mills and in Castle Thunder, of a little over $430.

No one would have blamed Mary Walker if she had decided she was finished with war work. She had been to the Front and she had been imprisoned—as much (and more) than most men had done. President Lincoln considered the young doctor's experiences so singular that he set aside time to talk with her about Castle Thunder. Struggling with persistent eye problems and still weak from weight loss, she told a reporter of her intention to "settle up her business and retire to private life." By the time the story ran, she had changed her mind.

After about two weeks in the capital, Mary Walker headed west to meet up with her compatriots from the 52nd Ohio Infantry, who had been with General William Tecumseh Sherman on the Atlanta Campaign over the summer. That was the big military push she had tried to assist with her intelligence gathering in Confederate territory around Lee and Gordon's Mills, and she wanted to know how it had successfully played out. But the doctor most likely wanted the details of what had happened to Colonel Daniel McCook Jr., her former commanding officer.

Daniel McCook belonged to the "Fighting McCooks" of Ohio, made up of two senior McCook men and their sons who took up arms to defend the Union. Daniel McCook Sr. headed up the "Tribe of Dan," which consisted of himself and his eight sons. McCook Sr.'s brother, Dr. John McCook, ran the "Tribe of John," with his three sons. The "Tribe of Dan" boasted five generals in its ranks, but had suffered heavy losses. Only four members of that side of the family survived the war. Daniel Jr. was not one of them. In late June 1864, while Mary Walker was imprisoned in Castle Thunder, McCook and the 52nd Ohio Infantry had moved with the Army of the Cumberland toward Marietta, Georgia, about twenty miles north of Atlanta. Confederate general Joseph E. Johnston's Army of Tennessee, determined to keep them out of Atlanta, had intended to stop them at Kennesaw Mountain.

General Sherman's three armies had been on the move since early May, cautiously but decisively making its way through Georgia, following the path of the Western and Atlantic Railroad. Johnston's men, numbering about half of Sherman's, managed to skirmish, snipe, and confront the Yankees along the way. Then the Confederates set up a defensive perimeter at Kennesaw Mountain, which Sherman could not maneuver around. A full-scale battle commenced on the morning of June 27 with the kind of head-on attack Sherman usually avoided. Colonel Daniel McCook Jr. commanded a five-regiment brigade that hit the Confederates' center line, charging up Cheatham Hill. He prepared his men by reciting a selection from "Horatius at the Bridge" by the British writer, Thomas Babington Macaulay, which includes the line: "And how can man die better than facing fearful odds."

When McCook and his men were within firing distance of the enemy, they crouched and began shooting. About a third of the brigade was cut down as it tried to advance. The colonel sustained serious wounds when he was shot on a Confederate parapet, his sword drawn as he shouted, "Surrender, you traitors!" The confrontation on Cheatham Hill devolved into hand-to-hand combat until it finally ended before eleven a.m. with a Union retreat. Daniel McCook was transported to his home in Steubenville, Ohio, where he died on July 17. Three thousand Union soldiers were killed or wounded at Kennesaw Mountain, the last time General Sherman would use a large-scale frontal assault on Southern troops.

After spending some time in Nashville learning these details about Daniel McCook's death, Dr. Walker traveled to Louisville, Kentucky. She decided to stay, likely because of a job opportunity, though in terms of life and liberty, remaining in the Bluegrass State was not the safest option. Kentucky was a border state with legalized slavery, evenly influenced by and tied to both the North and the South. Its northern border ran along the free states of Ohio, Indiana, and Illinois. On its southern end was a shared border with three slaveholding states.

Many of the North–South ties related to Kentucky's economy, which relied on slavery. Enslaved people made up 19.5 percent of the state's population in 1860, though the percentage had been dropping for decades. Louisville nevertheless became a prominent site for the slave trade. The Mississippi River, along Kentucky's western border, facilitated the exchange of human beings and agricultural products with Southern states. At the northern part of Kentucky, the Ohio River and, later, the railroad, established important trade links with the more-industrialized free states.

Internal state politics juggled a states' rights agenda with support for the Union. In the late 1790s, a few years after achieving statehood, the legislature adopted the Kentucky Resolution. Authored by Thomas Jefferson to defend states' rights over federal authority, the document made the controversial argument that a state possessed the power to nullify any federal law it disagreed with. In more-extreme cases, secession might be the only option. Yet rather than becoming insular loners, Kentuckians went on in the nineteenth century to support the national government in its wars against Great Britain and Mexico. They championed the political contributions native son and Whig Party leader Henry Clay made at the federal level, including his part in forging the Compromise of 1850 that temporarily kept the country from fracturing over slavery.

During the presidential election of 1860, Kentuckian John C. Breckinridge, the incumbent vice president, ran as the presidential candidate

of the Southern faction of the Democratic Party. Though he was a senti-
mental favorite and garnered a respectable number of votes, more people
gravitated toward John Bell, the Tennessee nominee of the Constitutional
Union Party, which promoted the preservation of the Union. Kentucky-
born Abraham Lincoln only racked up 1,364 votes and failed to carry a
single county.

While Southern states debated secession after the election, Kentucky
moved slowly. The decades of Henry Clay's leadership had cultivated a
penchant for compromise. Kentucky senator John Crittenden proposed
six constitutional amendments and four federal resolutions that would
preserve a North–South divide over slavery, constitutionally protecting
the institution in the South while keeping the North free. Neither side
would get everything it wanted, but the Union would remain intact. Congress failed to take them up. When Crittenden left the Senate in March
1861, he returned to Kentucky, where he exerted his influence to keep the
state from seceding.

Kentucky's governor, the Democrat Beriah Magoffin, supported
slavery and a state's right to secede. He also understood that Kentucky
legislators were divided over secession and union, so he did not push
for immediate secession. While Kentucky continued its search for an
agreement with the federal government about protecting slavery, the war
started. Magoffin rebuffed President Lincoln's call for volunteers to fight
the insurrection, stating, "Kentucky will furnish no troops for the wicked
purpose of subduing her sister Southern States." Yet the state refused to
follow those siblings out of the union.

In May 1861, Kentucky proclaimed it would act as "mediators and
friends" to both sides, but it would "during the contest, occupy a position of strict neutrality." State politicians continued to meet to figure out
how to maintain neutrality. Unionists raised the Home Guards to protect
the state from a possible Confederate invasion, and Southern Rightists
formed the State Guards to prevent a Northern attack. Meanwhile, young
men went off to join whichever army they supported. President Lincoln
accepted Kentucky's neutrality because it did not amount to outright
secession. As long as Kentucky "made no demonstration of force against
the United States, he would not molest her."

State elections in August 1861 returned a majority of Unionists to the legislature, and this made strict neutrality difficult to sustain. Confederate forces moved on Columbus the following month, eager to take over the strategic port town and cultivate support for the South. General Ulysses S. Grant responded by occupying Paducah and Smithland. Governor Magoffin objected to both actions, but the Unionist legislature viewed the Confederates as the aggressor and voted to expel them. Magoffin resigned and led a call for secession, which was approved by a special convention on November 18. The Confederate Congress in Richmond, Virginia, admitted Kentucky to the Confederacy on December 10.

Kentucky secessionists could not control the entire state; 35,000 Confederate forces occupied its southwest quarter, and a Confederate state government, with a new governor, established its capital in Bowling Green. The Unionist legislature, supported by 50,000 Federal troops, held the rest of Kentucky. By the end of February 1862, the Northern army had forced the collapse of the Bowling Green government and sent Confederates scurrying from the state. Union brigadier general Jeremiah Boyle, a native Kentuckian and supporter of the gradual emancipation of enslaved people, received command of what would be called the District of Kentucky. The harsh measures he implemented to end guerrilla warfare and Confederate incursions made him unpopular, but fortunately did not push more people to support the South. A Southern invasion in the fall of 1862 collapsed because the anticipated number of Kentucky volunteers failed to materialize. Only 2,500 out of an expected 20,000 to 30,000 young men signed on with the Confederate Army.

After the Union Army allowed the enlistment of black men for military service, General Boyle's resistance to allowing this in Kentucky caused his fall from favor. He lost his command in January 1864, and General Stephen Burbridge took over the following month. Guerrilla warfare and other unrest continued in Kentucky, and in July, President Lincoln put the state under martial law and suspended the writ of habeas corpus. Burbridge launched a retaliation policy against the guerrillas. For every Unionist they killed, four guerrilla prisoners would be shot. Any person who sympathized with the Confederacy and was within five miles of a guerrilla raid could be arrested and sent south.

Union authorities had not always been this harsh. Early in the war, they had tried to control the civilian population without giving it a reason to support the Confederacy. In September 1861, General John Anderson of the Department of the Cumberland ordered, "No one will be arrested for mere opinion's sake. All peaceable citizens of whatever opinion will be protected if they do not engage in giving aid in any manner to the enemies of our country." Women's most routine activities—keeping house, cooking, doing laundry, nursing—could be construed as "giving aid." Whenever they cared for any male family members who joined the Confederate cause, they risked arrest and imprisonment.

Kentucky's Confederate women did not confine their support for the cause to their domestic duties, which could be carried out behind closed doors; they also flaunted their loyalty in public places. Frances Peter, the nineteen-year-old daughter of a Unionist family in Lexington, described a couple of incidents at a concert in Louisville. As the band played songs of the Republic, the Confederate women stalked out. The following night, the hall manager announced that the band would again play those songs, and anyone who did not want to hear them should leave now. Once again, Confederate women walked out. This time the provost guard appeared at the door, and they took the women to jail.

Under General Boyle's command, the Union military established a prison at Newport Barracks, on the Ohio River across from Cincinnati, for disloyal women. During their incarceration, the women had to sew clothing for Union soldiers. Women who wanted to visit imprisoned Confederate men were not allowed to bring in food, newspapers, or letters. They also had to secure a visitor's pass, which required them to swear a loyalty oath to the federal government. During 1863 and into 1864, the Union toughened its policies. All persons, regardless of age or gender, who provided any kind of aid to the enemy would be considered spies or traitors, and could be put to death.

Adoption of the Lieber Code in April 1863 facilitated the change in treatment of "secesh women," or "she-rebels." For hundreds of years, international law regarded women as innocent civilians if they did not interfere with men who took up arms. But during the Civil War, women did interfere. General William Tecumseh Sherman observed, "We are not only fighting armies but a hostile people," and women were part of those people. President Lincoln, concerned about potential legal issues involved with fighting a domestic armed conflict, wanted the military to operate on a set of rules for dealing with civilians, prisoners, and fugitive slaves. Francis Lieber, an international lawyer and professor at the Columbia Law School, crafted 157 provisions outlining the conduct of US armies in the field. His code, also known as General Orders No. 100, recognized women's capacity to take sides and take action in wartime.

With the state under martial law beginning in July 1864, surveillance and arrests of Confederate women increased. Union authorities imprisoned Almeda Mason for writing a letter to her brother in the Confederate Army; arrested Lillie Parker for destroying an American flag, and Mary Burk for tearing one down; and sent Jennie Mann to jail for saying "she wished the President was dead and that nothing would please her better and she hoped that Jeff Davis would soon be in Washington as President of the United States."

Other women got into legal trouble for more-serious offenses. Minerva Rees, Emily Vaughn, Amanda Cook, and Mattie Patterson passed information to Confederates, some of it obtained by spying. Many others, including Lizzie Hardin, her mother, and her sister, provisioned the guerrilla forces operating in Kentucky. Despite the harsh language of the general orders governing this behavior, none of these women were executed for their crimes; it was more common for them to be imprisoned or sentenced to exile in Southern territory.

Despite the potential danger of remaining in this volatile area, on September 14, 1864, Dr. Mary Walker wrote to General Sherman, now headquartered in Atlanta, asking to stay in Louisville. "Having acted in *various* capacities, since the commencement of the rebellion, without a Commission from the Government," she requested a commission with the rank of major and an appointment as the surgeon for female prisoners and female refugees in Louisville, Kentucky. If Sherman had any reservations "on the ground that no *woman* had ever received *such a Commission*," Walker reminded him "there has not been a Woman who has served Government in such a variety of ways of importance to the great cause which has elicited patriotism that knows no sex."

Patriotism was not her only qualification. Mary Walker specified that she had "acted in the capacity of Extra Assistant Surgeon" for the army, "with entire satisfaction to my patients and the Surgeons by whom I have been put on duty." When she asked those doctors for a commission, they replied she could not have one "because I was a woman, and female Surgeons should confine their practice to their own sex." If this was the only thing in the way of the commission, Dr. Walker asked Sherman to assign her to the female hospital. By her logic, as a woman treating other women for the army, she was entitled to an officer's rank and pay. "I only ask that simple justice be done me as a 'military necessity.'"

Mary Walker had no reason to believe General Sherman would not support her. She had already corresponded with General Thomas, who had championed her back in 1863, despite the finding of the medical examination board. She sounded him out about the major's rank and the hospital appointment before she wrote to Sherman. Thomas forwarded his positive recommendation to his commanding general that same day. On September 22, Robert Wood, the assistant surgeon general, assigned Dr. Walker "to duty with female prisoners in this city" of Louisville. Without giving a reason—perhaps because he thought none necessary—Sherman approved the appointment but not the commission.

It was an official, paid position, so Mary Walker accepted, and she quickly spread the news. In early October, she received a congratulatory letter from her friend Susan Hall, who currently worked as a nurse at Hospital No. 1 in Chattanooga, Tennessee. The two women may have met as early as the late summer of 1861, shortly after Walker's arrival in Washington, DC. Hall, along with her friend Harriet "Hattie" Dada, had a nursing position at the Armory Square Hospital. Dr. Walker would not have had the time to get to know all the female nurses in the capital; thanks to Dorothea Dix's recruitment efforts, there were simply too many of them. But Mary Walker had developed a special bond with Hattie Dada and Susan Hall.

Dada grew up in Oswego County in New York during the 1830s and 1840s, and her years at the Falley Seminary in Fulton in the 1850s overlapped with the doctor's. After her graduation in 1855, the American Board of Commissioners for Foreign Missions hired Hattie Dada to teach the Choctaws in what was termed "Indian country." She returned east when tensions between the North and South threatened to erupt in violence. Dada may have been at the mass meeting organized by Dr. Elizabeth Blackwell at the Cooper Institute in New York City in late April 1861, which launched the Women's Central Relief Association. Inspired by Blackwell's call for nurses, Dada applied, was accepted, and completed a six-week training course.

Susan Hall met Hattie Dada during nurses' training. In 1861, Hall was attending medical school in New York City. Born in 1826, she grew up in the town of Ulysses in western New York, and she remained with her parents, taking care of them until they died. Then she set off for the city to fulfill her goal of becoming a doctor. At the end of her medical studies, after the war had started, Hall attended that meeting at the Cooper Institute. Susan Hall, like Hattie Dada, was motivated to volunteer as a nurse, and the two women became fast friends. They did so well in the training course that Dorothea Dix sent them to Alexandria, Virginia, to take care of soldiers wounded in the First Battle of Bull Run. During their next assignment at the Armory Square Hospital, they may have met Dr. Mary Walker.

The doctor likely crossed paths several more times with Susan Hall and Hattie Dada, who almost always took nursing assignments together: Antietam, Aquia Creek, Gettysburg. In late 1863, they moved west to Murfreesboro, Tennessee, where they found the medical director, Dr. Israel Moses of the 72nd New York Infantry Regiment, opposed to female nurses. He refused to allow Hall and Dada near the patients, confining them to kitchen duties. After several months, the two women settled at Hospital No. 1 in Chattanooga, after Dr. Walker had become a prisoner of the Confederacy. Hall and Dada appreciated Dr. Francis Salter's enlightened views about the abilities of women, and the 336-bed facility kept them busy with the nursing duties they had trained for.

Writing on US Christian Commission stationery in October 1864, Susan Hall addressed Miss Mary E. Walker, MD, as "My Dear Friend." She continued in the plural, a nod to the quarters she shared with Hattie Dada, "We were very glad to hear from you, of your success [but] wish you had given us more particulars of your charge, that we might have a better idea of what you have to do." The nurse understood that Walker had achieved a milestone in professional employment. "*Who* could object to the *propriety* of your position now?" Hall asked Walker how she liked Louisville, and if she had received the rank of major. Hall also inquired if the doctor had "been obliged to relinquish your anticipated visit home before the Presidential election."

Mary Walker did, in fact, request a leave of absence, and General Sherman granted twenty days, with the option of applying for an extension. Deeply committed to emancipation, she wanted to campaign on behalf of President Lincoln and the Republican Party in the 1864 election. However, she took up her post before the leave took effect. Her contract, signed on October 5, and which ran for three months, stipulated that she "perform the duties of a Medical Officer, agreeably to Army Regulations." The army set her salary at $100 per month for regular services, and $113.83 a month plus transportation for field services. She needed to provide her own instruments.

At the Louisville Female Military Prison, Dr. Walker worked for Dr. Edward E. Phelps, the medical director of the post. The sixty-one-year-old received an appointment in 1861 as the surgeon for the 1st Vermont Brigade, and went to Camp Griffin, near Washington, DC, to treat the soldiers of his unit. After serving in the Peninsula Campaign during the spring and summer of 1862, Phelps had returned to Vermont, where he worked at the brigade's camp and military hospital in Brattleboro. In 1864, he accepted a transfer west to Kentucky. Phelps considered Walker efficient "in her trying and complicated duties."

The elderly physician likely referred to Dr. Walker's alleged mistreatment of female patients and the hostility from a male doctor displaced by her arrival. Lieutenant Colonel Thomas Fairleigh, commander of the Kentucky volunteers, and Assistant Surgeon General Wood gave Walker the position of surgeon in charge of the female prisoners. This meant she had the authority to hire some of her own staff, including orderly Gary Conklin, who corroborated the antagonism she endured. She also supervised twenty-five guards.

Mary Walker's nemesis was Dr. Erasmus O. Brown, an assistant surgeon with the 26th Kentucky Infantry Regiment who had been placed in charge of the prison hospital in August 1864. Stung by the loss of control over part of the prison hospital, and resentful that a woman had achieved a position of power, he took a dislike to the female doctor. On October 4, Brown wrote to Assistant Surgeon General Wood: "I have the honor to State that I regard Dr. M. E. Walker as incompetent to prescribe for the Sick in the Female Prison, and would further State that her tyrannical conduct has been intolerable not only to the inmates of the Prison, but to myself." He asked Wood to either relieve Walker of her duties, or "to be relieved from that part of my charge." Brown likely believed the assistant surgeon general would take his word about the woman's ineptitude and dismiss her.

Instead, after receiving a letter from post commandant and assistant adjutant general Lieutenant Colonel John Henry Hammond, Colonel Wood reaffirmed Mary Walker's authority. "I think that Miss Walker should have control over her building and its inmates," Hammond wrote, "& that Dr. Brown should not be allowed to interfere." The assistant adjutant general reminded Wood that both generals Sherman and Thomas wanted Dr. Walker in charge of the female prisoners. "I will consider it a decided improvement to commit the whole management of the concern to her care." Hammond supported Walker's decision to replace the male cooks with women, which he considered more proper in a women's establishment, especially "as the prison has been no better than a brothel." Brown should be told to "stick to his own building and patients."

Aware of this attempted power play, Dr. Walker wrote to Lieutenant Colonel Hammond about events in the women's prison. She emphasized that her orders stipulated her authority over the female prisoners, with Dr. Brown in charge of the men. Yet he continued to treat the women, and Walker wanted something done to stop him. "He has prejudiced . . . the inmates, and informed them that they were not to have anyone to prescribe for them but himself *if they did not choose to have another*, and told them that they were not to obey any of the orders of any Surgeon but those given by himself." Brown also lied to the women, saying that Dr. Walker had been informed of this by Hammond, but she destroyed his orders. The next day, October 5, the Assistant Surgeon General's Office in Louisville announced that Dr. Mary Walker "is hereby assigned to duty in charge of the *Medical Department* of the Female Military Prison," and "will relieve *Asst. Surgeon E. O. Brown 26th KY* in this city."

The duties Walker performed at the prison extended beyond medical care. On October 7, she consulted Hammond about the three teenagers arrested across the Ohio River in Jeffersonville, Indiana, and sent to the Louisville prison. Walker told him she had encouraged them "to try to do better hereafter; they are all young, and there are extenuating circumstances connected with their early history, and they are anxious to do better." The trio of young women requested they be sent back to family members in Indiana, and Dr. Walker wanted Hammond to authorize transportation. "Without money and without friends, how are they to do better; if sent to the Civil Authorities, they will be discouraged, and the good resolutions they have formed will avail nothing."

Hammond wanted details of the charges brought against the women. In roundabout language, Dr. Walker told him they were prostitutes. They had come to the attention of an army surgeon in Jeffersonville, who had requested their arrest. Walker explained, "They had tents furnished by a couple of soldiers—and were sent here as disreputable females, which they do not pretend to deny." Their desire to return to family members was, for her, proof that they intended to "do better" with their lives and give up prostitution. Hammond approved the request.

It is likely that Mary Walker departed on her leave about the same time the three teenagers left Louisville. She applied for an extension of the twenty days granted so she could work through Election Day on November 8 and still have time to travel back to Louisville before the leave expired. The doctor went north to New York, spending most of her break in her hometown of Oswego. She appeared at several rallies, often speaking about her experiences as a doctor with the army, including her stint as a prisoner in Castle Thunder. Union soldiers in the audience showed their support with cheers whenever Democratic opponents attempted to boo Walker off the stage.

Abraham Lincoln, aware of the unpopularity of the Emancipation Proclamation and the toll the long war was taking on Northerners, had initially been pessimistic about his chances for reelection. To attract more voters, Lincoln's supporters had created the National Union Party and tapped him as their candidate. Lincoln selected Tennessee politician Andrew Johnson as his vice president. A Unionist, or War Democrat, Johnson currently served as the military governor of Tennessee. The Democrats ran George McClellan, who touted a negotiated peace with the South that would compromise emancipation. "The Union is the one condition of peace," McClellan announced; "we ask no more." This struck a chord with many potential voters—at least until General Sherman had concluded his ambitious Atlanta Campaign and occupied the city in early September. Victory over the Confederacy now seemed attainable.

Other women besides Mary Walker campaigned for Lincoln in 1864. Though they lacked direct access to the ballot, women understood they could persuade men in their choice of candidates. While the doctor focused her attention on New York, Sojourner Truth concentrated her efforts in the capital. An emancipated slave from Walker's home state, Truth was an accomplished and sought-after speaker on abolition and women's rights. In 1864 she took a job with the National Freedman's Relief Association in Washington. Devoted to emancipation, she campaigned for Lincoln's reelection.

Sojourner Truth wanted to meet Abraham Lincoln, with whom she believed she shared much in common, but she had difficulty getting into the White House. Truth prevailed on her friend and sister abolitionist, Lucy Colman, to make the arrangements. Colman, a white teacher and school superintendent in Washington, knew Elizabeth Keckley, the black dressmaker of Mary Todd Lincoln. Together they convinced the president to put Truth on a reception list at the end of October. Though Lincoln supported emancipation, he did not necessarily embrace racial equality, and the meeting with Sojourner Truth proceeded awkwardly. He rose and shook her hand when introduced, but he called her "aunty" rather than "Miss" or "Mrs." Still, when Truth admitted she knew nothing about him until he became president, Lincoln responded that he had heard much about her. Truth did not waver in her support.

To facilitate voting in 1864, Republican-controlled Northern states allowed soldiers to fill out and submit their ballots from wherever they were currently posted—no need for leaves to return home. Union states with Democratic governments refused that convenience, so the army granted furloughs to Republican soldiers to travel to vote, clogging train stations throughout the North, but especially in Washington. The campaigning and the furloughs worked out for Lincoln and the Republicans. Lincoln scored 55 percent of the popular vote, and for the first time since 1832, an incumbent president won reelection. Republicans captured 145 of 185 House seats, with a 41–10 majority in the Senate.

While Mary Walker was away, a dozen disgruntled female prisoners, likely encouraged by Dr. Erasmus Brown, petitioned Lieutenant Colonel Fairleigh for her removal. They gave no specific reason, only that "none of the inmates will receive her Medicine." If Fairleigh had no replacement for Walker, "let us remain without any Surgeon." They admitted they preferred Dr. Brown; "if you can let him return as we have had him once and all like him." Fairleigh forwarded the request to Colonel Wood at the surgeon general's office. About a week later, on November 1, Dr. Joseph B. Brown, an assistant surgeon general, replying on behalf of Wood, reminded Fairleigh that Dr. Walker's appointment had been at the direction of General Sherman. Moreover, "As she is now absent, no immediate action in the case is considered necessary."

On November 12, around the time Dr. Walker returned to duty in Louisville, Fairleigh asked the surgeon general's office to take action. Without repeating the content of the prisoners' petition, Fairleigh requested Walker be ordered to report to the Refugee Home. Hinting that Walker had difficulty treating Rebel women, he pointed out that "Female Patriots" at the home were "constantly in need of medical attention."

Dr. Joseph Brown's response was similar to the one he had sent nearly two weeks earlier. Brown believed he lacked the authority to remove someone supported by General Sherman, especially since there was "[n]o reason being assigned for the desire to relieve Dr. Mary E. Walker . . . other than the preference of certain of the prisoners for another medical officer." Brown assured Fairleigh, "Any statement of her unfitness for the charge of the Hospital . . . will at once be investigated by a Medical Inspector." The findings of such an investigation, if they went against Dr. Walker, would provide "satisfactory reasons to explain her removal" to General Sherman.

Joseph Brown's communication arrived at about the same time the Superintendent and Medical Director's Office of the US Army General Hospital in Louisville issued Special Orders No. 21, announcing Mary Walker's resumption of her position at the prison hospital. The document relieved a Dr. Rogers of "further duties at that place, and, will confine himself to his duties as A. A. Surgeon in charge of transportation." Dr. Walker again appeared to displace a man from his job, and criticisms of her and her work continued. One released prisoner claimed that the doctor treated inmates "in an inhumane manner," and that she "dresses in men's clothes and drinks at the public bars."

Aware of the ongoing assault on her character and credentials, Mary Walker tried to rein in the situation. On January 6, 1865, with the approval of Surgeon General Wood, she wrote to General Stephen Burbridge, commander of the District of Kentucky, that she wanted to see him. "If you are not coming here in the next few days, please order me to report to you *on business.*" It is not clear whether the meeting ever took place, but it is likely she wanted the same kind of endorsement from him that she had received from generals Sherman and Thomas, hoping to quiet the criticism.

Hostilities at the prison reached a critical point in mid-month when Lieutenant Stephenson passed along complaints to a new commanding officer, Lieutenant Colonel Coyle, from female prisoners that Dr. Walker had punished them for misbehaving. According to Gary Conklin, Mary Walker's orderly, Stephenson was wrong about what was happening in the prison. The doctor was "always kind and attentive" to both the prisoners and the guards, "so much so to the *prisoners* that some of the [U]nion people were very much displeased." Conklin believed Stephenson "seemed to take every opportunity and study to do whatever he thought would annoy and make the position of the Surgeon in Charge a very trying one."

Yet Lieutenant Colonel Coyle believed Stephenson. Outraged, Mary Walker penned a lengthy letter pointing out Stephenson's misperceptions of the situation. She accused Coyle of doing her a "gross injustice" for taking Stephenson's word over hers. "I thought you a man of efficient discretion and judgement to comprehend things as they exist—, and then

I thought you had sufficient moral courage to pursue a course consistent with an enlightened conscience."

In her point-by-point explanation, Dr. Walker illustrated what Lieutenant Colonel Fairleigh had earlier alluded to. As a staunchly pro-Union woman, she felt little sympathy for the Rebel women. She told Coyle that when she forbade the female inmates to sing Confederate songs or engage in "disloyal" talk, Lieutenant Stephenson accused her of being too harsh. "Oh, they are women," he told her—even though these utterances, under military rules of that time, would have gotten them arrested. The doctor monitored their visits with "[R]ebel friends," refusing to leave them unsupervised, and insisting on reading all letters sent in. Walker also forbade "familiarity" between the women and any of the prison staff. She expected the inmates to keep themselves and their quarters clean, and she would not tolerate them abusing each other. Some of the women had their young children in prison with them, and the doctor often provided them with child-care instructions, whether they wanted them or not.

Addressing the issue of punishments, Mary Walker admitted that she carried them out. She put one woman in handcuffs for two hours after she swore at a guard and threatened to kill other prisoners. She locked a few women in the storehouse when she caught them waving handkerchiefs and yelling "Jeff Davis" as Rebel prisoners passed their quarters. She dismissed as "a pretence" Lieutenant Stephenson's charge that the female cooks she hired served bad food to the prisoners. If he "had *three* grains of common sence [*sic*] he could see it. They complained every meal when there were *four men* cooks." Walker maintained that Lieutenant Stephenson had made "an outright idiot of himself" by making these charges against her.

She also expressed a low regard for the troublesome inmates. "Give them their filth, unrestrained disloyalty and immorality and it will be satisfactory times with them," Dr. Walker wrote in her concluding paragraph. She knew the female prisoners hated her because she was not a traditional woman. "I am an eye sore to them, and they want men Cooks again and a man Doctor." Her last sentence probably further alienated Coyle with an unfavorable comparison to his predecessor: "Col. Fairleigh has learned my true motive for all that I have done, and appreciates the trying position I hold, and all my greatest superior officers have confidence in my having done *well* under all circumstances, and that confidence is *merited*."

Two days later, Coyle forwarded the doctor's letter to Colonel Wood in the surgeon general's office, with only a brief note: "[A]ttention [is] invited to the contents of this communication." This likely prompted Wood to bring in a medical inspector—an officer who assisted medical directors in the supervision and education of surgeons—to examine Dr. Walker's actions at the female prison. Dr. Richard Henry Coolidge, a well-regarded surgeon with the army since 1841, made his investigation and submitted a report that apparently found no fault with Walker's medical abilities, but did find her punishments excessive.

Writing on behalf of the surgeon general on January 21, 1865, Dr. C. C. Gray told Mary Walker, "In view of facts and circumstances" reported by Coolidge, Colonel Wood "directs that in future your duties at the Female Military Prison in this City be strictly professional:—you will exercise no other authority than that of a physician and inflict no punishments." Gray warned her that "All cases of neglect or disobedience of your professional orders will be reported to the Commanding Officer of this Prison for his action."

It was a stinging rebuke. During this stressful time, Mary Walker may have been comforted, or at least amused, by a personal letter she received at the end of the month from an acquaintance known as "Doc." This rare glimpse into her private life offers no answers about it. The letterhead, embossed with an image of the Capitol building, and the return address 510 7th Street, East Side, with the initials J. H. W. scrawled below it. Doc's letter was a delighted response to the last communication he received from Walker, in which she used the word "love" in connection with her relationship with him.

Doc had been prepared to "settle down into a grave . . . & formal character; dispense stupid wisdom, and sensible nonsense" until "That word in your letter, around which revolves so many beautiful sentiments. That magic word *love* set my fancy in flights." He may have hoped for an admission of love but had not expected it. It is not clear what kind of love Mary Walker professed. There had been some mention of marriage: "Oh how happy such a reality will be, for us, when we are married; excuse my blunder—when we marry the companions of our choice." Doc quoted Shakespeare on love. "He says She loved me, for the dangers I had passed; and I, that she did pity them," and followed with, "How beautifully that would apply in your case were I to reverse the order of the pronoun."

Doc expressed deep ardor for Mary Walker. "Oh ye muses inspire my old goose quill, that I may sing of love . . . let it be moved by the hand of time until the clock of eternity runs down;—it could not half express, even in that length of time how I love your sex." Perhaps teasingly, he entreated, "Hoping you will not let my California inamorata know the expressions of my tendered philinks [*sic*] towards you." He closed with, "Subscribe myself yours till we meet on the other side." Mary Walker was a young woman, smart and attractive. Even with her long work hours, it is easy to believe she was still interested in romance. But whoever Doc was, their relationship must not have lasted long. No additional correspondence survived.

Throughout her adult life, Mary Walker's chosen profession—and the fact she selected a profession rather than marriage and family—and her style of dress raised questions about whether she was a "real" woman. She had been married, though she did not often share that personal information, and some men clearly found her attractive. How she felt about men as romantic, sexual partners, though, is not as clear. What Mary Walker understood of her own desires, she kept to herself.

As winter headed into spring in 1865, Dr. Walker performed her medical duties, knowing she lacked supporters close by. On March 21, Dr. Edward E. Phelps, the post's medical director who retained a high regard for her, wrote to Colonel Daniel J. Dill, the new post commander. "In view of the want of harmonious action between the medical and military officers at the Female Military Prison, it seems evident to me that the good of the services makes it expedient that Mrs. Dr. Mary E. Walker be relieved from duty." It is unclear whether a new incident prompted Phelps's request, but Dill jumped on it. The post commander sent a copy of the letter to Colonel Wood, with his own comments about Mary Walker. "Charges and specifications have been preferred against her and in my opinion the service will be greatly benefitted by her removal," Dill wrote, without mentioning if these were new complaints. "It is *perfectly impossible* for *anyone* to get along with her."

Prior to these communications, Mary Walker may have let Dr. Phelps know of her wish to move on from Louisville. The day after the decision was made to relieve her of duty, she wrote to Phelps and expressed no shock or outrage. Instead, she relayed that she knew "a number of Surgeons are being sent to the front [and] I most respectfully ask to be sent also." Walker noted that over the several months she worked at the prison, "it has been an untold task to keep this institution in a good condition *morally* & I am weary of the task & would much prefer to be where my services can be appreciated & I [can] do more good *directly* for the Cause." Yet a Louisville newspaper, in reporting about her departure, remarked that this surgeon of "fine ability" had received the approval of "all loyal people" in the city.

Dr. Walker's exit from Louisville probably pleased the officers who had resented her presence from the beginning, but she found herself in another difficult situation. The order from the assistant surgeon general's office, issued by Dr. Joseph Brown on March 22, pointed to Walker's cooperation with the transfer. "In conformity with the recommendation of the *Medical Director* of the Department of Kentucky, and the wishes of *Mary E. Walker*, Actg. Asst. Surgeon USA for duty in the front, she ... will proceed without delay to *Nashville, Tenn.* and report in person for duty to *Surgeon George E. Cooper.*" Her next assignment rested in the hands of the man who, a year earlier, had declared her unqualified for service.

Unwilling to shrink from confrontation, Dr. Walker packed up her meager belongings. At the end of March, the army furnished her transportation to Nashville, where she presented herself to Dr. Cooper. The meeting must have been awkward, but Walker admitted, "In justice to this officer I will say that he gave me a choice of places, and I, in pity for him, asked him to please send me as far from himself as possible." While she awaited that assignment, the war headed into its final days.

For about ten months, Confederate general Robert E. Lee had managed to keep Union forces out of Petersburg, Virginia, the final stronghold protecting Richmond, the Confederacy's capital. A Union victory at Five Forks, just southwest of Petersburg, on April 1, 1865, meant that

Lee's dwindling, undersupplied troops could not stand another Yankee onslaught. Petersburg and Richmond fell over the next two days. The night before Northern soldiers occupied Richmond, Confederate officials ordered the city's warehouses torched to keep the Union from stockpiles of tobacco, cotton, and food. The fires spread too rapidly, burning much of Richmond's city center. News of the capture of the Confederate capital sparked an eight-hundred-gun salute in Washington, shutting down the government and most private businesses in celebration.

Jubilation over Richmond's collapse continued in the Union's capital. On April 4, Secretary of State Seward recommended that the city illuminate itself at night, and owners of public and private buildings complied, adding flags to the lighting decorations. Five days later, General Lee surrendered to General Ulysses S. Grant at 1:00 in the afternoon. Grant allowed Lee's 25,000-man force to go home with their horses, and he provided three days' worth of rations to keep them from starving. Grant told all assembled, "The war is over. The rebels are our countrymen again."

It took time for this news to spread, for all Confederates to lay down their arms and stop fighting. On April 11, Dr. George Cooper issued Special Orders No. 87, directing Dr. Mary Walker to report to the surgeon in charge at the Refugee Hospital in Clarksville, about fifty miles northwest of Nashville. People displaced by the war, especially women and children, still required assistance, including lodging and medical care. Walker decided the position would be a good fit.

That same day, President Lincoln addressed an enthusiastic crowd in front of the Executive Mansion, the last speech he delivered. The war had been over for two days. Lincoln's message to the White House audience emphasized how the war had transformed the country. Using the example of Louisiana, he described the process of Reconstruction, how the Southern states would return to their place in the Union, and the significance of the ratification of the Thirteenth Amendment, which outlawed slavery. He acknowledged the importance of voting rights for African-American men, angering some of the people in the audience, including an actor named John Wilkes Booth.

Big upheavals for the United States lay ahead.

CHAPTER EIGHT

The Medal of Honor

THE WAR MAY HAVE ENDED, BUT NOT DR. MARY WALKER'S WORK. Tennessee had been under Union control since late 1863, yet guerrilla warfare spread as desperate Confederates tried to wrest the state from its Northern occupiers. Civilians, black and white, suffered, many of them fleeing their homes to stay out of the paths of guerrillas and soldiers. The Union Army set up refugee centers and contraband camps in several cities throughout the state to provide care and assistance. Though white Tennesseans appreciated the safety and services available in the refugee centers, many resented the Yankees and felt bitter about losing the war.

While Mary Walker believed her gender made her uniquely qualified to provide medical care for women, her dedication to the Union limited her empathy for Confederate sympathizers. As she had demonstrated in Louisville, she had a low tolerance for disloyalty. In Clarksville, this became very public as the result of a couple of incidents at the Episcopal Trinity Church in April 1865. The Reverend Samuel Ringgold, who became the church's rector the previous October, convinced occupation authorities to keep Trinity open because "decent and orderly worship" was above earthly political concerns. Yet he may not have been. Ringgold's sympathies seem to have skewed Confederate. He came from a prosperous plantation family in Maryland, and many slave owners interpreted Christianity as consistent with the practice of slavery. Both of Ringgold's ministries had been located in Union-occupied cities—first Louisville, then Clarksville—and he knew that Northern authorities worried churches could be hotbeds of resistance.·

Occupation officers kept an eye on Reverend Ringgold, monitoring his sermons for any hint of disloyalty or anti-Union agitation. Ringgold scrutinized his own writing, careful to obey the rules about unlawful speech, but he could not control how other people perceived his messages.

One night in April, when Samuel Ringgold returned from his missionary rounds to Trinity Church for the evening prayer service, his vestrymen warned him that Union soldiers had arrived to arrest him. The troops seated themselves with the congregation, however, and made no move to do so. Mary Walker was part of the Union contingent that listened to Ringgold's sermon about peace, assessing if anything sounded disloyal. After the sermon, she placed a small American flag on the collection plate, possibly a message to Samuel Ringgold about how she had interpreted his sermon. The minister accepted it without comment. "If the flag was her gift to God," he believed, "it was not his place to interfere."

Other Unionists in the congregation that night clearly resented the minister's sermon. The next morning, Samuel Ringgold found an envelope left at his door. Inside sat three bullets and a note demanding that he fly the American flag over the rectory or risk death. He ignored the threat and continued his duties as usual, ministering to Yankees and Rebels alike. After President Lincoln's assassination on Good Friday, Ringgold wrote a resolution of sorrow and spoke at a community memorial service at the Methodist church, a nondenominational event designed to bring together Northerners and Southerners.

On Easter Sunday, many American churches honored the slain president. In Washington, DC, it was known as "Black Easter" because of the churches that painted their Easter lilies black in mourning. Mary Walker may have been expecting something similarly somber at Trinity Church. Instead, when she arrived for the holiday service, she saw at the font in front of the chancel a display of red geraniums shaped into a cross, with a decorative white dove suspended above. Samuel Ringgold watched the doctor, attired in her blue uniform adorned with a series of red, white, and blue ribbons, cut off the blue ribbon with the dagger she wore in her belt. Walker took offense with the original red-and-white color scheme, largely recognized as Confederate colors. She pinned the blue ribbon to the dove to represent the United States of America.

As Samuel Ringgold passed the font, he removed the ribbon and put it on the collection plate. The minister found the bearing of the "colors of the nation" inappropriate for Easter Sunday. Mary Walker disagreed. She "rushed down to the font, seized the cross of flowers and stamped them under her army boots." Ringgold showed no reaction to her behavior and continued the service. A reporter for the Louisville *Journal* called the event a "sacrilige [*sic*]" and blamed Mary Walker for the disturbance. "The Major is sufficiently patriotic, but not modest enough by half." A Pittsburgh newspaper countered that "the truth would be better expressed" by the following change in wording: "The citizens of Clarksville are sufficiently modest but not patriotic enough by half."

A congregant identified only as "An Episcopalian" sent a letter to the Louisville *Journal*, providing his version of the events. The flower arrangement at the baptismal font, he insisted, was "*held sacred by us all.*" Dr. Walker's behavior at the church caused the Reverend Ringgold to stop the service and go complain to the military commandant, a Colonel Smith. It was the military officer who explained to Ringgold that Walker meant her actions to be taken as an offering, and the minister must be "content" with that. The letter writer criticized the Yankee doctor for inciting political tensions, pointing out, "If the flowers were typical of disloyalty, to the Colonel commanding belonged the right to remove or have them removed." Presuming to speak for the others in attendance, he cast a final aspersion. "We do not know whether Major Walker considers herself a lady or not. Judging from her costume we would suppose not, and certainly no gentleman would so desecrate the House of God."

Mary Walker objected to the Episcopalian's description of the Easter service, and fired off a response to the newspaper. "No one but a coward would make a personal attack without signing his name, and that the writer of that letter was guilty of false coloring, suppression of the truth— and base falsehood." The man did not accurately describe her outfit and incorrectly stated that she carried a "weapon of defense." The commandant had vindicated her actions, Walker reminded the *Journal* readers, and Mr. Ringgold only later made a "feeble attempt" to honor her offering. Her speculation that "a fear of military discipline" was a reason the letter writer remained anonymous reinforced the charged emotions of the weeks surrounding the Confederate surrender at Appomattox.

Tensions indeed remained high throughout the country in the aftermath of President Lincoln's death, as information spread about the precipitating conspiracy. That Confederates would resort to political assassination as a last-ditch effort to win the war outraged many Northerners. Secretary of War Stanton launched a massive manhunt for John Wilkes Booth, offering a $100,000 reward for the capture of the actor and his accomplices. Conspirators were tracked down within a few days, but Booth eluded authorities until April 26, when soldiers shot and killed him in a barn in Virginia. Gossip and innuendo about criminals dominated newspaper stories.

Andrew Johnson, Lincoln's successor, and Secretary of War Stanton arranged to bring the accused before a military commission rather than a civilian court. The judge advocate general of the army, Joseph Holt, served as prosecutor. Mary Walker likely followed these developments in the newspaper. As the government pulled together its plans for the trial, she received a letter from Dr. George Cooper on May 5. Addressing her as Madam rather than Doctor, he wrote, "I am informed that your services are not needed at the Refugee Home in Clarksville." The number of patients had dwindled to the point where the doctor in charge could care for them all. Dr. Walker could either report back to him in Nashville, or to the assistant surgeon general's office. Cooper, probably with some satisfaction, closed the letter by repeating that the medical department no longer required her services.

Twelve days later, Dr. Walker packed up and traveled to Nashville to talk to Cooper and figure out what she would do next. Her new orders sent her on to Washington, DC, where, at her own request, the army terminated her contract on June 15. She collected the rest of her pay, a sum of $766.16. Walker remained in the capital during the weeks of the trial of the Lincoln conspirators. Like other Americans, she would have closely followed the proceedings against the eight accused. On June 27, the military commission, having heard the last of the testimony from 361 witnesses, retired to review the evidence.

By then, Mary Walker had left the city, first heading south. While in Richmond at the end of June, she walked through Castle Thunder as a free woman, which probably gave her great satisfaction. The Richmond *Bulletin* reported Walker's presence on the city streets, beginning with a description of her outfit: "a blue coat with military buttons, and a very long skirt, a pair of nicely fitting blue pants . . . and gaiters, which fitted so as to display a pretty foot." The doctor attracted a lot of attention as she walked along Broad Street past the Powhatan Hotel. A small group of African-American children followed her. Men and boys "stopped along the sidewalk to comment upon the novel appearance of a lady in uniform."

When Dr. Walker reached 6th Street, a provost guard stopped and asked "by what authority she appeared upon the streets in the garb in which she was attired." Dr. Walker challenged, "By what authority do you make the inquiry?" The guard replied he was under orders of the provost marshal, which Walker would have known. "Then give him my compliments," she said, "and tell him I will call upon him." Bystanders watched as she "moved off as if nothing had occurred." Since she had started wearing reform dress more than ten years earlier, Mary Walker had always drawn notice while in public. Before long, verbal harassments would be compounded by arrests.

The doctor remained in the former Confederate capital until July 4, when she participated in the city's public celebration of Independence Day. The antislavery newspaper *The Liberator* reported on the subdued crowd, noting they were "not enthusiastic, except, perhaps, among a portion of the Union soldiers stationed there, and at the picnics of the freed people." The formal program began with a prayer from the Reverend George S. Stockwell of the First African Baptist Church. Dr. Walker, "late[ly a] surgeon in the army," dressed in her blue uniform, read the Declaration of Independence from the steps of the capitol building.

The next day, the military commission handed down its verdicts and sentences for the eight accused Lincoln conspirators. All were found guilty, and four, sentenced to death. On July 7, Lewis Powell, Mary Surratt, David Herold, and George Atzerodt were hanged at Fort McNair in Washington. The army strictly controlled the number of passes issued to those who wanted to witness the executions. Photographer Alexander

Gardner was on hand to record the event. In an odd example of Mary Walker's notoriety, one newspaper erroneously identified her as one of the army surgeons at the fort that day, and claimed, "When she left, she rode her horse after the masculine style."

Dr. Walker departed from Virginia around this time and traveled north to New York City, where she remained for a few weeks. She learned the unwelcome news that her soon-to-be-ex-husband, Albert Miller, had contacted her family in Oswego, looking for her. Miller expressed hope for a reconciliation. "I think she will yet see that haste does not always lead to the right & regret our separation." He also wanted to know if she needed "any of the comforts or necessities of life. I would willingly assist her at any time, should she need it." Mary Walker had no interest in anything Miller had to offer. She did not want him to interfere with the finalization of the divorce. Several months later, though, she would hear more unwelcome news from him.

From other correspondents, Mary Walker received advice on what she should do now that the war had ended. Edward Richards of Mound City, Kansas, secured an introduction through *The Sibyl*'s former editor, Lydia Hasbrouck, and proposed that the doctor write a pamphlet on dress reform. He had read her articles in that now-defunct reform journal and believed her uniquely qualified. Richards offered to take on the expense of publishing the pamphlet, then provide her with five hundred copies that she could distribute however she wished. Whether or not she accepted the offer, Richards hoped "to hear something of your past, & what you expect for the future." He told her that he was a hardworking man living on a farm, and "I have no wife now." He may have planned a marriage proposal to follow the publishing one.

Even Lydia Hasbrouck weighed in on Mary Walker's immediate future. "Sister Walker," Hasbrouck wrote on July 27, "Where in the name of common sense are you to be found?" After chiding her friend for not keeping in touch, Hasbrouck told the doctor she was needed in the North, "to work in earnest upon the question of woman's right[s] & suffrage & the Dress question." Hasbrouck planned a series of public lectures and wanted Walker to serve as "Sergeant Major to martial our forces." The idea of a public speaking tour held some attraction for the doctor. She had thought about it during the war, but the timing hadn't been right. Now she thought about it again.

Mary Walker knew this kind of work would attract criticism and controversy. From his law office at 128 Broadway in New York City, thirty-four-year-old Jacob W. Feeter wrote to her on August 2, advising her not to get involved with the women's suffrage movement. The two probably met somewhere in upstate New York in July, perhaps at the mountain vacation lodge where Feeter admitted to enjoying "several very enjoyable sensations." They struck up enough of a friendship that as he prepared to head back to the city, Walker requested he write and let her know that he had arrived safely.

Addressing her as "My Dear Major," Feeter complimented her patriotism before proposing his theory that the advancement of the American people "requires noble women to produce great men." He hoped she would not waste her energy "declaiming against the wrongs of women simply because they have not the right of suffrage." Feeter had no objection to women receiving an education and having access to the same kinds of jobs as men. He believed women made good doctors, and hinted that women's education should be geared toward that outcome. "I did not intend to deliver a lecture," Feeter wrote in closing, "but am certain and really feel there are many things you could explain from your thoughtful experience."

Jacob Feeter's letter indicated that he and Mary Walker had talked a lot about women's rights, especially women's access to education and jobs. She still worried about how to support herself. Her medical practice in Washington, DC, had declined during the last year of the war because she had spent so little time in the capital. Dr. Walker continued to hope for a commission as an assistant surgeon from the army. Because of her most recent assignment at Clarksville, she believed the army should appoint her to a position as a medical inspector for the Freedmen's Bureau in Washington, where Josephine White Griffing worked as the assistant to the assistant commissioner of the bureau.

An ardent abolitionist and women's rights supporter, in 1864 Josephine Griffing had left her husband home in Litchfield, Ohio, and moved to Washington with three of their daughters. After over ten years working as a traveling agent for the Western Anti-Slavery Society and nearly as many with the Ohio Women's Rights Association, she wanted to do something to directly help those newly freed from slavery. She became an agent for the National Freedman's Relief Association, a charitable organization founded in 1862 to provide material assistance and education to those liberated from enslavement. Griffing also opened two industrial schools designed to train African-American women for work in the paid-wages labor force.

Josephine Griffing believed this kind of assistance was so vital to the protection of a newly freed population that the federal government should sponsor it. She lobbied Radical Republicans in Congress to pass an act to create a bureau for the "Relief of Freedmen and Refugees." After nearly a year of congressional wrangling, President Lincoln signed it into law in March 1865. Griffing's efforts on behalf of the newly created Freedmen's Bureau were considered so essential that the man tapped as its commissioner, General Oliver Otis Howard, appointed her in June to the position of assistant to the assistant commissioner.

When Mary Walker learned that General Howard—who probably knew of her from his time with the Army of the Potomac and the Army of the Cumberland—was willing to hire a woman in the Freedmen's Bureau, she thought he might employ another. She secured letters of recommendation from several men she knew in Washington who worked for state military agencies. These state-funded organizations took care of the needs of their hometown soldiers, often working with the Sanitary Commission to provide medical care. The men all addressed their similarly worded letters to President Johnson. W. A. Benedict of Connecticut asserted, "Maj. Walker seems to me to be peculiarly fitted by her qualities of mind and heart, and her large experience, for the position she seeks." But to no avail. Johnson and Howard both already found Josephine Griffing outspoken and difficult to work with. They did not want to deal with another strong-minded woman.

At the end of August 1865, after receiving testimonials about Mary Walker's accomplishments, including a letter from Dr. Edward Phelps, President Johnson asked the secretary of war to find out "if there is any way in which or precedent by which" any recognition could be made of the doctor's wartime service. The use of the word *recognition* indicates that

Johnson considered something for Walker other than a job. An award or an honorary brevet seemed more likely.

It was not unusual for the army to reward a commissioned officer's exceptional service with a brevet title, which conferred status but not the authority or pay of the real rank. Another option was awarding the Medal of Honor. Congress passed an act in 1861 establishing one for the navy, which President Lincoln signed into law in December. Assistant adjutant general Edward Townsend pushed for the medal for the army, too. He saw the system of brevet promotions for officers rife with exaggeration and corruption, too often not recognizing true valor. Townsend also believed enlisted personnel deserved to be eligible. In July 1862, Congress followed suit for the army, creating a medal to award noncommissioned officers and privates who distinguished themselves "by their gallantry in action, and other soldier like qualities, during the present insurrection." In 1863 Congress expanded the Medal of Honor to include commissioned officers, and made it a permanent decoration.

President Johnson wanted to know if either of these could be applied to Mary Walker's situation, or if she could receive an army commission. At the end of September, perhaps hoping to quickly quash the matter, Edwin Stanton passed along some negative assessments of the doctor's abilities, including one from Dr. George Cooper. Addressing the surgeon general, Joseph Barnes, Cooper wrote that he learned the "so called Doctor Mary E. Walker was annoying you in Washington." Cooper recalled he had assigned Walker to the refugee home in Clarksville only because of the assistant surgeon general's order. Cooper "got rid of her as soon as practicable." He summed up his assessment of the doctor: "She is useless, ignorant, trifling and a consummate boor & I cannot imagine how she even had a contract made with her as Actg. Asst. Surgeon."

Such challenges to Mary Walker's accomplishments did not deter the president. Edwin Stanton, the secretary of war, wrote to him on October 27: "I have the honor to state that the legal question involved therein has been referred to the Judge Advocate General, whose report has not yet been received." Stanton and Joseph Holt developed a close working relationship. Stanton championed Holt's appointment as judge advocate general (JAG) in July 1862 when Congress expanded the scope and authority of the office. In addition to its original purpose of overseeing courts-martial, the JAG now maintained control over courts of inquiry, military commissions, and all matters of military law.

Attorney Joseph Holt entered federal employment as a patent commissioner in 1857, during James Buchanan's administration, and in 1859 became postmaster general. In the lame-duck months of the Buchanan presidency, Holt served as secretary of war. A Kentucky Democrat, Holt remained loyal to the Union after the war started, and in the fall of 1861, he began working in the War Department. Before Holt's current appointment, confirmed by the Senate in February 1863, he served as the commissioner of ordnance claims. During the summer of 1865, he prosecuted the Lincoln conspirators, and now he was tasked with determining what, if anything, the government could offer Mary Walker.

Holt's report opened with a clear explanation of Dr. Walker's expectations: "some formal acknowledgement of the value of her services, in the nature of a commission or brevet as U.S. surgeon." Recognition mattered the most. "While she asks that such appointment shall date from the period at which she first entered upon the performance of her work, she does not and will not apply for any *pay* as an officer, and will *resign* her commission upon its being once duly granted and accepted." Holt found "no *precedent* within the knowledge of this bureau" for appointment to either a full or brevet rank. Then he got to the main point. "Whether or not, however, her sex is to be deemed an *insuperable* obstacle to her receiving the official recognition which she asks, is a question which has not probably been heretofore presented to this Department."

Without the existence of a precedent, Joseph Holt declined to find in Mary Walker's favor. He summarized all the documents submitted on her behalf, then explained: "But not withstanding all this evidence as to her merit and efficiency in the public service, Miss Walker has not succeeded in satisfying the requirements of the medical department of the army." Those examiners found her incompetent, and the surgeon general, Joseph Barnes, would not approve her application for a commission. When Secretary Stanton communicated this to the president, Johnson wanted to know what could be done to honor Mary Walker that "may not be in conflict with law."

Joseph Holt admitted that though there was no precedent "for the commissioning of a female as an officer," and Mary Walker could not be awarded a brevet without having been commissioned first, there was "no *law* which prohibits it." Holt pointed out that other branches of the government, including the Treasury and Patent departments, hired women. With those precedents set, "it may with some force be claimed that, in the absence of a statutory prohibition, the granting of such an appointment as is now sought should depend upon the merits of the applicant alone." This opened the possibility of the female doctor's case establishing another precedent.

It would all come down to whether Mary Walker's job performance during the war could or should outweigh the findings of the medical examination board. While Joseph Holt noted that she "apparently performed with fidelity and efficiency the duties to which she was assigned," only the secretary of war could make the final determination. Still, Holt suggested that the adverse pronouncement of the medical board could serve as a barrier to Walker's future employment with the army, but "it can hardly fairly operate to preclude the desired recognition of services heretofore duly rendered, and commended by the officers referred to as valuable and important, and of which the authorities have enjoyed the full benefit."

The honorable thing, according to Joseph Holt, was to give Mary Walker an award. No one would have to worry that it set an "inconvenient precedent" because what she had done during the war—"her sacrifices, her fearless energy under circumstances of peril, her endurance of hardship and imprisonment at the hands of the enemy, and especially her active patriotism and eminent loyalty"—was so singular that it could not happen again. Along with the commendation, Dr. Walker "shall be officially advised of the final action upon her application." The government would not do anything more for her.

On November 2, Edward Townsend, assistant adjutant general, wrote to Mary Walker that the secretary of war had considered her request for a military commission but "decided adversely. There is no law or precedent which would authorize it." Before she received written notice of Stanton's decision, newspapers ran stories about the rejection of her application. In early September, a Vermont paper explained that the doctor had "been for some time expending the force of her woman's eloquence at the War Department to procure an appointment in the regular army." Walker wanted the position to pave the way for other women who might want to serve in the military. Her failure "must be accepted as fresh evidence of the strength of the secretary's character, and that downtrodden woman has yet to bide a considerable length of time." Another Vermont publication put it more succinctly, "Secretary Stanton declines to take the responsibility of the innovation."

Nine days after the secretary of war refused to commission Mary Walker, President Johnson awarded her the Medal of Honor. The citation identified her as an "Assistant Surgeon-in-Charge of female prisoners at Louisville" and as "Contract Surgeon in service to the United States." It lauded the "patriotic zeal" with which she approached her duties and "endured hardships as a prisoner of war four months in a Southern prison." Because Dr. Walker had not been a commissioned officer, she could not receive a brevet or honorary rank. Therefore, "in the opinion of the President, an honorable recognition of her services and sufferings should be made." Johnson ordered "the usual medal of honor for meritorious service be given her."

Newspapers across the country picked up the story. The *National Republican* of Washington, DC, printed the entirety of President Johnson's award statement, prefacing it with a clear explanation of why the Medal of Honor had been conferred on Mary Walker. Abraham Lincoln had wanted her to have the medal, and generals Sherman, Thomas, and McCook had all testified to her important contributions. "It is the only compensation, under the law, that the President is empowered to bestow upon the Doctor, because she happens to be a woman. Much of the service rendered by her to the Government could not have been accomplished by a man." The reporter held out hope that Congress might come up with "some degree of pecuniary justice" for Walker. And since many deserving generals were receiving medals they did not need, "why not make a small donation to a worthy woman who *does* need it? We merely throw out the suggestion."

Dr. Mary Walker received one of the 1,522 Medals of Honor awarded for Civil War service, and she was the only female recipient, a distinction she holds to this day. The medal was not conferred on many awardees until after the war, some not for decades afterward. Francis Brownell, a private with the 11th New York Volunteers, was not honored until 1877, but it was for the first meritorious act during the war. In Alexandria, Virginia, on May 24, Brownell killed innkeeper James Jackson, who killed Colonel Elmer Ellsworth for removing a Confederate flag from his property.

A potential awardee's status mattered. Only four civilian employees of the military received the medal for actions during the Civil War. The first Medals of Honor presented, in March 1863, went to the six surviving members of the Andrews Raiders who seized control of a train in Georgia to disrupt Confederate transportation. The raid's leader, James Andrews, was captured and hanged as a spy. Though additional participants in the action later got a posthumous medal, Andrews, a civilian, did not.

The Medal of Honor marked Mary Walker as a somebody, guaranteeing her place in history. No fanfare accompanied the award, only a parchment copy of the presidential statement and a medal designed by Philadelphia silversmiths William Wilson & Sons. The medal featured a spread-winged eagle holding a ribbon of the national colors above and a five-pointed star bearing Minerva's image below. The reverse side bore the inscription: "The Congress to Dr. Mary E. Walker, A-A. Surgeon, U.S.A., November 11, 1865." She wore the medal every day of her life.

This professional high point was followed by a personal low involving her divorce from Albert Miller. His communication with Mary Walker's family that summer had come out of the blue. He may have been sounding out Walker's determination to divorce, but, as she learned in late November, he only feigned an interest in a reconciliation. He continued to have affairs with women during the 1860s. In the spring of 1862, he was arrested for seducing Maria Hardy of Marlborough, New Hampshire. A millworker in her early twenties, Hardy had originally came to Miller for medical treatment while he was lecturing in the area, and the resulting affair may have produced a child. A colleague on the lecture circuit, Nelson Whittlesey, paid several hundred dollars "to settle the matter." Later in the year, another young woman informed authorities in South Paris, Maine, that Miller had fathered her child.

Sometime in the late winter or early spring of 1865, while in Boston, Albert Miller met Vesta Delphine Freeman, an allopathic medical school graduate and practicing physician. They embarked on an affair, and Miller decided he wanted to marry her. But as the guilty spouse in a divorce decree, he was legally barred from doing so, at least in New York. On November 24, 1865, two days before Mary Walker's birthday, the New York State supreme court took up the divorce petition Albert Miller had filed in Oneida County. The court granted Miller a divorce from Walker, effectively erasing her 1861 filing. She would not tolerate this stain on her character. Miller was the guilty party responsible for the dissolution of their marriage, and she refused to bear the public blame. Walker began the process of securing an act of relief from the New York State Assembly, to compel it to revisit the validity of the decree. In the meantime, Albert Miller married Delphine Freeman.

As 1865 drew to a close, the Thirteenth Amendment, which outlawed slavery throughout the country, was ratified and added to the Constitution. Congress and the states thereby fulfilled a major goal of the war. President Lincoln's 1863 Emancipation Proclamation had not freed all enslaved persons, though it made clear slavery would end with a Union victory. In April 1864, the US Senate passed a proposed amendment, but the many Democrats in the House of Representatives derailed it. After his reelection that November, Lincoln turned his persuasive powers on recalcitrant House Democrats, and within two months convinced enough to change their votes. On February 1, 1865, the president approved a joint congressional resolution that sent the amendment on to the states.

It took 309 days for three-fourths of the states to ratify. One sticking point was the question of state versus federal power, a debate as old as the Constitution itself. Another stemmed from white conservatives' fear that the national government would follow emancipation with a sweeping equal rights program. For them, legal freedom—and even equality before the law—did not mean racial equality. The New England states, with their strong abolitionist sentiments and weak Democratic parties, easily ratified the amendment. In New York, the strength of the Peace Democrats slowed ratification until after Lincoln's assassination. Former Confederates in the Southern states resented that confirmation of the amendment was an entrée ticket back into the Union. On December 6, 1865, Georgia became the twenty-seventh state to approve—at the time, all that was needed to add an amendment to the Constitution.

The national and state debates over the Thirteenth Amendment, in focusing on how much social and political change the amendment would generate, cast attention on women's roles and status. Democrats charged Republicans with a plot to dismantle all of society's foundations, including the patriarchal family structure. Republicans responded reassuringly that they would never meddle with "the rights of a husband to a wife." Edwin Lawrence Godkin, avid abolitionist and prominent writer and editor, spread this assertion widely. By upholding traditional families, Republicans soothed anxieties about emancipation.

They also distanced themselves from the women's rights movement. Many women's rights activists viewed emancipation as the first step toward a universal equality that would encompass all genders and races. In late December 1865, Massachusetts politician Charles Sumner told the Senate that the difference between slavery and freedom was "freedom of contract: the right to marry and have a family, and the right to sell one's labor for a wage." But he failed to acknowledge that this was gender-specific. While men had these rights, women, once they became wives, did not. Wives' labor and wages belonged to their husbands, and wives had no political or legal identity independent of their husbands'.

Before the war, the nascent women's rights movement began to change these laws, and had made small progress. Frances Dana Gage, a well-known abolitionist and women's rights activist, sat in the Senate gallery listening to Sumner on that December day. She realized Republicans would not be reliable allies in the quest for gender equality. "When I found that he meant only freedom for the male sex, I learned that Charles Sumner fell far short of the great idea of liberty."

Mary Walker emerged from the war with a strong sense of the meaning of liberty and equality, determined to see them apply to *all* people in the United States. At age thirty-three, with more than half of her life ahead of her, she plunged back into the battle for women's rights.

Mary Walker adopted this reform dress, commonly known as the "Bloomer costume," in the 1850s, and wore it for the rest of her life. CURRIER & IVES LITHOGRAPH, LIBRARY OF CONGRESS, PRINTS AND PHOTOGRAPHS DIVISION

Mary Walker visited Secretary of War Simon Cameron in 1861 when she arrived in Washington, DC, to ask for a commission as a US Army surgeon. CIVIL WAR PHOTOGRAPHS, 1861–1865, LIBRARY OF CONGRESS, PRINTS AND PHOTOGRAPHS DIVISION

Mary Walker worked as a volunteer physician at the Indiana Hospital, established in the Patent Office Building in 1861 after the Rhode Island troops moved out.
LIBRARY OF CONGRESS, PRINTS AND PHOTOGRAPHS DIVISION

Mary Walker volunteered at the behind-the-lines station at Lacy House in Falmouth, Virginia, in December 1862. ALEXANDER GARDNER PHOTOGRAPH, LIBRARY OF CONGRESS, PRINTS AND PHOTOGRAPHS DIVISION

A clerk in the Patent Office at the start of the war, Clara Barton's subsequent nursing duties caused her to cross paths with Mary Walker. The two women continued a cordial friendship after the war. CHARLES R. B. CLAFLIN PHOTOGRAPH, LILJENQUIST FAMILY COLLECTION OF CIVIL WAR PHOTOGRAPHS, LIBRARY OF CONGRESS, PRINTS AND PHOTOGRAPHS DIVISION

The poet Walt Whitman arrived at Lacy House in December 1862 to look for his wounded brother. He probably observed Mary Walker and Clara Barton at work. ALEXANDER GARDNER PHOTOGRAPH, FEINBERG-WHITMAN COLLECTION, LIBRARY OF CONGRESS, PRINTS AND PHOTOGRAPHS DIVISION

Known as the "Rock of Chickamauga," Major General George H. Thomas hired Mary Walker as a civilian contract surgeon for the US Army in 1864. CIVIL WAR PHOTOGRAPHS, 1861–1865, LIBRARY OF CONGRESS, PRINTS AND PHOTOGRAPHS DIVISION

Dr. Glover S. Perin, seated center front, medical director of the Army of the Cumberland and a member of the medical board examiners, opposed Dr. Mary Walker's employment as a contract surgeon in 1864. "COL. GROVER S. [SIC] PERIN SURROUNDED BY HIS MILITARY CORPS" (OHA271-001 00002). OHA 271: PERIN COLLECTION. OTIS HISTORICAL ARCHIVES, NATIONAL MUSEUM OF HEALTH AND MEDICINE.

In March 1864, Mary Walker reported for duty as a civilian contract surgeon to Colonel Daniel McCook, commander of the 52nd Ohio Volunteer Infantry at Lee and Gordon's Mills, Georgia. CIVIL WAR PHOTOGRAPHS, 1861–1865, LIBRARY OF CONGRESS, PRINTS AND PHOTOGRAPHS DIVISION

Castle Thunder Prison in Richmond, Virginia, was the site of Mary Walker's imprisonment by the Confederacy from April–August 1864. DAVID H. ANDERSON PHOTOGRAPH, MARIAN S. CARSON COLLECTION, LIBRARY OF CONGRESS, PRINTS AND PHOTOGRAPHS DIVISION

Dr. Mary Walker wearing the Medal of Honor decoration, c. 1866. MATHEW BRADY COLLECTION, NARA FILE #111-B-2112 WAR AND CONFLICT BOOK #216, NATIONAL ARCHIVES, WASHINGTON, DC

In 1866–1867, Mary Walker conducted a speaking tour in Great Britain and had her photograph taken in London.

Mary Walker's post–Civil War women's rights activism often put her at odds with the two prominent suffragists, Elizabeth Cady Stanton and Susan B. Anthony, pictured here c. 1880–1902.

Mary Walker pioneered the New Departure strategy in the late 1860s, which was briefly adopted by other suffragists, including Victoria Woodhull, pictured here addressing the House Judiciary Committee in 1871. *FRANK LESLIE'S ILLUSTRATED NEWSPAPER*, FEBRUARY 4, 1871, LIBRARY OF CONGRESS, PRINTS AND PHOTOGRAPHS DIVISION

During the late 1870s, Mary Walker began wearing more explicitly masculine attire.
C. M. BELL COLLECTION, LIBRARY OF CONGRESS, PRINTS AND PHOTOGRAPHS DIVISION

Mary Walker (r) standing next to her friend, the lawyer Belva Lockwood, with the Reverend Susanna Harris (l) in 1912. LIBRARY OF CONGRESS, PRINTS AND PHOTOGRAPHS DIVISION

Mary Walker in her standard formal dress attire, c. 1911. GEORGE GRANTHAM BAIN
COLLECTION, LIBRARY OF CONGRESS, PRINTS AND PHOTOGRAPHS DIVISION

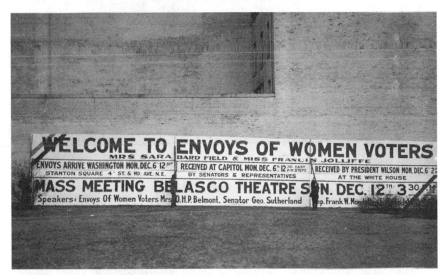

Despite her quarrels with the mainstream suffrage movement, Mary Walker
participated in various events, including this one welcoming suffragists from
the West to Washington, DC, in 1915. HARRIS & EWING COLLECTION, LIBRARY OF
CONGRESS, PRINTS AND PHOTOGRAPHS DIVISION

Mary Walker celebrated the Fourth of July in 1867 at a banquet in Paris, France, flaunting her patriotism by wearing a sash of the stars and stripes, which may have looked like this. Walker always considered herself a patriot. MARY EDWARDS WALKER PAPERS, SPECIAL COLLECTIONS RESEARCH CENTER, SYRACUSE UNIVERSITY LIBRARIES

CHAPTER NINE

Women's Rights during Radical Reconstruction

ALTHOUGH MARY WALKER PROUDLY WORE HER MEDAL OF HONOR, SHE understood that the award allowed the government to recognize her achievements without giving her the retroactive commission she desired. She wanted that designation as validation for the important duties she had performed for the Union Army during the war, and to lay the ground-work for women who aspired to a professional position in the military. This failure became a needling reminder of women's inequality, especially when the doctor realized that the deprivations she had endured while a prisoner of war had damaged her eyesight. She was forced to sideline surgery in the postwar years, always more lucrative than general-practice medicine. As a single woman, Walker could never stop thinking about how to support herself. While she expected to practice medicine, she also believed her years with the army entitled her to a government pension, which she doggedly pursued for the rest of her life.

Spending part of the spring of 1866 in New York allowed Mary Walker the opportunity to re-immerse herself in the women's rights movement. The Civil War created momentum for change in the way Americans viewed citizenship, suffrage, and equality. Indeed, in the wake of emancipation, both abolitionists and women's rights advocates focused on voting rights as the most important aspect of freedom and the corner-stone of human rights. Abolitionists wanted to make sure African Americans could vote. Women wanted to make sure they were not left out of any expansion of the franchise. In late 1865, congressional Republicans began drafting language about citizenship, representation, and voting for what would become the Fourteenth Amendment. If some women had been concerned about the content of the debates surrounding the Thirteenth Amendment, more of them, including Elizabeth Cady Stanton, raised an alarm about the wording of the Fourteenth.

The woman who had spearheaded the 1848 Seneca Falls Convention and led the prewar women's rights movement approved of the gender-neutral language of the first section. It identified "all persons born or naturalized in the United States" as citizens, forbade the states to pass laws that would interfere with the "privileges" of citizenship, and extended equal protection of the laws to all. Over the next decades, women's rights activists would cite this as the basis for their claims to women's equality. Mary Walker and others insisted it also conferred suffrage on women. However, section two proved problematic and devastating to the women's suffrage cause. In delineating representation and voting rights, Congress used gender-specific language: "But when the right to vote . . . is denied to any of the male inhabitants of such State, being twenty-one years of age, and citizens of the United States." All adult men, regardless of race or nationality, were eligible voters, but not women.

Republican politicians crafted this language because they believed that individual Southern states, still dominated by the Democratic Party, would never enfranchise black men. Yet Republicans themselves remained divided on the question of black men's suffrage. Radical Republicans—those dedicated to sweeping social and political changes in the defeated former Confederacy—viewed voting as an indispensable tool in reconstructing the postwar South. Conservative Republicans sided with Democrats to oppose suffrage, while moderates worried that the Republican Party would face a severe backlash for promoting it. The wording of the amendment's second section tied voting to representation. It did not directly bestow suffrage on African-American men, but it would decrease the South's representation in Congress if those men remained unenfranchised.

Elizabeth Cady Stanton unsuccessfully tried to get Congress to change this proposed language, making it gender-neutral like section one. She did not want the Republican Party to bypass an opportunity to grant women's suffrage. During the 1850s, though she supported abolition, Stanton had promoted voting rights for white women over those of African-American and immigrant men. After the Emancipation Proclamation, she supported voting rights for black men, briefly sidelining women's suffrage. Once the war ended, she shifted again and touted universal suffrage, linking the cause of black men and all women. But when pushed to prioritize, Stanton always chose white women. She resented that few male abolitionists supported universal suffrage. Now she was horrified that Congress intended to enshrine men's voting rights in the Constitution.

Through the first half of 1866, Congress debated the Fourteenth Amendment's final wording, a couple of times raising women's hopes that the word *male* would be left out. The amendment seemed particularly necessary to reinforce the Civil Rights Act, a piece of 1865 legislation guaranteeing citizenship and equal protection that had trouble getting through Congress. When it finally arrived on President Johnson's desk in late March 1866, he vetoed it. A congressional override made the bill a law on April 9, 1866. Johnson's resistance to the Radical Republicans' agenda for Reconstruction set up a battle between the president and Congress that lasted until his impeachment, in 1868.

As a divided Congress debated, women reformers were split on the subject of suffrage. Not all white women, especially those who had been ardent abolitionists, agreed with Elizabeth Cady Stanton's concerns about the Fourteenth Amendment, and they lauded any efforts to secure voting rights for African-American men. Prominent black women, including Harriet Tubman, Sojourner Truth, and Frances Ellen Watkins Harper, supported voting rights for women, but focused their energies on helping freed people and supporting suffrage for black men.

Elizabeth Cady Stanton and Susan B. Anthony decided to unite all factions in a group dedicated to universal suffrage. Their political partnership was now fifteen years old. Anthony excelled at organization and tactics, Stanton, at theory and prose. Together, slowly, and not always smoothly, they built a movement. The Eleventh National Women's Rights Convention, held in New York City at the Church of the Puritans on May 10, 1866, illuminated what the duo envisioned: "The question now, is, have we the wisdom and conscience, from the present upheavings of our political system, to reconstruct a government on the one enduring basis that has never yet been tried—'EQUAL RIGHTS TO ALL.'" Speeches from several well-known reformers, including Stanton, Anthony, Wendell Phillips, and Frances Ellen Watkins Harper, took up the morning session.

In the afternoon, the convention created the American Equal Rights Association (AERA). Lucretia Mott, one of the architects of the 1848 Seneca Falls meeting, served as the AERA's president, and Stanton held one of the vice presidencies. Anthony sat on the executive committee, along with Lucy Stone. When the Fourteenth Amendment passed both houses of Congress and was sent on to the states for ratification in June, AERA members found much in it to criticize, especially its weak language on suffrage.

Though Mary Walker did not attend the conference, as a universal suffrage supporter, she would have approved of the AERA's creation. It is likely she followed newspaper coverage of the convention and, since she was still in New York, she may have discussed its proceedings in person with Stanton and Anthony, with whom she maintained a cordial relationship. The doctor likely kept busy monitoring the progress of her pension application and preparing an address for the National Dress Reform Association (NDRA) that was scheduled for late June, in Syracuse. Walker had been involved with the organization since its founding in 1856 by abolitionist and health reformer James Caleb Jackson. Dr. Lydia Strowbridge of Cortland, New York, had invited Mary Walker to attend the 1866 meeting and speak. "We have watched with interest your course in helping put down the tyrant in the South," Strowbridge wrote in May, "and now we much desire your aid in crushing the tyranny of Fashion."

Before the NDRA convention, Mary Walker seized the opportunity to strike a blow against that tyranny when she was arrested in New York City. She had been staying at 13 Laight Street, near the Hygeio-Therapeutic College, close to Canal Street in southern Manhattan. On the afternoon of June 5, she took a walk. Though the doctor visited New York many times over the years, always wearing her reform dress, on this day her attire attracted a large crowd. When Walker stopped inside a millinery shop on Canal Street, the onlookers gathered around the door and windows, eager to see what she was doing. Concerned for her safety, the owner called over two policemen from the 8th Precinct, assuming they would disperse the crowd and escort Mary Walker home.

Instead, patrolman Patrick H. Pickett questioned her before taking her in for violating a city law that made it a misdemeanor for a woman to appear in public in male attire. Dr. Walker protested, telling Pickett that if he arrested her, "she would have him broken." But Pickett insisted, walking her—too roughly, she later charged—through the streets to the station house, where he made the situation worse by failing to offer her a chair. The desk sergeant found her "very defiant," though after talking with her, he released her without filing charges.

By the next day, word had spread throughout the city about Mary Walker's encounter with the police. Her friend, New York attorney Jacob Feeter, wrote to her on June 6: "I see by the *Times* this morning that a wooden headed Policeman arrested you." He advised her to try and see New York's attorney general, John Martindale, currently residing at the Fifth Avenue Hotel. Feeter likely believed Martindale would be sympathetic to the female doctor's situation because Martindale had been a general during the war, serving in the field with the Army of the Potomac, and in Washington, DC, as military governor. Feeter suggested the attorney general could write to Thomas C. Acton, president of the police commissioners' board, and ask for the "removal of the stupid Policeman."

Two days later, Mary Walker presented herself at police headquarters and filed a complaint for illegal arrest. On June 9 she was arrested again, this time by Officer Johnson of the 7th Precinct, for walking along Jefferson Street in her reform dress and attracting a crowd. "Instead of dispersing the rabble," the *New York Times* reported, Johnson "preferred to exercise his authority upon the unoffending lady." He took the doctor to the Essex Market Police Court and entered charges of disorderly conduct and appearing in "male costume" in public. Justice Mansfield set a $300 bail to compel her "to keep the peace for a year." She spent two hours in jail before her "counsel"—possibly Jacob Feeter, who later described Mansfield as a moral coward—came up with the money.

Mary Walker's complaint against Patrolman Pickett triggered a hearing before the police commission board, headed by Thomas Acton, on

June 13. The proceeding attracted a large crowd, and several people testified about the events of June 5, including Walker. Before describing what happened, she explained her ideas about fashion. She wore reform dress "from a high moral principle, and regarded the current female style of dress as immodest and immoral." Acton appeared genuinely interested in the doctor's ideology and her version of events. At the conclusion of the testimonies, he explained to her that Pickett was simply doing his duty. Policemen had to protect public safety, and Pickett had cause for concern about the size of the crowd that had gathered at the millinery shop. Wearing the attire of the opposite sex in public violated New York law, so Pickett was correct on that count, too. But Acton then ordered Pickett not to arrest Dr. Walker again. "She's smart enough to take care of herself."

With this final admonishment, Mary Walker felt vindicated, and she garnered much public sentiment to her side. A *New-York Tribune* reporter observed, "There is certainly nothing immodest in the costume." The *New York Times* commended the Canal Street desk sergeant for possessing "a small amount of common sense" when he decided the complaint against Walker was "trivial." The paper also derided Justice Mansfield for using his "high position . . . to dictate what shall constitute in future a lady's street costume." An article in the *Brooklyn Daily Eagle* reflected Commissioner Acton's mixed opinion. The doctor was "entitled to every respect as a lady, and to respect for her opinions. As an abstract principle she has a right to dress as she pleases." The reporter then emphasized that Walker had broken the law. "It is a question whether the public should suffer for the gratification of personal eccentricity."

This episode formed the core of the lecture Mary Walker gave at the meeting of the National Dress Reform Association in Syracuse about a week later. Her legal troubles may have been responsible for the convention's robust attendance, nearly eight hundred people. The talk, "forcible and suggestive," began with a detailed account of her arrest and "vindication." She addressed women's suffrage, making two predictions that would fail to come true. First, she believed voting rights would be achieved in ten years, and at the same time, women would start holding many elected offices. Second was her curious assertion that the South would emerge as the driving force for women's suffrage, with more Southern states enfranchising women than their Northern counterparts. Perhaps to avoid being considered too pro-Southern, Walker proposed that former Confederate president Jefferson Davis be forced to wear women's clothing while cleaning a four-story house. She finished with a denunciation of the corset, and urged immediate dress reform "as the only means of preserving the perpetuity of the American nationality."

Concern about safeguarding American nationality did not prevent Mary Walker from striving to make a bigger name for herself. When she received an invitation from the National Association for the Promotion of Social Science to attend its 1866 congress in Manchester, she seized the opportunity. The British group, founded in 1857, sought to improve public health, industrial relations, prisons, and women's education, all topics of interest to the doctor. She expected this visit would raise her international profile and amplify her professional reputation as a doctor and a reformer. It would underscore the fact that she *was* somebody.

Dr. Walker knew she would be something of a curiosity to the British. Dress reform had failed to catch on there, and women still faced obstacles to becoming licensed physicians. Elizabeth Garrett, whom Walker would meet in Manchester, had been denied admission to medical schools in Britain. After attending nursing school, the Englishwoman learned enough to pass the Society of Apothecaries examinations in 1865, and received her medical certification. The society then forbade other women to take the exams, and women were not allowed into the medical profession until 1876.

The Social Science Congress was scheduled for October, but Mary Walker decided to leave a few weeks early, giving her time to tour hospitals in Great Britain. The invitation to the congress did not come with an offer to cover expenses, so she scraped together her own funding. On her behalf, a friend reached out to Daniel H. Craig, general agent of the New-York Associated Press, for help getting her a pass from the ship to travel for free, or an appointment as the ship's doctor. Craig believed it would be pointless to ask because vessels rarely made such accommodations. He admitted he knew of Walker, and said, "I should take great pleasure in assisting her, pecuniarily, if her necessities require it." Her trip, it seems, was financed by generous friends.

Mary Walker had some agreeable company on the *Caledonia* when it set sail to Liverpool in August. Dr. Susannah Way Dodds, an eclectic medical practitioner and devoted dress reformer, was traveling with her husband Andrew, a Scotsman. Susannah Way had been born in Indiana in 1830 and spent most of her teens and early twenties pursuing an education, often interrupted by family duties. After she married Andrew Dodds in 1857 and settled in Yellow Springs, Ohio, she attended and graduated from Antioch College. While her husband served with the Union Army, Susannah Dodds completed her medical degree at the New York Hygeio-Therapeutic College in 1864. She may have met Mary Walker then, and they likely kept in touch after the war. The Doddses were probably among the friends who helped with Walker's travel expenses.

After the *Caledonia* docked in England, the trio traveled to Glasgow, where Mary Walker had arranged to tour the Royal Infirmary. The facility likely intrigued her because of its surgical department, run by Joseph Lister, a pioneer in the use of antiseptics. Susannah Dodds accompanied Walker to the Royal Infirmary and other hospitals in the area, as well as on additional nonmedical sightseeing excursions. In early October, Mary Walker left Scotland for Manchester to fulfill the main purpose of her overseas travel: attending the Social Science Congress.

The general theme that year, "Legislation on Social Subjects," held great interest, and she attended many different sessions. "The Repression of Crime," attended mostly by women, focused on finding the best way to prevent infanticide. Mary Walker, who had established a refuge for women and children in Washington, DC, during the war, contributed to this discussion. Identified as "an American lady" dressed in a Bloomer costume, decorated with a "war service" medal, she claimed that infanticide stemmed from women's desire to hide the sex they had out of wedlock, "and to escape the scorn of their own sex." In other sessions, she talked about dress reform and women's suffrage. Though the doctor did not convince everyone that her reform methods were the best, the *London Globe* pronounced her a *prima donna assoluta*.

Mary Walker was a hit. While the Social Science Congress met, people who read the newspaper coverage reached out, sometimes simply to make her acquaintance. Moncure Conway, an American minister, sent a letter in October while she was still at the congress, complimenting her on the "excellent address" she had delivered. He wanted to meet her. "I am an American and a radical," he explained. Conway, born in 1832 to a socially and politically prominent Virginia family, became an itinerant Methodist preacher in 1851, two years after graduating from Dickinson College in Pennsylvania. He soon embraced Unitarianism, became an acolyte of Ralph Waldo Emerson, and graduated from Harvard's Divinity School.

Moncure Conway worked briefly in Washington, DC, before moving in 1855 to Cincinnati, where his pro-abolitionist views stood out less. In April 1863, he traveled to London at the behest of Northern abolitionists to educate the British on the Union cause. He overstepped his authority when he asserted that American antislavery proponents would stop supporting the war if the Confederacy immediately freed its slaves. US abolitionists disavowed him, and Conway was forced to apologize to the American ambassador in London, Charles Francis Adams. The minister soon accepted a position at the South Place Chapel in London, where he cultivated relationships with other intellectuals, including Algernon Charles Swinburne and C. A. and Maria Rosetti. After reading about Mary Walker, he decided she was worth knowing. It was early November 1866 before they could find a time to meet to discuss topics of mutual interest: "woman, marriage, dress . . . and negro-equality."

Various reform groups, including temperance and suffrage societies, invited Dr. Walker to speak, lectures that provided a comfortable income. The talk that sealed her success—and inspired her to extend her overseas stay for almost a year—took place at St. James's Hall in London on November 20, 1866. Andrew Nimmo, a well-known London theatrical agent, planned the event, which was heavily advertised in British newspapers and by handbills distributed on the streets. Admission was pricey for the time for a lecture by a woman; seats ranged from one to seven shillings. Charles Dickens's appearance two years later generated the same admission prices.

St. James's Hall held over two thousand seats. By the time Mary Walker began speaking at 8:00 that Tuesday evening, she faced a standing-room-only crowd eager to hear "The Experiences of a Female Physician in College, Private Practice and in the Federal Army." A group of medical students, concentrated in the gallery seats, interrupted her several times with shouts and laughter, especially when she talked about dress reform. Andrew Nimmo, who introduced Dr. Walker, had to quiet their boisterous singing even before the speech began. At one point, she sat down for a few minutes until their ruckus stopped, and finally the police took the young men out of the building and arrested them.

Despite the disturbances, the American doctor realized she could make money from an extended speaking tour. Andrew Nimmo did, too, and tried repeatedly to convince her to let him continue as her agent. She declined, irritated that he tried to take more than his contracted share from the St. James's Hall lecture. Mary Walker sifted through advice, both solicited and not, about the quality of her lecture, and worked to tailor it for a British audience. Journalist and lecturer P. F. André sent a lengthy letter on November 21, offering "candid advice" as a thank-you for how much he had enjoyed her talk. It was "too naive" to believe she could describe letting a soldier kiss her, even if he was dying. He also encouraged her not to dwell on the Republican Party and the war, since "people did not come to hear a political lecture."

Press coverage of Mary Walker's public appearances ranged from laudatory to derisive. A particularly vicious attempt to destroy her reputation originated in the United States with an anonymous letter sent by "A Medical Student" to a variety of British newspapers in January 1867. The writer claimed that Walker was a nurse, not a doctor, and included a letter from Dr. Charles H. Crane, assistant surgeon general of the US Army. Crane's letter, however, did not prove the allegation. While Crane acknowledged the outcome of Dr. Mary Walker's 1863 medical board examination, he confirmed she received pay as a "contract-physician." Walker countered this "false" report and others by sharing her own documents attesting to her Medal of Honor and endorsements from doctors she had worked with during the war.

Another attack came from within the United States in January 1867 from the *New York Medical Journal*, which did not support women entering the medical profession. The journal devoted three pages to excerpts from British periodicals that criticized Mary Walker's public lectures. In its introduction, the article described how Walker had created "a heavy sensation in London, but her experiences there, we judge, will not prove among the sweetest of the 'pleasures of memory,' nor will they tend either to advance the cause of which she had voluntarily assumed the championship or add greatly to her individual reputation." The piece closed with a quote from the *Medical Press and Circular*, which "suggests as an attractive subject for her public entertainments, 'Why Not? or, Clitoridectomy and its Uses.'"

Press coverage, both positive and negative, ensured that Mary Walker would continue to receive lecture invitations into 1867. She returned to St. James's Hall in February, this time as a benefit for the Bermondsey Poor Schools, and presented a talk on her "Capture and Four Months' Imprisonment with the Confederates." Among the "fashionable audience" was another group of rowdy medical students who heckled the doctor until the police ejected them.

In the spring of 1867, England's House of Commons debated a bill about political representation and suffrage that would become the Second Reform Act. Like the discussion in the United States about the wording of the Fourteenth Amendment, this bill generated much talk about using the word *male* instead of *person*. In May, political philosopher John Stuart Mill, elected to Parliament in 1865, pushed for the latter, and for the right of women to vote. Organized support for women's enfranchisement was in its early stages. Leigh Smith Bodichon, an educator and artist, established a Women's Suffrage Committee in 1865. Two years later, the Manchester Society for Women's Suffrage formed. In June 1867 at London's Cleveland Hall in Fitzroy Square, Mary Walker chaired a women's suffrage meeting and gave a talk on the link between voting rights and marriage laws. Her lecture followed Harriet Law, a secular freethinker, who spoke about Mill's support for women's suffrage.

To embellish her international reputation and promote dress reform, Mary Walker traveled to France. As numerous newspapers reported in July, she was "just now walking the hospitals of Paris." She was keen to tour medical establishments in the City of Light, but some less-generous reports put it out that the doctor had been "haw-hawed out of London" and was now "exciting the polite curiosity of Paris." Of particular interest to Mary Walker—and some eleven million people—was the Exposition

Universelle, which had opened April 1. Organized by Emperor Napoleon III, the fair highlighted the history of labor and the culture of forty-two countries.

The United States was well represented in each of the ten labor-related exhibition categories. It earned five grand prizes, including one for the US Sanitary Commission, for its use of ambulances and medical instruments for treating those wounded in the Civil War. Surgeon General Joseph Barnes received one of America's seventy-six silver medals for the surgical instruments and hospital apparatus he developed during the war. Mary Walker likely toured these exhibits and took pride in her connection to them. But one of the American displays, which included photographs of Robert E. Lee and other Confederate generals, caused her to lose her temper. She tore at the accompanying card that described Lee in flattering terms. Nelson M. Beckwith, the commissioner general and president of the American commission to the exposition, tried to stop her, explaining his duty to protect the exhibition items. When the doctor ignored him, he took her by the arm and led her from the room.

Mary Walker also flaunted her patriotism at an American Fourth of July banquet held at the Grand Hotel in Paris. Strained relations existed between the United States and France that summer of 1867. In June, the president of the Mexican Republic, Benito Juarez, had ordered the execution of Mexico's emperor, Ferdinand Maximilian. Napoleon III had arranged this position for the Austrian archduke so France could extend its reach in the Western Hemisphere. Napoleon blamed the United States for supporting Juarez, and for pressuring France to remove its troops from Mexico, leaving the unpopular Maximilian at the mercy of the republicans. Napoleon snubbed American achievements at the exposition, and his government tried to prevent the Fourth of July celebration.

The Americans refused to cancel, and three hundred guests showed up, all fashionably attired, but none so spectacularly as Mary Walker. She donned her usual reform dress, but over that she had draped a large sash of stars and stripes, so it appeared she was wearing the American flag. She walked up to the head table and interrupted a long string of toasts with her own a "To our soldiers and sailors." Since Walker abstained from alcohol, she kissed the flag she wore before returning to her seat.

Her appearance at the banquet provoked "a grand ovation from the large crowd of French people collected in the hall."

At the beginning of August, Mary Walker was back in London, preparing for her return to the United States. She considered her time in Paris a success. She had been, one London paper reported, "the object of many courteous attentions on the part of the leading authorities of the hospitals and other influential persons." The American gave "A Farewell Lecture to the Ladies of London, on Ladies' Dress Reform" at three o'clock in the afternoon on August 17, 1867, at the National Temperance League Rooms. The full audience confirmed her popularity.

When she reached home, however, she found she would have to work hard to remain an influential public figure. Dr. Walker had been overseas during a critical year of the women's rights movement. While it had once addressed a broad range of issues, it now focused on suffrage, assuming equality would take root once women could vote. And it was mired in debates about the meaning of citizenship and political loyalties, with racism injecting an ugly dimension.

While Mary Walker toured Great Britain and Paris, the Republican Party had made a strong showing in the midterm elections of 1866, which allowed it to move forward with its version of Reconstruction that focused on citizenship and voting. President Johnson continued to resist, and encouraged Southern states not to ratify the Fourteenth Amendment. Frustrated over the lack of true change in the South, Radical Republicans in Congress devised a reconstruction plan for the former seceded states, and passed it over Johnson's veto, in March 1867. The Reconstruction Act divided the South into five military districts until the states wrote new constitutions acceptable to Congress. Those constitutions had to establish universal manhood suffrage, and the states had to ratify the Fourteenth Amendment before they could be readmitted to the Union.

The national debate over race, gender, and voting rights continued into late 1866, after the midterms. Congressional Republicans drafted a law to provide suffrage to African-American men in Washington, DC. Edgar Cowan, a Republican senator from Pennsylvania who supported President Johnson's lenient approach to the former Confederate states, offered an amendment that removed the word *male* from the bill. The tactic, designed to scuttle the legislation by introducing universal suffrage, also exposed divisions in the Party over support for women's voting rights.

This was not the first time Edgar Cowan, a conservative Republican, had demonstrated an antipathy toward women's rights. He had questioned the wording of the Thirteenth Amendment, which outlawed slavery, because of the term *involuntary servitude*. Cowan believed it could be interpreted to interfere with the right of a husband to claim his wife's services. He opposed passage of the Civil Rights Act of 1866 because its provision about allowing free persons to enter into legal contracts would allow wives to do so without permission from their husbands. Such a liberty violated the long-standing tradition of coverture, under which married women lost their legal rights.

Edgar Cowan had no intention of allowing the federal government to facilitate the goals of the women's rights movement. In December 1866, he anticipated that not even Radical Republicans would support a planned law granting women the right to vote. But his proposed amendment gave a boost to the fledgling women's suffrage movement. Suffrage activists in Washington, DC, converged on the Capitol building, seeking out members of Congress and encouraging them to vote for the amendment to the bill.

Over three days in December, senators debated voting rights for women, but in the end only nine supported Edgar Cowan's amendment. In early 1867, Congress passed the bill in its original form, granting suffrage in the nation's capital to all men over twenty-one. That spring, Josephine White Griffing, who Mary Walker knew through her work with the Freedmen's Bureau, Belva Lockwood, and several other supporters of universal suffrage formed the Universal Franchise Association (UFA). The organization's objective was to "secure equal rights to all American citizens, and especially the right of women to vote." It welcomed male and female members, both black and white, though white women dominated its leadership. The UFA supported the endeavors of Elizabeth Cady Stanton and Susan B. Anthony's American Equal Rights Association (AERA), and vowed to hold public meetings to discuss the benefits of universal suffrage.

Belva Lockwood was a native New Yorker, born in 1830 in Royalton, along Lake Ontario, about 140 miles west of Mary Walker's hometown of Oswego. Like Walker, Belva Ann Bennett McNall Lockwood grew up on a farm with several siblings. She worked in the fields as needed and acquired enough education to become a teacher in a rural schoolhouse. Lockwood's realization that she earned only half of what male teachers did sparked her interest in women's rights, and convinced her to look for another profession.

Unable to find the money for the additional education that would qualify her to do something besides teach, the eighteen-year-old Lockwood married Uriah McNall in 1848. A steady, reliable young man from Royalton, McNall died four and a half years later, leaving his wife with a young daughter to support. Belva Lockwood inherited enough money from her husband's modest estate to fund her studies at the coeducational Genesee College in Lima, New York, graduating with honors in 1857. She accepted a teaching position about eighty miles west at Lockport Union School, and involved herself in several of the town's reform organizations. She met Susan B. Anthony, the temperance and women's rights advocate, and the two worked closely on a variety of issues, including girls' education.

After years of trying—and failing—to create the kind of administrative career she wanted from teaching, Belva Lockwood sent her teenage daughter Lura to boarding school, and in February 1866 she moved to Washington, DC. For a while, she still relied on the schoolroom to earn money. Lockwood began teaching at the Young Ladies' Seminary on 13th Street NW, between G and H Streets. She spent her spare time in the Ladies' Gallery of the Senate chamber, listening to debates on legislation, or at the Supreme Court, hearing oral arguments. She tried, unsuccessfully, to secure a position with the US Foreign Service. She immersed herself in reform organizations, and became particularly attracted to suffrage issues.

Sometime after September 1867, Belva Lockwood met Dr. Mary Walker, likely through the UFA. Soon after returning from abroad, Mary Walker joined both that organization and the American Equal Rights Association. AERA members, although disappointed in the wording of the Fourteenth Amendment, decided not to actively oppose it. Instead, the organization directed its efforts toward state campaigns for universal suffrage. When New York announced it would hold a state constitutional convention in June 1867, Susan B. Anthony coordinated a petition drive to remove the word *male* from the constitution and to abolish its discriminatory property qualifications for black male voters. Though the AERA-backed campaign collected 28,000 signatures, both measures failed.

The AERA also got involved with cultivating support for a pair of suffrage bills—one for African-American men, the other, for women—that had been submitted for a November 1867 referendum in Kansas. Samuel N. Wood, a lawyer and Republican politician, formed the Impartial Suffrage movement, and in early 1867 invited the AERA to promote the twin causes. The organization sent its best speakers, Henry Blackwell and Lucy Stone, to Kansas to assist Wood's endeavors. State Republican leaders favored black suffrage but regarded the inclusion of women's voting rights as a divisive measure. They ignored the work of the Moneka Woman's Rights Association, which backed women's suffrage, and had already secured for Kansas women equal rights in terms of property ownership and child custody, plus the right to vote in school elections.

The recent failure of the New York state legislature to pass women's suffrage had an adverse effect on the cause in Kansas. State Republicans believed chances for women's voting rights in Kansas were nil, and in their determination to secure suffrage for black men, they began to campaign against women. Even the arrival in September of the venerable team of Elizabeth Cady Stanton and Susan B. Anthony achieved little for the women's suffrage cause. Stung by the rejection of their former Republican allies, the two women looked to the Democratic Party. There they found help from some rebel Democrats willing to do just about anything—including supporting women's voting rights—to make the Republicans look bad.

In October, Stanton and Anthony accepted help from George Francis Train, a wealthy Democrat and notorious white supremacist. He bankrolled their speaking tour and funded their short-lived women's rights publication, *The Revolution*. Train was not a silent partner. He shared a podium with Anthony and sometimes cloaked his racism by promoting a literate or educated electorate, which prioritized white women's suffrage. But most of the time he did not bother. Stanton and Anthony's willingness to align themselves with Train cut them off from the Republicans and former abolitionists and drove a wedge into the women's suffrage movement. The executive committee of the AERA, horrified that the duo associated with Train, disavowed their public events. Both Kansas referenda went down in defeat in November.

During the election season, Mary Walker decided to put into action her beliefs about women's suffrage. One was based on history. She interpreted the American Revolution's rallying cry of "No taxation without representation" as a genderless principle. As a property owner and taxpayer in New York State, Walker insisted on her right to cast a ballot. The other was based on current events. Though the Fourteenth Amendment had not yet been ratified, its language had been established. The doctor focused on section one, which outlined citizenship qualifications. She reasoned that being born in the United States made her a citizen, and as such, she was entitled to vote. But when she attempted to cast a ballot in her hometown of Oswego, perhaps the first woman to do so in New York, an election inspector "placed his hand over the box and told me to get out." She protested until another inspector showed her the state law that stipulated only male citizens could vote. Unless she swore an oath that she was a male citizen, she could not vote. Mary Walker refused to perjure herself and abandoned her scheme.

Suffragists later dubbed this tactic the "New Departure." Based on an interpretation of the Fourteenth Amendment, and later, the Fifteenth Amendment, they argued that the Constitution implicitly granted women's voting rights. Suffrage advocates encouraged women to show up at polling places and try to cast a ballot. It was a legal strategy; suffragists wanted to pressure Congress to pass enabling legislation or the courts to weigh in on the matter. Mary Walker believed congressional action would suffice, and she pushed for that for decades. In a few years, though, the Supreme Court would settle the legal question at the heart of the New Departure.

Mary Walker's ideas about women's suffrage were shaped by the vibrant circle of accomplished women she surrounded herself with. In addition to Belva Lockwood, who was contemplating a career as a law-yer, Walker renewed acquaintances with the major leaders of the wom-en's suffrage movement: Lucy Stone, Elizabeth Cady Stanton, Susan B. Anthony. The doctor also cultivated a cordial, though not close, relation-ship with Clara Barton. The two women crossed paths during the Civil War, and in its aftermath, Barton settled in Washington, DC. The nurse's experiences in the war led to a deep commitment to women's rights, and she became a popular speaker on the subject, often attending Universal Franchise Association meetings.

Suffrage activism in Washington, DC, increased through the spring of 1868, and Mary Walker participated when she was in the city. Belva Lockwood, who married her second husband in March, realized she was pregnant in late May. Unlike other white, middle-class women who cur-tailed their public outings once they knew a baby was on the way, Lock-wood continued her reform activities and remained an influential figure in the UFA. It may have been at her invitation that Mary Walker spoke at the May meeting. She was "the last named speaker, who appeared in bloomer costume, giving account of the progress of [the] female suffrage movement in England, as she observed during a recent visit."

Though pleased to be singled out as an expert on British women's suffrage, Dr. Walker struggled to fit into the American movement. An innovator of the New Departure, which put her on the cutting edge of suffrage tactics, she blundered in dealing with racial issues. Walker had always maintained that she supported universal suffrage, but in early June 1868, she convened a meeting at city hall to form the White Woman's Franchise Association. She never explained why she established this group. Since she took pride in living her principles—as she did with her reform dress—the logical explanation is that she believed, along with Elizabeth Cady Stanton and Susan B. Anthony, that white women deserved suffrage more than black men. About thirty people showed up that night, includ-ing Josephine Griffing and other UFA members. Dr. Walker proposed two resolutions for debate. The first stated "That to deny to white women the right of suffrage is most positively and practically to assert that white women are inferior to black men." The second identified Washington, DC, as a location "suitable for the experiment of doing tardy justice to woman."

Mary Walker chaired the meeting and was elected president. She explained that she wanted to make sure that all Washington women who could read their names and write a ballot "shall have all the rights of a male citizen." In the ensuing discussion, Josephine Griffing said she preferred to have "white" left out of the resolution. Annie Denton Cridge, a British-born writer, spiritualist, and outspoken member of the UFA, was willing to support white women receiving suffrage first, followed by black women. Dr. Walker offered the final remarks of the evening, admitting that "her blood boiled when she heard men talk about the inferiority of women," and stressing that educated women should be able to vote. The meeting adjourned without any action taken on the resolutions.

The White Woman's Franchise Association floundered after that first meeting, and it is not clear a second took place. The justifications Mary Walker put forth that night reached few sympathetic ears. A few days later at a UFA meeting, some of the speakers "took occasion to disclaim connection" with her organization, and "thought its promulgation not calculated to do much good for the sex." Yet when the doctor appeared at the next UFA meeting and spoke in her capacity as president of the White Woman's Franchise Association, she received some applause.

Most of Mary Walker's colleagues in the UFA proved unwilling to engage in such blatantly racist tactics. Julia Archibald Holmes, one of the UFA's officers, wrote to the *Evening Star* in June 1868, to clarify that three women's suffrage groups existed in Washington. The Universal Franchise Association promoted the "advancement of the cause of Suffrage and Education throughout the world." The Equal Franchise Association pursued suffrage for women in the capital city. Finally, the "White Woman's Intelligent Franchise Association," of which "Mrs. Dr. Mary Walker" was president, was a local organization "whose name sufficiently expresses its objects." Such a dismissive description likely cut Walker, especially coming from Holmes, who she must have admired. In 1858, clad in reform dress, Holmes climbed Pikes Peak in Colorado, the first white woman to do so. By later in the summer of 1868, Walker's association dissolved.

In July 1868, the Fourteenth Amendment was ratified. Now the word *male* appeared in the Constitution in connection with voter qualifications. Dr. Walker had demonstrated a willingness to ally with Stanton and Anthony's tactic of pushing for a white educated electorate, but when she realized she had few followers in Washington, she gave it up. She may have worried about losing her closest friends—an unpleasant prospect, especially for a single woman who frequently relied on their generosity. But she had made known her views on race.

During that politically intense spring and summer, Mary Walker also found time for romance, the last one in her life for which any documentation exists. Stephen R. Harrington, a lawyer from Virginia, was prominent enough in the state Republican Party to be selected as one of its delegates to the national Party convention in November 1868. He spent a lot of time in Washington, on business with Congress, and socially, with the doctor. Harrington addressed his letter *"Mon cher ami,"* and alluded to a memorable incident that had occurred four weeks earlier. Responding to a "little missive" he had received from her, detailing some recent activities that might have involved the White Woman's Suffrage Association, he commented, "It shows what one heroic, determined woman can do, armed by justice alone and opposed by law and public opinion." After the flattery came the love. "I would like to see you *very much* this morning,—from my heart, but what is[,] is written, and my wild wandering thoughts must stay."

Stephen Harrington described himself as a man with a "restless brain, spirred [*sic*] on by cold, blind ambition, a heart throbing [*sic*] with warmest impulses,—a conflict that of course achieves nothing and unfits me for companionship even to myself." He lamented these qualities, perhaps hinting that they made him unsuitable for marriage. Harrington wished he "could plant my feet on solid earth, go on wrestling with the present practical realities, and content with to-day's experience and gain." He may not have recognized similar traits in Mary Walker, whose own aspirations were unusual for a woman of her time. Women were not expected to have professions, to engage in public life. Many who did were not married. Walker's negative experience with marriage may have convinced her to remain single. Like "Doc" a few years earlier, Stephen Harrington disappeared from her life.

The struggle between the president and Congress over the scope and progress of Reconstruction ended in 1868. In early February, the House of Representatives voted to impeach President Johnson for violating the Tenure of Office Act when he removed Edwin Stanton from his position as secretary of war. The impeachment trial in the Senate began in March and lasted for about three months. The president cut deals to ensure he would not be convicted, including a promise he would no longer interfere with Reconstruction. On May 26, a single vote saved Johnson from conviction and removal from office. That evening, throngs of well-wishers crowded into the Executive Mansion to congratulate him on his acquittal. He received the Democratic members of Congress first, then some members of the public, including Dr. Mary Walker, "who engaged the President some time in pleasant conversation." As an abolitionist and suffragist, Walker generally supported the Republican Party, but she felt a loyalty to the man who had awarded her the Medal of Honor.

The Democratic Party held its convention in New York City in July, and Andrew Johnson sought the nomination as its presidential candidate for the 1868 election. His popularity among Southern whites was not enough, and Horatio Seymour, a former New York governor, received the nod. Seymour had remained a Unionist during the war, though he often criticized President Lincoln's conduct of it, and he supported Johnson's Reconstruction policies. Susan B. Anthony and Elizabeth Cady Stanton again tried to ally with the Democrats. They attended the convention to present their "Tammany Hall Platform," calling for universal suffrage, but the Democrats refused to endorse it.

Republicans, anxious to hold on to their political power by appealing to as many voters as possible, bypassed the radical contenders in their party and chose a war hero, Ulysses S. Grant. Reformers were wary, especially abolitionists, though many believed the Republican Party was still their best hope for securing civil rights and suffrage. Frederick Douglass endorsed Grant's candidacy. Both the American Equal Rights Association and the Universal Franchise Association encouraged its female members to vote. While hundreds attempted—the women of Vineland, New Jersey, even carried their own ballot box to the polls to underscore the seriousness of their action—none succeeded. Grant won the election in

November, but by an uncomfortably narrow margin, convincing Republicans of the necessity of protecting black men's suffrage—although still not adding women's voting rights—to sustain their political power.

Like many reformers, Mary Walker was wary of Ulysses Grant's commitment to equal rights and women's suffrage. Some remained willing to give him a chance. At a postelection UFA meeting, one of the African-American members predicted that the former general would help the progress of women's suffrage. Walker disagreed, arguing that suffragists should not support Grant "because of his indifference to the 'rights' of woman." Her concern was well placed. In December, congressional Republicans began work on the Fifteenth Amendment, which would explicitly confer suffrage on African-American men. They had the backing of a new organization, the New England Woman Suffrage Association, fronted by the poet and social reformer Julia Ward Howe. The NEWSA stood against Elizabeth Cady Stanton and Susan B. Anthony to support the new amendment, with the understanding that another one, granting women's suffrage, would immediately follow.

This did not seem an unattainable dream. Lucy Stone and other NEWSA members remained committed to universal suffrage, as did some politicians. Indiana congressman George W. Julian proposed that the Fifteenth Amendment read: "The right of suffrage in the United States shall be based on citizenship, and shall be regulated by Congress, and all citizens of the United States, whether native or naturalized, shall enjoy this right equally, without any distinction or discrimination whatever founded on race, color, or sex." After Congress rejected that phrasing in favor of "race, color, or previous condition of servitude" in February 1869, Julian reworded and resubmitted his proposal for women's suffrage as a possible Sixteenth Amendment.

While Congress debated the Fifteenth Amendment, the Universal Franchise Association hosted a suffrage conference, called at the behest of Elizabeth Cady Stanton and Susan B. Anthony, in January 1869 in Washington, DC. By the time it opened, Mary Walker's divorce case against Albert Miller had been settled in her favor during a special session of the New York State supreme court. The court determined that Miller, the defendant, had committed adultery, and as the injured party,

Walker was free to marry again. Although barred from remarrying during his former spouse's lifetime, Miller had, out of New York's jurisdiction, taken a second wife.

Mary Walker was relieved to put it all behind her. The press had gotten wind of the story, and throughout 1868 garbled accounts of the couple's suit and countersuit appeared in print across the country, almost always making the female doctor look foolish. A Vermont paper, for instance, reported that she wanted "to marry her husband who has been divorced from her several years. Unfortunately he has another wife!"

The topics of marriage and divorce became an integral part of Mary Walker's writings and lectures about women's rights. On January 19, 1869, a week after her divorce case was decided, the National Woman's Rights Convention opened in the capital at Carroll Hall, on 10th Street NW. About sixty people attended, and the elderly Lucretia Mott presided. Dr. Walker took a seat at the front of the room with her friend, Dr. Ellen Beard Harman, who she met at the Hygeio-Therapeutic College in New York City. Harman lived in Illinois with her husband, and she wrote frequently on medical and reform topics and served as an officer of the World's Health Association, an eclectic medicine organization. Walker and Harman, both attired in reform dress, attracted much attention. Sara Jane Clarke Lippincott, a popular author who used the pen name Grace Greenwood, disparagingly described Walker's bloomers as "emancipated garments."

Mary Walker was one of the scheduled speakers. She began with a statement reminiscent of her reason for starting the White Woman's Suffrage Association. She told the audience she "had labored, suffered for the colored man, the white man and the women, but she was not willing to see another man made a voter until the whole female population of this country was enfranchised." She then launched into the part that elicited hisses from others on the stage and prompted Lucretia Mott to ask her several times to stop. Dr. Walker recounted the details of her divorce case, "more entertaining than instructive," according to one reporter. She continued her "long-winded dissertation" of the "hardships and sufferings of her sex, caused by inhuman man, as experienced at the hands of her husband" until several people left the hall, "so indecent was the language used by her in relating her grievances."

Most published reports portrayed Mary Walker in a negative or condescending light, if they covered her contributions to the conference at all. Sara Jane Lippincott's account, reprinted in many contemporary newspapers, was then included in the *History of Woman Suffrage*, Stanton and Anthony's mammoth undertaking to document the movement. That version nearly erased Walker. Lippincott did not mention her speech at all. After the snide reference to Walker's clothing, Lippincott may have been targeting the doctor when she denigrated "certain anomalous creatures, in fearful hybrid costumes, who, a-thirst for distinction, and not possessing the brain, culture, or moral force to acquire it, content themselves with a vulgar notoriety, gained by the defiance of social laws, proprieties, and decencies, by measureless assumption and vanity, and by idiotic eccentricity of dress."

Mary Walker made many of the suffrage leaders uncomfortable. During this 1869 convention they began to sideline and marginalize her, mostly because of her reform dress and for her critiques of marriage and divorce. She also spoke up about racial issues again, although this did not necessarily put her out of step with other white suffragists. During a discussion of a resolution, she stated, "A *man's* government is worse than a *white* man's government; because, as you increase the number of tyrants, you make the condition of the disfranchised class more hopeless and degraded." She also objected to Dr. Charles Purvis's comment that white women were "the bitterest enemies of the negro." Walker wanted to know what white women had done to African Americans. George Downing, another black delegate, pointed out women's contributions to the brutality of enslavement. When the female doctor insisted that none of the women at the convention had done such things, the men had to agree.

The resolutions passed at the end of the conference delineated the meaning of the postwar movement. First, suffrage should be accompanied by the right to hold public office. Second, women and African Americans should be able to "choose their own occupations, and be paid always equally with men for equal work." Finally, suffrage should be based on "loyalty and intelligence, and nowhere be limited by odious distinctions on account of color, people or sex." If Mary Walker had any designs on a leadership role in the suffrage movement, this 1869 meeting showed how difficult that would be. Though she had been elected as one of the convention's vice presidents, she did not find a way into the inner circle that Elizabeth Cady Stanton and Susan B. Anthony increasingly controlled.

The generally positive responses to the gathering propelled Washington, DC's, suffrage movement forward, giving Mary Walker hope for a chance to carve out a local leadership role. She had the opportunity to spend additional time with Stanton, Anthony, and Lucretia Mott, who remained in the capital for a few more days. Walker joined them at a meeting of the Universal Peace Union, an organization Mott had cofounded in 1866 with Philadelphia reformer Alfred H. Love. Walker must have been pleased when she was asked to speak along with Stanton and Anthony.

The Universal Franchise Association, which had decided to disband after organizing and hosting the national suffrage meeting, was revived, and a new suffrage organization for Washington, DC, women was founded. Activists still hoped in January 1869 that Congress would give women in the capital voting rights. It had already done so for black men, and for over a month, the Senate had discussed women's suffrage. But with progress on the Fifteenth Amendment stalled in Congress in early 1869, suffragists worried that support would evaporate. They intensified their efforts to make sure this did not happen.

On January 22, 1869, about a hundred women gathered at Union League Hall to talk about the best ways to secure women's suffrage and women's social and civil rights. Belva Lockwood called the meeting to order, and several women, including Susan B. Anthony and Mary Walker, gave speeches. Although the women agreed they must act, working out the details took up most of the meeting. Walker once again found herself at odds with the other leaders. Lockwood proposed that this new group accept only women as members, but Walker "advocated a meeting of the women and men of the District that the objects of the movement might be explained." When she moved the establishment of a committee to plan a new organization, Anthony opined that this was premature, and the motion failed. Walker then started to talk about unjust laws, and Lockwood called her to order. "With sharpness," the doctor responded, "I am very sorry that I am such a disturbing element here, for it seems that whenever I rise to speak everybody else has desire to speak also."

Before the meeting adjourned, the women agreed on a system for canvassing to secure signatures for petitions in favor of women's suffrage that would be presented to Congress. They met twice the following week, beginning on January 28, the day Republican senators Roscoe Conkling and Samuel Pomeroy raised the topic of women's voting rights in the Senate. These meetings led to the creation of the Central Woman's Suffrage Bureau (CWSB), which combined Mary Walker's canvassing strategy with Susan B. Anthony's proposal for an agency to provide women with information about suffrage and equal rights. Universal Franchise Association members dominated the CWSB, but Belva Lockwood was largely absent during its early months. She had given birth to a daughter on January 28, and the newborn kept her busy.

Mary Walker attended these founding meetings of the CWSB, speaking at both. During the first, she clarified her views about the opposite sex. She did not believe all men were bad; rather, "There were many noble men, but there [are] too many ignorant ones." She found one right in the Union League Hall, who asserted that when the state of New Jersey temporarily granted women's suffrage in the Revolutionary period, only "disreputable" women had voted. The doctor challenged him about what made them disreputable, and the room erupted with a variety of opinions.

The next day's meeting revealed the persistent divisions within the women's suffrage movement. As CWSB members worked out the particulars of canvassing, Mrs. Hathaway, a woman from Boston who presided over the session, urged everyone to read and circulate women's rights publications, including Stanton and Anthony's *The Revolution*. Many women raised concerns over that paper's ties to George Francis Train and the Democratic Party, but Hathaway defended it, approving of its "course." Mary Walker spoke up in favor of the planned ward meetings that would facilitate the petition canvasses, then addressed the topic of universal suffrage. "As to the negro question," a reporter wrote, "she was not in favor of another person, be he negro, Indian, Hottentot, or otherwise, being granted a vote before the women."

In February 1869, Congress finally passed the Fifteenth Amendment and sent it to the states for ratification. The lengthy debates over scope and wording produced language that most reformers found anemic: "The right of citizens of the United States to vote shall not be denied or abridged by the United States or by any State on account of race, color, or previous condition of servitude." The Stanton and Anthony branch of the suffrage movement considered it a travesty for leaving out women. Mary Walker, too, must have been unhappy, since the amendment meant a lot of people would receive voting rights before women. Stanton and Anthony vigorously protested the Fifteenth, and in three months, the suffrage movement would fracture because of it.

In April 1869, Mary Walker appeared at a women's rights conference in Cincinnati, Ohio, with Susan B. Anthony, Lucy Stone, and Mary Livermore, a journalist and reformer who had worked for the US Sanitary Commission during the Civil War. The doctor was back in Washington on April 28 to chair a two-day meeting of the Mutual Dress Reform and Equal Rights Association, which replaced the defunct National Dress Reform Association. The new organization had been founded by Dr. Lydia Sayer Hasbrouck, and Walker served as its president. The two women showed up at the Union League Hall wearing black reform dress, and Hasbrouck delivered the first speech, which was frequently interrupted by a group of unruly young men. The elderly Dr. Ezekiel Lockwood, Belva's husband, periodically restored order by rapping his cane on the floor.

Part of Lydia Hasbrouck's address criticized President Grant for refusing to meet with Dr. Walker until she adopted traditional female attire. Walker was no fan of the new president. Probably in recognition of her Medal of Honor, she had been invited to and attended Grant's inauguration the previous month. Among all the dignitaries present in the Senate chamber gallery, she was the lone woman. She also appeared at the inaugural ball, decked out in reform dress made of green satin. But as much as she disliked President Grant because of his lack of interest in women's rights, she would not be party to spreading lies about him. Walker explained to the assembled that this story about Grant declining to meet with her was a falsehood likely concocted by the press to weaken the dress reform movement.

The second night of the meeting was less somber than the first. Both Mary Walker and Lydia Hasbrouck smartened up their outfits. Walker wore green, with a white shirt and patent leather boots. She must have been pleased to see her friend Belva Lockwood, reentering public life after the birth of her daughter, accompanied by her husband. The rowdy men were there again, but this time Dr. Walker engaged them with humor. They especially enjoyed her demonstration of the health risks of women's traditional dress by using a one-legged skeleton. The meeting adjourned on a cordial note, with Walker satisfied she had made her points.

In May 1869, the uneasy coalition of women's rights activists finally fractured. After a contentious meeting of the American Equal Rights Association in New York City, during which Elizabeth Cady Stanton and Susan B. Anthony intensified their criticisms of the Fifteenth Amendment, they left the organization. They founded the National Woman Suffrage Association (NWSA), which opposed passage of the Fifteenth Amendment because it did not provide for women's voting rights. They advocated for a constitutional amendment on women's suffrage, which they optimistically assumed would be the Sixteenth, and emphasized that the NWSA would focus on suffrage rather than equal rights. In a matter of weeks, the New England Suffrage Association, in an effort spearheaded by Lucy Stone, announced its intention to create the American Woman Suffrage Association (AWSA). This group preferred universal suffrage sanctioned by the individual states, but was willing to prioritize voting rights for black men first, followed by voting rights for women. The AWSA fully supported the Fifteenth Amendment.

Like other suffragists, Mary Walker now faced a question. Which side was she on?

CHAPTER TEN

Outcast and Erased

IN THE GREAT DIVIDE OF THE WOMEN'S SUFFRAGE MOVEMENT, MARY Walker took her own path. She found some acceptable ideas and tactics along with some congenial people in the National Woman Suffrage Association (NWSA) and the American Woman Suffrage Association (AWSA). Dr. Walker interacted with both groups as she rose first to prominence, then notoriety in the movement. Though Elizabeth Cady Stanton and Susan B. Anthony, founders of the NWSA and publishers of *The Revolution*, had national reputations as women's rights advocates, they were not yet national leaders of the movement. Suffragists pursued their goal from too many directions in too many ways during the years after the war to settle on undisputed leaders, or even a single organization.

Mary Walker was one of many women angling for position. In the summer of 1869, she tried to secure it by forging an alliance with working women. She believed she had much in common with them, especially their struggle to earn a decent income. Most of these women toiled in low-wage factory jobs and even lower-paying domestic positions. Dr. Walker had a level of education and training they lacked, which gave her more options. After the war, she chose not to restart a formal medical practice; she traveled too much and had too many other interests. She tried different ways of earning a living. The overseas lecture tour tested Walker's professional speaking abilities and boosted her income, but she wanted to come back to the States. Since she had been employed by the army during the war, she figured the federal government would be eager to hire her for a peacetime position. First, she tried the State Department, then the Post Office and the Treasury. Despite the doctor's many contacts and supporters in Washington, DC, none of these hoped-for appointments came through.

Frustrations with finding a job led Mary Walker to think more deeply about how the lives of all working women would improve if they had the right to vote. She decided to join Susan B. Anthony at the National Labor Congress in Philadelphia in August 1869, to forge a link between the suffrage movement and working women's rights. It was the third such meeting sponsored by the National Labor Union (NLU), founded in 1866 to bring together the 200,000 workers who had formed local unions across the United States. The NLU supported skilled and unskilled laborers as well as farmers, and its major goal was to secure a nationwide commitment by employers to implement an eight-hour workday. Unlike individual local unions of the time, the NLU also tried to address the needs of female and African-American laborers.

Susan B. Anthony had only recently begun organizing working women. She and Elizabeth Cady Stanton recognized that these hundreds of thousands of mostly nonunionized women would make powerful allies in the suffrage cause. Many white middle-class reformers believed the vote was key to all desired change, and Stanton and Anthony assumed that women who worked for wages, regardless of their race or class, would see the franchise in the same way. In September 1868, the duo created the Working Women's Association. The WWA remained small, perhaps about one hundred members, and few actually came from the working class. Moreover, they were not as keen on suffrage as Stanton and Anthony expected. WWA members declined to openly support women's voting rights until their own organization was firmly established.

In mid-August of 1869, Mary Walker and Belva Lockwood issued a call for a meeting of working women at the Union League Hall in Washington, DC, to select a delegate to the National Labor Congress. They may have also been looking to boost the WWA's membership. Four women showed up—including Walker and Lockwood, who were mystified at the low turnout. It may have been because they announced the meeting with only a day's notice. A newspaper reporter suggested that most women who labored during the day did not have the time to spend at evening meetings. One of the attendees played the piano for over an hour, waiting for more people to arrive. When Walker and Lockwood realized no one else was going to show, they made official the already-made decision that Walker would serve as the delegate to represent the women of the capital.

Armed with a letter of introduction written by Belva Lockwood, Mary Walker headed to Philadelphia. The letter identified her as "connected with the Woman's Labor Movement" in Washington, and an "accredited Delegate for the Working Women" of the capital. No one questioned her presence at the National Labor Congress when she arrived on August 16, but Susan B. Anthony received a chilly reception from some of the 150 attendees. A male delegate from the Typographical Union (TU), an organization involved in the printing trade, challenged Anthony's credentials from the WWA. Until the matter was settled, she remained at the meeting as an observer rather than a participant.

The delegates' objection to Susan B. Anthony did not stem from her gender, "[a]s the [National Labor] Union makes no distinction as to color, sex or creed." The congress had also accepted a "representative from the Woman's Suffrage Convention, of Saratoga," prompting a *New York Times* reporter's observation that "there is an attempt being made to mingle together very incongruous elements." But the opposition to Anthony was clear. During a recent printers' strike, "as proprietress of the *Revolution* newspaper," Anthony had hired "rat compositors," or female workers willing to take the places of men who walked off their jobs. Additionally, she encouraged the movement of women into these positions knowing they would replace men because owners could pay them a smaller salary. Therefore, the TU delegate argued, Anthony's Working Women's Association was not a bona fide labor group, and she had no standing at the congress.

The National Labor Congress put the issue to a vote and rejected Susan B. Anthony's credentials. Mary Walker stood by her during the ordeal, offering support and consolation. Anthony received permission to remain, and she and the doctor addressed the congress's female labor committee, arguing that women's suffrage would advance the cause of equal pay for working women. Though the committee accepted this strategy, writing it into its report, the congress refused the proposal linking voting rights with equal pay. Instead, the larger body adopted a version that supported equal opportunity for women and their "rights in every field of enterprise and labor." The WWA folded at the end of 1869, by which time Mary Walker had moved on to other projects. Though she gave up on organizing working women for suffrage, she never lost sight of their needs for medical care and education, contributing to these causes when she could.

Working closely with Susan B. Anthony at the labor meeting may have firmed up Dr. Walker's decision to undertake a lecture tour. The biggest names of the women's movement—Anthony, Elizabeth Cady Stanton, Lucy Stone—toured, and Walker understood this as a mark of leadership. Other women did as well, so she became part of a crowded field, as an "invasion" of female lecturers booked public halls to stump for suffrage, which many people viewed as public entertainment. The doctor did not represent any one group, had her own repertoire, and made her own arrangements, including negotiating her fees. During the first part of her travels, which commenced in September and included parts of the Midwest and the Plains states, she shared the stage with other notable women's rights activists. They all exhorted women to join state suffrage organizations as well as the National Woman Suffrage Association or the American Woman Suffrage Association. From the start, though, Dr. Walker realized the other suffragists did not always welcome her.

Mary Walker began in Cincinnati, which she had visited a few months before, where local women called together the Ohio State Woman's Suffrage Society on September 15 at Pike's Music Hall. The organization attracted a cross section of women's suffragists. Both Lucy Stone and Susan B. Anthony were featured speakers, but because of Mary Walker's emphasis on dress reform, organizers did not want the doctor to speak. According to a local reporter, Walker was "the thorn in the flesh of the manager of the Convention. She was constantly anxious to be seen and heard, and the curiosity-hunting audience making calls for her." However, not all the delegates felt the same. One from Ohio, citing the importance of Dr. Walker's Civil War work, asked that she be allowed to speak. The audience concurred, and she gave remarks twice the following day, "more speaking than was her right," the reporter sourly observed. Most newspaper coverage of the event failed to mention Walker's participation at all.

Mary Livermore, the Illinois reformer who had worked with the US Sanitary Commission during the war, and had recently embraced the suffrage cause, provided her own interpretation of Mary Walker's appearance at the convention. In a letter to the press, Livermore began with a harsh assessment of the "pea-green pantaloon and frock-coated little woman" who "uninvited, unsolicited, and . . . undesired . . . took her seat boldly on the platform." Then she conceded that while Walker's style of dress was unusual, it was not immodest. The Illinoisan acknowledged the annoyance of the organizers over Walker's presumptive action of placing herself in a location equal to Susan B. Anthony and Lucy Stone.

But Mary Livermore stressed that though they disapproved of Mary Walker's reform dress, they believed women had the right to dress however they chose. Livermore criticized the men and boys who followed the doctor along the streets, turning her into a spectacle as she went about her business. Those people, Livermore insisted, "behaved like ninnies." Still, she had little praise for Walker's contributions to the suffrage conference, where she "spoke once or twice, in a manner that lacked magnetism and power, her dress creating a sensation that her speech cannot." Livermore concluded what other women's rights activists had about a decade earlier. Wearing reform dress detracted from important goals of the movement.

Mary Walker convinced few people with her arguments about reform dress, only occasionally making converts. In Cincinnati, at least one young woman, Ida Price, decided to emulate the doctor and wear "semi-male attire" around town. A policeman arrested Price, but not Walker and her companion, Dr. Ellen Harman, who had attracted a crowd of "ill-bred loafers" while they waited for a streetcar. "We should like to know under what statute women are persecuted for wearing a convenient dress," asked the suffragist newspaper *The Revolution*, "that may chance to bear some resemblance to male attire?"

From Ohio, Mary Walker traveled on to St. Louis, Missouri, in October 1869. Missouri's Woman's Suffrage Association planned a large meeting on October 6–7 to coincide with the St. Louis Annual Fair. Delegates from every state were anticipated, and Virginia Minor, the conference organizer and future defendant in a landmark women's suffrage court case, expected Elizabeth Cady Stanton, Susan B. Anthony, and Julia Ward Howe to speak. Dr. Walker arrived on October 2; though not a delegate, one newspaper predicted she "[would] probably attend the convention." Another advised that the event was worth attending to hear Howe and Mary Livermore, but "You will see Dr. Mary Walker squelched if she tries to put in." The people of St. Louis disliked Walker because of her "pantaloons." Much of the press she received from her time in that city repeated the false story that her lecture focused on "the necessity of a law compelling men to marry before they reached the age of forty."

After spending most of October in Missouri, in places like Fulton and Kansas City, Mary Walker moved on to Kansas. She delivered different lectures in different places, usually about suffrage and dress reform, but sometimes on issues of fairness in the law and on health and medical matters. Kansans generally received her well, except for her arrest in the third week of November in Kansas City, Kansas, "for appearing on the street in her usual garb." A policeman hauled the doctor before a local magistrate, who quickly dismissed the case. At least one state reporter found the incident silly. "As it is about the only sensible dress sensible women have adopted in this senseless age, we cannot understand why it is sensible men deride it."

When Mary Walker arrived in Lawrence, Kansas, at the end of November, people were already gossiping about her. She had attracted considerable attention on the train, where the conductor told her she did not have the correct ticket and would have to pay the proper fare. Walker argued with him, stating that she had paid the right amount but apparently did not receive a layover ticket. As the doctor related to a reporter, "she emphatically denies having made use of the epithets accredited to her . . . and adds that, in endeavoring to make people coincide with her way of thinking, she is strictly argumentative." It was not coincidental that Walker chose to focus her Lawrence lecture on the topic, "Blessed are ye when men shall revile you and persecute for righteousness' sake."

Dr. Walker decided not to leave Kansas to attend the first formal meeting of the American Woman Suffrage Association (AWSA) in Cleveland, Ohio, on November 24 and 25, 1869. Carrying out a formal split of the women's suffrage movement, members of the former New England Suffrage Association had created an alternative to Elizabeth Cady Stanton and Susan B. Anthony's National Woman Suffrage Association (NWSA). About a thousand people crowded into the large Cleveland lecture hall Lucy Stone had reserved. The driving force behind the AWSA's creation, Stone had determined to have a group that "shall embody the deliberate action of the State organizations, and shall carry with it their united weight."

The AWSA believed in the power of individual states to decide on voter qualifications. Its members did not oppose the Fifteenth Amendment, still working itself through the ratification process, but argued that federal action had grown out of a national emergency. They did not consider women's suffrage a crisis on par with protecting freedmen's civil rights. Susan B. Anthony attended the AWSA convention and observed the organization's commitment to a state-by-state suffrage campaign. Her request that the association support a Sixteenth Amendment on women's suffrage received no backing. The AWSA also made clear that it would "limit the range of discussion to woman suffrage" and not become involved with other reforms that might taint the suffrage cause with radicalism. Mary Walker, because of her devotion to reform dress and her belief that the Constitution already held the authority for women's voting rights, realized she would not find a welcome home in the group.

While in Leavenworth, Kansas, in mid-December 1869, she received a letter from Mary L. Reed of Port Gibson, Mississippi. A group of ladies in the town had met at the beginning of November and decided they should "form themselves into a sisterhood for the promotion of those interests which should be so dear to every woman, and for which the sex is so nobly battling elsewhere." They wanted to bring in an "eminent lecturer" who could explain women's rights to the group members and the general public. Reed asked Dr. Walker to come to Port Gibson in December to deliver this talk "on account of the eminent position which you hold in the ranks of the supporters of our noble cause." The society would pay $600, and it had already collected $450.

The invitation intrigued Mary Walker. The South lagged behind other areas of the country in its support for equal rights and suffrage, but many of its residents discussed these issues as Reconstruction swept the country. Mary Reed mentioned the necessity of Southern women working with their Northern sisters. If Walker could facilitate that important relationship, she might cement her leadership position in the movement. Anxious to add Mississippi to her lecture schedule, she telegrammed her acceptance to Reed in advance of sending a letter that explained her travel details. Walker promised she could be in Port Gibson by December 28 to meet with Reed's group, and explained that she had postponed other engagements so she could "be at liberty to visit other parts of Miss. and also respond to calls in other Southern states."

It was a hoax. After paying her way to Port Gibson, a trip of nearly seven hundred miles, Mary Walker found no one in the town with the name Mary Reed, and no local women's rights organization. The Port Gibson *Standard* reported that Walker gave a speech anyway, but provided no details of what she said. It identified "the *cause* of the lecture . . . an insatiable thirst for notoriety, and a shrew's determination to be heard." But the rest of the article consisted of a condemnation of the boys or young men who "resolved to have some fun" at Dr. Walker's expense, which was literally considerable. Although Port Gibsonites surely found Walker's promotion of women's suffrage and dress reform distasteful, she had not imposed herself on local affairs. She believed she was responding to a legitimate invitation. "There is and can be no excuse for so scurvy a trick, and it should be condemned, as we believe it is, by this entire community."

Despite this disappointing start to the Southern portion of her extended lecture tour, Mary Walker persevered, determined to overcome whatever apathy and hostility she might face. In Mississippi, she visited Vicksburg and Jackson, drawing tiny audiences in each place. The *Vicksburg Herald* referred to her as the "famous 'man-woman' Mrs. Dr. Mary Walker." She faced similar-sized crowds in small towns in Louisiana in early 1870, but believed she would find more-receptive listeners in New Orleans. With public transportation unavailable through the stretch from Clinton to Bayou Sara, Walker accepted an offer from Captain Thomas Jenks to accompany him on February 3 in his buggy. In the late afternoon, three miles from their destination, armed bandits forced them to stop the vehicle, get out, and throw their money on the ground. The doctor escaped with her life—she prevented Jenks from pulling his pistol on the robbers, who outnumbered them—but she lost about sixty dollars of her hard-earned lecture money.

Newspapers across the country reported on the event. One Pennsylvania publication condemned the attack but held Mary Walker partially to blame. If she "will persist in dressing like a man, she must expect to be mistaken for a man, and sometimes enjoy the inalienable right of being robbed like any other man." Another in Minnesota described the robbery as a "villainous wrong," and opined, "there is nobody in the country but is doubtless sorry that she was not more of a man than she ever pretended to be, that she might somehow have given the scamps their just dues."

Mary Walker remained in New Orleans for a couple of months. During this time, the Fifteenth Amendment was finally ratified, so many people had suffrage on their minds. She found more interest in her lectures but, as usual, they provoked a divided opinion among the population because of her focus on women's voting rights. Though some white Southerners embraced white women's suffrage to uphold white supremacy by countering the votes of black men, the Northern doctor did not include such a racially charged argument in her lectures. She had either abandoned her earlier commitment to securing white women's voting rights before those of black men, or decided, with the passage of the Fifteenth, that the point was moot. On February 16, she gave a noontime lecture on "Men's Rights, Woman's Wrongs" to "an immense array of empty chairs and benches" at the St. Charles Theatre that was described as "droning and monotonous." One New Orleans newspaper lamented, "God help us! It has begun—the invasion of the strong-minded. Already the enemy is lodged within the gates of our city, in the person of Mrs. Dr. Mary Walker, the renowned champion of Woman's Rights."

The local police force targeted Mary Walker, arresting her at least twice when she appeared on New Orleans streets in her reform dress. The charge was dismissed both times, but she complained about her treatment to George L. Cain, superintendent of the Metropolitan Police, asserting her "right to protect herself from the weather by whatever apparel she chose." Cain responded that any lady would prefer to jump in the

Mississippi River rather than wear "that unheard of garb" in public. He was not sure if Walker was really a woman. When she responded that he "would never have an opportunity of knowing," their confrontation escalated, with the doctor's "sarcasms becoming a little more personal." Captain Cain ended their encounter by telling her to leave his office, and warning that every time she appeared in public in her reform dress, "he would lock her up." The doctor swayed enough public opinion to her side by detailing these events in a letter to the editor of the *New Orleans Republican* that the city police did not bother her again.

During the third week of March 1870, the *New Orleans Republican*, perhaps encouraged by the positive response it had received from publishing Mary Walker's letter, sent a reporter to conduct an in-depth interview with her before she left town. It was a lengthy exchange, during which the reporter observed that Walker responded to his questions "with feminine promptness and profuseness." Dr. Walker spoke rather daringly when she criticized people who reduced all the problems between the sexes to sexual relations. "It is perfectly disgusting to see the ideas of sex dragged into everything," she told the reporter. "Women and men should regard each other as human beings and not simply as men and women."

Mary Walker insisted women's suffrage would "do more to elevate the moral condition of the country" than anyone could imagine. She explained that she "[had] been for over twenty years working in the cause of woman's equality with man, and the more I have been oppressed, the more zealous have I become in the cause." The interview concluded with a discussion of dress reform, the cause Walker had been promoting the longest. She defended the Bloomer-style costume on health and hygiene grounds. Many female reformers approved of it but lacked "the moral courage to live out their intelligent convictions." She concluded by saying, "All people are not heroes in all things."

With her women's rights ideology clearly and publicly expressed, Mary Walker headed to Texas, the last destination of her Southern tour. Audiences in the Lone Star State were not always receptive. In late April 1870, B. F. Luce, a cotton merchant in Calvert, wrote to her that his work had kept him so busy, "I have had no leisure to ascertain how the good people of this place would patronize or receive a lecture from you on your favorite theme, 'Woman's Rights.'" Calvert was a new town about 130 miles northwest of Houston, founded after the Civil War, and train service had just been established. Luce believed that Walker would find a "very respectable audience" in Calvert. He wished her "God Speed—And should this great principle, now just beginning to percolate, ever arrive at Maturity, you may justly claim to be its greatest expounder."

At Brenham, Texas, Dr. Walker spoke before a small "select" audience made up of one woman and several men. When she claimed that "before long the white women of Texas would think nothing of marrying negroes, owing to the 'social development'" of Reconstruction, most of the crowd walked out. If she really made this assertion, it is little wonder she often faced hostile whites. Texas state senator Henry R. Latimer arranged for a sheriff at her lecture in the capital city of Austin, stressing that the officer was "simply discharging his Duty," because Latimer wanted to make her "visit as pleasant as profitable."

The Texas portion of the tour ended up being a bit of both, with respectable turnouts in Austin and San Antonio. Next, Mary Walker returned to Washington, DC, where she again decided against fitting the AWSA and NWSA meetings into her schedule. Both organizations met earlier in May on the same day in New York City, forcing suffragists to choose one or the other, rapidly becoming the most powerful women's rights groups in the country. The AWSA's commitment to state campaigns appeared to bear fruit. The territorial governments of Wyoming and Utah wrote women's suffrage into their constitutions, and Lucy Stone and others believed that more states would soon follow. The AWSA, then, gained an early advantage in recruiting followers to its cause.

Yet Mary Walker continued to operate outside both of these organizations, forging her own path to prominence. For the rest of 1870 she traveled between Washington and New York, giving speeches on a variety of reform topics. While in New York City in October, Walker cultivated a new relationship that underscored her radical ideas about women's rights. At least a couple of events brought her to the city. In early October, she attended the funeral service of Admiral David Farragut, riding in one of the procession carriages as his body was taken to Woodlawn Cemetery in the Bronx. The Sons of Temperance invited her to address them at their

Sunday-night services at the Cooper Institute. The audience "vehemently hissed" at one lecture when she brought up the subject of women's rights. At another, Dr. Walker, "attired in her particular style of dress, delivered an entertaining and effective temperance speech."

Her "particular style" attracted considerable attention when she was in New York City. In the midafternoon of October 12, she walked along Broad Street near the Stock Exchange and Delmonico's, wearing light brown pants and a matching coat, with a black bow tied over her lace collar, and a "jaunty jockey hat." Hundreds of men and boys followed Mary Walker, taunting, until she went into the Wall Street office of Woodhull, Claflin & Company, a new brokerage firm run by two sisters, Victoria Woodhull and Tennessee "Tennie" Claflin. The siblings, born seven years apart in rural Ohio, had little formal schooling. Woodhull married at fifteen, divorced her alcoholic husband but kept his name, and remarried in 1866. She and her sister had concocted a traveling clairvoyant act, which facilitated an introduction to millionaire businessman Cornelius Vanderbilt. He became so smitten with Tennie Claflin that he helped the sisters set up their brokerage in January 1870.

Victoria Woodhull used her business notoriety to leverage herself into prominence in the women's rights movement. She received early support from Susan B. Anthony and Elizabeth Cady Stanton, who wrote about her in *The Revolution*. They admired how Woodhull cracked the male bastion of Wall Street, and lauded her embrace of the New Departure. Stanton especially appreciated Woodhull's willingness to talk about divorce reform. With the profits from their brokerage company, in May 1870 the sisters launched *Woodhull & Claflin's Weekly*, a publication that promoted women's suffrage, spiritualism, free love, and Woodhull's political ambitions, including a campaign for the presidency.

Woodhull, Claflin & Company was Mary Walker's destination on October 12, 1870. She had known about the sisters since her return to Washington that spring, and she understood the controversial, radical reputation Victoria Woodhull had already gained. Washington's Central Woman's Suffrage Bureau nearly fractured because some members, including Walker, insisted on endorsing the businesswoman's flamboyant tactics. The doctor concurred with many of Victoria Woodhull's ideas, especially on women's suffrage. Woodhull believed the Constitution already extended voting rights to women; Congress only had to pass enabling legislation. Like Walker, she supported divorce reform. The women had much to talk about, and Mary Walker remained in the Wall Street office for an hour, likely honing her ideas about women's rights and suffrage.

Though Mary Walker did not agree with the basic tenet of the American Woman Suffrage Association—state-by-state campaigns to secure women's voting rights—she attended its convention in Cleveland on November 22–23, 1870. She approved of the AWSA's broader commitment to universal suffrage, and participated in a debate on whether the Constitution already provided women's suffrage. Lucy Stone said that while she believed this about the original Constitution and the Fourteenth and Fifteenth Amendments, "there was great doubt" that women would receive voting rights based on them, and "thought it best to seek also for a XVI Amendment." Dr. Walker weighed in: "The fact of women attempting to vote in Washington had done more for woman suffrage than all the Conventions ever held. We want a declaratory law . . . passed by the Congress of the United States, giving women the right to vote." This, she believed, would save all the effort that would have to go into state campaigns.

At the beginning of the new year the doctor was in New York City again, attending the annual meeting of the Woman's Suffrage Society, a state organization dedicated to eliminating the word *male* from the Constitution. Although Mary Walker did not give a speech, she was singled out in press accounts, along with "other feminine celebrities." In the meantime, Victoria Woodhull went to Washington to address the Judiciary Committee of the House of Representatives. She circulated a version of her argument, based on the legal analysis written by Virginia and Francis Minor, to Congress ahead of her January 11 appearance before the committee. Belva Lockwood, Susan B. Anthony, and several other suffragists accompanied her. Though the Judiciary Committee overwhelmingly rejected Woodhull's proposal, it gave Lockwood ideas for future actions in Washington, DC.

By early February 1871, Mary Walker found herself linked to Victoria Woodhull, not always in the most flattering way. An unexpected criticism came from *The Independent*, a weekly magazine published in New York City that supported abolition and women's suffrage. Now under the editorship of its founder, Henry C. Bowen, it condemned any interpretation of the Constitution that allowed for women's voting rights. Bowen considered this "impolitic," and an ill-advised shortcut. Only the courts could determine the meaning of the Constitution, not individuals. People like George Francis Train, Victoria Woodhull, and Mary Walker "keep up a perpetual flutter, and are always seen first. They are often thought to be leaders because they persist in walking in front."

Buried at the end of the article was the other reason Victoria Woodhull and Mary Walker were ostracized by Henry Bowen and many women's suffrage supporters. "It is of the utmost importance that the real leaders of the movement let it be understood that Woman Suffrage is not on deposit in Mrs. Woodhull's office, and that it has no relationship near or remote to anybody's doctrines of divorce." Both Woodhull and Walker considered divorce a core component of women's rights and equality under the law. Most suffragists, especially those allied with the AWSA, did not want any other causes, especially one as controversial as divorce, to taint their efforts on behalf of voting rights. But neither Woodhull nor Walker backed down.

As Mary Walker worked through her ideas about the Constitution, she pushed for congressional support for women's suffrage, even a limited version. In February 1871, while she assisted former Civil War nurses in their quest for pensions, she linked war service to equal rights and voting rights. The doctor petitioned the House of Representatives to provide "the women who labored for the sick and wounded, during the late war, and grant unto them the same bounties, the same grants of land, and the same pensions that the United States is giving to the men who served Government as soldiers." Ohio congressman William Lawrence presented the petition, which also asked that suffrage "not be denied any of the women citizens of the U.S. or Territories, who labored 90 days, in hospitals for the sick or wounded of the late war." The House forwarded the document to the Committee on Invalid Pensions.

Understanding the power of the written word to promote her causes and her leadership abilities, Mary Walker turned the many lectures she had delivered over the years into a book-length manuscript. Advance notices of the book, titled *Hit*—a reference to the verbal assaults female reformers routinely faced when they took their messages public—began appearing in newspapers in late 1870. A female correspondent from the Boston *Courier* met Walker on a night train from New York to Washington in early March 1871. The doctor had overheard the reporter and her companion, still wide awake from cups of coffee, talking about the printing business in the United States and England. Walker joined them, explaining that she was very interested in the topic because she was about to publish a book. She told them it was about women's rights, and seemed offended they did not know who she was. "Well, we know her now," the reporter wrote. "Steadily and incessantly, volubly and incoherently did that woman talk on politics, religion, literature, physics, and metaphysics and every other known subject."

The American News Company in New York published *Hit* that spring. Its eight chapters—love and marriage, divorce, religion, temperance, tobacco, suffrage, work, and dress reform—explored different facets of women's rights. Mary Walker's overarching argument was that women needed to be self-sufficient and develop their strengths before committing to a marriage truly equal in nature. Despite her own failed marriage, she still believed in it as a viable, important institution that nevertheless required reform. *Hit* garnered a wide-enough readership that year to further solidify Walker's standing as one of the most well-known leaders of the women's rights movement.

The Central Woman's Suffrage Bureau had a busy spring during 1871 as Congress debated allowing home rule in Washington, DC. Mary Walker and Belva Lockwood, inspired by Victoria Woodhull's House Judiciary Committee appearance, considered this an opportune time to once again raise the issue of voting rights. They drafted a universal suffrage amendment to the bill, and when that failed, the CWSB launched a petition drive for female voter registration. Members collected some sixty signatures, including those of Josephine Griffing, journalist Sara Lippincott, popular novelist E. D. E. N. Southworth, and two African-American women, Amanda Wall and Mary Anderson. In an April 14 event that "created a decided sensation in the city," Walker and Lockwood led a "large delegation" of women to city hall and presented the petition to the chief registrar. Lockwood, who had recently enrolled in law school, hoped to find legal grounds to force a court decision on women's suffrage.

Mary Walker and the others startled all the men who had come that day to sign up to vote, especially when they saw the women "each carried a bouquet for the gallant clerk who should register her." As the women filled out the forms, the doctor explained to the men in the room, "These women have assembled to exercise the right of citizens of a professed-to-be republican country, and if you debar them of the right to register, you but add new proof that this is a tyrannical government, sustained by force and not by justice." Underscoring the language of the American Revolution, Walker charged, "As long as you tax women and deprive them of the right of franchise, you but make yourselves tyrants." The registrar accepted the completed forms from the women but did not record them.

The action did not secure voting rights for DC women. Though blocked from registration, they tried to cast ballots in the April 20 local elections and were turned away. In May, Mary Walker spoke at an NWSA meeting about these events, where her efforts were lauded by Victoria Woodhull, Susan B. Anthony, and Isabella Beecher Hooker. Now in her late forties, Hooker, half-sister to popular novelist Harriet Beecher Stowe, had become interested in women's rights after reading works by John Stuart Mill, and took on a leadership role in the NWSA. These women were disappointed when, later in that summer of 1871, the Supreme Court in Washington, DC, rejected the suffragists' arguments—that "natural rights" and the Fourteenth and Fifteenth Amendments conferred voting rights on women. It was a blow to the New Departure strategy, but activists did not give up. An appeal was in the works, with at least one other major suffrage case on the horizon.

Mary Walker continued to cultivate an association with Victoria Woodhull, though the two women did not agree on all points of women's rights. While in Oswego during the summer of 1871, Walker established a Victoria League to support Woodhull's candidacy in the 1872 presidential election. The doctor also maintained ties with the NWSA, though during the January 1872 convention in Washington, DC, they showed signs of strain. Still considered important enough to merit a place onstage, Walker nonetheless provoked divided opinions about her views on women's suffrage. She spoke on the evening of January 10, first correcting Elizabeth Cady Stanton, who introduced her as Mrs. Walker. Then she criticized Woodhull for advocating a new Constitution that would eliminate the executive and legislative branches of government. "No, the [C]onstitution is as ever," the doctor insisted.

On the morning of the second day of meetings at Lincoln Hall, when Mary Walker took her place on the platform, she was "greeted as no other woman . . . by a confusion of cheers and hisses." After listening to speeches about the failure of Republicans and Democrats to support women's suffrage, and about Victoria Woodhull's contributions to the cause, she moved forward to speak in defense of Congress, claiming it had been unjustly criticized. Susan B. Anthony cut her off, saying it was time to adjourn the meeting. Walker pleaded for five minutes, but Anthony insisted on breaking for lunch. One reporter observed the various factions evident among the convention delegates, with the doctor "the most thoroughly abused of the entire lot."

The NWSA appointed a committee, including Stanton, Anthony, Woodhull, and Isabella Hooker, to appear before the Senate Judiciary Committee, currently meeting in Washington. Dozens of women flocked in the hallways, trying to press into the committee room, until Capitol police were called for crowd control. When it seemed that most of the women would be prevented from attending the proceedings, Mary Walker, who also turned up, encouraged the women to "stand just where you are—don't budge an inch." She took a position at the committee room door, making sure as many women as possible got in. Hooker spoke first, outlining the New Departure argument for the senators, and she presented them with a book containing about six thousand signatures from women, asking for their rights. Stanton and Anthony followed, expanding on Hooker's argument. Belva Lockwood delivered a petition from DC women requesting the right to vote. Senator Lyman Trumbull, a Republican from Illinois, and the rest of the committee then moved to a closed meeting, promising they would let the suffragists know the result of their deliberations.

Mary Walker tangled with Isabella Hooker on January 24 at a meeting with the House Judiciary Committee. The doctor and Belva Lockwood arranged to present a 35,000-signature suffrage petition through committee member Benjamin Butler. A former major general of the Union Army, Butler currently represented Massachusetts's fifth district in Congress, and was a staunch proponent of civil rights and women's suffrage. Hooker showed up to inform Butler that Walker and Lockwood were acting without authority from the NWSA. In fact, Hooker claimed that Lockwood had taken the petition from Josephine Griffing, who intended to submit it to the NWSA first. "Dr. Mary Walker jumped to her feet and declared it was all right, and Mrs. Hooker was mistaken." Lockwood told Butler that the women looked to him as a leader of their cause, and he said he was honored and would present their case to the House.

The election of 1872 further marginalized Mary Walker from the mainstream women's suffrage movement. Though she had founded a Victoria League to support Victoria Woodhull's candidacy, she knew the female broker had no chance of winning. It was a symbolic gesture. In May 1872, in a move that alienated Susan B. Anthony and endeared her to Elizabeth Cady Stanton, Woodhull organized an Equal Rights Party to challenge the Republican Party. That new political party nominated Woodhull as its presidential candidate, with Frederick Douglass as the vice presidential candidate, an honor he never acknowledged.

Mary Walker chose to support Horace Greeley for president. The owner and editor of the *New-York Tribune* had helped found the Republican Party and championed many nineteenth-century reforms, including abolition and women's rights. But he did not favor women's suffrage, which, of course, made him a problematic politician for many suffragists. Walker approved of Greeley's support for Radical Republicans, and shared his disenchantment with the corruption of Ulysses S. Grant's administration. Both the Liberal Republican Party and the Democrats, in their attempts to unseat Grant in the 1872 election, nominated Greeley as their presidential candidate. This election marked the beginning of Mary Walker's turn toward the Democratic Party.

As suffragists—mostly those aligned with the NWSA—planned to implement the New Departure in force, Victoria Woodhull complicated their chances for success, and her own, as well, when she used *Woodhull & Claflin's Weekly* to expose an alleged affair between minister Henry Ward Beecher, half-brother of Isabella Beecher Hooker, and his parishioner, Elizabeth Tilton. Woodhull pointed out the hypocrisy of the sexual double standard by revealing the intimate life of the popular Beecher, first president of the AWSA and one of the most influential religious figures of the nineteenth century. Not only was Tilton a member of his congregation, she was also the wife of his best friend.

Because of Victoria Woodhull's connection with suffrage and because she identified Elizabeth Cady Stanton as the source of her information about the Beecher-Tilton affair, the movement became tainted with free love, still generally viewed as immoral behavior. And Woodhull was stung by the same double standard she tried to erase. Many people blamed her for publicizing the affair rather than Beecher for carrying it out. The minister's criminal adultery trial resulted in a hung jury, and the Congregational Church exonerated him of the charge. Woodhull was arrested on New York State obscenity charges; the NWSA ostracized her; and, after a brief speaking tour in the West and the Midwest, she moved to England in 1877.

Despite this cloud hanging over their movement, suffragists deployed the New Departure during the 1872 election season, encouraging women to register to vote and cast ballots on Election Day. They hoped to force either Congress or the courts to act on women's suffrage. Though women did not turn out in the large numbers the suffragists had hoped for, the courts were compelled to weigh in on the ideology behind the New Departure. One case was immediately high-profile; the other took two years to make its way to the US Supreme Court.

"Well, I have been & gone & done it!!—positively voted the Republican ticket," Susan B. Anthony wrote to Elizabeth Cady Stanton from Rochester, New York, on November 5, 1872. On the Friday before the election, Anthony and fifteen other townswomen had successfully registered to vote, inspiring dozens more in Rochester to do the same. City officials, concerned with the legalities, warned election officials of the consequences of allowing illegal voting. Still, Anthony and the other women of the eighth ward managed to have their ballots accepted and counted on Election Day. Newspapers across the country picked up the story.

At the end of November, a deputy marshal arrived at Susan B. Anthony's home to arrest her for illegal voting, a violation of an act of the US Congress. Arrest warrants were served on the other fifteen women, including three of her sisters. Under questioning, Anthony admitted she had voted to test the question of whether women's suffrage was allowed under the Fourteenth Amendment. Anthony would go on trial the following June; the government selected hers as the representative case. Free on bail, she spent the intervening months lecturing about her situation, hoping to sway public opinion to her side.

Because of this extensive publicity, the June 1873 trial was moved to Canandaigua, about thirty miles from Rochester. The jury consisted of all white men, many of the same social standing and with the same level of education as Susan B. Anthony. After hearing testimony, the judge, to everyone's astonishment, directed what appeared to be a sympathetic jury to find Anthony guilty. Before the judge pronounced sentence the next day, the suffragist took the opportunity to have her say. "I am degraded from the status of citizen to that of a subject," she said, as "all of my sex are by your honor's verdict, doomed to political subjugation under this so-called form of government." She refused to ask for leniency, but instead, requested that the "full rigors of the law" be applied. She received a fine of one hundred dollars, and vowed to "never pay a dollar of your unjust penalty." By refusing to compel her, the judge cut off her chance for appeal. Susan B. Anthony's case would not go to the US Supreme Court.

Virginia Minor's did. In 1869, the Missouri suffragist, along with her lawyer husband Francis, devised the interpretation of the Constitution, based on the first section of the Fourteenth Amendment, that served as the ideological foundation of the New Departure. In mid-October 1872, Virginia Minor attempted to register to vote in St. Louis. When her district's registrar, Reese Happersett, refused the application because of her gender, her husband filed a civil suit against Happersett on her behalf. As a married woman, Virginia Minor lacked standing in the Missouri courts to sue on her own. The Minors argued that women had been guaranteed citizenship rights under the Fourteenth Amendment, which does not give the states any power to prevent a citizen from voting.

After losing in a lower court in 1873, the Minors appealed to the Missouri State Supreme Court, which declined to overturn the original ruling. The clear intention of the Fourteenth Amendment, the higher court decided, was to protect the voting rights of African-American men. Francis Minor took the matter to the US Supreme Court, where he claimed that denying women the right to vote in individual states was a matter of practice rather than law. The Supreme Court rejected this argument in a unanimous decision handed down in 1875. The court found no natural link between citizenship and voting rights, and it reaffirmed the power of the states to decide which of their inhabitants could vote.

Mary Walker would have closely followed both cases. She had adopted the New Departure before it even had a name, and she continued to urge women to cast ballots at every election. To help the cause along, she wrote a pamphlet that she published in January 1873 as the "Crowning Constitutional Argument." Unlike Susan B. Anthony and Virginia Minor, who wanted the courts to settle the matter, Dr. Walker believed Congress needed to pass enabling legislation to clarify women's voting rights. To support another amendment to the Constitution, she maintained, only denied women's citizenship status.

Addressed to the members of the Senate and the House of Representatives, the pamphlet's argument was based more on a wishful reading of the Constitution and American history than on facts. Mary Walker claimed that since the Constitution opened with "We the people" rather than "We the men," the Founding Fathers meant to promote gender equality in the new government. She also provided an inaccurate explanation of the circumstances that surrounded the brief time in the Revolutionary period when some New Jersey women received voting rights.

Dr. Walker sent advance copies of the pamphlet to two old acquaintances, Radical Republican senator Charles Sumner and Chief Justice Salmon P. Chase. She used their positive responses to promote the "Crowning Constitutional Argument," which many newspapers covered, and it went through at least eight printings. She circulated the tract among her reform acquaintances, too. Dr. Preston Day, who Walker may have met during the war, wrote to her and provided Angelina Grimké Weld's mailing address, and suggested additional names as likely sympathetic recipients. Day praised Walker—"Your mission is good"—but predicted that "The Republican Party will probably deny you; the 'Liberals' are sure to reject you; the politicians will wait for the *voters* to push them on." He saw a "long and tedious process of agitation and teaching" ahead before women would be able to vote.

Timed to garner maximum publicity, Mary Walker arranged to present her argument to Congress on January 15, 1873, the day before the NWSA convention opened. Her attendance at the suffrage meeting, held in Washington, DC's, Lincoln Hall, provoked more than the usual amount of controversy. Elizabeth Cady Stanton and Susan B. Anthony— the latter out on bail since her November 1872 arrest—resented all the attention heaped on Walker. Anthony expected the spotlight because of her current legal predicament, and she and Stanton still hoped the court would side with Anthony. But if Anthony's case failed, they wanted the NWSA to reevaluate the New Departure strategy. It was one thing to encourage women to flock to polling places to force the issue of voting; it was quite another for them to knowingly break the law. If Anthony lost her case, the NWSA would instead focus its energies on a campaign for a constitutional amendment.

Mary Walker publicized her "Crowning Constitutional Argument" to boost the momentum of the New Departure, challenging Stanton and Anthony's leadership in the process. Walker's name was listed among the NWSA speakers in 1873, but according to one reporter, she was "an unwelcome intruder . . . who insisted upon being heard." Walker also took a seat on the stage, and Anthony tried to diminish her importance by inviting all interested parties to do the same. Another reporter repeated the intruder comment and observed, "There seems to be a disposition of the women composing this convention to ignore Dr. Mary Walker . . . and some of them expressed regret that she should make herself so conspicuous." The doctor was "told very decidedly that the convention . . . could do without her company."

Not everyone wanted to do without Mary Walker at the meeting. Enough calls came from the floor for her to speak about her constitutional argument that she took the podium. After a brief recitation, she asked the convention for an official motion of thanks to Kansas senator Alexander Caldwell, who had presented her pamphlet to Congress. When Susan B. Anthony called "Miss" Mary Walker's motion to a vote, the doctor insisted on being addressed by her proper title. It was probably with considerable frost that Anthony responded, "Oh, I beg pardon—Dr. Mary Walker." The motion carried. The next day, some NWSA members asked her privately not to sit on the stage, but she ignored them, earning some applause when she belatedly entered.

When one speech ended, Mary Walker took the floor without first being recognized, though Susan B. Anthony hastily introduced her. Walker claimed she was being ostracized because she knew more than most of the organization's leaders and had accomplished more than they had. She accused Anthony of having sworn she was a "male" so she could vote in the last election. Walker then launched into a criticism of the NWSA and its leaders, chiding them for abandoning dress reform, for not supporting the racial civil rights outlined in the Fourteenth and Fifteenth Amendments, and for failing to understand exactly how the Constitution already provided women's voting rights.

The speech drew both applause and hisses. "As much as I have done for the cause of woman suffrage," Mary Walker told the audience, "I shall continue to work in the same direction—even for you who hissed, for you need it more than anyone else." Anthony declined to respond to any of the doctor's assertions. Elizabeth Cady Stanton, not present at that daytime session, later commented privately to a friend, "I endured untold crucifixion at Washington. I supposed as I sat there I looked patient & submissive, but I could have boxed Mary Walker's ears with a vengeance." Instead of resorting to physical violence, Stanton wrote Walker out of the NWSA's official convention report, a tactic Anthony did not support.

The "long and tedious process of agitation and teaching" Preston Day had predicted settled in, with Mary Walker lacking the support of both the largest women's suffrage organizations and many of the most influential women in the movement. She knew about Elizabeth Cady Stanton's slight with the convention report, which she considered "a clear case of jealousy and petty spite, unworthy of her sex." Walker claimed that Stanton and Anthony "would see woman's suffrage postponed ten years rather than have the honor of success crowning with its laurel wreath any other brow" than their own.

Mary Walker's insistence on living out her principles by wearing reform dress interfered with her ability to secure a federal job. During the spring of 1873, she set her sights on a clerkship in the Treasury Department. It would provide a steady income while allowing time in the evening to occasionally treat patients and to continue writing and speaking. The doctor knew Francis Spinner, Treasurer of the United States, and knew he had hired female employees during the Civil War. When the appointment failed to materialize, she set up camp in the East Room of the president's Executive Mansion, vowing to remain until she received a job. President Ulysses S. Grant capitulated and promised her work if she swore never again to occupy the building.

Grant extracted the promise before telling Mary Walker she would have to wear traditional women's attire at the workplace. She accepted the clerkship, with its $1,200 annual salary, but the doorkeepers at the Treasury Building refused her access because of her reform dress. Undaunted, she reported for work almost every morning wearing her bloomers, and each time she was turned away. The doctor likely did not attract much public sympathy. She was attempting to convince Congress to pay her a $10,000 settlement for the health problems she continued to suffer as a result of her wartime work. Most Americans knew she had received a physician's pay during the war and saw this request as a "humbug and a nuisance." In January 1874, Walker began receiving a modest pension of $8.50 a month because of the damage she sustained to her eyesight while a Confederate prisoner.

This news may have helped to soften the reports Mary Walker read about the upcoming NWSA convention. The hostilities against her that surfaced during the 1873 meeting had not lessened. When she announced she would "make one of her usual eloquent and learned addresses" at the 1874 meeting, Professor J. K. H. Willcox, a journalist and well-known reformer in both Washington, DC, and New York City, sent a note to one of the DC newspapers. It contained an "awful warning" that if the doctor tried to do so, "there will be a row; that, in fact, the base minions of the law will be called in to squelch her." Willcox insisted that Walker had no "standing" in the women's suffrage movement.

The NWSA members convened in Washington, DC, at the Union League Hall in mid-January 1874 without Mary Walker. One reporter described the proceedings as a "cross between a mutual admiration society and an indignation meeting. Dr. Mary Walker and her irrepressible pantaloons appears to have been, this time, temporarily repressed." Suffragists had much to be indignant about. Susan B. Anthony talked about her arrest and conviction for illegal voting. Without identifying her by name, Anthony refuted Walker's allegation from last year that Anthony had sworn she was "male" in order to cast her ballot. The older suffragist insisted she took an oath that she was a citizen. She then urged "every woman should get her ballot into the ballot-box wherever she can find a judge of election who will receive it." Anthony also encouraged women who owned taxable property to refuse to pay the tax until they had the right to vote. The convention resolutions focused on appeals to Congress to change national laws, including amending the Constitution.

Mary Walker could not stay away from the next year's convention. Determined to air her grievances over her treatment by Elizabeth Cady Stanton and Susan B. Anthony, she showed up at Lincoln Hall on January 14, 1875, the first meeting day, and sat on the stage, earning a round of applause. She contributed nothing to the morning or afternoon sessions, but after the first speech of the evening she stepped up to the podium and addressed Stanton as "Mrs. Presidentress," to get recognized as the next speaker. Stanton reminded the doctor that the NWSA had an established roster and her allotted speaking time was not until the next evening. Stanton polled the audience about whether "Mrs." Walker should address them, and Mary Walker objected to the use of this incorrect title.

The audience did not want to hear from Mary Walker then, and amid hisses and catcalls she continued to try to speak until Susan B. Anthony intervened. "We all believe in the freedom of speech," Anthony said, but "we foot the bills and want to do this to suit ourselves." Walker replied to the assembled, "Yes, she foots the bills and asks you people to pay for it." After the session adjourned, the doctor spoke with a reporter and explained that the whole dust-up was rooted in jealousy. She said, "That was a show of fairness to talk of to-morrow," intimating she would be prevented from doing so.

Susan B. Anthony opened the next day's meeting. Mary Walker's late arrival interrupted the suffragist's speech about working women. The doctor took a seat on the stage, as she had the previous day, "attired in her Sunday-go-to-meeting clothes, and was received with prolonged applause." When the audience quieted, Anthony continued her talk, not pausing when Elizabeth Cady Stanton walked in. Looking "unusually prim and stately," Stanton approached Mary Walker and the two conversed for a moment before the older woman sat down. When Anthony finished, Stanton rose and recapped last night's episode with Walker. As promised, the doctor was then invited to address the convention.

Mary Walker admitted she had difficulty speaking under such circumstances. "She had been repeatedly insulted by the officers and delegates of this association on the stand and on the streets." She felt hurt by this treatment. She explained how the NWSA had tried to erase her contributions to the suffrage movement even though she had been one of the first women in Washington to embrace the cause. Moreover, none of the money the NWSA raised came to her for payment for her lectures and writings. Anthony interrupted and asked the audience if they wanted to listen to Walker's personal grievances. Amid the responses of "No, no," the doctor admonished Anthony to stop "dictating" to her. Walker said, "If the truth is a tirade, all right," and to a swell of applause, she continued.

Women's suffrage and dress reform occupied most of Mary Walker's remarks. In conclusion, she proposed a resolution requesting Congress to pass a law defining appropriate attire for women, and someone seconded it. "There not being much feeling manifested toward the resolution, she appealed to her audience not to sit still and see a woman suffer." Laughter erupted in the hall, then Elizabeth Cady Stanton said the resolution had to go through a committee first. Walker insisted on calling the question, and as others tried to be heard, Anthony adjourned the meeting until the afternoon. But most people remained, along with the doctor, airing additional grievances. At a delegate's suggestion, she stepped up to the podium and read her "Crowning Constitutional Argument," following it with a recitation of her wartime accomplishments. The audience responded with a burst of applause.

Twice during the convention Mary Walker brought up the issue of age. She claimed that now she was no longer young and attractive, the NWSA leaders wanted nothing to do with her. When she stumbled through parts of her constitutional argument, she put it down to poor eyesight. She was forty-two years old and had been fighting for women's rights for at least twenty years. Though Dr. Walker endured laughter, hissing, and catcalls from the NWSA delegates, she did not abandon her causes, but over the next year she distanced herself from Stanton and Anthony by focusing on dress reform.

The more Mary Walker concentrated on that cause, the more she connected it to issues of the body, sexuality, and marriage. In August 1875 she headed west on another lecture tour. Dr. Charlotte A. Von Cort, a client of attorney Belva Lockwood, accompanied the doctor through Utah, where Walker spoke on dress reform in Salt Lake City and Ogden. So many people turned up in Ogden that it was standing room only in the hall, with even more turned away at the door. In September, the two women parted. Von Cort spent her time in California establishing a women's medical college, and Dr. Walker continued to lecture. In her San Francisco talk, she argued that women's current fashion was so expensive that it was a hindrance to marriage, and, she maintained, women of "natural feelings" wanted to marry. When couples postponed marriage because of costly clothing bills, "much immorality" resulted.

As Mary Walker focused her lectures on love and marriage, she practically guaranteed her split with the NWSA leadership would be permanent. In Petaluma, California, during January 1876, she debuted "Pure Love and Sacred Marriage" for an all-woman audience. The next night, she talked about "Woman" to an audience of men. Some of these ideas came from her book *Hit*, but Walker extended her analysis of sexual relations, possibly planning for a new publication. Her public discussions of sexuality risked reviving the "free love" stigma against the suffrage movement. The Beecher-Tilton affair, fanned by Victoria Woodhull, had concluded in July 1875 with an acquittal for the Reverend Henry Beecher, but the aftereffects of the scandal still tainted the suffrage movement.

Mary Walker remained in the West until the spring of 1876. Upon her return to the East Coast, she may have been involved in planning some of the women's exhibits at the Centennial International Exposition in Philadelphia. The members of the Women's Centennial Executive Committee, headed by Elizabeth Duane Gillespie, a great-granddaughter of Benjamin Franklin, raised over $30,000 to build a Woman's Pavilion. Its entryway was adorned with a banner containing the words from Proverbs 31: "Let Her Works Praise Her in the Gates." The exhibits highlighted women's work both inside and outside the home. Dr. Walker would have assisted with displays on clothing and medicine.

The NWSA refused to get involved with the formal planning and execution of the centennial's exhibits. Despite the emphasis on women's labor, Gillespie's committee declined to include suffrage and women's rights work. So the NWSA rented rooms near the exposition grounds and set up its own displays, using the location to recruit new members to the suffrage cause. Mary Walker was not present for Susan B. Anthony's dramatic public protest on July 4, the day of the exposition's Grand Ceremonies, though she likely would have approved. Anthony forced her way to the stage while her compatriots distributed copies of her "Declaration of Rights for Women" to a startled audience. The suffragist read the declaration, modeled after the original 1776 version, with a nod to Elizabeth Cady Stanton's 1848 "Declaration of Sentiments."

During the summer, Mary Walker started supporting the Democratic Party ticket for the upcoming presidential election—New York governor Samuel Tilden as the presidential nominee, with Indiana governor Thomas Hendricks as his running mate. Though the Democrats did not embrace women's suffrage, the doctor approved of the Party's broadbased reform agenda. In July, she became involved with the Tilden and Hendricks Campaign Reform Club in Washington, DC. The following month she tried to link women's suffrage to Tilden's candidacy, holding an event at Lincoln Hall to ratify Tilden and Hendricks's nomination. Though about two hundred people showed up, most drifted away during Walker's speech, in which, according to a reporter, she "assailed the

Administration, got mad because she couldn't vote, and looked lovingly towards S. J. Tilden as the man who was going to protect her."

That August, Mary Walker warned the Tilden and Hendricks Club of a "radical plot to carry the next Presidential election by fraud and corruption . . . to secure the electoral vote." To prevent this, she advised that "the brain of woman must be engaged." After all, the Republican Party had remained in power for so long because of the many women who supported it. Walker continued to alienate herself from most women suffragists, who still backed the Republicans and their candidate, Rutherford B. Hayes. But her warning proved prophetic. Though Tilden won the popular vote that November, twenty disputed electoral votes—and the presidency—ultimately went to Hayes in return for his promise to end Reconstruction.

The NWSA spent most of the campaign season promoting a Sixteenth Amendment. Though the 1875 *Minor* decision undercut arguments for federal action on women's suffrage, Elizabeth Cady Stanton and Susan B. Anthony pointed out that since the Fourteenth and Fifteenth Amendments protected black men's voting rights, the Constitution could do the same for women. But a white population weary of Reconstruction considered any new emphasis on federal power unwelcome. The American Woman Suffrage Association continued its state campaigns. The NWSA's timing was poor, but Stanton and Anthony refused to give up.

To coincide with the January 1877 NWSA convention at Lincoln Hall in Washington, DC, Mary Walker arranged to have a women's suffrage bill presented to Congress. One of the first to arrive for the opening of the meeting, she carried an "additional masculine 'fixin'," a cane. Walker took a seat on the stage but remained silent during the proceedings. Elizabeth Cady Stanton opened the morning session on the second day with a speech about the necessity for congressional action on suffrage, explaining that the movement had been going on for so long that many activists would probably die before receiving their voting rights. The audience then called to hear from Walker. She acknowledged she held a minority view: "She wanted her rights restored, not an amendment to give her a right that she already has." The doctor then read the documents she submitted to Congress.

The cloud of the contested election, which would not be settled until March, hung over the suffrage meeting. The second day's morning session concluded with the adoption of Belva Lockwood's resolution that the NWSA appoint a committee of women to oversee any vote recounts in Washington. Mary Walker caused a commotion in the evening session when she interrupted Phoebe Couzens's speech to offer a resolution. About half of the audience called for Couzens, a well-known suffragist and lawyer from St. Louis, the other half, for Walker. An exasperated Susan B. Anthony brought in the police to restore order and arrest Mary Walker. The doctor avoided this by taking her seat, but she had the last word with Stanton and Anthony, admonishing them, "You are not working for the cause, but for yourselves."

With the end of Reconstruction at hand and with her alienation from the NWSA, Dr. Mary Walker intensified her efforts to direct the movement for women's rights.

CHAPTER ELEVEN

The Old "New Woman"

BRUSHING OFF THE HARSH TREATMENT SHE HAD RECEIVED FROM Susan B. Anthony and other delegates of the National Woman Suffrage Association, Mary Walker blazed her own women's rights path, emphasizing dress reform while stumping for suffrage. She remained in Washington, DC, where she spoke to the First Independent Congregation at the Masonic Temple on February 4, 1877. In what by now seemed a common tactic, she entered the room during the first speech, attracting considerable attention. As the fourth speaker, the doctor's "remarks were entirely devoted to the hobby of dress reform," which she pronounced the "biggest" question of the day. The audience did not appear convinced. Several members left the hall as Walker spoke; more took interest in a subsequent lecturer who dealt "heavy blows at the dress-reform movement, by which very hearty demonstrations of approval were elicited."

Wearing her reform dress, Mary Walker went to the Treasury building on March 16, 1877, to see the new secretary of the treasury, John Sherman. She intended to talk to him about the position she had been given under the Grant administration but was not allowed to take up. When the building's doorkeeper, Walter R. Baker, saw her in Sherman's waiting room, he physically removed her. Walker filed charges against Baker, claiming he violated her rights as a citizen, and he was ordered to appear in police court on March 23. One newspaper described Baker's action as an "outrage upon woman's rights," but most reports had a fine time poking fun at the doctor for her behavior, some articles even claiming that she swore at the doorkeeper and waved a pistol at him. The court, however, found in her favor, determining her rights deserved to be respected as much as anyone else's.

Despite her poor experience at the previous NWSA convention, Mary Walker attended a smaller mid-year one in New York City in May 1877. Her presence in the city attracted attention, with children and adults following her whenever she went out on the streets. She used that notoriety to invite reporters to come hear a private lecture on "The Reform in Women's Dress" in her lodgings at 334 Bowery. A reporter for the *New-York Tribune* noted her appearance. "Her face is thin but attractive, with a touch of color upon each cheek, and a pair of sparkling, laughing eyes." She wore blue silk trousers with a matching coat and a man's hat perched on her head. Walker broke the ice with a bit of levity, dispelling the rumor that the former presidential candidate Samuel Tilden had proposed marriage to her, but reassured the reporters, "I don't hate all the men by any means." She then launched into her topic, which she illustrated with drawings and diagrams. The New York reporter found Dr. Walker "very enthusiastic in her commendation of the attire of men as compared with that of women."

As she probably expected, Dr. Walker received a much less cordial reception at the NWSA convention. She had not been included on the speakers' roster—the first insult. Then Lillie Devereux Blake, a prominent New York City suffragist, delivered a more public one. She "acted as Sergeant-at-arms" of the meeting and told Walker she was not wanted. Blake prevented the doctor from sitting on the platform. Walker responded that Blake would "catch it, and that the spirit of illiberality displayed by this so-called liberal meeting should be duly punished in the newspapers." The doctor moved away from the stage area and tried to "converse pleasantly of political and social topics with those about her," only to be rebuffed. Blake pronounced her "crazy" and a "nuisance," and called in a policeman in case the doctor became disorderly. Mary Walker did not further disrupt the meeting, but the incident underscored how few supporters she had.

Someone who followed these newspaper reports concocted a practical joke that Mary Walker learned about while in Oswego in June. That person sent out bogus wedding invitations for a July 4 ceremony, featuring Walker as the bride. The doctor sent letters to newspapers advising she was not getting married. She described the hoax as a cruel way of trying to harm the reputation of a "distinguished gentleman." None of those invitations has survived, and Mary Walker did not identify her alleged groom, but at least one newspaper speculated it was Samuel Tilden.

As hostility toward Mary Walker increased, she altered her appearance, making her outfit more tailored and masculine. She stopped wearing ruffles, ribbons, and flowers at her neckline. She cut off her hair, fashioning it in the contemporary men's style. The words *manly* and *masculine* turned up more routinely in public descriptions of the doctor. Some articles commented on or joked about her unmarried state, but without explicit speculation about her sexuality. Like Victoria Woodhull's accusations about Henry Ward Beecher, that would have been an improper topic for public discussion.

Mary Walker may have been signaling her sexual identity with this change in attire, which would have been a daring thing at the time. Most nineteenth-century Americans condemned sexual activity between people of the same gender, pronouncing it immoral or unnatural. Same sex relationships occurred, although how many were "romantic" friendships and how many were sexual relationships is impossible to know because of public reticence on the topic. Many women forged close relationships with other women, sometimes using passionate and romantic language to describe their feelings for each other. Until the 1880s, these attachments did not raise concerns, since many people believed they were not sexual. But during the last two decades of the 1800s, medical experts began labeling and stigmatizing these friendships as sexually perverted.

Throughout her life, Dr. Walker developed friendships with many women, some closer than others, but they rarely lasted more than a few years. Her relationship with Belva Lockwood, for instance, waxed and waned over the years. The doctor's social and professional circles—dress reform, suffrage, women's health issues—kept her in regular contact with women. She may have confided in some of them—she may have had sexual relations, too—but she left no conclusive evidence about this part of her life. It is intriguing, however, that she published her second book, one that explicitly addressed sexuality issues, as she went through her sartorial transformation.

Unmasked, or the Science of Immorality was published on January 1, 1878. Addressed "To Gentlemen," Mary Walker reasoned that since so many male doctors had written books for women, "it is but fair to suppose that men generally may be benfited [*sic*] by women physicians writing 'private treatises' to men, embodying advice, facts, observations, discoveries, etc., that are all important for men to learn in a pure way as matters of science." Written as an extended critique of the double sexual standard that pervaded American society, the doctor wanted men to learn the facts about sexuality from an expert instead of relying on the "most degraded ideas" they picked up elsewhere.

In twelve chapters, Dr. Walker examined topics including pure manhood, kissing, hymens, and seminal weaknesses. She began by positing that "If men would only reason, they would very soon understand that the true position of women is always one of equality with themselves in all the relations of life"—public and private. The more "selfhood" a woman possessed, the more willing she would be to engage in "pure monogamic love." Love and respect must accompany sexual activity, she asserted; otherwise, "it is an injury to both parties in the transaction."

If men expected women to remain virgins until they married, Mary Walker claimed, men should likewise abstain from sex until after marriage. "But very few men ever stop to consider their own inconsistency in demanding such purity from their wives, since, if they were themselves pure, they could not so readily doubt the chastity of women." Though most of her advice sounded reasonable, much of it would have been debatable within the nineteenth-century medical community. For instance, she disapproved of kissing because of the diseases it spread, including syphilis, and because of the "animal passions" it aroused in men. She believed seminal weakness, or a low sperm count, was caused "by masturbation, excessive copulation, and by shaving the beard." She defined hermaphrodites as "legitimate results of abuse of either or both soul and body."

Mary Walker published *Unmasked* anonymously. She lectured widely on its contents, though, and took copies with her for sale, so she was not afraid to claim authorship on these occasions. Considering her determination to be somebody, she may have been looking for some notoriety by picking a fight with Anthony Comstock, the self-appointed morality sheriff of the United States. While serving in the Union Army, the young Comstock, a devout Christian, was stunned at the lewdness of his fellow soldiers. Determined to clean up vice in the country, he settled in New York City after the war, where he launched a morality crusade against all print material and images he deemed obscene.

At Comstock's urging, in March 1873, Congress passed the Act for the Suppression of Trade in, and Circulation of, Obscene Literature and Articles of Immoral Use. Widely known as the Comstock Act, the law prohibited the use of the mail service to send any lewd items or devices. The postmaster general appointed Comstock as a special agent of the Post Office to decide what was indecent, and then to enforce the law. Upon conviction, violators could be fined up to $5,000, sentenced for up to ten years' hard labor, or both. If Mary Walker intended to challenge Comstock, she risked losing money she did not have, and/or her liberty. She did not pursue a confrontation.

—◦—

By the beginning of 1878, Mary Walker felt like a somebody. In December 1877, she had been vindicated in her fight with the Treasury Department, which had prevented her from taking up her job there because of her attire, and was awarded $900 in back pay. She had published her second book. Now, she felt ready to challenge the NWSA delegates again, so she attended the 1878 convention in Washington, DC. On the morning of January 10, the women met in the Ladies' Reception Room of the Senate, the day California senator Aaron Sargent introduced the Sixteenth Amendment as Senate Resolution 12. Elizabeth Cady Stanton crafted the wording, using the Fifteenth Amendment as her guide: "The right of citizens of the United States to vote shall not be denied or abridged by the United States or by any state on account of sex."

Isabella Beecher Hooker's opening prayer on January 10 sparked a controversy over the substance and direction of the NWSA. Calls came from the floor for Dr. Walker to speak, and she stood on a chair to be seen over the crush of people, some trying to prevent her from addressing the meeting. She "created some merriment" by predicting that all the African-American women would vote in the next presidential election because they had been enfranchised by the Fourteenth Amendment.

After the convention, Mary Walker accompanied NWSA members to meetings of the Senate Committee on Privileges and Elections, which agreed to hear arguments about women's suffrage. The event was so well attended that a larger meeting room had to be procured, and the audience received instructions not to interrupt the proceedings with applause or boos. Elizabeth Cady Stanton maintained that while states had the right to regulate suffrage, they could not deny citizens the right to vote. The committee praised the propriety and dignity of the suffragists who spoke—Walker was not among them—and promised to take up their "important questions" at one of its future meetings. When the doctor appeared at the House Judiciary Committee meeting on January 16 to argue for women's voting rights through their existing citizenship rights, a Virginia newspaper predicted, "The talk will have no effect as the committee seem obdurate."

Twelve days later, the doctor, invited by George Q. Cannon, Utah's congressional territorial delegate, spoke to the House Subcommittee on Territories to oppose efforts to strip Utah women of their voting rights because they were Mormons. Sara Jane Andrews Spencer, an NWSA officer and supporter of the New Departure, joined her in objecting to federal interference. While the territorial government of Utah had recognized women's voting rights in 1870, its application for statehood had raised concerns in Congress about the morality of polygamy.

Mary Walker claimed that the practice of a man taking more than one wife, "from a physiological standpoint, is an improvement upon monogamy and a more enlightened phase of the social evil." Sara Spencer raised the "bad taste" of the hypocrisy of the sexual double standard because so many members of Congress were "practical polygamists." Not all Utahans appreciated Walker's support; she was too radical for their taste. The *Salt Lake Tribune* proclaimed her argument "brazen" and "astonishing."

The attention Mary Walker received for her views on polygamy provoked an increase in the harassment she faced on the street. Frustrated that law enforcement officials declined to ensure her safety, on March 7,

1878, she appeared before the Board of Metropolitan Police to explain why she had applied for a job as an officer. She cited her work with the army during the war as the best qualification. The doctor believed that wearing a badge would significantly cut down on incidents of provocations against her and other reform women, but newspapers reported that what she really wanted was revenge against the young boys who tormented her. The board declined her application.

All of this rejection took a toll. In April 1878, Mary Walker fell ill, reportedly with a near-fatal case of pneumonia. Except for persistent eye trouble, this was the first time the forty-five-year-old doctor had contended with poor health. The episode was likely triggered by unrealized worries that the Washington, DC, police force, irritated by her job application, might press obscenity charges against her for *Unmasked*. Rumors circulated during the year that city authorities had threatened to stop the sale of the book. Victoria Woodhull's entanglement with the New York state obscenity laws remained a topic of discussion among suffragists. Now with the federal Comstock Act in effect, Walker must have realized that this was not the kind of notoriety she wanted. After a few days in Washington's Providence Hospital, she recuperated at the home of her two aunts in Massachusetts before resuming her routine activities.

The NWSA held a thirtieth anniversary commemoration of the Seneca Falls Convention with a daylong celebration of women's rights in Rochester, New York, on July 19. Lucretia Mott, Elizabeth Cady Stanton, and Susan B. Anthony attended, along with other luminaries of the movement. But Mary Walker was absent. At least one newspaper noticed and asked, "Was it lack of funds, or anger because the convention did not come to her?" The lingering effects of her sickness likely prevented her attendance. By the fall, Walker felt well enough to undertake a lecture tour in New England and New York, "advocating greenbacks, pantaloons, etc.," as well as "Pure Love and Sacred Marriage."

In early December 1878, Mary Walker had another encounter with New York City police. An officer arrested her for creating a public nuisance because she wore her reform dress while walking along Broadway. The superintendent let her go after talking to her, but Walker filed a complaint against the policeman, which was later dropped. Before leaving the building, the doctor insisted the superintendent guarantee his officers would stop harassing her. She told him "she was a citizen . . . and she had served as a United States Army surgeon during the war, so the least she could ask was the right of passing through the street without annoyance at the hands of officials." He declined to give his assurance.

Women's citizenship rights occupied Mary Walker from 1879 into the new decade. In March 1879, she sat in the courtroom the day her friend, attorney Belva Lockwood, won the right to argue cases before the Supreme Court. The next month the doctor presented a petition to Congress requesting that in cases of female defendants in jury trials in Washington, DC, half the jury consist of women. In May, she attended hearings of the Potter Committee, convened by Congress to investigate the 1878 presidential election. Sitting in the ladies' gallery, she pounded her umbrella on the floor when she agreed with an argument. The door-keeper threatened to eject her, and she claimed it would take four of them to "remove her from the people's Senate." As a woman and a citizen, Mary Walker believed she had every right to express her opinions.

Based on her recent experiences with the NWSA, the doctor avoided large organizations. Even the Woman's Christian Temperance Union (WCTU), which might have offered her a congenial home for her suffrage work, held no attraction. Founded in 1874, its members became adept at petitioning and other political actions to stop the sale and consumption of alcohol. It soon became the largest women's organization of the 1800s. Beginning in 1879 with Frances Willard's leadership, the WCTU endorsed women's suffrage. Only through the vote, Willard asserted, could women save their homes from the evils of liquor. Many women like suffragist Mary Livermore belonged to the WCTU and a suffrage organization. Livermore described the two movements as entangled, as difficult to tell apart as the famous conjoined twins of the era, Chang and Eng. Dr. Mary Walker had been a temperance advocate since childhood—and a women's rights supporter for about as long—but she did not agree with all of Willard's tactics, so she never joined the WCTU.

In the late summer of 1879, the doctor traveled through Pennsylvania and Ohio, where she attended the Tri-State Reunion of Civil War veterans in Steubenville. Since the end of the war, she had often heard from men who served, whether they had been her patients or not, sometimes providing them with assistance in filing pension claims. Over the years, she had attended many functions of the Grand Army of the Republic, a Civil War veterans' organization. Mary Walker felt particularly close to the 52nd Ohio, and always held a high regard for Colonel Daniel McCook, who hired her as a contract surgeon. Mortally wounded at Kennesaw Mountain in June 1864, McCook was taken home to Steubenville, where he died the following month. Walker's visit would have been doubly poignant.

The Tri-State Reunion on August 28 attracted about 25,000 people. Approximately 6,200 veterans participated in a parade through the city streets that ended at Stokely's Grove, where a grandstand, festooned with flags and flowers, held the visiting dignitaries. On the platform, amid the politicians and generals, sat Dr. Mary Walker. She was identified as an assistant surgeon with the 52nd Ohio, but newspapers reported she was the only "veteran" onstage who did not give a speech. The use of quotation marks around the word *veteran* served as a reminder that the doctor had not been inducted into the army. That day, Walker did not employ her usual tactic of simply taking the podium, perhaps satisfied that one speaker lauded the contributions of women during the war, and another delivered a tribute to Colonel McCook.

The beginning of 1880 found Mary Walker in Washington, DC, working for suffrage. The NWSA held its annual meeting on January 21–22 at Lincoln Hall, and newspapers reported that conference organizers prevented Walker from attending. If she stayed away from those sessions, she refused to be left out of a private meeting with members of the Senate Judiciary Committee. They had agreed to meet with a few of the NWSA suffragists, but the doctor was not supposed to be among them. When she showed up anyway, Susan B. Anthony and the other women demanded her removal. The doorkeeper, perhaps familiar with Walker's reputation, declined to eject her.

Mary Walker spent much of the year dealing with family matters. Her father, Alvah, died in April, at age eighty-two, and Alvah Jr. contested his will, challenging his sister Mary's possession of some family property. He was unsuccessful, and relations between the siblings remained strained. Though she normally looked forward to her frequent visits to Oswego as a break from her political work, going home now added to her stress rather than relieved it. Nevertheless, she returned to her hometown for Election Day. She had never given up on the New Departure strategy, and she intended to vote for the Democratic presidential candidate, Winfield Hancock, who had served the Union as a general during the Civil War.

The Oswego election inspectors declined to accept Mary Walker's ballot, pointing out that she was not a "legally qualified voter." She insisted, claiming that since "female" included "male" and that since she was a citizen, she was entitled to vote. The inspectors repeated their refusal, and she threatened to sue them. They did not relent. As the doctor prepared to leave the polling place, a young man said that if she was going to vote, they should get all the women in town to dress as men and come out and do the same. "I don't wear men's clothes," she told him. "I wear my own clothes."

Though not a qualified voter, on June 21, 1881, Dr. Walker declared her candidacy as the Democratic senator from New York. She wrote to the state legislature, responsible for making the selection, saying she believed "her duty to her native State demands her services in the present exigency." She presented a long list of qualifications that included knowledge of parliamentary procedure, speaking experience, moral courage, and "ownership of a brain that is never made abnormal by the use of anodynes or stimulants." Walker's candidacy was an extension of the New Departure strategy. She believed that as a citizen, she had the right to run for office, and she intended to exercise that right. The legislature did not agree.

The attention Mary Walker received from her senatorial bid—newspapers across the country carried the story, which spawned endless quips about a woman serving in Congress—likely helped to soothe her hurt feelings and fury over being erased from the "official" history of the women's suffrage movement. The first two volumes of *History of Woman Suffrage*, written by Elizabeth Cady Stanton, Susan B. Anthony, and Matilda Joslyn Gage, and published in 1881, hardly mentioned the doctor's contributions to the suffrage movement. Stanton and Anthony conceived the series to cement their leadership and control the direction of the movement. Its publication was widely reported, with emphases on its historical importance. One Boston newspaper, for instance, declined to comment on the books' literary merits, but asserted that they deserved a "place among the records of new social and political movements during the last thirty-five years."

Volume I covered 1848–1861, years during which Mary Walker did not engage in suffrage work. Her pursuit of dress reform as the key to conquering women's inequality was viewed by women's rights supporters as a side issue—and an unnecessarily distracting one. The second volume, 1861–1876, recognized the doctor's contributions to the war effort, but relegated her to a footnote. It highlighted Dr. Walker's medical credentials but failed to explain she had worked as a contract surgeon for the US Army. Her appearance at the 1869 NWSA convention was acknowledged only by a description of what she wore, not what she said. Her comments in support of the New Departure strategy merited a small paragraph in a lengthy section on the 1871 NWSA meeting. According to the NWSA leadership, Mary Walker was a nobody.

In 1882 she found herself in the public eye. She opposed the execution of Charles Guiteau, convicted of assassinating President James Garfield in the summer of 1881. Dr. Walker believed, along with many other physicians, that Guiteau's mental instability should exempt him from the death penalty. "I think it would be a burning disgrace to the country" to hang Guiteau, she told a reporter. "He is a monomaniac . . . and he has shown himself insane throughout the trial." Walker tried to intervene with President Chester Arthur, to ask that he grant clemency, but he refused to see her, and Guiteau's execution proceeded as scheduled on June 30.

Newspaper stories about the doctor's views on capital punishment vied with reports that on May 1, 1882, she landed a position as a mailroom clerk in the pension office of the Interior Department. She was not required to wear a dress. For the first few months, Mary Walker seemed the ideal employee, and she received a promotion in September. But she did not get along with her supervisor, D. L. Gitt. He claimed she refused to complete some of her assigned duties. She countered that he had singled her out because she knew about an affair he was having with another female clerk. Walker was terminated from the job the following summer.

Just when it seemed that the doctor had hit a plateau in her reform career, she experienced a resurgence. In 1886, the year she turned fifty-four, Americans responded to a poll about the country's greatest social reformers. Walker came in second place, behind the two women who tied for first, Elizabeth Cady Stanton and Frances Willard. Because of this reputation, the budding feminist Charlotte Perkins Gilman came to visit her in November. Gilman, known at the time by her first married name of Stetson, was the great-granddaughter of the famous minister Lyman Beecher, and her great-aunts were Isabella Beecher Hooker and Harriet Beecher Stowe. As a young woman, Gilman loved literature and art, and she planned to earn a living by creating them.

But in 1884, bowing to social conventions—and against her better judgment—Charlotte Gilman wed the Rhode Island painter Charles Walter Stetson. The birth of their only daughter, Katharine, in 1885 added stress to the already-fragile marriage, and Gilman began to suffer from postpartum depression. Her meeting with Mary Walker in November 1886 occurred at a critical time in her life. During the next year, Gilman would be put under the care of Dr. S. Weir Mitchell, known for his rest cure for "nervous" women. That treatment proved almost worse than the depression for Gilman, who would write chillingly of it in her 1890 short story, "The Yellow Wallpaper."

Charlotte Perkins Gilman and Mary Walker discussed politics and reform that afternoon, including marriage and fashion. Gilman and her husband would divorce in 1888, and she likely talked to Dr. Walker about the unequal system of laws women faced to dissolve their marriages. Dress reform was also a topic of interest. In October 1886, Gilman published "Why Women Do Not Reform Their Dress" in the *Woman's Journal*, Lucy Stone's suffrage publication. She answered her own question, "But to offend and grieve instead of pleasing, to meet opposition and contempt instead of praise and flattery, to change pride for shame,—this is suffering which no woman will accept unless it is proved her duty. And this is why women do not reform their dress." This gave the two women much to converse about.

Energized by the renewed attention and frustrated by suffrage setbacks, Dr. Walker went out on the lecture circuit in 1887. She wanted to do something to reverse the tide. In January, for the first time, the US Senate voted on the woman suffrage amendment, but failed to pass it. Also that year, a Washington territorial court repealed women's voting rights, which women in that far west location had been granted in 1883. And after much discussion about the Mormon practice of polygamy, Congress took suffrage away from Utah women. More than twenty years of intensified suffrage activism had resulted in little progress. The public seemed less interested than ever before.

And it was not only suffrage. Americans' appetite for reform began declining during the Grant administration. Interest in paying money to listen to talk about reform, including suffrage, dropped during the 1880s, as people spent their time and money on minstrel shows and other similar stage performances. In a strategic move, Dr. Walker booked popular entertainment venues known as dime museums, determined to reach as many people as possible throughout the Mid-Atlantic and the Northeast. She had no independent wealth to bankroll such an undertaking, nor would any of the suffrage organizations sponsor her. Only a few of Walker's lectures would focus specifically on suffrage. Instead, she covered a variety of topics, including work, the evils of tobacco, and dress reform.

Mary Walker traveled to Philadelphia in early March 1887 to arrange for two weeks' worth of "short talks to women" at the Dime Museum on 9th and Arch Streets, beginning April 4. Her appearance in the city in March caused its usual stir, since she was "dressed like a gentleman." She told a reporter that "the time is not far distant when the greatest scientists in the country will adopt the stage of a dime museum as the best place from which to disseminate knowledge." The Philadelphia engagement was well advertised but attracted little press attention. She subsequently forged a profitable relationship with M. S. Robinson, amusement manager, who operated several museums, including the Wonderland in Buffalo, New York. Walker appeared at his establishments every four to six months over the next several years. She became so well known for these lectures that Austin's Nickelodeon in Boston created a wax figure in her likeness to keep on display.

The NWSA's distancing from Mary Walker was made evident on the last day of Philadelphia's centennial celebration in September 1887.

President Grover Cleveland received visitors—about 3,200 per hour—in city hall on the morning of September 17. Lillie Devereux Blake, the NWSA's vice president, was one of them. She used the opportunity to give Cleveland a copy of the organization's "Protest Against the Unjust Interpretation of the Constitution," signed by the NWSA officers. It made the same argument Dr. Walker had always promoted, most recently in April to a Philadelphia reporter. "The women who are agitating the question now," she said, "are trying to get an amendment to the Constitution, which is absurd. We have the right to vote by the Constitution, and we do not need an amendment." The NWSA promoted the same interpretation in its pamphlet, but did not acknowledge the doctor's contributions.

Susan B. Anthony delivered a more-public slap in the face in March 1888 at the meeting of the International Council of Women (ICW) in Washington, DC. Created by Anthony and Elizabeth Cady Stanton to mark the fortieth anniversary of Seneca Falls, the ICW focused on a variety of women's issues, including suffrage. Its participants included suffragists from about fifty organizations, including the American Woman Suffrage Association. A truly international event, delegates from eight countries attended. The meeting's inclusivity signaled a willingness to create one unified suffrage group.

The conference opened on March 25, an unseasonably cold day that pelted the city with icy rain. Anthony, Stanton, Matilda Joslyn Gage, and Lillie Devereux Blake arrived at Albaugh's Opera House around ten o'clock and took seats on the stage. But Mary Walker was not there. The day before, she had turned up at a House Judiciary Committee meeting where Stanton had been invited to read a statement encouraging Congress to pass a women's suffrage amendment. Committee members did not publicize the meeting, nor did the NWSA officers who accompanied Stanton. The doctor's appearance was an unwelcome surprise. She insisted on having time to speak, claiming she represented more women than Stanton. The committee declined.

A furious Susan B. Anthony barred Mary Walker from the ICW sessions, allegedly calling the doctor a "woman's franchise backslider." Anthony's controversial move sparked much discussion among the attendees who had looked forward to meeting and hearing from the doctor.

The doctor showed up at one gathering on March 31, and Anthony and Elizabeth Cady Stanton ignored her. They probably figured they had the final say on Dr. Walker's status in the movement, when, that same day, the ICW celebrated a "Conference of the Pioneers." The forty men and women—including six women who had attended Seneca Falls—designated as pioneer suffragists sat on the stage and received a special purple badge and lavender ribbon to mark their status. Mary Walker was not among them.

She was also absent when the National Woman Suffrage Association and the American Woman Suffrage Association met in Washington, DC, on February 18, 1890, to formalize their merger. Negotiations had begun in 1887. An emerging new generation of suffragists, unconnected with the Civil War–era divisiveness of the organizations, had pushed for it. Also, given how long it had taken to secure a few state suffrage victories, more and more members believed it made sense to combine resources to secure their goal. Alice Stone Blackwell, Lucy Stone's daughter, contacted Susan B. Anthony to start the discussion. A joint committee of NWSA and AWSA members began working out the details, a long process complicated by disagreements over tactics and leadership. The NWSA pushed for a constitutional amendment, while the AWSA maintained suffrage laws had to be changed at the state level.

The National American Woman Suffrage Association (NAWSA) was created at that joint meeting of the NWSA and AWSA in February 1890. Anthony aspired to its presidency, but she knew her sometimes-rigid leadership style made her a controversial candidate. She pushed for Elizabeth Cady Stanton, who was elected president of NAWSA. Lucy Stone, longtime AWSA leader, became chair of NAWSA's executive committee. Anthony settled for vice president, and, in reality, she ran the organization. The elderly Stanton was more than content to serve as a figurehead. She attended her last NAWSA conference in 1892. Stone, also aged, resigned her position after a year, unable to mesh with the new group.

Dr. Walker may have declined to attend because of her treatment at the 1888 ICW meeting, but it was more likely because of her health. In the spring of 1889, the fifty-six-year-old fell and broke her leg. Before it had completely healed, she fell again. Her convalescence was slow, and for months at a time she had to curtail her activities. Reporter Robert Graves visited her in Washington in April 1890 and found her bedridden in a cramped attic room in an old house. The doctor wore a loose-fitting blouse with a tie, her face "pale and wan, the eyes look tired." She told Graves, "I am alone, helpless, penniless, and no one will help me. It is a shame and an outrage the way this government has treated me!" After she recounted her contributions to the Civil War, the reporter concluded: "[H]er life has been one of sacrifice and of devotion to her idea of principle . . . When well Dr. Walker supports herself very nicely by practicing medicine and lecturing. But it is not likely she will ever be able to work again."

The article was well timed to gain sympathy for her latest request to Congress. Because of her condition, she applied for an increase in her pension. Newspapers across the country reported on her reduced circumstances, cultivating a strong showing of public support. Some people sent Mary Walker money and other necessities. One article acknowledged that she had "true friends in the past, but they were forced to give up all efforts to reform her; she has never been considered anything worse than a crank." But her army record "was an honorable one. People who are cognizant of it have nothing but good words for the poor woman now."

Congress remained impervious to public opinion on the matter of Dr. Walker. In September 1890, it denied her most recent petition for a pension increase for reasons, she believed, that had nothing to do with her actual circumstances. Walker maintained that the refusal stemmed from Congress's disapproval of her reform dress and resentment that she spoke—or argued—in person with congressmen about her request. In response to this refusal, the doctor sent another petition to Congress, asking for a constitutional amendment that would establish a "national costumer" to determine appropriate attire for women.

The next month some New York friends of Mary Walker nominated her as an independent candidate for the state's 27th Congressional District. She accepted, hoping to call attention to the New Departure, but because of state election laws her name failed to appear on the ballot. The doctor's interest in party politics grew in the 1890s, and in 1892, a nonpartisan group in Oswego selected her as its representative to the Democratic National Convention in June in Chicago. She had no voting rights at the convention, but other attendees were interested in her opinions on Grover Cleveland's failings, and rival New York senator David Hill's virtues. During the nomination speech for Cleveland on June 22, which was ultimately successful, Walker got up on a chair and waved a white handkerchief as Hill supporters called out for their candidate. Susan B. Anthony was there, too, to speak to the Party's resolutions committee; though they traveled on the same train, she avoided the doctor.

While in Chicago for the convention, Mary Walker made a bid for heading up a costume department for the World's Columbian Exposition that was opening there in 1893. On June 24, she brought a letter to director general George G. Davis at his office at the Tremont Hotel on Michigan Avenue. She wrote that she believed "a costume department under my charge would be of interest to the people, and I most respectfully ask for such to be announced, and that I be appointed as manager of such department." Davis's private secretary informed the doctor that he was not available to see her, but her request would be considered.

A few days later, Bertha Palmer, president of the Board of Lady Managers for the exposition, still had not received the request for her board's consideration. But she thought the dress reform movement had "attracted so much attention of late that it might be productive of much good." During the 1890s, women across the United States attended college in increasing numbers, engaged in sports and leisure activities that encouraged them to don new outfits, took up jobs in previously all-male occupations, and talked openly about sexuality. These "new women" did not hesitate to match attire to circumstances. Bertha Palmer believed that Mary Walker had given "much thought and attention to the subject" and would make a success of the costume department. The doctor did not get the appointment, but she was honored as one of the few women in the country to receive a special invitation to the exposition reserved for "distinguished" Americans.

Now in her early sixties, Mary Walker remained an active lecturer. She stayed away from organized women's groups, especially the new NAWSA, as she continued to promote equal rights. In a great burst of ambition, in late September 1895 she publicized "A Colony for New Women." Through an attorney, she purchased a 135-acre farm about seven miles outside of Oswego that she intended to turn into a community to teach women economic independence. Walker planned to build a "large commodious farmhouse" big enough for seventy-five women, all single, all wearing reform dress, who would live and work together in a self-sustaining enterprise. She decided to give her "personal supervision to the establishment," but the residents would elect representatives for self-government, and a court system would be established. Besides working on the farm, the women would receive a university-level education, all in pursuit of the doctor's goal to "turn out new women" for American society. Though new women proliferated during the 1890s, they did not come from Mary Walker's colony, which never quite jelled.

After an absence of several years the doctor returned to Washington, DC—mostly to look after some pension matters, but also to continue her reform work. Her reappearance attracted attention, and reporters wanted to know what she was up to. One from the city's *Evening Star* reminded readers that Mary Walker was famous "as the first woman to adopt man's apparel in this country." Now she noticed that some versions of bloomers were acceptable. "Women have adopted this form of dress for bicycling and for mountain climbing to a very large extent." She had come to the capital, she told the reporter, "to see if I can interest people in the establishment of a hospital for consumptives." Dr. Walker proposed to donate some of her New York farmland to the project, along with her own medical expertise.

While in Washington, she went to the Health Office to register as a practicing physician, in compliance with a new district law. On February 17, the doctor attended the Congress of Mothers at the Arlington Hotel. Over three days, its sessions explored all aspects of "child nature" and the mother's role in its development. Mary Walker's presence caused a bit of a stir, especially on the last day. When she tried to speak on dress reform, her attempt was laughed off. At the evening session, she insisted on discussing the resolutions that were presented for approval and was cut off then, too. But if she felt discouraged by this response to her offered contributions, she would have been buoyed by her inclusion in Frances

Willard and Mary Livermore's 1897 massive encyclopedia of nineteenth-century American women. Mary Walker's entry covered a full page, and included a photo of her in reform dress decorated with her Civil War medals.

This distinction did not matter at the next NAWSA convention, held in Washington, DC, in February 1898. That year, members marked successes for women's suffrage in Colorado, Idaho, Utah, and Wyoming. The conference also celebrated the fiftieth anniversary of Seneca Falls. Elizabeth Cady Stanton, elderly and infirm, was unable to attend. Susan B. Anthony, who planned much of the event, did not want her political partner forgotten, and arranged to display the table on which Stanton wrote the Declaration of Sentiments in 1848. A copy of the declaration graced the table, and conference participants received their own copy.

Mary Walker, who had not been involved with the national organization since the 1880s, probably decided to attend the convention because she was already in Washington. Arriving in early January 1898 to take up the anti-imperialist cause, she lectured against the annexation of Hawaii. She viewed it as a violation of the Constitution's prohibition against the involvement of domestic matters in foreign nations. The doctor arranged a meeting with the deposed Queen Liliuokalani to extend her sympathy over what was happening in the islands. Walker lobbied individual members of Congress, trying to convince them to oppose annexation. When she tried to meet with the Senate's Territories Committee, none of its members responded to her invitation. By the time the suffragists arrived in the capital, Mary Walker was once again a spectacle.

The NAWSA conference opened on the morning of February 15 at the Columbia Theater with a session honoring the pioneers of the suffrage movement. Susan B. Anthony had not invited Mary Walker, nor did she show up for it. But the doctor arrived late in the afternoon and tried to take the floor to speak. Carrie Chapman Catt, an Iowa suffragist and the future president of the NAWSA, recognized a woman from Missouri instead. Walker protested that she had risen first, and the other woman deferred. Dr. Walker said she was "proud of the movement, but it was not being directed properly, and she offered a number of suggestions." Catt called her on a point of order—that the session focused on press issues and Walker must stick to the topic. But the older woman continued with her speech "until her voice was inaudible because of the rapping of the gavel." Catt cut her off.

The doctor returned the next day and encountered similar rejection. She tried to enter one session and found the door locked. Mary Walker believed that had been done solely to keep her out. At the end of the previous day's session, she talked to some women who wanted to hear about her "Crowning Constitutional Argument." When organizers realized the extent of interest in Walker's ideas, they prevented her from getting into the morning session. It was because they found her "such a forcible speaker, she will make these Delegates believe we have been on the wrong track all these years, and it is a question we disgrace *one* woman, or all of us be made out simpletons" for pushing for a constitutional amendment. Walker was again refused permission to speak in the afternoon. After the convention, the NAWSA refunded her annual dues.

Susan B. Anthony wanted nothing more to do with Mary Walker. The doctor continued to criticize the NAWSA's leader, asserting that she did not really want women's suffrage, because when it was achieved, she would be out of a job. "The love of power is the keynote of her character," claimed the doctor about Anthony. The public, however, seemed more interested in Walker's lifelong dedication to dress reform than her disagreements with suffrage leaders. In the spring of 1898, newspapers across the country published a lengthy story about "the only woman in the United States who wears trousers and doesn't wish she were a man." Walker explained, "This is a free country and as I was not responsible for being a woman, I failed to see the reason why I should be compelled to endure the discomfort of skirts for a lifetime simply because I didn't happen to be born a man." She found it "very funny" that young women tried to flirt with her. She did not consider herself a "dude" because she did not follow current fashion, only selected clothes that looked nice and fit comfortably. During the late 1890s, the term "Mary Walkers" came into popular usage as a synonym for women's trousers.

In the early 1900s, as Mary Walker headed into her early seventies, she was often referred to as the old, or veteran, "New Woman." She assisted people who encountered trouble because their choice of clothing did not reflect their biological gender. In early February 1905, the doctor offered to care for Frances Lamousche, a young woman from Cincinnati who fell ill while working as a hotel barber. Using the name Frank Williams, she had been dressing in masculine attire since childhood. Her decision to dress this way, Walker said, "shows her superior intelligence." That spring, Randolph Milbourne of Washington Courthouse, Ohio, asked her for help with his legal case. After being banished by the mayor for wearing women's clothing in public, Milbourne appealed to the attorney general for the right to "wear that clothing which is to him most comfortable and convenient." He argued that "but little question is raised now as to Dr. Mary Walker's right to wear men's clothes." Milbourne wanted her support of his contention, but she advised him that there might be an issue of "disguise" at stake in his case. The attorney general declined to weigh in on the matter.

Mary Walker's willingness to associate herself with these cases attracted the attention of doctors who pathologized behavior that did not conform to what were considered traditional heterosexual gender norms of the time. They paid particular attention to what medical professionals at the time called "sexual inversion"—when a person of one gender adopted the appearance and actions of the other. In his 1906 book on human sexuality, Dr. Joseph Parke, formerly an acting assistant surgeon in the Union Army, speculated that Walker suffered from "delusional masculinity." He found it "regrettable" that she had not been "investigated by any competent medico-psychologist," which would have "afforded some enlightenment in this interesting field of research."

~~~

After the turn of the new century, the suffrage movement lost its two great leaders. Elizabeth Cady Stanton died at age eighty-six in 1902, and four years later, Susan B. Anthony, also eighty-six, followed. Lucy Stone had died in 1893, not long after her AWSA merged with the NWSA. Lucretia Mott, who planned Seneca Falls with Stanton, had been gone since 1880, Sojourner Truth, since 1883. The NAWSA continued with able leaders like Iowa's Carrie Chapman Catt and Anna Howard Shaw, an ordained minister with a medical degree from Boston University.

In 1907, Mary Walker released a new edition of the "Crowning Constitutional Argument." She opened it with a statement that "Franchise was not a creation of the United States Constitution, any more than it was a creation of the soil of the United States. It expressed the Ideal of Birthright." She once again argued that the Constitution already provided women's suffrage and encouraged women to exercise that right. The doctor added a couple of pages about her grievances with the NAWSA, explaining that if Elizabeth Cady Stanton and Susan B. Anthony had not controlled the suffrage movement for as long as they did, women would already be voting. "The wheels of progress have been held back by them, and all others whom they could influence, because their brains did not originate the CROWNING CONSTITUTIONAL ARGUMENT."

The doctor wanted to argue her point before the New York state legislature in March 1910. After referring to some of the members of the suffrage movements as "grafters and notoriety seekers," she assured reporters that she favored women's suffrage, but "the manner in which the campaign is being conducted is pretty nearly a farce." She attended the suffrage debate in Albany, where many New Yorkers voiced their opinions, but she was not granted the opportunity to speak. When she tried to do so anyway, the committee chair gaveled her into silence.

The seventy-nine-year-old Mary Walker returned to Washington, DC, in January 1912, lecturing extensively about tuberculosis, still hoping to raise funds to build a sanitarium in Oswego. On February 14, she appeared before the House Judiciary Committee to explain her constitutional argument about women's suffrage. Committee chair Henry D. Clayton of Alabama reminded her of the 1898 Supreme Court decision in *Williams v. Mississippi*, which affirmed the role of states in determining voter qualifications. Walker countered that the court obviously had not read her "Crowning Constitutional Argument," which she believed would withstand its scrutiny, since "Truths are immortal."

Later that year, Dr. Walker traveled to Chicago, where she spent about four months lecturing. She immediately alienated many of the city's dedicated reformers when she publicly criticized Jane Addams, founder of Hull House, and perhaps the most well-known and highly regarded social worker in the country. Walker took issue with Addams's approval of Theodore Roosevelt, the former president who broke with the Republican Party to create the Progressive Party. "I am at a loss to understand" how Addams could support Roosevelt, Walker said, "unless she was a crass seeker of popularity and publicity." When informed of this charge, Addams responded, "I don't mind. I'll just keep on with my work."

Not everyone reacted like Jane Addams. Within twenty-four hours, word went out that "Dr. Mary Walker, dean of American suffragists, is to be officially 'snubbed' by the organized suffrage associations of Chicago." Now it was Walker's turn to say she did not care; she had other engagements to keep her busy. She attended the Illinois state suffrage meeting, but the organizers ignored her. In early February 1913, Chicago patrolman Peter Cleary arrested Dr. Walker, now eighty years old, for wearing men's clothing in public. She insisted, "These are not men's pants. They belong to me and they are a woman's." Soon after her arrival at the Englewood station, the acting lieutenant released her. Despite her notoriety in the city, Cleary later admitted he had never heard of Mary Walker.

Hospitalized briefly after another fall, the doctor did not return to Washington in time for Alice Paul's massive suffrage parade on March 3. Timed to maximize attention with Woodrow Wilson's upcoming inauguration, the event drew thousands of participants and thousands of spectators. Paul, a young, well-educated Quaker from Philadelphia, joined the NAWSA in 1912 and took over its constitutional committee. She mobilized her small subset of members to work exclusively on securing a suffrage amendment to the Constitution. Anna Howard Shaw, now the NAWSA's president, disliked Paul's tactics but did not interfere. The young Quaker never felt comfortable in the NAWSA and soon broke away, first forming the Congressional Union, then the National Woman's Party. For Alice Paul, a constitutional amendment was the key to women's equality.

Mary Walker believed it was a wasted effort. She never deviated from her belief that women already had voting rights. In January 1914, she resumed lecturing on the topic, first appearing at Hammerstein's Victoria Theatre in New York City, where she delivered a "twenty minute discourse on woman's rights and other issues of the day." She continued the presentations in Washington, DC, and found enough interest in her ideas to form the American Constitutional Association. Serving as its president provided the doctor an official status for appearing in front of government bodies like Congress, to push for suffrage. On March 3, she appeared at a House Judiciary Committee meeting to present her "Crowning" argument.

Dress reform, marriage, and divorce all factored into Mary Walker's lectures on women's rights. During a discussion of marriage in late March 1914, she revived the old story of President Chester Arthur's marriage proposals. Reporter Robert Graves had written about it back in 1890 as an example of how the doctor could not tell when she was the victim of a practical joke—the proposals had not been made in person, but had arrived by the "instrumentality of a mutual friend." Now Walker still insisted Arthur had proposed twice, but she had turned him down because he smoked tobacco, something she could not abide. Even if he gave it up, though, she would not have married him. "I would not lose my identity in his," she insisted. "I will always be somebody."

With the onset of World War I in Europe that summer, Mary Walker responded like most other American women—by promoting peace through a diplomatic settlement of hostilities. It was not a foregone conclusion that the United States would get involved in the conflict. In November 1914 she traveled to the forty-sixth annual NAWSA convention, held in Nashville, Tennessee, and chaired by Anna Howard Shaw. The doctor's appearance sparked no controversy. She asked to speak for ten minutes, which she spent "scoring the suffragists and saying that women already had the right to vote under the National Constitution." On December 14, 1915, Walker brought this argument to the White House when President Wilson invited two thousand suffrage supporters and opponents. Shaw spoke first on women's voting rights, and the doctor, introduced as having "another phase of the situation," explained her unique perspective.

Though she shared the Reverend Shaw's distaste for such actions, Mary Walker agreed to head a section of marchers in a huge suffrage parade held in New York City on October 24, 1915. Between 25,000 and 30,000 women from twenty countries participated. Since Alice Paul's extravaganza in March 1913, these kinds of public demonstrations had become increasingly popular to promote the suffrage cause. Walker made an exception in this case because she approved of the parade's inclusivity, and because it was timed to encourage New York voters to approve women's suffrage in an upcoming election. The doctor then joined a group of capital suffragists to welcome their Western counterparts, who arrived in December bearing a 500,000-signature petition to submit to Congress.

In January 1917, Alice Paul placed "Silent Sentinels" at the White House to pressure President Wilson into supporting a suffrage amendment. Wilson claimed he did not oppose voting rights for women, but he believed it a state matter, not federal. Paul determined to change his mind. Members of her National Woman's Party stationed themselves on the sidewalk, holding signs with various slogans, some of them bearing Wilson's own words about democracy. Over more than two years, about two thousand women participated, and hundreds of them, including Paul and her political partner, Lucy Burns, were arrested and jailed on bogus charges.

Dr. Mary Walker did not approve. The eighty-four-year-old, describing herself to a reporter as the "head of the suffrage movement in America," wanted to let President Wilson know she did not like "such acts as the sentinels are committing in front of the White House." She said she did not believe the "suffragists will ever be able to gain their point until they cease such tactics." During a lecture to the Secular League at the Pythian Temple in Washington on January 28, 1917, Walker referred to the "silent suffs" as "simpletons, grafters and publicity seekers." They were "ignorant" of how government works because they aimed their protest at the president, who has no role in the amendment process. Then she took aim at that procedure, claiming that neither the suffragists nor members of Congress had read the Constitution well enough to know that "Women already have the same rights under the Constitution as men, and to pass an amendment in their favor would be ridiculous."

In her lecture, the elderly doctor managed to alienate members of both the National Woman's Party and the NAWSA. Ida Husted Harper, the Indiana suffragist in charge of the NAWSA's press relations and official biographer of Susan B. Anthony, publicly corrected Mary Walker's assertions. In a letter to the editor of the *Washington Herald*, Harper pointed out that Walker had been making this constitutional argument for years. Harper then inaccurately stated that the doctor never tried to vote in New York, "which would have been the surest way of proving whether she was correct in her belief." Both Anthony and Virginia Minor had tested this in the 1870s, Harper reminded readers, and the Supreme Court had determined the Constitution "did not confer this right on women." Members of the NAWSA "have never attempted to defy" the Constitution or any legal authority; that was why they pursued an amendment.

While much of the nation focused its attention on the Silent Sentinels and the latest developments in the European war, Dr. Walker learned that the army had rescinded her Medal of Honor. It was nothing personal. In the spring of 1916, Congress passed H.R. 4701, an act to establish in the War Department a Medal of Honor Roll that entitled recipients to a ten-dollar monthly pension after the age of sixty-five. A review board consisting of five retired army generals convened to investigate each medal that had been awarded. It began meeting in October under the leadership of Lieutenant General Nelson Miles. Each file was anonymous, identified with a number rather than a name. The review board released its findings in February 1917 and revoked 911 medals. Because she had not engaged with the enemy in combat, the board ruled, Mary Walker was ineligible for the award.

She had been keeping track of these developments. When the 1916 act passed, she wrote to the pension office and the War Department to find out when her payments would begin. In late June she learned that nothing would be processed until her name had been "certified" by the War Department. This letter signaled a potential problem with her award. Though her pension had finally been increased in 1898 to twenty dollars a month, extra money was always welcome. When the War Department notified Mary Walker in 1917 that it had removed her name from the honor roll, she refused to acknowledge the rescission and continued to wear the decoration.

In April 1917, the United States declared war against Germany and entered the European conflict on the Allied side. President Wilson asked Congress for the declaration because Germany harassed American vessels on the high seas with its use of unrestricted submarine warfare. It had also tried to get the Mexican government involved in a Southern border scheme that would have violated US territorial sovereignty. A disappointed Mary Walker telegrammed Germany's Kaiser Wilhelm, offering him and other European leaders the use of her Oswego home for a peace conference. He did not respond.

The doctor intended to work for the Red Cross and the American Women's Hospitals during the war, but ill health prevented her from doing so. About a month after the war declaration, she was at the Capitol building, probably trying to talk to someone about her Medal of Honor or her pension. She later claimed that while outside on the steps, a gust of wind knocked her over. It is more likely the eighty-five-year-old doctor fell. Though Mary Walker sustained serious injuries—further damage to her bad leg, three broken fingers, and a bruised face—she insisted on recuperating in her room at the Lochraven Hotel.

Though she recovered enough to return to Oswego, it took many months, and she was never really well again. Mary Walker died in her home in the morning of February 22, 1919. She had been a somebody. Newspapers across the country, including the *New York Times*, published lengthy obituaries, often accompanied by a photograph of her in reform dress. Little is known of her last days except that her mind remained clear while neighbors cared for her. Dr. Walker must have known that in the United States' determination to beat Germany in the European war, the military utilized female labor.

In the first decade of the 1900s, Congress had authorized the army and navy to establish a nurse corps and enroll women. During World War I, the navy and marine corps enlisted women into their reserves. The army held out, only hiring women as contract workers. Mary Walker may have been aware that the war in Europe ended in November 1918 with an Allied victory. Because of her pacifist interests, she would have followed the role President Wilson and the United States played in the peace process.

She did not live long enough to see women achieve suffrage. Both houses of Congress finally passed the Nineteenth Amendment in the spring of 1919, a few months after she died. State ratification would take until August 1920. It had been a long battle, and in the end, the

National Woman's Party, the NAWSA, and myriad smaller organizations marshaled their forces to secure voting rights for women. Mary Walker would have celebrated the fact of women voting, but she would have had something sharp to say about the method with which it was achieved.

EPILOGUE:
THE MEDAL OF HONOR RESTORED

A SOMEBODY IN HER LIFETIME, MARY WALKER WAS NOT FORGOTTEN after she died. Her name surfaced in the newspapers a dozen or so times a year, especially in connection to changes in women's fashion. After World War I, women discarded the long skirts and bulky undergarments that impeded movement and damaged their health. In the late 1920s, Lida Poynter of Omaha, Nebraska, began a decades-long project of researching and writing a biography of the doctor. Republican congressman Frances D. Culkin, who grew up in Oswego, became interested in Walker's wartime service, perhaps intending a historical display for their mutual hometown at the end of the 1930s. During World War II, when American women could choose which branch of the military to enlist in for the duration, including the army, stories of Mary Walker once again circulated in the newspapers, stressing her patriotism and dedication. In June 1948, President Harry Truman signed the Women's Armed Services Integration Act, which allowed women to become permanent members of the military. Mary Walker had pushed for that more than eighty years earlier.

In early November 1957, the Medical Museum of the Armed Forces Institute of Pathology in Washington, DC, opened an exhibit on "Women and Medicine." One of its main attractions was a small portrait purporting to be Dr. Mary Walker as a spy during the Civil War. Bearing the artist's signature, J. B. Hudson, the painting had been in the museum's possession at least since 1888. Though the figure in Hudson's artwork looks nothing like the doctor, her inclusion in an exhibition of fifty notable medical women was quite an honor. During the Cold War of the 1950s, as Americans worried about the communist threat from the Soviet Union and China, women continued their push into the professions and engaged in politics from the grassroots to the national level. Mary Walker's story served as an inspiration.

The 1960s launched what is often called the "second wave," a feminist movement dedicated to the achievement of gender equality. Journalist Betty Friedan helped it along with the publication of *The Feminine Mystique* in 1963, a bestseller that exposed the negative consequences of underutilizing women's abilities. Three years later, she was instrumental in the creation of the National Organization for Women. The federal government acted on women's issues, too. Congress passed an Equal Pay Act in 1963, and Title VII of the 1964 Civil Rights Act forbade gender discrimination in employment. There was renewed interest in the passage of the Equal Rights Amendment, first introduced into Congress in 1923 by National Woman's Party founder Alice Paul. By 1972, both the House of Representatives and the Senate approved it and sent it on to the states for ratification. A hundred years earlier, when Mary Walker promoted similar ideas, she was labeled a radical.

The women's rights movement dealt blows to gender inequality in the military. In the early 1970s, Air Force lieutenant Sharron Frontiero sued the secretary of defense when her request for housing and medical dependent benefits for her husband was denied. Wives of male service members automatically received these benefits, but married women in the military had to prove they provided more than half of the support for their husbands. Ruth Bader Ginsburg, future Supreme Court justice, represented the American Civil Liberties Union and appeared in the high court to argue on Frontiero's behalf. In 1973, the court decided in the lieutenant's favor; the air force rule had discriminated based on gender. Two years later, Congress authorized the admission of women to the national service academies, and over one hundred enrolled at West Point in 1976, the year the United States celebrated its two hundredth birthday.

This reinvigorated women's movement intersected with rising patriotism over the bicentennial celebration of 1976. Anne Walker, a freelance medical writer and distant relative of the famous doctor, and Helen Hay Wilson, a nurse and a grandniece, capitalized on that perfect confluence of sentiment to campaign for the restoration of Mary Walker's Medal of Honor. Both women had been laying the groundwork for several years. Anne Walker made contacts in the medical community and through her congressmen. Wilson did the same; plus she cultivated support by donating some of Dr. Walker's belongings to museums, including the Smithsonian. In April 1976, the city of Oswego passed a resolution recommending and encouraging Congress to return the doctor's name to the Medal of Honor Roll. A copy of the resolution was sent to President Gerald Ford and several members of Congress.

The personnel subcommittee of the House Armed Services Committee took up the matter. Birch Bayh, a Democrat from Indiana, introduced a resolution, one of several in recent years, to the Senate. But the army moved more quickly. On May 4, 1977, the Army Board for the Correction of Military Records held a hearing at the Pentagon, which Helen Hay Wilson attended, along with her counsel, Donald Boardman of the American Red Cross. The five members of the board were all male civilian employees of the army. Boardman delivered a history of Dr. Walker's wartime activities, and Wilson answered follow-up questions about her grandaunt and the long process of seeking restoration of the Medal of Honor.

Helen Wilson explained that she had started talking to senators about Mary Walker in 1927. They had told her that now was not "quite the right time. Women aren't strong enough yet." Wilson waited. "But I am seventy-two now, and I don't have time to wait any longer. So I want to get this done." Now was the right time, she told the board. "Many organizations all over the country have contacted me about this. As you probably know, many of the broadcast companies have programs and are very much interested in it." Wilson referred to the rescission as unjust because it changed the rules retroactively. Under the original terms—"gallantry in action and other soldier-like qualities"—Dr. Walker had qualified for and received the Medal of Honor. Only a later change in the criteria made her ineligible.

The army board agreed and forwarded the results of its findings to Army Secretary Clifford Alexander Jr. In June 1977, he announced that the army had restored Dr. Walker's Medal of Honor. "There was ample evidence of her frontline gallantry and bravery as a physician," he said, and she had probably been a victim of gender discrimination during the war. The army instructed the National Archives to correct the doctor's records to reflect that "the action taken in 1917 to remove her name from the Medal of Honor Roll is void and of no force or affect [*sic*]." Helen Wilson was "quite thrilled" with the decision.

Dr. Mary Walker likely would not have been thrilled. She never recognized that the medal had been taken away—never believed that the review board of 1917 had the authority to undo the action taken by President Johnson after the war—and an acknowledgment of this action would have meant accepting that she had lost it in 1917.

As of this writing, Mary Walker remains the only female recipient of the Medal of Honor. While she cherished the commendation, she would likely be disappointed that no other women have earned the distinction. With the medal's criteria refocused on service members' demonstrated bravery under enemy fire, women's opportunity to qualify has been restricted. Though they have served as regular members of the military since 1948, not until 2013 did the Department of Defense remove a ban on women having combat positions. Recently, there have been discussions about requiring eighteen-year-old women to register with the Selective Service, just like their male counterparts. Mary Walker's patriotism and dedication to gender equality would have led her to support these changes.

In 1977, the year the army restored Mary Walker's Medal of Honor, Congress funded a National Women's Conference, held in Houston, Texas, November 18–21. This congressional decision attested to the widespread bipartisan enthusiasm for pursuing women's rights during the second wave. The United Nations had proclaimed 1975 as International Women's Year, and Republican president Gerald Ford created a National Commission on the Observance of International Women's Year. The thirty-five-member group explored ways to promote gender equality. At New York congresswoman Bella Abzug's urging, Congress designated $5 million for state and national conferences devoted to working out women's rights issues. In 1977, President Jimmy Carter, a Democrat, put in new commission members and named Abzug as its head.

From the late winter through the summer of 1977, women from each of the fifty states met at conferences to talk about problems of gender inequality and to select delegates for a national meeting in Houston, where a plan of action would be formalized. On September 29, a crowd of organizers and supporters gathered at Seneca Falls, New York, and lit a torch that relay runners, including tennis player Billie Jean King, carried 2,600 miles to the conference site. African-American poet Maya Angelou's updated rendering of the Declaration of Sentiments, "To Form a More Perfect Union," accompanied the torch, and thousands of people signed it along the way. Angelou emphasized the inclusivity of this movement: "We promise to accept nothing less than justice for every woman."

More than 2,000 delegates from fifty states came to Houston on November 18, about 20,000 additional observers, and 1,500 members of the press. The conference was nonpartisan, racially and ethnically diverse, multidenominational, and cut across class lines. The twenty-six resolutions submitted by the states for the National Plan of Action sparked varying levels of debate, the most heated centering on the Equal Rights Amendment, reproductive rights, and sexual orientation. After four days, the delegates had worked out a comprehensive plan that addressed issues ranging from equal access to credit to legal protection for battered women. Mary Walker would have been pleased with the wide range of women attending the conference, and she would have lauded their reform efforts. She would have been delighted to see so many wearing trousers.

Another meeting took place five miles away from the National Women's Conference. A rally of about 15,000 "pro-family" advocates gathered under the auspices of the Citizens' Review Committee (CRC), an organization opposed to the feminist agenda of the larger Houston conference. The CRC event was spearheaded by Phyllis Schlafly, the conservative Republican leader of Stop ERA, the anti–equal rights group that would accomplish its goal in a few short years. Outraged that Congress had spent federal money on promoting feminist ideals, Schlafly and the CRC mobilized thousands of women determined to protect women's traditional roles as wives, homemakers, and mothers. They especially objected to abortion, legalized by the 1973 Supreme Court decision in the *Roe v. Wade* case, the Equal Rights Amendment, and equal rights for lesbians. Mary Walker would have been appalled. She likely would have pushed past Schlafly to get to the podium and deliver a speech about how wrong they were. She would have been frustrated that even after all this time, the work she had begun was not yet complete.

ACKNOWLEDGMENTS

AT TIMES—AND FOR VERY LONG STRETCHES—WRITING SEEMS LIKE A solitary endeavor, but it is not. I welcome the opportunity to thank those who made this book possible.

Charles Clark, my husband, read the entire manuscript and flagged all the problem areas. I am so grateful for all his support over the years. As a historian, he understands my work, and he knew that my retirement from my university faculty position did not mean I would stop writing books. Sam Clark smoothed out computer glitches and patiently answered technology questions. He and Marta Rusten provided my favorite diversion from too much writing; the world is a sunnier place with Oscar in it. My mother, Irene Kaminski, remains my biggest booster. She never fails to ask when my next book will be published, then tells everyone about it.

The idea for this book came from Stephanie Scott, associate editor at Lyons Press, who believed that Dr. Mary Edwards Walker deserved a fresh look. My agent, Jacqueline Flynn, who always tells me I really can write faster than I think I can, made the deal happen. I could not pass up the opportunity to combine the two topics that have fascinated me since graduate school: war, and women's rights.

I was a history professor for over twenty-five years, and every year I taught undergraduates about the Civil War and the women's rights movement. I read countless books and articles to prepare the best lectures I could, and I had to revisit those publications, plus delve into new ones as I wrote this book. I owe huge intellectual debts to these academic historians and literary scholars whose work laid the foundation for my interpretation of Mary Walker: Sharon Harris, Elizabeth D. Leonard, Lisa Tetrault, and Faye E. Dudden. (A fuller discussion of their works is included in the Note on Sources and Recommended Readings.)

I usually travel to archives to conduct research, but for this project I was fortunate to be able to hire the services of expert researchers. Morgan Kolakowski, a PhD student specializing in nineteenth-century women's history at Syracuse University, navigated the Mary Edwards Walker Papers in the Special Collections Research Center at the Syracuse University Libraries and at the Oswego Town Historical Society. Dr. Kelly O'Donnell, historian of gender, activism, and health care in modern America, delved into the Lida Poynter Collection at the Drexel University College of Medicine, Legacy Center: Archives and Special Collections on Women in Medicine and Homeopathy. R. Dennis Pool, professional historical researcher, found Mary Walker items at the National Archives in Washington, DC.

The following archivists and librarians also provided research assistance: Matthew Herbison, archivist at the Drexel University College of Medicine, Legacy Center; Trenton Streck-Havill, assistant archivist at the Defense Health Agency, US Army Garrison-Fort Glen, National Museum of Health and Medicine; and Nicole Westerdahl, reference and access services librarian, Special Collections Research Center at the Syracuse University Libraries.

Many people shared their expertise with me and provided encouragement for the project. Anna J. Clutterbuck-Cook, reference librarian extraordinaire, gave helpful leads on studies of transgender people. The members of the Writing Challenge group on Facebook kept me accountable, day by day, month by month, to reach my publication goal. Our fearless leader, the historian and writer Pamela Toler, and scholars Elizabeth DeWolfe and Sunny Stalter-Pace provided feedback on the project, and Jessica Parr provided an invaluable research contact.

NOTE ON SOURCES
AND RECOMMENDED READINGS

THIS SECTION IS FOR READERS WHO LIKE TO LEARN HOW WRITERS KNOW what they know but do not necessarily want to read through the Sources section that follows. This is a work of nonfiction; I did not make up anything. All of my information came from primary and secondary sources.

Primary source material—that which was generated during Mary Walker's lifetime—forms the core of this book. The following collections were instrumental in illuminating her beliefs and actions: the Mary Edwards Walker Papers in the Special Collections Research Center at Syracuse University Libraries; the Lida Poynter Collection on Dr. Mary E. Walker at the Drexel University College of Medicine, Legacy Center: Archives and Special Collections on Women in Medicine and Homeopathy; Military Service Records Relating to Mary Edwards Walker, MD, Record Group 94, Records of the Adjutant General's Office and Record Group 15, Records of the Veteran's Administration, National Archives and Records Administration, Washington, DC; and the Mary Edwards Walker Collection at the Oswego Town Historical Society. I also tracked Dr. Walker's activities in contemporary newspapers, mostly through the databases of Newspapers.com and the *New York Times*. The Wisconsin Historical Society houses a microfilmed run of *The Sibyl: A Review of the Tastes, Errors and Fashions of Society*, an invaluable source of Walker's early writings.

Numerous published books—secondary sources—provided additional information, insights, and arguments on Mary Walker's life and times. Of those included in the Sources section, the following warrant special mention because they shaped the way I thought about Walker's world and her place in it. I also highly recommend them to readers who enjoy serious historical nonfiction. Sharon M. Harris's *Dr. Mary Walker: An American Radical, 1832–1919* (Rutgers University Press, 2009) established a timeline of Walker's activities and gave me leads on additional sources. It is the most comprehensive biography of the Medal of Honor winner and provides full discussions of Walker's family and her interest in criminal legal trials. Elizabeth D. Leonard wrote an insightful account of Mary Walker's Civil War years in *Yankee Women: Gender Battles in the Civil War* (W. W. Norton, 1994), centering on the pervasive sexism the doctor encountered. Leonard includes biographical examinations of other important but little-known women in her book. My understanding of the complexities of the nineteenth-century women's rights movement was greatly expanded by Lisa Tetrault's *The Myth of Seneca Falls: Memory and the Women's Suffrage Movement, 1848–1898* (University of North Carolina Press, 2014) and Faye E. Dudden's *Fighting Chance: The Struggle Over Woman Suffrage and Black Suffrage in Reconstruction America* (Oxford University Press, 2011).

Though I did not quote from them for this book, the following will be of interest to those who want to know more about women and the Civil War and the suffrage movement: Karen Abbott, *Liar, Temptress, Soldier, Spy: Four Women Undercover in the Civil War* (Harper, 2014); Ellen Carol DuBois, *Feminism and Suffrage: The Emergence of an Independent Women's Movement in America, 1848–1869* (Cornell University Press, 1978) and *Suffrage: Women's Long Battle for the Vote* (Simon & Schuster, 2020); Stephanie McCurry, *Women's War: Fighting and Surviving the American Civil War* (Belknap Press, 2019); Pamela D. Toler, *Heroines of Mercy Street: The Real Nurses of the Civil War* (Little, Brown and Company, 2016); Elizabeth Varon, *Southern Lady, Yankee Spy: The True Story of Elizabeth Van Lew, a Union Agent in the Heart of the Confederacy* (Oxford University Press, 2003) and *Armies of Deliverance: A New History of the Civil War* (Oxford University Press, 2019); Susan Ware, *Why They Marched: Untold Stories of the Women Who Fought for the Right to Vote* (Belknap Press, 2019); and Elaine Weiss, *The Woman's Hour: The Great Fight to Win the Vote* (Viking, 2018).

SOURCES

EPIGRAPH

Mary Edwards Walker, "Soldiers' Appreciation of Noble Women," *The Sibyl* 8:1 (July 1863), 1157 (see page vi).

INTRODUCTION: "I WILL ALWAYS BE SOMEBODY"

Nixon B. Stewart, *Dan. McCook's Regiment, 52nd O.V.I.: A History of the Regiment, Its Campaigns and Battles* (Alliant, OH: Published by the Author, 1900; reprinted Huntington, WV: Blue Acorn Press, 1999), 80 (see page viii).

James M. McPherson, *Battle Cry of Freedom: The Civil War Era* (New York: Oxford University Press, 1988), 670–74; Battle of Chickamauga, www.battlefields.org/learn/civil-war/battles/chickamauga, accessed January 25, 2019 (see page viii).

Robert P. Broadwater, *General George H. Thomas: A Biography of the Union's "Rock of Chickamauga"* (Jefferson, NC: McFarland and Company, 2009), 161–62 (see page ix).

McPherson, *Battle Cry of Freedom*, 743–44; Stewart, *Dan. McCook's Regiment*, 84; Sharon M. Harris, *Dr. Mary Walker: An American Radical, 1832–1919* (New Brunswick, NJ: Rutgers University Press, 2009), 52 (see page ix).

Stewart, *Dan. McCook's Regiment*, 91; Harris, *Dr. Mary Walker*, 54 (see page ix).

Harris, *Dr. Mary Walker*, 55; Mary Edwards Walker, "Incidents Connected with the Army," Box 4, Mary Edwards Walker Papers, Special Collections Research Center, Syracuse University Libraries, Syracuse, New York, hereafter abbreviated SCSU (see page x).

Harris, *Dr. Mary Walker*, 54–55; Walker, "Incidents Connected with the Army," hereafter abbreviated "Incidents" (see page x).

"Petition of Dr. Mary E. Walker, Praying Compensation for Services During the Late War, August 25, 1890," *The Miscellaneous Documents of the Senate of the United States for the First Session of the Fifty-First Congress* (Washington: Government Printing Office, 1890), 9; Stacey Graham, "Samuel 'Champ' Ferguson (1821–1865)," *Tennessee Encyclopedia*, https://tennesseeencyclopedia.net/entries/samuel-ferguson/, accessed online January 31, 2019. More than twenty years after the war, Walker saw a photo of Ferguson and connected him with the incident. She was likely mistaken (see page x).

Troy D. Smith, "Champ Ferguson: An American Civil War Rebel Guerrilla," History Net, June 12, 2006, www.historynet.com/champ-ferguson-an-american-civil-war-rebel-guerrilla.htm, accessed January 31, 2019 (see page xi).

Stewart, *Dan. McCook's Regiment*, 91 (see page xi).

Harris, *Dr. Mary Walker*, 57; Mary Edwards Walker to Edwin Stanton, September 1862, RG 94, Dr. Mary E. Walker file, National Archives and Records Administration, Washington, DC, hereafter abbreviated NARA (see page xi).

Elizabeth D. Leonard, *Yankee Women: Gender Battles in the Civil War* (New York: W. W. Norton, 1994), 138; Harris, *Dr. Mary Walker*, 58 (see page xii).

"Refused Hand of Pres. Arthur," *New Castle* (PA) *News*, March 28, 1914, 13 (see page xii).

CHAPTER ONE: GETTING TO WASHINGTON

James M. McPherson, *Battle Cry of Freedom: The Civil War Era* (New York: Oxford University Press, 1988), 318 (see page 1).

Jim Cullen, " 'I's a Man Now': Gender and African American Men," in Catherine Clinton and Nina Silber, eds., *Divided Houses: Gender and the Civil War* (New York: Oxford University Press, 1992), 78, 80 (see page 2).

Louisa May Alcott, *Hospital Sketches* (Boston: James Redpath, 1863), 9, www.gutenberg .org/files/3837/3837-h/3837-h.htm, accessed January 3, 2019 (see page 2).

Jeanie Attie, "Warwork and the Crisis of Domesticity in the North," in Catherine Clinton and Nina Silber, eds., *Divided Houses: Gender and the Civil War* (New York: Oxford University Press, 1992), 248–49; Nina Silber, *Daughters of the Union: Northern Women Fight the Civil War* (Cambridge: Harvard University Press, 2005), 162–65 (see page 3).

Attie, "Warwork and the Crisis of Domesticity in the North," 247–48; Louisa May Alcott, *Her Life, Letters, and Journals*, edited by Ednah D. Cheney (Boston: Little, Brown, 1898), 127, www.gutenberg.org/files/38049/38049-h/38049-h.htm, accessed January 10, 2019; Jeanie Attie, *Patriotic Toil: Northern Women and the American Civil War* (Ithaca: Cornell University Press, 1998), 25, 31 (see page 3).

The scant evidence available on Ancestry.com about Albert Miller shows that he was born in April 1831 in Covert, New York (see page 3).

Samuel J. May, *The Rights and Condition of Women: A Sermon, Preached in Syracuse, Nov., 1845*, www.loc.gov/item/09002749/, accessed January 7, 2019. See also Donald Yacovone, *Samuel Joseph May and the Dilemmas of the Liberal Persuasion, 1797–1871* (Philadelphia: Temple University Press, 1991) (see page 4).

Sharon M. Harris, *Dr. Mary Walker: An American Radical, 1832–1919* (New Brunswick, NJ: Rutgers University Press, 2009), 15 (see page 4).

Elisabeth Griffith, *In Her Own Right: The Life of Elizabeth Cady Stanton* (New York: Oxford University Press, 1984), 33 (see page 5).

T. W. [Thomas Wentworth] Higginson, "Marriage of Lucy Stone Under Protest." *The Liberator*, 25: 18 (May 4, 1855), 71, www.historyisaweapon.com/defcon1/stone blackwellmarriageprotest.html, accessed January 7, 2019 (see page 5).

Harris, *Dr. Mary Walker*, 15, 25–26 (see page 5).

Harris, *Dr. Mary Walker*, 27 (see page 5).

Mary E. Miller Walker, MD, "New York State Foundling Hospital," *The Sibyl*, 4:3 (August 1, 1859), 593–95 (see page 6).

Amy Kesselman, "The 'Freedom Suit': Feminism and Dress Reform in the United States, 1848–1875," *Gender and Society* 5:4 (December 1991), 503 (see page 6).

Amy Kesselman, "Lydia Sayer Hasbrouck and '*The Sibyl*': Bloomers, Feminism and the Laws of Life." *OCHS Journal* 14 (November 1, 1985), www.orangecountyhistorical-society.org/J-1985_Lydia_Sayer_Hasbrouck.html, accessed February 14, 2019 (see page 6).

Harris, *Dr. Mary Walker*, 37 (see page 7).

Women of the Hudson Valley, https://omeka.hrvh.org/exhibits/show/women-of-the-hudson-valley/in-reform, accessed February 18, 2019 (see page 7).

Harris, *Dr. Mary Walker*, 20–21; Dr. W., "Extracts from Correspondence," *The Sibyl*, 1:13 (January 1, 1857), 102 (see page 7).

"The Canastota Convention," *The Sibyl*, 1:14 (January 15, 1857), 109; Mary E. Miller Walker, MD, "Dress Reform Convention," *The Sibyl*, 1:14 (January 15, 1857), 105 (see page 8).

L. J. Worden to "To Whom It May Concern," March 21, 1866, Mary Edwards Walker Papers, Box 2, SCSU; "Dr. Mary Walker, The Forgotten Woman," unpublished manuscript, 66–67, Lida Poynter Collection, #026, Drexel University College of Medicine, Archives and Special Collections on Women in Medicine and Homeopathy; "National Union League," *National Republican* (Washington, DC), May 4, 1863, 179 (see page 8).

John D'Emilio and Estelle B. Freedman, *Intimate Matters: A History of Sexuality in America*, 3rd ed. (Chicago: University of Chicago Press, 2012), 58–59 (see page 8).

D'Emilio and Freedman, *Intimate Matters*, 61–63 (see page 9).

D'Emilio and Freedman, *Intimate Matters*, 71 (see page 9).

Harris, *Dr. Mary Walker*, 27; L. J. Worden to "To Whom It May Concern," March 21, 1866 (see page 11).

Nancy F. Cott, *Public Vows: A History of Marriage and the Nation* (Cambridge: Harvard University Press, 2000), 28–29, 48–51 (see page 11).

For additional details about this divorce case, see Di Long, "Divorce in New York from 1850s to 1920s," Master's Thesis, University of Georgia, 2013. https://getd.libs.uga .edu/pdfs/long_di_201312_ma.pdf, accessed January 4, 2019 (see page 11).

L. J. Worden to "To Whom It May Concern," March 21, 1866; D'Emilio and Freedman, *Intimate Matters*, 115–16 (see page 12).

L. J. Worden to "To Whom It May Concern," March 21, 1866 (see page 12).

Revised Statutes of the Territory of Iowa (Iowa City: Hughes and Williams, 1843), 169–70. www.legis.iowa.gov/docs/shelves/code/ocr/1843%20Revised%20Statutes%20 of%20the%20Territory%20of%20Iowa.pdf, accessed January 11, 2019 (see page 12).

Harris, *Dr. Mary Walker*, 28. Additional details about Albert House's life are available on Ancestry.com (see page 13).

Harris, Dr. Mary Walker, 28 (see page 13).

The History of Delaware County, Iowa (Chicago: Western Historical Company, 1878), 463–64. https://books.google.com/books?id=-AguAAAAYAAJ&printsec=front cover&dq=the+history+of+delaware+county+iowa&hl=en&sa=X&ved=0ahUK EwjtoNvOgPDfAhWjxYMKHSbxCEAQ6AEIKjAA#v=onepage&q=the%20

history%20of%20delaware%20county%20iowa&f=false, accessed January 15, 2019 (see page 13).

The History of Delaware County, Iowa, 464 (see page 13).

Diane Fannon-Langton, "Time Machine: Bowen Collegiate Institute." *The Gazette* (Cedar Rapids, IA), January 30, 2017, www.thegazette.com/subject/news/archive/ time-machine-bowen-collegiate-institute-hopkinton-builds-a-college-in-the-1850s-20170130, accessed January 12, 2019; *The History of Delaware County, Iowa*, 464. Scant information exists about Cooley's life, but documents on Ancestry.com confirm she was born in 1832, the same year as Mary Walker (see page 14).

Fannon-Langton, "Time Machine: Bowen Collegiate Institute" (see page 14).

Harris, *Dr. Mary Walker*, 29 (see page 15).

Harris, *Dr. Mary Walker*, 31; State of New York Supreme Court Decree, Mary E. Miller agt. Albert E. Miller, September 16, 1861, Mary Edwards Walker Papers, Box 2, SCSU (see page 15).

Kenneth J. Winkle, *Lincoln's Citadel: The Civil War in Washington, DC* (New York: W. W. Norton, 2013), 98–104; Harris, *Dr. Mary Walker*, 57 (see page 15).

McPherson, *Battle Cry of Freedom*, 308. As McPherson put it, "amateurs went to war" (see page 16).

McPherson, *Battle Cry of Freedom*, 347. These figures vary from source to source, as McPherson acknowledged (see page 16).

Elizabeth D. Leonard, *Yankee Women: Gender Battles in the Civil War* (New York: W. W. Norton, 1994), 7, Winkle, *Lincoln's Citadel*, 213–14 (see page 17).

Ira M. Rutkow, *Bleeding Blue and Gray: Civil War Surgery and the Evolution of American Medicine* (New York: Random House, 2005), 6–8; Winkle, *Lincoln's Citadel*, 217–18 (see page 17).

Winkle, *Lincoln's Citadel*, 218; Leonard, *Yankee Women*, 7 (see page 18).

Leonard, *Yankee Women*, 7 (see page 18).

Leonard, *Yankee Women*, 16–17; Silber, *Daughters of the Union*, 113–15 (see page 18).

CHAPTER TWO: COMMISSION SEEKER

"The Election Case of Simon Cameron of Pennsylvania (1857)," www.senate.gov/artand history/history/common/contested_elections/031Simon_Cameron.htm, accessed November 29, 2018; Ida M. Street, "The Simon Cameron Indian Commission of 1838." *The Annals of Iowa* 7 (1905), 115–39. http://dx.doi.org/10.17077/0003 -4827.3189, accessed November 29, 2018 (see page 20).

Sharon M. Harris, *Dr. Mary Walker: An American Radical, 1832–1919* (New Brunswick, NJ: Rutgers University Press, 2009), 1–2 (see page 21).

The City of Oswego, www.oswegony.org/explore/history, accessed December 5, 2018 (see page 21).

Karen Abbot, "The Fox Sisters and the Rap on Spiritualism," Smithsonian.com, October 30, 2012. www.smithsonianmag.com/history/the-fox-sisters-and-the-rap-on-spiritualism-99663697/, accessed December 6, 2018. See also Anne Braude, *Radical Spirits: Spiritualism and Women's Rights in Nineteenth-Century America*, 2nd ed. (Bloomington: Indiana University Press), 2001, and Barbara Weisberg, *Talking to the Dead: Kate and Maggie Fox and the Rise of Spiritualism* (New York: Harper One, 2004) (see page 22).

Adele Oltman, "The Hidden History of Slavery in New York," *The Nation*, October 24, 2005, www.thenation.com/article/hidden-history-slavery-new-york/, accessed December 11, 2018; Slavery in New York, www.slaveryinnewyork.org/history.htm, accessed December 11, 2018; When Did Slavery End in New York State? www .nyhistory.org/community/slavery-end-new-york-state, accessed December 11, 2018 (see page 23).

Dr. Walker, "Women Soldiers," *The Sibyl*, 4:5 (September 1, 1859), 610–11 (see page 23).

Nina Silber, *Daughters of the Union: Northern Women Fight the Civil War* (Cambridge: Harvard University Press, 2005), 177, 163. See also Jeanie Attie, *Patriotic Toil: Northern Women and the American Civil War* (Ithaca: Cornell University Press, 1998) (see page 25).

Elizabeth D. Leonard, *Yankee Women: Gender Battles in the Civil War* (New York: W. W. Norton, 1994), 10 (see page 25).

Silber, *Daughters of the Union*, 176–77; Kristie Ross, "Arranging a Doll's House: Refined Women as Union Nurses," in Catherine Clinton and Nina Silber, eds. *Divided Houses: Gender and the Civil War* (New York: Oxford University Press, 1992), 98 (see page 25).

For more on Mary Gove Nichols, see Jean L. Silver-Isenstadt, *Shameless: The Visionary Life of Mary Gove Nichols* (Baltimore: Johns Hopkins University Press, 2002) (see page 27).

Elisabeth Griffith, *In Her Own Right: The Life of Elizabeth Cady Stanton* (New York: Oxford University Press, 1984), 43 (see page 27).

Harris, *Dr. Mary Walker*, 5–6; *The Falley Seminary, of the Black River Conference, Fulton, NY, 1836–1855* (Fulton, NY: The Gazette Office, 1855), 47, Ancestry.com (see page 27).

Jean V. Matthews, "Consciousness of Self and Consciousness of Sex in Antebellum Feminism," *Journal of Women's History*, 5:1 (Spring 1993): 70; Harris, *Dr. Mary Walker*, 18 (see page 28).

Griffith, *In Her Own Right*, 8, 17, 24, 26, 33 (see page 29).

Griffith, *In Her Own Right*, 34 (see page 29).

Griffith, *In Her Own Right*, 36–38; Lisa Tetrault, *The Myth of Seneca Falls: Memory and the Women's Suffrage Movement, 1848–1898* (Chapel Hill: University of North Carolina Press, 2014), 10–12 (see page 29).

Griffith, *In Her Own Right*, 43 (see page 29).

Griffith, *In Her Own Right*, 50–57; Tetrault, *The Myth of Seneca Falls*, 12–13 (see page 30).

Griffith, *In Her Own Right*, 57–60; Tetrault, *The Myth of Seneca Falls*, 14–15 (see page 30).

Elizabeth Cady Stanton, *Eighty Years and More: Reminiscences, 1815–1897* (New York: T. Fisher Unwin, 1898, reprint ed., New York: Schocken Books, 1971), 201–02 (see page 30).

"The Visit of Jenny Lind to America," *New York Herald*," May 6, 1850, 7, accessed December 28, 2018 (see page 31).

Keith S. Hambrick, "The Swedish Nightingale in New Orleans: Jenny Lind's Visit of 1851," *Louisiana History: The Journal of the Louisiana Historical Association*, Vol. 22, No. 4 (Autumn, 1981), 387–88 (see page 31).

Regan Shrumm, "Meet Jenny Lind, One of America's First Female Celebrities," Smithsonian Blog, March 16, 2016, http://americanhistory.si.edu/blog/jenny-lind, accessed online December 27, 2018; Harris, *Dr. Mary Walker*, 8–9; Hambrick, "The Swedish Nightingale in New Orleans," 391–92, 398 (see page 31).

Harris, *Dr. Mary Walker*, 9 (see page 32).

John S. Haller, *Medical Protestants: The Eclectics in American Medicine* (Carbondale: Southern Illinois University Press, 1994), 152–53 (see page 32).

John K. Scudder, MD, ed., *The Eclectic Medical Journal*. Vol. LVII (Cincinnati, OH: The Scudder Brothers Company, 1897), 429; Haller, *Medical Protestants*, 153–54; Harris, *Dr. Mary Walker*, 9 (see page 33).

Haller, *Medical Protestants*, 128, 140; Leonard, *Yankee Women*, n. 14, 242–43; Robert G. Slawson, MD, "Medical Training in the United States Prior to the Civil War," *Journal of Evidence-Based Complementary and Alternative Medicine*. 17:1 (2012), 13; Harris, *Dr. Mary Walker*, 10 (see page 33).

Harris, *Dr. Mary Walker*, 11 (see page 33).

CHAPTER THREE: VOLUNTEER SURGEON

"The Drama of the Civil War at the Patent Office," www.streetsofwashington .com/2015/06/the-drama-of-civil-war-at-patent-office.html, accessed December 18, 2018; Elizabeth D. Leonard, *Yankee Women: Gender Battles in the Civil War* (New York: W. W. Norton, 1994), 115; Kenneth J. Winkle, *Lincoln's Citadel: The Civil War in Washington, DC* (New York: W.W. Norton, 2013), 215 (see page 35).

Mary E. Walker, MD, "What Can Woman Do?" *The Sibyl*, 6:7 (January 1862), 1011 (see page 36).

Letter from E. H. Stockwell to "To Whomsoever it May Concern," June 3, 1855, Records of the War Department, Office of the Adjutant General, Records Group 94, Re: Dr. Mary Walker, NARA; John S. Haller Jr., *Kindly Medicine: Physio-Medicalism in America, 1836–1911* (Kent, OH: Kent State University Press, 1997), 39; Leonard, *Yankee Women*, 116; Sharon M. Harris, *Dr. Mary Walker: An American Radical, 1832–1919* (New Brunswick, NJ: Rutgers University Press, 2009), 32 (see page 36).

John Bell, *Confederate Seadog: John Taylor Wood in War and Exile* (Jefferson, NC: McFarland and Company, 2002), 12–15 (see page 37).

Ira M. Rutkow, *Bleeding Blue and Gray: Civil War Surgery and the Evolution of American Medicine* (New York: Random House, 2005), 67, 73–74; Judith Ann Giesberg, *Civil War Sisterhood: The U.S. Sanitary Commission and Women's Politics in Transition* (Boston: Northeastern University Press, 2000), 5 (see page 37).

Harris, *Dr. Mary Walker*, 32 (see page 37).

Mary Edwards Walker, "Incidents Connected with the Army," Mary Edwards Walker Papers, Box 4, SCSU; Harris, *Dr. Mary Walker*, 32–33 (see page 38).

Walker, "Incidents" (see page 38).

Carole Emberton, "The Minister of Death," *New York Times*, August 17, 2012, https://opinionator.blogs.nytimes.com/2012/08/17/the-minister-of-death/, accessed February 19, 2019 (see page 38).

Emberton, "The Minister of Death" (see page 39).

Rutkow, *Bleeding Blue and Gray*, 16; Harris, *Dr. Mary Walker*, 33; Winkle, *Lincoln's Citadel*, 219 (see page 39).

Walker, "Incidents" (see page 39).

Walker, "Incidents" (see page 40).

Walker, "Incidents" (see page 40).

Walker, "Incidents" (see page 40).

Walker, "Incidents" (see page 40).

Rutkow, *Bleeding Blue and Gray*, 78–81; 88–95 (see page 41).

Edwin M. Stone to Mary Walker, December 9, 1861 and January 7, 1861 [*sic* 1862], Mary Edwards Walker Papers, Box 1, SCSU. Additional biographical information on Stone is available in the Edwin M. Stone Papers, Rhode Island Historical Society, www.rihs.org/mssinv/Mss854.htm (see page 41).

Mary Walker to Brother and Sister, November 13, 1861, Mary Edwards Walker file, Gerald R. Ford Presidential Library; Harris, *Dr. Mary Walker*, 33; Leonard, *Yankee Women*, 115 (see page 42).

Winkle, *Lincoln's Citadel*, 156–57 (see page 42).

Winkle, *Lincoln's Citadel*, 158 (see page 42).

Judith E. Harper, *Women During the Civil War: An Encyclopedia* (New York: Routledge, 2003), 176–77; Kate Lineberry, "The Wild Rose of Washington," *New York Times*, August 22, 2011, https://opinionator.blogs.nytimes.com/2011/08/22/the-wild-rose-of-washington/, accessed February 13, 2019; Ann Blackman, *Wild Rose: Rose O'Neale Greenhow, Civil War Spy* (New York: Random House, 2005), 9–11, 15, 21; Edwin C. Fishel, *The Secret War for the Union: The Untold Story of Military Intelligence in the Civil War* (New York: Houghton Mifflin Company, 1996), 58 (see page 43).

Blackman, *Wild Rose*, 36–37; Fishel, *The Secret War for the Union*, 59 (see page 43).

Lineberry, "The Wild Rose of Washington"; Michael Farquhar, " 'Rebel Rose,' A Spy of Grande Dame Proportions," *Washington Post*, September 18, 2000, A1, www.washingtonpost.com/wp-srv/WPcap/2000-09/18/057r-091800-idx.html, accessed February 13, 2019; Blackman, *Wild Rose*, 3–6, 39; Fishel, *The Secret War for the Union*, 59–60 (see page 44).

Lineberry, "The Wild Rose of Washington"; Blackman, *Wild Rose*, 47–48, 52–56, 183–87. Fishel is skeptical about much of Greenhow's story. *See* Fishel, *The Secret War for the Union*, 60–66 (see page 44).

Lineberry, "The Wild Rose of Washington"; Blackman, *Wild Rose*, 188–203; Fishel, *The Secret War for the Union*, 66–70 (see page 44).

"The Washington Diary of Horatio Taft," Library of Congress, www.loc.gov/collections/diary-of-horatio-taft/articles-and-essays/the-washington-diary-of-horatio-taft/, accessed March 8, 2019 (see page 45).

Julia Taft Bayne, *Tad Lincoln's Father* (Boston: Little, Brown, and Company, 1931), 53–56; Charles Lachman, *The Last Lincolns: The Rise and Fall of a Great American Family* (New York: Union Square Press, 2008), 84–86 (see page 45).

Bayne, *Tad Lincoln's Father*, 64 (see page 45).

Bayne, *Tad Lincoln's Father*, 65 (see page 46).

Bayne, *Tad Lincoln's Father*, 172 (see page 46).

Bayne, *Tad Lincoln's Father*, 93–95 (see page 47).

Bayne, *Tad Lincoln's Father*, 95–97 (see page 47).

Bayne, *Tad Lincoln's Father*, 172 (see page 47).

Mary E. Walker, MD, "What Can Woman Do?" *The Sibyl*, 6:7 (January 1862), 1011 (see page 48).

Mrs. F. R. Harris Reid, "Wisconsin Florence Nightingale Union," Circular Letter, May 1861, Berlin, Wisconsin, Harris Reid Papers, Wisconsin State Historical Society, Madison, Wisconsin (see page 48).

Mrs. F. R. Harris Reid, "Short Dresses in the Army," *The Sibyl*, 5:23 (June 1, 1861), 947 (see page 48).

Letter from J. M. Mackenzie to "To Whom It May Concern," October 28, 1861, Mary Edwards Walker Papers, Box 1, SCSU. Mackenzie was a prominent member of the Sacramento community, serving on its city council. See "Sacramento Historic City Cemetery Established in Mid-19th Century," *Valley Community Newspapers*, January 29, 2014, www.valcomnews.com/?p=13275, accessed December 18, 2018 (see page 48).

Walker, "Incidents" (see page 49).

Walker, "Incidents" (see page 49).

Walker, "Incidents" (see page 50).

Walker, "Incidents" (see page 50).

Robert McNamara, "Why Amputations Became Common In the Civil War," ThoughtCo., www.thoughtco.com/amputations-became-common-in-the-civil-war-1773715, accessed February 23, 2019; Rutkow, *Bleeding Blue and Gray*, 30–31, 216–18 (see page 50).

Harris, *Dr. Mary Walker*, 9–10 (see page 51).

Sherry Ceniza, *Walt Whitman and 19th-Century Women Reformers* (Tuscaloosa: University of Alabama Press, 1998), 47 (see page 51).

"Lydia Folger Fowler," Women History Blog, www.womenhistoryblog.com/2014/09/lydia-folger-fowler.html, accessed February 23, 2019; Madeleine B. Stern, *Heads & Headlines: The Phrenological Fowlers* (Norman: University of Oklahoma Press, 1971), 181 (see page 52).

"The Hygeio-Therapeutic College," *The Water-Cure Journal*, May 1862, 109–10, https://archive.org/details/McGillLibrary-osl-water-cure-v33n5-18742/page/n11, accessed February 23, 2019 (see page 52).

CHAPTER FOUR: FIELD SURGEON

James M. McPherson, *Battle Cry of Freedom: The Civil War Era* (New York: Oxford University Press, 1988), 396–403 (see page 53).

Quoted in McPherson, *Battle Cry of Freedom*, 414 (see page 54).

Ira M. Rutkow, *Bleeding Blue and Gray: Civil War Surgery and the Evolution of American Medicine* (New York: Random House, 2005), 115–16 (see page 54).

Rutkow, *Bleeding Blue and Gray*, 131; Judith E. Harper, *Women During the Civil War: An Encyclopedia* (New York: Routledge, 2003), 199; Katharine [*sic*] Prescott Wormeley, *The Other Side of War: With the Army of the Potomac* (Boston: Ticknor and Company, 1889), 13 (see page 54).

Wormeley, *The Other Side of War*, 15–17 (see page 55).

Wormeley, *The Other Side of War*, 72–73, 89, 103–04; Harper, *Women During the Civil War*, 201 (see page 55).

Mary Clemmer Ames, *Ten Years in Washington: Life and Scenes in the National Capital, As a Woman Sees Them* (Hartford, CT: A. D. Worthington & Co., 1873), 67, 69 (see page 55).

Ames, *Ten Years in Washington*, 69 (see page 56).

Kenneth J. Winkle, *Lincoln's Citadel: The Civil War in Washington, DC* (New York: W. W. Norton, 2013), 182–84 (see page 56).

Winkle, *Lincoln's Citadel*, 187, 190–91 (see page 56).

Winkle, *Lincoln's Citadel*, 192–94 (see page 56).

Winkle, *Lincoln's Citadel*, 201; "Miss Belle Boyd," *The Spirit of the Age* (Raleigh, NC), October 27, 1862, 4 (see page 57).

Edwin C. Fishel, *The Secret War for the Union: The Untold Story of Military Intelligence in the Civil War* (New York: Houghton Mifflin Company, 1996), 174–76; McPherson, *Battle Cry of Freedom*, 456; Winkle, *Lincoln's Citadel*, 201; "Another Account of the Retreat of Banks," *The Wheeling* (WV) *Daily Intelligencer*, May 31, 1862, 3 (see page 57).

Winkle, *Lincoln's Citadel*, 201 (see page 57).

Fishel, *The Secret War for the Union*, 176; "Belle Boyd," *The Buffalo* (NY) *Commercial*, August 6, 1862, 4 (see page 58).

Nancy Isenberg, *Sex and Citizenship in Antebellum America* (Chapel Hill: University of North Carolina Press, 1998), 53 (see page 58).

Letter from Dr. Mary E. Walker, *The Sibyl* 7:11 (July 1862), 1059 (see page 58).

Letter from Dr. Mary E. Walker, *The Sibyl* 7:11 (July 1862), 1059; Sharon M. Harris, *Dr. Mary Walker: An American Radical, 1832–1919* (New Brunswick, NJ: Rutgers University Press, 2009), 38–39 (see page 58).

Damani Davis, "Slavery and Emancipation in the Nation's Capital," *Prologue Magazine*, Spring 2010www.archives.gov/publications/prologue/2010/spring/dcslavery.html, accessed March 2, 2019 (see page 59).

Quoted in McPherson, *Battle Cry of Freedom*, 495 (see page 60).

McPherson, *Battle Cry of Freedom*, 497; Matthew Pinsker, "Contrabands of War," Emancipation Digital Classroom, http://housedivided.dickinson.edu/sites/emancipation/2012/07/14/contraband-of-war/, accessed March 5, 2019 (see page 60).

McPherson, *Battle Cry of Freedom*, 352–54. The full text of the 1861 Confiscation Act can be found at the Freedmen & Southern Society Project website, www.freedmen.umd.edu/conact1.htm, accessed March 5, 2019 (see page 61).

McPherson, *Battle Cry of Freedom*, 528–32 (see page 62).

McPherson, *Battle Cry of Freedom*, 540–45; Winkle, *Lincoln's Citadel*, 363 (see page 62).

Elizabeth Brown Pryor, *Clara Barton, Professional Angel* (Philadelphia: University of Pennsylvania Press, 1988), 23, 26, 33, 48, 52, 56–59, 62, 64 (see page 63).

Pryor, *Clara Barton*, 79–81 (see page 63).

Pryor, *Clara Barton*, 81, 84, 87 (see page 63).

Pryor, *Clara Barton*, 93, 97 (see page 64).

Stephen B. Oates, *A Woman of Valor: Clara Barton and the Civil War* (New York: The Free Press, 1994), 91–93, 97–98; Pryor, *Clara Barton*, 99; F. H. Harwood, "An Army Surgeon's Story," *St. Louis Illustrated* 24:150 (April 1883), 137–50 (see page 64).

Laura Leedy Gansler, *The Mysterious Private Thompson: The Double Life of Sarah Emma Edmonds, Civil War Soldier* (New York: Free Press, 2005), chapters 1, 3, 4 (see page 65).

Gansler, *The Mysterious Private Thompson*, chapters 4–7; DeAnne Blanton and Lauren M. Cook, *They Fought Like Demons: Women Soldiers in the Civil War* (Baton Rouge: Louisiana State University Press, 2002), 98; "Sarah Emma Edmonds," Civil War Biography, American Battlefield Trust, www.battlefields.org/learn/biographies/ sarah-emma-edmonds, accessed April 10, 2019 (see page 65).

Gansler, *The Mysterious Private Thompson*, 136–40; Blanton and Cook, *They Fought Like Demons*, 92; S. Emma E. Edmonds, *Nurse and Spy in the Union Army: Comprising the Adventures and Experiences of a Woman in Hospitals, Camps, and Battle-Fields* (Hartford, CT: W. S. Williams & Co., 1865), 271–73, www.gutenberg.org/ files/38497/38497-h/38497-h.htm#CHAPTER_XX, accessed April 10, 2019 (see page 65).

Gansler, *The Mysterious Private Thompson*, 180–84 (see page 66).

Blanton and Cook, *They Fought Like Demons*, 98–99, 157–58, 167–69; "Sarah Emma Edmonds"; Edmonds, *Nurse and Spy in the Union Army*, 6; McPherson, *Battle Cry of Freedom*, 483; Gansler, *The Mysterious Private Thompson*, 172–73, 185, 188–89, 193–96 (see page 66).

Alfred Young, *Masquerade: The Life and Times of Deborah Sampson, Continental Soldier* (New York: Vintage Books, 2004), 13, 86, 114 (see page 66).

"A Female Soldier," *Holmes County* (OH) *Republican*, May 23, 1861, 1; "Our Camp Correspondence," *Cincinnati Daily Press*, May 14, 1861, 3. The theme of romance is also covered in Blanton and Cook, *They Fought Like Demons*, 145–46 (see page 67).

"Our Camp Correspondence"; "A Female Soldier." These stories can be found throughout the war years. For example, the exploits of "Frank Martin" were also widely reported in 1863. See "A Romantic History—The Story of a Female Soldier—How Women Join the Army," *The Brooklyn* (NY) *Daily Eagle*, May 13, 1863, 1 (see page 67).

McPherson, *Battle Cry of Freedom*, 557 (see page 68).

Hobbs v. Fogg, 6 Watts 553, Pennsylvania Supreme Court, 1837, 17, www.ravellaw.com/ opinions/cf3af59a823d5fe51f588c4fadffc510, accessed April 18, 2019 (see page 68).

Leonard, *Yankee Women*, 120; Mary Edwards Walker, "On Washington, the Seat of the Government." Mary Edwards Walker Papers, Box 4, SCSU (see page 68).

Walker, "On Washington" (see page 68).

"Petition of Dr. Mary E. Walker, Praying Compensation for Services During the Late War, August 25, 1890," *The Miscellaneous Documents of the Senate of the United States for the First Session of the Fifty-First Congress* (Washington: Government Printing Office, 1890), 4–5; "Women in the Army," *The Sibyl* 8:5 (November 1863), 1188 (see page 69).

McPherson, *Battle Cry of Freedom*, 568–69 (see page 69).

Mary Edwards Walker, "Incidents Connected with the Army," Mary Edwards Walker Papers, Box 4, SCSU (see page 70).

Walker, "Incidents" (see page 71).

"Petition of Dr. Mary E. Walker, 3; https://books.google.com/books?id=UKH9jcGYoAw C&pg=RA18-PA3&lpg=RA18-PA3&dq=ambrose+burnside+and+mary+walker +warrenton+va&source=bl&ots=mubfncpSv6&sig=ACfU3U2LDZvz2NnNd-2k _C3cndARJY4Gxw&hl=en&sa=X&ved=2ahUKEwjzysKsocvhAhUEba0KHR9 cAYI4ChDoATAPegQICBAB#v=onepage&q=ambrose%20burnside%20and%20 mary%20walker%20warrenton%20va&f=false, accessed April 12, 2019 (see page 71).

Walker, "Incidents" (see page 71).

Walker, "Incidents" (see page 72).

"Petition of Dr. Mary E. Walker"; Walker, "Incidents." Walker misremembered Cutting as a captain (see page 72).

Walker, "Incidents" (see page 72).

Walker, "Incidents"; "Petition of Dr. Mary E. Walker." Walker gave two slightly different accounts of where the train stopped (see page 73).

Walker, "Incidents" (see page 73).

Walker, "Incidents" (see page 73).

Drew Gilpin Faust, *This Republic of Suffering: Death and the American Civil War* (New York: Alfred A. Knopf, 2008), xiii, 6–11 (see page 73).

Walker, "Incidents" (see page 73).

McPherson, *Battle Cry of Freedom*, 570–71 (see page 74).

McPherson, *Battle Cry of Freedom*, 571–72; Rutkow, *Bleeding Blue and Gray*, 206–07 (see page 74).

Rutkow, *Bleeding Blue and Gray*, 146, 182 (see page 74).

Rutkow, *Bleeding Blue and Gray*, 196–99, 201 (see page 75).

Rutkow, *Bleeding Blue and Gray*, 206–09; Oates, *A Woman of Valor*, 104 (see page 75).

Oates, *A Woman of Valor*, 94–96, 98, 100, 103; Pryor, *Clara Barton*, 103–04 (see page 76).

Oates, *A Woman of Valor*, 101–06; Pryor, *Clara Barton*, 104–05 (see page 76).

Oates, *A Woman of Valor*, 108–09; Pryor, *Clara Barton*, 106 (see page 76).

Oates, *A Woman of Valor*, 111–15; Pryor, *Clara Barton*, 106 (see page 77).

Rutkow, *Bleeding Blue and Gray*, 218; Pryor, *Clara Barton*, 107; Oates, *A Woman of Valor*, 117–18 (see page 77).

Walker, "Incidents" (see page 77).

Roy Morris Jr., *Better Angel: Walt Whitman in the Civil War* (New York: Oxford University Press, 2000), 54 (see page 77).

Morris, *Better Angel*, 56–60 (see page 78).
Morris, *Better Angel*, 70 (see page 78).
Elizabeth Brown Pryor, *Clara Barton, Professional Angel* (Philadelphia: University of Pennsylvania Press, 1988), 107 (see page 78).
Stephen B. Oates, *A Woman of Valor: Clara Barton and the Civil War* (New York: The Free Press, 1994), 119–21; Pryor, *Clara Barton*, 107; Morris, *Better Angel*, 78 (see page 79).
Morris, *Better Angel*, ch. 3; Oates, *A Woman of Valor*, 120; Pryor, *Clara Barton*, 108 (see page 79).
Walker, "Incidents" (see page 79).

CHAPTER FIVE: IN THE FIELD, IN THE CITY

Kenneth J. Winkle, *Lincoln's Citadel: The Civil War in Washington, DC* (New York: W. W. Norton, 2013), 323–24 (see page 80).
Winkle, *Lincoln's Citadel*, 324–25; Sharon M. Harris, *Dr. Mary Walker: An American Radical, 1832–1919* (New Brunswick, NJ: Rutgers University Press, 2009), 43 (see page 80).
Preston King to Mary Walker, January 10, 1863, RG 94, Mary E. Walker file, NARA (see page 81).
Harris, *Dr. Mary Walker*, 44 (see page 82).
Oates, *A Woman of Valor*, 124–25, 132–33 (see page 82).
James M. McPherson, *Battle Cry of Freedom: The Civil War Era* (New York: Oxford University Press, 1988), 600–01 (see page 82).
McPherson, *Battle Cry of Freedom*, 601; Winkle, *Lincoln's Citadel*, 341 (see page 82).
McPherson, *Battle Cry of Freedom*, 584–85 (see page 83).
McPherson, *Battle Cry of Freedom*, 639–45 (see page 83).
"Dr. Mary E. Walker," *Weekly Commonwealth* (Topeka, KS), July 22, 1863, 3; McPherson, *Battle Cry of Freedom*, 644 (see page 84).
Harris, *Dr. Mary Walker*, 41–42; "Petition of Dr. Mary E. Walker, Praying Compensation for Services During the Late War, August 25, 1890," *The Miscellaneous Documents of the Senate of the United States for the First Session of the Fifty-First Congress* (Washington: Government Printing Office, 1890), 6 (see page 84).
Quoted in Morris, *Better Angel*, 117–18 (see page 84).
Harris, *Dr. Mary Walker*, 45; McPherson, *Battle Cry of Freedom*, 645 (see page 85).
Mary Edwards Walker, "Soldiers' Appreciation of Noble Women," *The Sibyl* 8:1 (July 1863), 1157 (see page 85).
McPherson, *Battle Cry of Freedom*, 647 (see page 85).
McPherson, *Battle Cry of Freedom*, 648–49 (see page 85).
McPherson, *Battle Cry of Freedom*, 652 (see page 86).
Ira M. Rutkow, *Bleeding Blue and Gray: Civil War Surgery and the Evolution of American Medicine* (New York: Random House, 2005), 275–76 (see page 86).
McPherson, *Battle Cry of Freedom*, 663–65; Drew Gilpin Faust, *This Republic of Suffering: Death and the American Civil War* (New York: Alfred A. Knopf, 2008), 69; Rutkow, *Bleeding Blue and Gray*, 275 (see page 86).

Rutkow, *Bleeding Blue and Gray*, 276 (see page 86).

Sophronia E. Bucklin, *In Hospital and Camp: A Woman's Record of Thrilling Incidents Among the Wounded in the Late War* (Philadelphia: John E. Potter and Company, 1869), 36 (see page 87).

Bucklin, *In Hospital and Camp*, 33–34 (see page 87).

Bucklin, *In Hospital and Camp*, 37–40; Elizabeth D. Leonard, *Yankee Women: Gender Battles in the Civil War* (New York: W. W. Norton, 1994), 29 (see page 87).

Bucklin, *In Hospital and Camp*, 45–46, 66–67, 72, 132, 134, 137–38; Leonard, *Yankee Women*, 13, 19, 32 (see page 88).

Bucklin, *In Hospital and Camp*, 138–39 (see page 88).

Bucklin, *In Hospital and Camp*, 141–43 (see page 88).

Bucklin, *In Hospital and Camp*, 143–44, 152, 158, 184–86, 195–96. Bucklin was in the audience on November 19 when President Lincoln delivered his Gettysburg Address (see page 88).

"Petition of Dr. Mary E. Walker," 7 (see page 89).

Congressional Records Containing the Proceedings and Debates of the Fiftieth Congress, First Session, Volume XIX (Washington, DC: Government Printing Office, 1888), 2529; John Y. Foster, *New Jersey and the Rebellion: History of the Services of the Troops and People of New Jersey in Aid of the Union Cause* (Newark, NJ: Martin R. Dennis & Co., 1868), 29, https://archive.org/details/newjerseyrebell00fost/page/n7, accessed May 2, 2019. According to records on Ancestry.com and Find A Grave, Joseph H. Painter was born in Pennsylvania in 1817 or 1818. He married Esther Kersey in 1840. During the war he first served as a quartermaster sergeant with the 1st New Jersey Infantry, then with the 7th. At some point he received a promotion to lieutenant. The 1850 census showed the family living in Hardy, Ohio, where he worked as a telegrapher. After the war, Hettie Painter's request for an invalid pension (H.R. 3839) was reduced from $25 to $12 a month (see page 89).

Rutkow, *Bleeding Blue and Gray*, 280–81; *Congressional Records*, Volume XIX, 1888, 2529. In 1863, Barnes was appointed surgeon general (see page 89).

Congressional Records, Volume XIX, 1888, 2529 (see page 89).

Congressional Records, Volume XIX, 1888, 2529 (see page 90).

"Petition of Dr. Mary E. Walker," 7 (see page 90).

"Petition of Dr. Mary E. Walker," 7 (see page 90).

"Petition of Dr. Mary E. Walker," 7 (see page 91).

This information comes from the 1830, 1840, 1850, and 1860 census records available on Ancestry.com (see page 91).

"Petition of Dr. Mary E. Walker," 7 (see page 91).

"Petition of Dr. Mary E. Walker," 7 (see page 92).

"Petition of Dr. Mary E. Walker," 7 (see page 92).

"Dr. Mary E. Walker," *The Weekly Commonwealth* (Topeka, KS), July 22, 1863, 3. See also "Gleanings from our Exchanges," *Buffalo* (NY) *Courier*, June 19, 1863, 2. This second article was attributed to the *New-York Tribune*'s Army of the Potomac correspondent. In fact, both, and others like them, may have all been variations on the *Tribune* article (see page 92).

Sharon M. Harris, *Dr. Mary Walker: An American Radical, 1832–1919* (New Brunswick, NJ: Rutgers University Press, 2009), 43 (see page 92).

Mary Edwards Walker, "The True Spirit, Go on Faithfully," *The Sibyl*, 7 (March 1863), 1123 (see page 92).

Untitled, *The Sibyl* 7:9 (March 1863), 1126 (see page 93).

Harris, *Dr. Mary Walker*, 44; Walker, "Woman's Mind," *The Sibyl*, 7 (April 1863), 1133 (see page 93).

Newspapers gave the title of the poem as "My Dear Old Flag." However, it was probably George Cooper's poem "For the Dear Old Flag," which Stephen Foster put to music after Gettysburg, turning it into a popular wartime song. See "Grand Fair at Odd Fellows' Hall," *Evening Star* (Washington, DC), February 27, 1863, 2. The *National Republican* ran a similar article the same day (see page 94).

Rutkow, *Bleeding Blue and Gray*, 277 (see page 94).

Winkle, *Lincoln's Citadel*, 387 (see page 94).

Winkle, *Lincoln's Citadel*, 388–89 (see page 94).

Winkle, *Lincoln's Citadel*, 388; "New Military Prison," *Philadelphia Inquirer*, September 11, 1862, 4 (see page 95).

Winkle, *Lincoln's Citadel*, 389; "Petition of Dr. Mary E. Walker," 2; William Lawyer to Mary E. Walker, November 4, 1863, Mary Edwards Walker Papers, Box 1, SCSU (see page 95).

"Petition of Dr. Mary E. Walker," 2–3 (see page 95).

"Petition of Dr. Mary E. Walker," 5 (see page 96).

"Petition of Dr. Mary E. Walker," 6 (see page 96).

"Petition of Dr. Mary E. Walker," 6; Winkle, *Lincoln's Citadel*, 391 (see page 96).

Lida Poynter, "Dr. Mary Walker, The Forgotten Woman," unpublished manuscript, 66–67, Lida Poynter Collection, #026, Drexel University College of Medicine, Archives and Special Collections on Women in Medicine and Homeopathy; "National Union League," *National Republican* (Washington, DC), May 4, 1863, 4; https://newscomwc.newspapers.com/image/46410379/?terms=%22union%2Bleag ue%2Bof%2BWashington%22&pqsid=-TD73njyliCHtSjIOvUDLw%3A267000 %3A1699894606, accessed May 12, 2019 (see page 96).

T. M. N, "Women in the Army," *The Sibyl*, 8:3 (September 1863), 1171 (see page 97).

Kaitlin Mihalov, "Vivandieres: Forgotten Women of the Civil War," https://www.army .mil/article/11458/vivandieres_forgotten_women_of_the_civil_war, accessed May 13, 2019; Peter Cozzens, "Fearless French Mary," https://www.historynet.com/ fearless-french-mary.htm, accessed May 13, 2019 (see page 97).

T. M. N, "Women in the Army," 1171 (see page 97).

T. M. N, "Women in the Army" (see page 98).

T. M. N, "Women in the Army"; "Remarks," *The Sibyl* 8:3 (September 1863), 1171 (see page 98).

McPherson, *Battle Cry of Freedom*, 670–74; Battle of Chickamauga, www.battlefields .org/learn/civil-war/battles/chickamauga, accessed January 25, 2019 (see page 99).

McPherson, *Battle Cry of Freedom*, 675; Robert P. Broadwater, *General George H. Thomas: A Biography of the Union's "Rock of Chickamauga"* (Jefferson, NC: McFarland and Company, 2009), 161–62 (see page 99).

McPherson, *Battle Cry of Freedom*, 675–76 (see page 99).

Harris, *Dr. Mary Walker*, 46; Mary Edwards Walker to the Hon. Mr. Stanton, November 2, 1863, RG 94, Dr. Mary E. Walker file, NARA (see page 99).

McPherson, *Battle Cry of Freedom*, 676 (see page 100).

Ezra D. Simons, *The One Hundred and Twenty-Fifth New York State Volunteers: A Regimental History* (New York: The Judson Printing Company, 1888), 167–68. Biographical information on Springsteen can be found on Ancestry.com (see page 100).

Chelsea Gilmour, "The Mystery of the Civil War's Camp Casey," *Consortium News*, February 26, 2015, https://consortiumnews.com/2015/02/26/the-mystery-of-the-civil-wars-camp-casey/, accessed May 14, 2019; Alexander Springsteen to Mary Walker, November 19, 1863, Mary Edwards Walker Papers, Box 1, SCSU (see page 100).

Springsteen to Mary Walker, November 19, 1863. The captain died a year later in Key West, Florida, of yellow fever (see page 100).

"Eccentric Garb of a Lady," *Vermont Journal*, November 28, 1863, 2 (see page 101).

"Eccentric Garb of a Lady" (see page 101).

Untitled, *The Sibyl* 8:6 (December 1863), 1193; Mary Edwards Walker, "Positions that Women Ought of Right to Occupy," *The Sibyl* 8:6 (December 1863), 1196 (see page 101).

Walker, "Positions that Women Ought of Right to Occupy" (see page 101).

Walker, "Positions that Women Ought of Right to Occupy" (see page 102).

Harris, *Dr. Mary Walker*, 48; Matt Blitz, "Meet the Madam on the Mall," Smithsonian.com, February 20, 2015, www.smithsonianmag.com/history/meet-madam-mall-180954371/, accessed May 17, 2019; T. Rees Shapiro, "Washington's Civil War Madam Could Keep a Secret," *Washington Post*, April 27, 2013, www.washingtonpost.com/lifestyle/style/washingtons-civil-war-madam-could-keep-a-secret/2013/04/26/515aa746-7143-11e2-ac36-3d8d9dcaa2e2_story.html?utm_term=.a59f41d83bfe, accessed May 17, 2019 (see page 102).

Mary Edwards Walker, "Incidents Connected with the Army," Mary Edwards Walker Papers, Box 4, SCSU (see page 102).

Walker, "Incidents" (see page 103).

Walker, "Incidents" (see page 103).

Walker, "Incidents"; "A New and Benevolent Idea," *Evening Star* (Washington, DC), December 21, 1863, 2 (see page 103).

Walker, "Incidents" (see page 104).

"Lodging Rooms for Homeless Women," *National Republican* (Washington, DC), December 17, 1863, 3; "Women's Free Lodging Rooms," *National Republican* (Washington, DC), December 21, 1863, 2 (see page 104).

"A New and Benevolent Idea"; Walker, "Incidents"; Walker, "Petition of Dr. Mary E. Walker," 4 (see page 104).

"Ladies' Relief Association," *National Republican* (Washington, DC), January 18, 1864, 3; "Women's Free Lodging Rooms and Relief Association," *National Republican* (Washington, DC), January 26, 1864, 2; "Women's Relief Association," *National Republican* (Washington, DC), January 29, 1864, 2 (see page 105).

"The Women's Relief Association," *National Republican* (Washington, DC), February 2, 1864, 3; "Women's Relief Association," *National Republican* (Washington, DC), February 17, 1864, 2; "Petition of Dr. Mary E. Walker," 4 (see page 105).

"Women's Relief Association," *National Republican* (Washington, DC), February 17, 1864, 2 (see page 105).

Letter from Dr. Mary E. Walker. *National Republican* (Washington, DC). February 20, 1864, 3 (see page 105).

CHAPTER SIX: UNION SPY

Elizabeth Cady Stanton, *Eighty Years and More: Reminiscences, 1815–1897* (New York: T. Fisher Unwin, 1898), Chapter XV, https://digital.library.upenn.edu/women/stanton/years/years.html#XV, accessed May 21, 2019; Elisabeth Griffith, *In Her Own Right: The Life of Elizabeth Cady Stanton* (New York: Oxford University Press, 1984), 112 (see page 106).

Elizabeth Cady Stanton, Susan B. Anthony, and Matilda Joslyn Gage, eds., *History of Woman Suffrage. Volume II, 1861–1876* (Rochester, NY: Charles Mann, 1887), 57–66 (see page 106).

Stanton, Anthony, and Gage, eds., *History of Woman Suffrage. Volume II*, 85; Coxe poem quoted in Sharon M. Harris, *Dr. Mary Walker: An American Radical, 1832–1919* (New Brunswick, NJ: Rutgers University Press, 2009), 49 (see page 107).

Mary E. Walker, MD, to Abraham Lincoln, January 11, 1864, RG 94, Mary E. Walker file, NARA. See also Harris, *Dr. Mary Walker*, 49, and Elizabeth D. Leonard, *Yankee Women: Gender Battles in the Civil War* (New York: W. W. Norton, 1994), 129–30 (see page 107).

Mary E. Walker, MD, to Abraham Lincoln, January 11, 1864; "Petition of Dr. Mary E. Walker, Praying Compensation for Services During the Late War, August 25, 1890," *The Miscellaneous Documents of the Senate of the United States for the First Session of the Fifty-First Congress* (Washington: Government Printing Office, 1890), 13; Leonard, *Yankee Women*, 130 (see page 108).

Kenneth J. Winkle, *Lincoln's Citadel: The Civil War in Washington, DC* (New York: W. W. Norton, 2013), 216; Harris, *Dr. Mary Walker*, 50; Nic Rowan, "Nuns on the Battlefield," *Wall Street Journal*, April 26, 2019, A: 13 (see page 108).

Mary E. Walker, MD, to Abraham Lincoln, January 11, 1864; Harris, *Dr. Mary Walker*, 50; Leonard, *Yankee Women*, 130. Lincoln wrote his response on Walker's letter and sent it back to her (see page 108).

"A Gallant Female Soldier—Romantic History," *National Republican* (Washington, DC), March 16, 1864, 2. The article was republished in *The Sibyl* in April 1864 (see page 109).

"Female Soldiers," *Pittsburgh Daily Commercial*, April 23, 1864, 2; "A Gallant Female Soldier," 2 (see page 109).

"A Gallant Female Soldier," 2 (see page 109).

Leonard, *Yankee Women*, 130 (see page 110).

J. F. Farnsworth to Dr. Wood, February 30 [*sic*], 1864, RG 94, Mary E. Walker file, NARA (see page 110).

Leonard, *Yankee Women*, 131; Ira M. Rutkow, *Bleeding Blue and Gray: Civil War Surgery and the Evolution of American Medicine* (New York: Random House, 2005), 114, 242–44 (see page 111).

Rutkow, *Bleeding Blue and Gray*, 244–45 (see page 111).

David A. Rubenstein, "A Study of the Medical Support to the Union and Confederate Armies During the Battle of Chickamauga: Lessons and Implications for Today's US Army Medical Department Leaders," Master of Military Art and Science Thesis, US Army Command and General Staff College, 1990, 21–22 (see page 111).

Rubenstein, "A Study of the Medical Support," 72–74, 81–83, 103; Mary C. Gillett, *The Army Medical Department, 1818–1865* (Washington, DC: Center of Military History, 1987), 221 (see page 111).

Roberts Bartholow, Letter to the Editor, *New York Medical Journal* 5:2 (May 1867), 168, https://babel.hathitrust.org/cgi/pt?id=ien.35558002136642;view=1up;seq=191, accessed May 24, 2019 (see page 112).

Bartholow, Letter to the Editor, 168 (see page 112).

Bartholow, Letter to the Editor, 168 (see page 113).

G. Perin to Miss Mary E. Walker, March 14, 1864; Mary Walker to Andrew Johnson, September 30, 1865, RG 94, Mary E. Walker file, NARA (see page 113).

Bartholow, Letter to the Editor, 168–69; G. Perin to Headquarters Department of the Cumberland, March 11, 1864, RG 94, Mary E. Walker file, NARA (see page 113).

Mary Walker to Andrew Johnson, September 30, 1865; "Petition of Dr. Mary E. Walker," 13 (see page 113).

Mary Walker to Andrew Johnson, September 30, 1865; "Petition of Dr. Mary E. Walker," 14 (see page 114).

Mary Walker to Andrew Johnson, September 30, 1865 (see page 114).

"Petition of Dr. Mary E. Walker," 14; Mary Walker to Andrew Johnson, September 30, 1865 (see page 114).

Timothy J. Orr, ed., *Last to Leave the Field: The Life and Letters of First Sergeant Ambrose Henry Hayward, 28th Pennsylvania Volunteer Infantry* (Knoxville: University of Tennessee Press, 2010), 300 n34; Walker, 1890 Petition, 8, 14; *A History of the Eleventh Regiment (Ohio Volunteer Infantry)* (Dayton, OH: W.J. Shuey, Printer and Publisher, 1866), 162, https://archive.org/stream/historyofeleven00hort#page/n5/mode/2up, accessed May 9, 2019. Dr. Salter had been in Chattanooga since Chickamauga. See Robert D. Richardson, "Rosecrans' Staff at Chickamauga: The Significance of Major General William S. Rosecrans' Staff on the Outcome of the Chickamauga Campaign," Master of Military Art and Science Thesis, U.S. Army Command and General Staff College, 1977, 128–29, https://apps.dtic.mil/dtic/tr/fulltext/u2/a211801.pdf, accessed May 28, 2019 (see page 114).

Headquarters Department Cumberland to Surg. G. Perin, March 10, 1864, RG 94, Mary E. Walker file, NARA (see page 115).

G. Perin to Headquarters Department of the Cumberland, March 11, 1864 (see page 115).

G. Perin to Miss Mary Walker, March 11, 1864, RG 94, Mary E. Walker file, NARA (see page 115).

"Petition of Dr. Mary E. Walker," 14; Bartholow, Letter to the Editor, 169 (see page 115).

Special Orders No. 8, March 14, 1864, RG 94, Mary Walker file, NARA; Brigadier General and A.A.G. [William Whipple] to Col. D. McCook, March 17, 1864, RG 94, Mary E. Walker file, NARA; Untitled, *The Sibyl*, 8:10 (April 1864), 1228 (see page 116).

Mary Edwards Walker, "Incidents Connected with the Army," Box 4, Mary Edwards Walker Papers, SCSU; "Petition of Dr. Mary E. Walker," 14 (see page 116).

Sharon M. Harris, *Dr. Mary Walker: An American Radical, 1832–1919* (New Brunswick, NJ: Rutgers University Press, 2009), 54; Nixon B. Stewart, *Dan. McCook's Regiment, 52nd O.V.I.: A History of the Regiment, Its Campaigns and Battles* (Alliant, OH: Published by the Author, 1900), 91 (see page 116).

Walker, "Incidents"; "Petition of Dr. Mary E. Walker," 14 (see page 117).

"Petition of Dr. Mary E. Walker," 14; Walker, "Incidents" (see page 117).

Walker, "Incidents" (see page 117).

Walker, "Incidents" (see page 118).

Walker, "Incidents" (see page 118).

"Petition of Dr. Mary E. Walker," 9; Walker, "Incidents." Walker remembered the number of children differently in these two sources. Writing after the war, she always referred to McCook as a general, though he was not breveted to major general until mortally wounded at Kennesaw Mountain in late June 1864, when he was twenty-nine (see page 118).

Walker, "Incidents" (see page 119).

Adee Braun, "The Once-Common Practice of Communal Sleeping," *Atlas Obscura*, June 22, 2017, www.atlasobscura.com/articles/communal-sleeping-history-sharing-bed, accessed May 30, 2019 (see page 119).

Walker, "Incidents" (see page 119).

Walker, "Incidents" (see page 119).

Walker, "Incidents" (see page 119).

Walker, "Incidents" (see page 120).

Walker, "Incidents" (see page 120).

Walker, "Incidents" (see page 120).

Walker, "Incidents" (see page 120).

Walker "Incidents"; "Petition of Dr. Mary E. Walker," 9 (see page 121).

Walker, "Incidents" (see page 121).

Walker, "Incidents" (see page 121).

Walker, "Incidents" (see page 121).

Walker, "Incidents" (see page 122).

"Petition of Dr. Mary E. Walker," 9; Walker, "Incidents" (see page 123).

Harris, *Dr. Mary Walker*, 57; Mary Edwards Walker to Edwin Stanton, September 1862, RG 94, Mary Walker file, NARA (see page 123).

Leonard, *Yankee Women*, 136–37; E. D. Townsend to Commissioner of Pensions, May 20, 1873, RG 94, Mary E. Walker file, NARA; Stewart, *Dan. McCook's Regiment, 52nd O.V.I.*, 91 (see page 123).

Harris, *Dr. Mary Walker*, 58; "Petition of Dr. Mary E. Walker," 14; Leonard, *Yankee Women*, n103, 259; Lida Poynter, "Dr. Mary Walker, The Forgotten Woman," 85, unpublished manuscript in the Lida Poynter Collection, #026, Drexel University College of Medicine, Archives and Special Collections on Women in Medicine and Homeopathy (see page 124).

James Wylie Ratchford, *Some Reminiscences of Persons and Incidents of the Civil War* (Richmond, VA: Whittet and Shepperson, Printers, 1909), reprint edition (Toccoa, GA: The Confederate Reprint Company, 2015), 31 (see page 124).

Ratchford, *Some Reminiscences of Persons and Incidents of the Civil War*, 32; *Representative Men of the South* (Philadelphia: Chas. Robson & Co., 1880), 530; quoted in Leonard, *Yankee Women*, 139 (see page 124).

Quoted in Leonard, *Yankee Women*, 139; Poynter, "Dr. Mary Walker," 86 (see page 125).

"Isaac H. Carrington," *Richmond Dispatch*, February 1, 1887, 1; Paul J. Springer, *America's Captives: Treatment of POWs from the Revolutionary War to the War on Terror* (Lawrence: University Press of Kansas, 2010), 82 (see page 125).

Quoted in Leonard, *Yankee Women*, 139 (see page 125).

Angela M. Zombeck, "Castle Thunder Prison," *Encyclopedia Virginia*. www.encyclopediavirginia.org/Castle_Thunder_Prison#start_entry, accessed June 4, 2019 (see page 126).

DeAnne Blanton and Lauren M. Cook, *They Fought Like Demons: Women Soldiers in the Civil War* (Baton Rouge: Louisiana State University Press, 2002), 9–10, 153–54; William C. Davis, "Confederate Con Artist," *Civil War Times Magazine*, June 2017, www.historynet.com/confederate-con-artist.htm, accessed June 5, 2019 (see page 126).

Quoted in Zombeck, "Castle Thunder Prison" (see page 127).

Mary Edwards Walker, Letter to the Editor, *Richmond Dispatch*, April 26, 1864, 1; Untitled, *The Sibyl*, 8:12 (June 1864), 1245 (see page 127).

The article was reprinted in the *Buffalo* (NY) *Commercial*, May 25, 1864, 2 (see page 127).

"Dr. Mary Walker," *National Republican*, June 24, 1864, 2 (see page 127).

James M. McPherson, *Battle Cry of Freedom: The Civil War Era* (New York: Oxford University Press, 1988), 791 (see page 128).

Springer, *America's Captives*, 80 (see page 128).

General Order No. 252, July 20, 1863, War Department, http://rmc.library.cornell.edu/lincoln/exhibition/question/index.html, accessed June 5, 2019 (see page 128).

Quoted in McPherson, *Battle Cry of Freedom*, 793; Harris, *Dr. Mary Walker*, 58 (see page 128).

Dr. Mary E. Walker, "Hotel de Castle Thunder," *National Republican*, August 25, 1864, 1; Poynter, "Dr. Mary Walker," 88 (see page 129).

"Petition of Dr. Mary E. Walker," 10 (see page 129).

J. L. Burrows, "Recollections of Libby Prison," *Southern Historical Society Papers* XI (1883), 89, https://archive.org/details/southernhistoricv11sout/page/82, accessed June 5, 2019; Springer, *America's Captives*, 94–95 (see page 129).

"Petition of Dr. Mary E. Walker," 11 (see page 130).

"Petition of Dr. Mary E. Walker," 10 (see page 130).

"Petition of Dr. Mary E. Walker," 10 (see page 131).

"Petition of Dr. Mary E. Walker," 10. Additional biographical information on McKean can be found on Ancestry.com (see page 131).

"Miss Walker, the Yankee Surgeoness," *Richmond Examiner*, June 29, 1864, n.p., www.mdgorman.com/Written_Accounts/Examiner/1864/richmond_examiner_6291864a.htm, accessed June 7, 2019 (see page 131).

"Dr. Mary E. Walker," *Richmond Sentinel*, May 2, 1864, 2, www.mdgorman.com/Written_Accounts/Sentinel/1864/richmond_sentinel,_5_2_18642.htm, accessed June 7, 2019 (see page 131).

R. Finn to Edwin M. Stanton, June 30, 1864, RG 94, Mary E. Walker file, NARA (see page 131).

Poynter, "Dr. Mary Walker," 88; "Attractive Young Woman," *Richmond Whig*, July 26, 1864, 2, www.mdgorman.com/Written_Accounts/Whig/1864/richmond_whig,_7_26_1864.htm, accessed June 7, 2019 (see page 132).

Winkle, *Lincoln's Citadel* (New York: W. W. Norton, 2013), 392–93 (see page 132).

Untitled, *Buffalo* (NY) *Weekly Express*, November 8, 1864, 1; Poynter, "Dr. Mary Walker," 89 (see page 132).

Poynter, "Dr. Mary Walker," 91; "Telegraphic News," *Evening Star* (Washington, DC), August 15, 1864, 2; "Arrived," *Evening Star* (Washington, DC), August 18, 1864, 2 (see page 133).

CHAPTER SEVEN: SURGEON IN CHARGE

E. D. Townsend to Major Genl. G. H. Thomas, August 21, 1864, RG 94, Mary E. Walker file, NARA; Sharon M. Harris, *Dr. Mary Walker: An American Radical, 1832–1919* (New Brunswick, NJ: Rutgers University Press, 2009), 62 (see page 133).

Harris, *Dr. Mary Walker*, 61; Lida Poynter, "Dr. Mary Walker, The Forgotten Woman," 93, unpublished manuscript in the Lida Poynter Collection, #026, Drexel University College of Medicine, Archives and Special Collections on Women in Medicine and Homeopathy; Untitled, *National Republican*, September 16, 1864, 1 (see page 134).

"Daniel McCook, Jr.," *Ohio Civil War Central*, August 26, 2011, www.ohiocivilwarcentral.com/entry.php?rec=858, accessed June 10, 2019 (see page 135).

"Colonel Daniel McCook's Brigade at the Battle of Kennesaw Mountain, June 27th, 1864," *Iron Brigade*, June 9, 2014, https://ironbrigader.com/2014/06/09/colonel-daniel-mccooks-brigade-battle-kennesaw-mountain-june-27th-1864/, accessed June 11, 2019 (see page 135).

Re-union of Col. Dan McCook's Third Brigade, Second Division, Fourteenth A.C. (Chicago, IL: [privately printed] 1900), 85, https://archive.org/details/reunionofcoldanm

00mcco/page/n11, accessed June 11, 2019. McCook's exact words vary according to the other participants, but are very similar (see page 136).

Lowell H. Harrison, *The Civil War in Kentucky* (Lexington: University Press of Kentucky, 1975, 1 (see page 136).

Harrison, *The Civil War in Kentucky*, 2, 5 (see page 136).

Harrison, *The Civil War in Kentucky*, 4–5 (see page 137).

James M. McPherson, *Battle Cry of Freedom: The Civil War Era* (New York: Oxford University Press, 1988), 293 (see page 137).

Quoted in Harrison, *The Civil War in Kentucky*, 8 (see page 137).

Harrison, *The Civil War in Kentucky*, 9–10; McPherson, *Battle Cry of Freedom*, 293–94 (see page 137).

Harrison, *The Civil War in Kentucky*, 11; McPherson, *Battle Cry of Freedom*, 294–97 (see page 138).

McPherson, *Battle Cry of Freedom*, 297; Harrison, *The Civil War in Kentucky*, 19, 22, 32, 34, 54–55 (see page 138).

Untitled, *National Republican*, September 16, 1864, 1; Harrison, *The Civil War in Kentucky*, 77–78 (see page 138).

Quoted in Kristen L. Streater, " 'Not much a friend to traiters no matter how beautiful': The Union Military and Confederate Women in Civil War Kentucky," in Kent T. Dollar, Larry H. Whiteaker, and W. Calvin Dickinson, *Sister States, Enemy States: The Civil War in Kentucky and Tennessee* (Lexington: University Press of Kentucky, 2009), 245 (see page 139).

Streater, " 'Not much a friend to traiters no matter how beautiful'," 246 (see page 139).

Streater, " 'Not much a friend to traiters no matter how beautiful'," 247–49 (see page 139).

Kristen L. Streater, " 'She-Rebels' on the Supply Line: Gender Conventions in Civil War Kentucky," in LeeAnn Whites and Alecia P. Long, eds., *Occupied Women: Gender, Military Occupation, and the American Civil War* (Baton Rouge: Louisiana State University Press, 2009), 88, 93; Stephanie McCurry, "Enemy Women and the Laws of War in the American Civil War," *Law and History Review*, 35:3 (August 2017), 667–71 (see page 140).

Streater, " 'Not much a friend to traiters no matter how beautiful'," 250–51 (see page 140).

Streater, " 'Not much a friend to traiters no matter how beautiful'," 252–53, 256 (see page 140).

Mary E. Walker, MD, to Maj. Genl. Sherman, September 14, 1864, RG 94, Mary E. Walker file, NARA (see page 140).

Walker to Sherman, September 14, 1864 (see page 141).

R. C. Wood to Major General Sherman, September 22, 1864, RG 94, Mary E. Walker file, NARA; "Petition of Dr. Mary E. Walker, Praying Compensation for Services During the Late War, August 25, 1890," *The Miscellaneous Documents of the Senate of the United States for the First Session of the Fifty-First Congress*. Washington: Government Printing Office, 1890, 15 (see page 141).

"Dr. Susan E. Hall Barry," www.findagrave.com/memorial/9622873/susan-e-barry, accessed June 13, 2019. Sources vary on the details of Hall's medical education and whether she graduated. There is no evidence that she practiced medicine after the war (see page 142).

Edmund J. Raus Jr., ed., *Ministering Angel: The Reminiscences of Harriet A. Dada, a Union Army Nurse in the Civil War* (Gettysburg, PA: Thomas Publications, 2004), 39, 43, 46 (see page 142).

Susan E. Hall to Miss Mary E. Walker, MD, October 10, 1864, Mary Edwards Walker Papers, Box 1, SCSU (see page 143).

Order of the Assistant Surgeon General, September 24, 1864; W. T. Sherman to R. C. Wood, September 24, 1864, RG 94, Mary Walker file, NARA; Contract with a Private Physician, October 5, 1864, Mary Edwards Walker Papers, Box 3, SCSU (see page 143).

"Petition of Dr. Mary E. Walker," 12 (see page 143).

Affidavit of Gary C. Conklin, July 8, 1873, Mary Edwards Walker Papers, Box 3, SCSU; "Petition of Dr. Mary E. Walker," 12 (see page 143).

E. O. Brown to Col. R. C. Wood, October 4, 1864, RG 94, Mary E. Walker file, NARA (see page 144).

J. H. Hammond to Col. R. C. Wood, October 4, 1864, RG 94, Mary E. Walker file, NARA (see page 144).

Mary E. Walker, MD, to Lt. Col. Hammond, October 4, 1864; Order from the Assistant Surgeon General's Office, October 5, 1864, RG 94, Mary E. Walker file, NARA (see page 145).

Mary E. Walker, MD, to Lt. Col. Hammond, October 7, 1864, RG 94, Mary E. Walker file, NARA (see page 145).

Notes between Mary E. Walker and J. H. Hammond, October 7, 1864, RG 94, Mary Walker E. file, NARA (see page 145).

Order of the Assistant Surgeon General, September 24, 1864; W. T. Sherman to R. C. Wood, September 24, 1864, RG 94, Mary E. Walker file, NARA; Harris, *Dr. Mary Walker*, 63 (see page 145).

Quoted in Kenneth J. Winkle, *Lincoln's Citadel: The Civil War in Washington, DC* (New York: W. W. Norton, 2013), 401 (see page 146).

Winkle, *Lincoln's Citadel*, 399–400 (see page 146).

Winkle, *Lincoln's Citadel*, 402 (see page 147).

Mrs. E. Cobb, et al. to Col. Fairleigh, October 24, 1864; Joseph B. Brown to Col. T. B. Fairleigh, November 1, 1864, RG 94, Mary E. Walker file, NARA (see page 147).

Lt. Col. Thomas Fairleigh to Col. Wood, November 12, 1864, NARA (see page 147).

Joseph B. Brown to Lt. Col. Fairleigh, November 13, 1864, RG 94, Mary Walker file, NARA (see page 147).

Special Orders No. 21, November 13, 1864; Initialed Note in Mary E. Walker's File, February 8, 1865, RG 94, Mary Walker file, NARA (see page 148).

Dr. Mary E. Walker to Gen. Burbridge, January 6, 1864 [*sic*], RG 94, Mary E. Walker file, NARA (see page 148).

Affidavit of Gary Conklin, July 8, 1873 (see page 148).

Dr. Mary E. Walker to Lieut.-Col. Coyne, January 15, 1865, Mary Edwards Walker Papers, Box 1, SCSU (see page 149).

Dr. Mary E. Walker to Lieut.-Col. Coyne, January 15, 1865 (see page 149).

Dr. Mary E. Walker to Lieut.-Col. Coyne, January 15, 1865 (see page 149).

Dr. Mary E. Walker to Lieut.-Col. Coyne, January 15, 1865 (see page 150).

Lt. Col. Coyne to Col. Wood, January 17, 1865, Mary Edwards Walker Papers, Box 1, SCSU (see page 150).

C. C. Gray to Mary E. Walker, January 21, 1865, RG 94, Mary E. Walker file, NARA (see page 150).

Doc to Dear Doctor, January 31, 1865, Mary Edwards Walker Papers, Box 1, SCSU (see page 151).

Doc to Dear Doctor, January 31, 1865 (see page 151).

Edw. E. Phelps to Col. J. [sic] Dill, March 21, 1865; Col. Danl. J. Dill to R. C. Wood, March 21, 1865, RG 94, Mary Walker file, NARA (see page 152).

Mary E. Walker to Surgeon E. E. Phelps, March 22, 1865, RG 15, Mary E. Walker file, NARA; "Tribute to a Female Surgeon," *Racine* (WI) *Advocate*, June 7, 1865, 2. The *Advocate* reprinted this article from the Louisville *Journal* (see page 152).

Joseph B. Brown to Mary E. Walker, March 22, 1865, Mary Edwards Walker Papers, Box 3, SCSU (see page 152).

"Petition of Dr. Mary E. Walker," 15 (see page 152).

Noah Brooks, *Washington in Lincoln's Time* (New York: The Century Company, 1896), 244–45 (see page 153).

Brooks, *Washington in Lincoln's Time*, 248; McPherson, *Battle Cry of Freedom*, 849–50 (see page 153).

Geo. E. Cooper, Special Orders No. 87, April 11, 1865, RG 94, Mary E. Walker file, NARA (see page 153).

McPherson, *Battle Cry of Freedom*, 849–50 (see page 153).

CHAPTER EIGHT: THE MEDAL OF HONOR

Paul G. Ashdown, "Commission from a Higher Source: Church and State in the Civil War," *Historical Magazine of the Protestant Episcopal Church* 48:3 (September 1979), 322, 327; Trinity Episcopal Parish, http://trinityparish.com/about-us/ accessed June 25, 2019 (see page 154).

Ashdown, "Commission from a Higher Source," 328 (see page 155).

"Personal," *Pittsburgh Daily Commercial*, May 2, 1865, 2; Ashdown, "Commission from a Higher Source," 328 (see page 155).

Ashdown, "Commission from a Higher Source," 329; "Personal," *Pittsburgh Daily Commercial*, 2 (see page 156).

Lida Poynter, "Dr. Mary Walker, The Forgotten Woman," 141, unpublished manuscript in the Lida Poynter Collection, #026, Drexel University College of Medicine, Archives and Special Collections on Women in Medicine and Homeopathy (see page 156).

Poynter, "Dr. Mary Walker," 142–43 (see page 157).

James L. Swanson and Daniel R. Weinberg, *Lincoln's Assassins: Their Trial and Execution* (New York: William Morrow, 2001), 13–15 (see page 157).

Dr. George E. Cooper to Madam [Mary E. Walker], May 5, 1865, Mary Edwards Walker Papers, Box 1, SCSU (see page 157).

Surgeon Genl's Office to Mary E. Walker, June 15, 1865, RG 94, Mary E. Walker file, NARA; Sharon M. Harris, *Dr. Mary Walker: An American Radical, 1832–1919* (New Brunswick, NJ: Rutgers University Press, 2009), 69; Mary E. Walker brief, July 29, 1890, RG 94, Mary E. Walker file, NARA; Swanson and Weinberg, *Lincoln's Assassins*, 22 (see page 157).

"Miss Dr. Mary E. Walker," *New York Times*, July 9, 1865, 8. This was a reprint of the Richmond *Bulletin* article from June 28 (see page 158).

"Miss Dr. Mary E. Walker" (see page 158).

"The Fourth in Virginia," *The Liberator*, July 21, 1865, 3; Harris, *Dr. Mary Walker*, 69 (see page 158).

Swanson and Weinberg, *Lincoln's Assassins*, 24–25; Untitled, *Staunton* (VA) *Spectator*, August 8, 1865, 2 (see page 159).

A. E. Miller to Mr. Coates, July 12, 1865, Mary Edwards Walker Papers, Box 1, SCSU (see page 159).

Edward M. Richards to Dear Madam [Mary Walker], July 10, 1865, Mary Edwards Walker Papers, Box 1, SCSU (see page 159).

L. Sayer Hasbrouck to Sister Walker, July 27, 1865, Mary Edwards Walker Papers, Box 1, SCSU (see page 159).

J. W. Feeter to My Dear Major [Mary Walker], August 2, 1865, Mary Edwards Walker Papers, Box 1, SCSU (see page 160).

J. W. Feeter to My Dear Major, August 2, 1865 (see page 160).

Harris, *Dr. Mary Walker*, 70 (see page 160).

"Freedmen's Bureau Acts of 1865 and 1866," US Senate, www.senate.gov/artandhistory/history/common/generic/FreedmensBureau.htm, accessed July 1, 2019; Harris, *Dr. Mary Walker*, 70 (see page 161).

W. H. DeMotte to Andrew Johnson, June 12, 1865; D. E. Millard to Andrew Johnson, June 16, 1865; W. A. Benedict to Andrew Johnson, June 15, 1865, RG 94, Mary E. Walker file, NARA (see page 161).

Edward E. Phelps to [no name], August 10, 1865; Andrew Johnson to the Secretary of War, August 24, 1865, RG 94, Mary E. Walker file, NARA (see page 161).

The Editors of the Boston Publishing Company, *The Medal of Honor: A History of Service Above and Beyond* (Minneapolis: Zenith Press, 2014), 13–15; James H. Willbanks, ed., *America's Heroes: Medal of Honor Recipients from the Civil War to Afghanistan* (Santa Barbara, CA: ABC-CLIO, 2011), xvii–xviii (see page 162).

Edwin Stanton to the President, September 30, 1865; Andrew Johnson to the Secretary of War, October 23, 1865; Edwin Stanton to the President, October 27, 1865; Geo. E. Cooper to Surgeon General, September 10, 1865, RG 94, Mary E. Walker file, NARA (see page 162).

Edwin Stanton to the President, October 27, 1865, RG 94, Mary E. Walker file, NARA; Elizabeth D. Leonard, *Lincoln's Forgotten Ally: Judge Advocate General Joseph Holt of Kentucky* (Chapel Hill: University of North Carolina Press, 2011), 158 (see page 163).

J. Holt to Hon. E. M. Stanton, October 30, 1865, RG 94, Mary E. Walker file, NARA (see page 163).

J. Holt to Hon. E. M. Stanton, October 30, 1865 (see page 163).

J. Holt to Hon. E. M. Stanton, October 30, 1865 (see page 164).

J. Holt to Hon. E. M. Stanton, October 30, 1865 (see page 164).

J. Holt to Hon. E. M. Stanton, October 30, 1865 (see page 164).

E. D. Townsend to Miss Mary E. Walker, MD, November 2, 1865, RG 94, Mary E. Walker file, NARA; Untitled, *Manchester* (VT) *Journal*, September 7, 1865, 2; Untitled, *Rutland* (VT) *Weekly Herald*, September 14, 1865, 3 (see page 165).

"A Testimonial and Medal of Honor to Doctor Mary E. Walker," *National Republican* (Washington, DC), November 22, 1865, 2 (see page 165).

"A Testimonial and Medal of Honor to Doctor Mary E. Walker" (see page 165).

"Medal of Honor Statistics," The Army Center of Military History, https://history.army.mil/moh/mohstats.html, accessed July 4, 2019; Willbanks, *America's Heroes*, xviii, 95 (see page 166).

The Editors of the Boston Publishing Company, *The Medal of Honor*, 14–15; Poynter, "Dr. Mary Walker," 110 (see page 166).

Harris, *Dr. Mary Walker*, 28, 31; State of New York Supreme Court Decree, Mary E. Miller agt. Albert E. Miller, September 16, 1861; Nelson Whittlesey to New York Supreme Court, January 17, 1867, Mary Edwards Walker Papers, Box 2, SCSU. Additional biographical information on Miller and Maria L. Hardy can be found on Ancestry.com (see page 166).

Nelson Whittlesey to New York Supreme Court, January 17, 1867; Poynter, "Dr. Mary Walker," 110; Harris, *Dr. Mary Walker*, 76–77. Miller embraced allopathy in the 1860s, graduating from the University of Pennsylvania's medical school in 1864. See Poynter, 180–81 (see page 167).

Michael Vorenberg, *Final Freedom: The Civil War, the Abolition of Slavery, and the Thirteenth Amendment* (Cambridge: Cambridge University Press, 2001), 178, 180 (see page 167).

Vorenberg, *Final Freedom*, 188–90, 213, 228, 233 (see page 168).

Vorenberg, *Final Freedom*, 194–95 (see page 168).

Amy Dru Stanley, "Conjugal Bonds and Wage Labor: Rights of Contract in the Age of Emancipation," *Journal of American History*, 75:2 (September 1988), 471 (see page 168).

Stanley, "Conjugal Bonds and Wage Labor" (see page 168)

CHAPTER NINE: WOMEN'S RIGHTS DURING RADICAL RECONSTRUCTION

Lisa Tetrault, *The Myth of Seneca Falls: Memory and the Women's Suffrage Movement, 1848–1898* (Chapel Hill: University of North Carolina Press, 2014), 20–21 (see page 170).

Faye E. Dudden, *Fighting Chance: The Struggle Over Woman Suffrage and Black Suffrage in Reconstruction America* (New York: Oxford University Press, 2011), 79 (see page 170).

Dudden, *Fighting Chance*, 67 (see page 170).

Dudden, *Fighting Chance*, 45–46, 57, 61–62; Tetrault, *The Myth of Seneca Falls*, 21 (see page 171).

H. M. Parkhurst, *Proceedings of the Eleventh National Women's Rights Convention* (New York: Robert J. Johnston, Printer, 1866), 3, https://search-alexanderstreet-com .ezproxy.uwsp.edu/view/work/bibliographic_entity%7Cbibliographic_details %7C2533630#page/2/mode/1/chapter/bibliographic_entity%7Cdocument% 7C2533631, accessed July 12, 2019 (see page 172).

Dudden, *Fighting Chance*, 83, 87, 89 (see page 172).

Sharon M. Harris, *Dr. Mary Walker: An American Radical, 1832–1919* (New Brunswick, NJ: Rutgers University Press, 2009), 19; Lydia A. Strowbridge to Dr. Mary E. Walker, May 7, 1866, Mary Edwards Walker Papers, Box 1, SCSU (see page 172).

"Local News," *The Sun* (New York), June 5, 1866, 4; "Male versus Female Attire," *New-York Tribune*, June 14, 1866, 8; Lida Poynter, "Dr. Mary Walker, The Forgotten Woman," 118, unpublished manuscript in the Lida Poynter Collection, #026, Drexel University College of Medicine, Archives and Special Collections on Women in Medicine and Homeopathy (see page 173).

"Male versus Female Attire" (see page 173).

J. W. Feeter to Dr. Mary E. Walker, June 6, 1866, Mary Edwards Walker Papers, Box 1, SCSU (see page 173).

"Essex Market—Before Justice Mansfield," *New York Times*, June 10, 1866, 8; J. W. Feeter to Dear Dr., June 29, 1866, Mary Edwards Walker Papers, Box 1, SCSU (see page 173).

"Dr. Mary E. Walker Arrested," *Evening Telegraph* (Philadelphia), June 9, 1866, 4; "Male versus Female Attire" (see page 174).

"Male versus Female Attire"; "Essex Market—Before Justice Mansfield"; "The Dress Question," *Brooklyn Daily Eagle*, June 14, 1866, 2 (see page 174)

Harris, *Dr. Mary Walker*, 79, "Dress Reform Convention at Syracuse," *The Sun* (New York), June 23, 1866, 1 (see page 175).

Harris, *Dr. Mary Walker*, 84, 86; D. H. Craig to Friend Spear, August 7, 1866, Lida Poynter Collection, #026, Box 3, Drexel University College of Medicine, Archives and Special Collections on Women in Medicine and Homeopathy. Craig also sent a letter of introduction on Walker's behalf to AP's Liverpool agent. See D. H. Craig to Richard Stuart, August 11, 1866, Lida Poynter Collection, #026, Box 3. Harris points out that the invitation likely came from Sheldon Amos of Manchester's Social Science Association (see page 175).

Harris, *Dr. Mary Walker*, 84; Poynter, "Dr. Mary Walker," 124. Biographical information on the Dodds is available on Ancestry.com (see page 176).

Poynter, "Dr. Mary Walker," 127. Walker continued correspondence with the Dodds, even visiting with them while she was still in Great Britain. See A. Dodds to Dr. Walker, November 1, 1866, Lida Poynter Collection, #026, Box 3, Drexel University College of Medicine, Archives and Special Collections on Women in Medicine and Homeopathy (see page 176).

"The Social Science Congress," *Sydney* (N.S.W.) *Empire*, December 20, 1866, 2; Harris, *Dr. Mary Walker*, 85; Poynter, "Dr. Mary Walker," 129–30 (see page 176).

"Moncure D. Conway to My Dear Dr. Walker," October 8, 1866, Lida Poynter Collection, #026, Box 3 (see page 177).

"Moncure D. Conway to My Dear Dr. Walker," October 8, 1866; M. D. Conway to Dear Dr. Walker, November 1, 1866 (see page 177).

Poynter, "Dr. Mary Walker," 141; "American Doctress in London," *Buffalo* (NY) *Commercial*, December 21, 1866, 4. Advertisements for the talk appeared in many London newspapers, including the *Daily News*, *The Examiner*, and *The Observer*, sometimes on page 1 (see page 177).

Poynter, "Dr. Mary Walker,"141, 144; Harris, *Dr. Mary Walker*, 87–88; "Varia," *New York Medical Journal* 4 (January 1867), 314, https://babel.hathitrust.org/cgi/pt?id=ien.3 5558002136634;view=1up;seq=326, accessed May 24, 2019; "American Doctress in London" (see page 178).

Nimmo correspondence, Lida Poynter Collection, #026, Box 3; P. F. André to Dr. Mary E. Walker, November 21, 1866, Mary Edwards Walker Papers, Box 1, SCSU (see page 178).

Poynter, "Dr. Mary Walker," 144–49, 153–54; "Dr. Mary E. Walker," *The Leeds* (England) *Mercury*, April 8, 1867, 3 (see page 178).

"Varia," 314, 316 (see page 179).

"Charities," *The Observer* (London), February 24, 1867, 8 (see page 179).

"Suffrage for Women," *Border Sentinel* (Mound City, KS), June 21, 1867, 1; Harris, *Dr. Mary Walker*, 97; Poynter, "Dr. Mary Walker," 167–68 (see page 179).

"Foreign Miscellany and Gossip," *Huddersfield Chronicle and West Yorkshire Advertiser*, July 13, 1867, 3; Untitled, *Fort Wayne* (IN) *Gazette*, July 31, 1867, 4 (see page 180).

Universal Exhibition, Paris, 1867, Report of the Hon. N. M. Beckwith, Commissioner General, and President of the Commission (Washington, DC: Government Printing Office, 1868), 11–12; Poynter, "Dr. Mary Walker," 173–74; Harris, Dr. Mary Walker, 99 (see page 180).

"The Fourth of July in Paris," *New-York Tribune*, July 23, 1867, 2; Harris, *Dr. Mary Walker*, 98 (see page 180).

"The Fourth of July in Paris"; Poynter, "Dr. Mary Walker," 171 (see page 181).

"Dr. Mary Walker," *The Observer* (London), August 4, 1867, 8; "Dr. Mary E. Walker, MD, Farewell Lecture to the Ladies of London, on Ladies' Reform Dress," Lida Poynter Collection, #026, Box 3; Poynter, "Dr. Mary Walker," 174; Tetrault, *The Myth of Seneca Falls*, 20 (see page 181).

Jill Norgren, *Belva Lockwood: The Woman Who Would Be President* (New York: New York University Press, 2007), 21 (see page 182).

Amy Dru Stanley, *From Bondage to Contract: Wage Labor, Marriage, and the Market in the Age of Slave Emancipation* (New York: Cambridge University Press, 1998), 57 (see page 182).

Norgren, *Belva Lockwood*, 21 (see page 182).

Norgren, *Belva Lockwood*, 22–23; "Congressional Reports," *National Republican* (Washington, DC), December 11, 1866, 1; "Congressional," *National Republican*,

December 12, 1866; "Suffrage in the District," *National Republican*, December 14, 1866, 2; "Local News," *Evening Star* (Washington, DC), September 21, 1867, 3 (see page 182).

Norgren, *Belva Lockwood*, xiii–xvi, 3. Though Lockwood was known as Belva McNall during her first two years in Washington, I've used her second married name throughout to avoid confusion (see page 183).

Norgren, *Belva Lockwood*, 4–11 (see page 183).

Norgren, *Belva Lockwood*, 13–20 (see page 183).

Norgren, *Belva Lockwood*, 23–24 (see page 184).

Tetrault, *The Myth of Seneca Falls*, 22 (see page 184).

Tetrault, *The Myth of Seneca Falls*, 24; Dudden, *Fighting Chance*, 139 (see page 185).

Harris, *Dr. Mary Walker*, 101; Poynter, "Dr. Mary Walker," 176 (see page 185).

Dudden, *Fighting Chance*, 189; Tetrault, *The Myth of Seneca Falls*, 58–59 (see page 185).

Poynter, "Dr. Mary Walker," 198; Elizabeth Brown Pryor, *Clara Barton, Professional Angel* (Philadelphia: University of Pennsylvania Press, 1988), 151–53 (see page 186).

Norgren, *Belva Lockwood*, 25; "Universal Franchise Association," *Evening Star* (Washington, DC), May 24, 1868, 4 (see page 186).

"Local Department," *National Republican*, June 6, 1868, 3; Jas. A. Durbin to Mr. Atkinson, May 27, 1868, Mary Edwards Walker Papers, Box 1, SCSU (see page 186).

"Local Department," *National Republican*, June 6, 1868, 3 (see page 187).

"Universal Franchise Association," *Evening Star*, June 10, 1868, 4; "Universal Franchise Association," *Leavenworth* (KS) *Times*, June 19, 1868, 1 (see page 187).

Julia Archibald Holmes, "Letter to the Editor," *Evening Star*, June 12, 1868, 4. For another fine discussion of these race and gender issues, see Laura E. Free, *Suffrage Reconstructed: Gender, Race, and Voting Rights in the Civil War Era* (Ithaca: Cornell University Press, 2015), ch. 6 (see page 187).

S. R. Harrington to *Mon cher ami* [Mary Walker], July 27, 1868, Lida Poynter Collection, #026, Drexel Medical Archives (see page 188).

S. R. Harrington to *Mon cher ami*, July 27, 1868; Harris, *Dr. Mary Walker*, 103–04 (see page 188).

"A Delegation of Democratal Members of Congress Visit the President," *New York Daily Herald*, May 27, 1868, 3 (see page 189).

Dudden, *Fighting Chance*, 153–54 (see page 189).

Ann D. Gordon, "Looking for a Right to Vote: Introducing the Nineteenth Amendment," National Park Service, www.nps.gov/articles/introducing-the-19th-amendment.htm., accessed July 25, 2019 (see page 190).

"Washington Letter," *Richmond* (VA) *Dispatch*, November 13, 1868, 2; Dudden, *Fighting Chance*, 163; Tetrault, *The Myth of Seneca Falls*, 27 (see page 190).

Gordon, "Looking for a Right to Vote" (see page 190).

Mary E. Miller agt. Albert E. Miller, New York State Supreme Court, Utica, New York, Second Tuesday of January 1869 [January 12, 1869], Mary Edwards Walker Papers, Box 2, SCSU (see page 191).

Untitled, *Orleans Independent Standard* (Irasburg, VT), April 10, 1861, 1 (see page 191).

Letter from Washington, *Daily Evening Express* (Lancaster, PA), January 26, 1869, 2; Grace Greenwood [Sara Jane Clarke Lippincott], "Washington Suffrage Convention," *Philadelphia Press*, January 21, 1869, http://womenwriters.digitalscholarship.emory.edu/advocacy/content.php?level=div&id=suffragist_017&document=suffragist, accessed July 9, 2019 (see page 191).

"Local Department," *National Republican* (Washington, DC), January 20, 1869, 4; "From Washington," *Muscatine* (IA) *Weekly Journal*, January 29, 1869, 4; "From Washington," *Brooklyn* (NY) *Daily Times*, January 27, 1869, 2 (see page 191).

Grace Greenwood [Sara Jane Clarke Lippincott], "Washington Suffrage Convention" (see page 192).

Harris, *Dr. Mary Walker*, 110–11; Dudden, *Fighting Chance*, 172 (see page 192).

"Review," *Evening Star*, January 21, 1869, 4; "National Woman's Rights Convention," *New York Daily Herald*, January 22, 1869, 3 (see page 193).

"The Universal Peace Union," *Evening Star*, January 22, 1869, 4 (see page 193).

Dudden, *Fighting Chance*, 165 (see page 194).

"Woman's Meeting," *Evening Star*, January 22, 1869, 4; "Woman's Rights," *National Republican*, January 23, 1869, 4 (see page 194).

"Fortieth Congress—Third Session," *National Republican*, January 29, 1869, 1; "Woman's Rights," *National Republican*, January 23, 1869, 4; Norgen, *Belva Lockwood*, 31–32 (see page 194).

"Woman's Suffrage," *National Republican*, January 29, 1869, 4 (see page 194).

"Woman's Rights," *National Republican*, January 30, 1869, 4 (see page 194).

Dudden, *Fighting Chance*, 173; Tetrault, *The Myth of Seneca Falls*, 27–28 (see page 195).

"Woman's Dress Reform Meeting," *National Republican*, April 29, 1869, 4; "Woman's Dress Reform Convention," *New York Herald*, April 29, 1869, 5 (see page 195).

Harris, *Dr. Mary Walker*, 113; "The Inaugural Ball—Who Was There and How They Looked," *Semi-Weekly Wisconsin* (Milwaukee, WI), March 17, 1869, 1 (see page 195).

"The Dress Reformers," *New York Daily Herald*, April 30, 1869, 3 (see page 196).

Tetrault, *The Myth of Seneca Falls*, 31–33; Harris, *Dr. Mary Walker*, 115–16 (see page 196).

CHAPTER TEN: OUTCAST AND ERASED

Sharon M. Harris, *Dr. Mary Walker: An American Radical, 1832–1919* (New Brunswick, NJ: Rutgers University Press, 2009), 116–17 (see page 198).

"Working Women's Meeting," *National Republican* (Washington, DC), August 16, 1869, 4; "The Workingwomen's Movement," *Evening Star* (Washington, DC), August 16, 1869, 4 (see page 199).

Jill Norgren, *Belva Lockwood: The Woman Who Would Be President* (New York: New York University Press, 2007), 33; Belva Lockwood to the National Working Men's Convention, August 14, 1869, Mary Edwards Walker Papers, Box 1, SCSU; "National Labor Congress in Philadelphia," *New York Times*, August 15, 1869, 5; "The National Labor Congress," *New York Times*, August 17, 1869, 8 (see page 199).

"The National Labor Congress," *New York Times*, August 17, 1869, 8; "Labor: Work of the National Convention at Philadelphia," *New York Times*, August 18, 1869, 1 (see page 199).

Harris, *Dr. Mary Walker*, 117–18; "National Labor Congress," *New York Herald*, August 19, 1869, 4; "Proceedings of the National Labor Congress," *Pittsburgh Weekly Gazette*, August 21, 1869, 1; Lida Poynter, "Dr. Mary Walker, The Forgotten Woman," 194, unpublished manuscript in the Lida Poynter Collection, #026, Drexel University College of Medicine, Archives and Special Collections on Women in Medicine and Homeopathy (see page 200).

Lisa Tetrault, *The Myth of Seneca Falls: Memory and the Women's Suffrage Movement*, 1848-1898 (Chapel Hill: University of North Carolina Press, 2014), 51 (see page 200)

Poynter, "Dr. Mary Walker," 234; Untitled, *The American Israelite* (Cincinnati, OH), September 24, 1869, 7; Harris, *Dr. Mary Walker*, 119 (see page 201).

"Mrs. Livermore on Dr. Mary E. Walker," *Holt County Sentinel* (Oregon, MO), October 8, 1869, 4 (see page 201).

"Mrs. Livermore on Dr. Mary E. Walker" (see page 201).

Poynter, "Dr. Mary Walker," 190; "Girls and Gowns," *The Revolution*, October 7, 1869, 217 (see page 201).

"Female Suffrage," *St. Louis Globe-Democrat*, September 8, 1869, 4; "Meeting of the Women's Suffrage Association," *Evansville* (IN) *Daily Journal*, October 4, 1869, 1; "Letter From St. Louis," *Pittsburgh Weekly Gazette*, October 11, 1869, 2; "Personal," *National Republican* (Washington, DC), October 22, 1869, 2 (see page 202).

Untitled, *Leavenworth* (KS) *Daily Commercial*, November 21, 1869, 4 (see page 202).

"Dr. Mary Walker," *Daily Kansas Tribune* (Lawrence, KS), November 28, 1869, 3 (see page 202).

Lisa Tetrault, *The Myth of Seneca Falls*, 2 (see page 203).

Tetrault, *The Myth of Seneca Falls*, 35 (see page 203).

Mary L. Reed to Madam [Mary E. Walker], undated, Mary Edwards Walker Papers, Box 1, SCSU (see page 203).

Mary E. Walker, MD, to Mary L. Reed, December 16, 1869, Mary Edwards Walker Papers, Box 1, SCSU (see page 204).

"Dr. Mary Walker," *Memphis Daily Appeal*, January 15, 1870, 4. This newspaper reprinted the Port Gibson *Standard* article (see page 204).

Untitled, *The Vicksburg Herald*, December 29, 1869, 2; "Mrs. Dr. Walker Robbed by Highwaymen in Louisiana," *Vermont Union* (Lyndon, VT), February 18, 1870, 2; Harris, *Dr. Mary Walker*, 122; Poynter, "Dr. Mary Walker," 201 (see page 205).

"The News in Brief," *Daily Evening Express* (Lancaster, PA), February 21, 1870, 2; "Mrs. Dr. Mary Walker in Trouble," *Star Tribune* (Minneapolis, MN), February 16, 1870, 2 (see page 205).

Tetrault, *The Myth of Seneca Falls*, 48–49; Advertisement, *Times-Picayune* (New Orleans, LA), February 15, 1870, 7; "The Dr. Mary Walker Matinee," *Times-Picayune* (New Orleans, LA), February 17, 1870, 6; "Mrs. Doctor Mary Walker," *Times-Democrat* (New Orleans, LA), February 27, 1870, 7 (see page 205).

"Local Paragraphs," *Memphis* (TN) *Daily Appeal*, February 28, 1870, 4; Harris, *Dr. Mary Walker*, 123; Poynter, "Dr. Mary Walker," 208 (see page 206).

"Dr. Mary Walker Interviewed," *New Orleans Republican*, March 20, 1870, 8 (see page 206).

"Dr. Mary Walker Interviewed" (see page 206).

B. F. Luce to Dr. Mary E. Walker, April 26, 1870, Mary Edwards Walker Papers, Box 1, SCSU; "One of the Radical Strong-Minded Makes a Social Development," *Clarion-Ledger* (Jackson, MS), July 7, 1870, 1; "Doctor Mary," *Southern Home* (Charlotte, NC), June 2, 1870, 1 (see page 207).

Latimer quoted in Harris, *Dr. Mary Walker*, 124 (see page 207).

"Personal," *Buffalo* (NY) *Commercial*, October 7, 1870, 2; "Personal," *Times Union* (Brooklyn, NY), October 10, 1870, 2; Untitled, *Lancaster* (PA) *Intelligencer*, October 21, 1870, 2 (see page 208).

"A Woman Bombarded," *Walnut Valley Times* (El Dorado, KS), October 28, 1870, 2. This was a reprint of a *New York World* article (see page 208).

"Is Mr. Thacher Friendly to Woman Suffrage?" *Lawrence* (KS) *Tribune*, June 1, 1870, 4; "A Woman Bombarded" (see page 209).

Elizabeth Cady Stanton, Susan B. Anthony, and Matilda Joslyn Gage, eds., *History of Woman Suffrage. Volume II, 1861–1876* (Rochester, NY: Charles Mann, 1887), 792 (see page 209).

"Woman Suffrage," *New York Daily Herald*, January 21, 1871, 6; Jill Norgren, *Belva Lockwood: The Woman Who Would Be President* (New York: New York University Press, 2007), 56; Jason Jones, "Breathing Life into a Public Woman: Victoria Woodhull's Defense of Woman's Suffrage," *Rhetoric Review* 28:4 (2009), 352; Tetrault, *The Myth of Seneca Falls*, 57–60 (see page 209).

"The Independent," *Vermont Watchman and State Journal* (Montpelier, VT), February 8, 1871, 2 (see page 210).

"The Independent" (see page 210).

Harris, *Dr. Mary Walker*, 127 (see page 210).

"Mrs. Dr. Mary A. [*sic*] Walker," *Ogden* (UT) *Junction*, March 22, 1871, 4 (see page 211).

Mary E. Walker, MD, *Hit* (New York: The American News Company, 1871), 14–15, ch. 1; Harris, *Dr. Mary Walker*, 129–30 (see page 211).

"Suffrage Demanded," *Janesville* (WI) *Daily Gazette*, April 15, 1871, 1; Harris, *Dr. Mary Walker*, 135; Norgren, *Belva Lockwood*, 59 (see page 212).

"Suffrage Demanded"; Harris, *Dr. Mary Walker*, 135 (see page 212).

Harris, *Dr. Mary Walker*, 136; Norgren, *Belva Lockwood*, 62 (see page 212).

Harris, *Dr. Mary Walker*, 137; "Woman Suffrage," *Evening Star* (Washington, DC), January 11, 1872, 4 (see page 213).

"Washington," *Daily Commonwealth* (Topeka, KS), January 19, 1872, 2; "The Suffragists," *National Republican* (Washington, DC), January 12, 1872, 1; Untitled, *The Tribune* (Scranton, PA), January 13, 1872, 2; "Woman Suffrage" (see page 213).

"The Right of Women to Vote," *Evening Star*, January 12, 1872, 1; "The Female Swell-Mob," *Leavenworth* (KS) *Daily Commercial*, January 21, 1872, 2 (see page 214).

"Woman's Suffrage," *Pittsburgh Daily Commercial*, January 25, 1872, 1 (see page 214).

Tetrault, *The Myth of Seneca Falls*, 61–64 (see page 219).

Tetrault, *The Myth of Seneca Falls*, 89–90; Holly Jackson, *American Radicals: How Nineteenth-Century Protest Shaped the Nation* (New York: Crown, 2019), 292 (see page 215).

Quoted in Tetrault, *The Myth of Seneca Falls*, 66–67; Godfrey D. Lehman, "Susan B. Anthony Cast Her Ballot for Ulysses S. Grant," *American Heritage*, December 1985, accessed August 2, 2019, www.americanheritage.com/susan-b-anthony-cast-her-ballot-ulysses-s-grant (see page 216).

Quoted in Lehman, "Susan B. Anthony Cast Her Ballot" (see page 216).

"Virginia Minor and Women's Right to Vote," www.nps.gov/jeff/learn/historyculture/the-virginia-minor-case.htm, accessed August 24, 2019 (see page 217).

Mary E. Walker, MD, "Crowning Constitutional Argument of Mary E. Walker, MD," Oswego, NY, 1907 (originally published 1873), 3–5, Mary Edwards Walker Papers, Box 4, SCSU (see page 217).

Harris, *Dr. Mary Walker*, 143; Preston [Day] to D. D. [Mary Walker], February 18, 1873, Mary Edwards Walker Papers, Box 2, SCSU (see page 218).

"Woman Suffrage," *Evening Star*, January 17, 1873, 4; "Woman Suffrage," *Evening Star*, January 16, 1873, 4; "Woman Suffrage Association Convention," *Buffalo* (NY) *Commercial*, January 16, 1873, 3 (see page 218).

"Woman Suffrage," *Evening Star*, January 16 and January 17, 1873. Caldwell resigned his seat about two months later under a cloud of alleged bribery and corruption in the senate campaign (see page 219).

"The National Woman's Suffrage Association," *Inter-Ocean* (Chicago, IL), January 25, 1873, 4; "Woman Suffrage," *Evening Star*, January 17, 1873 (see page 219).

"Woman Suffrage," *Evening Star*, January 17, 1873, 4; Harris, *Dr. Mary Walker*, 141–42 (see page 219).

Untitled, *Leavenworth* (KS) *Daily Commercial*, February 9, 1873, 1 (see page 220).

Untitled, *Brooklyn* (NY) *Daily Eagle*, February 7, 1873, 2; Harris, *Dr. Mary Walker*, 146 (see page 220).

Untitled, *National Republican*, January 14, 1874, 2 (see page 221).

"Our Washington Letter," *Somerset* (PA) *Herald*, January 21, 1874, 2; "Woman Suffrage," *Evening Star*, January 15, 1874, 4; "Woman Suffrage," *Evening Star*, January 16, 1874, 4 (see page 221).

"The Woman Suffragists," *National Republican*, January 15, 1875, 4 (see page 222).

"The Woman Suffragists," *National Republican* (see page 222).

"Down-Trodden Woman," *National Republican*, January 16, 1875, 4 (see page 222).

"Down-Trodden Woman," *National Republican* (see page 223).

"Down-Trodden Woman," *National Republican* (see page 223).

"Woman and the Ballot," *Evening Star*, January 15, 1875, 4 (see page 223).

"Distinguished Visitors," *Daily Ogden* (UT) *Junction*, August 24, 1875, 2; "Lecture on Dress Reform," *Ogden* (UT) *Junction*, August 28, 1875, 6; "Dr. Mary Walker on Dress," *New York Daily Herald*, September 26, 1875, 6 (see page 223).

Harris, *Dr. Mary Walker*, 150; "To Men Only," *Petaluma* (CA) *Weekly Argus*, January 7, 1876, 3; Untitled, *National Republican*, January 19, 1876, 2 (see page 223).

Tetrault, *The Myth of Seneca Falls*, 98–99; Mary Frances Cordato, "Toward a New Century: Women and the Philadelphia Centennial Exhibition, 1876," *Pennsylvania Magazine of History and Biography* 107:1 (January 1983), 116–18 (see page 224).

Tetrault, *The Myth of Seneca Falls*, 100–01. See also Cordato, "Toward a New Century," 113–35 (see page 224).

"The Tilden and Hendricks Club," *Evening Star*, July 5, 1876, 1; "The Female Democracy," *National Republican*, August 7, 1876, 4 (see page 225).

"The Young Democracy," *Evening Star*, August 2, 1876, 4 (see page 225).

Tetrault, *The Myth of Seneca Falls*, 97–98, 102 (see page 225).

"Congress: The House of Representatives," *Alexandria* (VA) *Gazette*, January 16, 1877, 3; "They Want to Vote," *National Republican*, January 16, 1877, 1; "Asking for the Ballot," *National Republican*, January 17, 1877, 4 (see page 225).

"Asking for the Ballot" (see page 226).

CHAPTER ELEVEN: THE OLD "NEW WOMAN"

"Fighting the Devil," *National Republican* (Washington, DC), February 5, 1877, 4 (see page 227).

"Dr. Mary Walker 'Bounced'," *The Times* (Philadelphia, PA), March 24, 1877, 1; Untitled, *The Times* (Philadelphia, PA), March 24, 1877, 2; "Woman's Rights," *Boston Globe*, March 24, 1877, 1 (see page 228).

"Mary Walker's Clothes," *Boston Globe*, May 25, 1877, 5. This was a reprint of the *New-York Tribune* article (see page 228).

"Women's Rights," *Harrisburg* (PA) *Daily Independent*, May 26, 1877, 2; Untitled, *St. Louis Post-Dispatch*, May 30, 1877, 2; Lida Poynter, "Dr. Mary Walker, The Forgotten Woman," 251, unpublished manuscript in the Lida Poynter Collection, #026, Drexel University College of Medicine, Archives and Special Collections on Women in Medicine and Homeopathy; "An Incident at the Woman Suffrage Convention," *Topeka* (KS) *Weekly Times*, June 15, 1877, 2. This last was a reprint of a *New York World* article (see page 228).

"Current Comment," *Brooklyn* (NY) *Union*, June 27, 1877, 2 (see page 229).

John D'Emilio and Estelle B. Freedman, *Intimate Matters: A History of Sexuality in America*, 3rd ed. (Chicago: University of Chicago Press, 2012), 121 (see page 229).

A Woman Physician and Surgeon [Mary Walker], *Unmasked, or the Science of Immorality* (Philadelphia: William H. Boyd, 1878), 1, 7 (see page 230).

Walker, *Unmasked*, 10–11 (see page 230).

Walker, *Unmasked*, 17, 19, 49–50, 59, 32 (see page 230).

Holly Jackson, *American Radicals: How Nineteenth-Century Protest Shaped the Nation* (New York: Crown, 2019), 291–92 (see page 231).

"Dr. Mary Walker Triumphs," *Boston Globe*, December 10, 1877, 1; "Woman Suffragists at the Capitol," *Evening Star* (Washington, DC), January 10, 1878, 1; Lisa Tetrault, *The Myth of Seneca Falls: Memory and the Women's Suffrage Movement, 1848–1898* (Chapel Hill: University of North Carolina Press, 2014), 103 (see page 231).

"Woman Suffragists at the Capitol" (see page 232).

"Woman Suffragists at the Capitol," *Evening Star*, January 12, 1878, 1; "Woman's Rights," *Alexandria* (VA) *Gazette*, January 16, 1878, 2; Tetrault, *The Myth of Seneca Falls*, 103 (see page 232).

"Utah Matters," *Nebraska State Journal*, January 29, 1878, 1; "The Marked Ballot," *Salt Lake Tribune*, January 30, 1878, 2 (see page 232).

Untitled, *Inter Ocean* (Chicago, IL), March 7, 1878, 4; "Dr. Mary Walker's Appeal," *Times Union* (Brooklyn, NY), March 8, 1878, 4; Untitled, *Evening Star*, March 8, 1878, 4 (see page 233).

"Personal Mentions," *Boston Globe*, April 18, 1878, 4; "Personal," *Star Tribune* (Minneapolis, MN), November 18, 1878, 2; Sharon M. Harris, *Dr. Mary Walker: An American Radical, 1832–1919* (New Brunswick, NJ: Rutgers University Press, 2009), 162–64; Untitled, *The Fort Wayne* (IN) *Sentinel*, August 3, 1878, 4 (see page 233).

Untitled, *Buffalo* (NY) *Morning Express*, July 22, 1878, 2 (see page 233).

" 'Dr.' Mary Walker Arrested," *New York Daily Herald*, December 6, 1878, 5 (see page 233).

Jill Norgren, *Belva Lockwood: The Woman Who Would Be President* (New York: New York University Press, 2007), 83; "Politics," *Buffalo* (NY) *Courier*, April 30, 1879, 1; "Last Speeches of the Debate," *Daily Gazette* (Wilmington, DE), May 21, 1879, 1 (see page 234).

Tetrault, *The Myth of Seneca Falls*, 87–89; Harris, *Dr. Mary Walker*, 182 (see page 234).

"Tri-State Reunion," *Wheeling* (WV) *Daily Intelligencer*, August 29, 1879, 1 (see page 234).

"Tri-State Reunion" (see page 235).

"Letter from Washington," *Centre Democrat* (Bellefonte, PA), January 29, 1880, 4; "Politics," *Topeka* (KS) *Daily Capital*, January 26, 1880, 1 (see page 235).

"Dr. Mary Walker at the Polls," *Onaga* (KS) *Democrat*, November 25, 1880, 1. This article was originally published in the *New York Sun* (see page 236).

"A New Applicant," *National Republican* (Washington, DC), June 30, 1881, 2. This article appeared in many papers across the country (see page 236).

"History of Woman Suffrage," *Boston Post*, May 20, 1881, 1 (see page 237).

Elizabeth Cady Stanton, Susan B. Anthony, and Matilda Joslyn Gage, eds., *History of Woman Suffrage. Volume II, 1861–1876* (Rochester, NY: Charles Mann, 1887), 20, 360, 813 (see page 237).

Untitled, *Decatur* (IL) *Daily Republican*, January 14, 1882, 2; Harris, *Dr. Mary Walker*, 173 (see page 237).

"Our Washington Letter," *Valley Sentinel* (Carlisle, PA), May 4, 1882, 4; "The Woman's National Labor League," *Philadelphia Inquirer*, September 8, 1882, 8; " 'Dr.' Mary Walker Dismissed," *Journal Times* (Racine, WI), July 13, 1883, 1; Harris, *Dr. Mary Walker*, 174–76 (see page 237).

Harris, *Dr. Mary Walker*, 182 (see page 238).

Rob Schorman, *Selling Style: Clothing and Social Change at the Turn of the Century* (Philadelphia: University of Pennsylvania Press, 2003), n. 80, 183; Charlotte P. Stetson, "Why Women Do Not Reform Their Dress," http://essays.quotidiana.org/gilman/why_women_do_not_reform/, accessed May 24, 2019 (see page 238).

Tetrault, *The Myth of Seneca Falls*, 167 (see page 239).

"Popular Entertainments," *Philadelphia Inquirer*, April 4, 1887, 3; "Dr. Mary Walker's New Role," *New York Times*, March 8, 1887, 1; M. S. Robinson to Mary Walker,

MD, December 13, 1887, Mary Edwards Walker Papers, Box 2, SCSU; Harris, *Dr. Mary Walker*, 181; Austin's Nickelodeon advertisement, *Boston Globe*, April 27, 1890, 11 (see page 239).

"Memorial Day," *Sunday Leader* (Wilkes-Barre, PA), September 18, 1887, 1; "Dr. Mary Walker's Views," *Indianapolis Journal*, April 12, 1887, 4 (see page 240).

"The Woman's Congress," *Evening Star*, March 26, 1888, 5; "For Female Suffrage," *Buffalo* (NY) *Evening News*, March 26, 1888, 1 (see page 240).

Tetrault, *The Myth of Seneca Falls*, 147–48, 150–51; Harris, *Dr. Mary Walker*, 182–83; National Woman Suffrage Association, *International Council of Women* (Washington, DC: Rufus H. Darby, Printer, 1888), 322–23, https://archive.org/details/ofinternatreport00interich/page/n7, accessed August 15, 2019 (see page 241).

Tetrault, *The Myth of Seneca Falls*, 155–57 (see page 241).

Tetrault, *The Myth of Seneca Falls*, 162–64, 166; "Mrs. Stanton's Farewell," *Evening Star*, February 18, 1890, 2 (see page 241).

Robert Graves, "Of Dr. Mary E. Walker," *Topeka* (KS) *Daily Capital*, April 20, 1890, 10 (see page 242).

"A Worthy Crank," *St. Joseph* (MO) *Daily News*, April 29, 1890, 1 (see page 242).

"Dr. Mary Walker Heard From," *St. Louis Globe-Democrat*, September 13, 1890, 1 (see page 242).

"Mary Walker for Congress," *Boston Globe*, October 10, 1890, 6; "On the First Ballot," *Indianapolis Journal*, June 23, 1892, 1; "Dr. Mary Breathing Fire," *Boston Globe*, June 20, 1892; Harris, *Dr. Mary Walker*, 194–95 (see page 243).

"A Costume Department," *Buffalo* (NY) *Commercial*, June 27, 1892, 1 (see page 243).

"A Costume Department"; R. E. A. Dorr, "The Exposition of 1893," *Arthur's Home Magazine*, 62 (July 1892), 599–600, https://babel.hathitrust.org/cgi/pt?id=njp.32101064461963&view=2up&seq=626, accessed August 16, 2019 (see page 243).

"A Bloomer Colony," *Leavenworth* (KS) *Standard*, September 30, 1895, 1; "The New Woman Factory," *Lebanon* (PA) *Semi-Weekly News*, September 30, 1895, 1 (see page 244).

"Dr. Mary Walker," *Evening Star*, January 13, 1897, 2 (see page 244).

"She Wished to Register," *Washington Times*, January 14, 1897, 3; "The Congress of Mothers," *Evening Times*, February 17, 1897, 1, 5; "Their Labors Completed," *Washington Times*, February 20, 1897, 1, 5; Frances E. Willard and Mary A. Livermore, eds., *American Women* (New York: Mast, Crowell & Kirkpatrick), 740, https://babel.hathitrust.org/cgi/pt?id=yale.39002004528981&view=2up&seq=8, accessed August 16, 2019 (see page 245).

Tetrault, *The Myth of Seneca Falls*, 174–76 (see page 245).

"Not a Senator Appears," *Washington Times*, January 9, 1898, 9; "Works for Queen Lil," *Berkshire Eagle* (Pittsfield, MA), February 12, 1898, 2, Harris, *Dr. Mary Walker*, 211–12 (see page 245).

"Want Their Rights," *Evening Star*, February 16, 1898, 7, 9 (see page 246).

Mary E. Walker, MD, "Crowning Constitutional Argument," 1907, Mary Edwards Walker Papers, Box 4, SCSU (see page 246).

Harris, *Dr. Mary Walker*, 214–15, 217; "Her Thirty Years' Experience in Trousers," *San Francisco Call*, March 20, 1898, 20 (see page 246).

"Dr. Mary E. Walker," *Our Mountain Home* (Talladega, AL), September 21, 1904, 10; "Girl Wore Trousers," *Iola* (KS) *Daily Record*, February 1, 1905, 1; "Wants to Wear Skirts," *Sedalia* (MO) *Weekly Democrat*, April 20, 1905, 10; Harris, *Dr. Mary Walker*, 234–35 (see page 247).

Joseph Richardson Parke, MD, *Human Sexuality: A Medico-Literary Treatise on the Laws, Anomalies, and Relations of Sex with Especial Reference to Contrary Sexual Desire* (Philadelphia: Professional Publishing, 1906), 264, https://archive.org/details/humansexualitya00parkgoog/page/n236, accessed August 17, 2019 (see page 247).

Walker, "Crowning Constitutional Argument" (see page 248).

"Campaign Like a Real Farce," *Post-Standard* (Syracuse, NY), March 8, 1910, 7; "Woman Suffrage Fight in Albany," *Buffalo Commercial*, March 9, 1910, 1 (see page 248).

Harris, *Dr. Mary Walker*, 243 (see page 248).

"After Jane Addams," *Evening Star*, December 2, 1912, 4 (see page 249).

"Dr. Mary Walker Will Be 'Snubbed'," *Inter Ocean* (Chicago, IL), December 3, 1912, 1; "Man's Attire Lands Dr. Walker in Jail," *Inter Ocean* (Chicago, IL), February 2, 1913 (see page 249).

"Dr. Mary Walker Enters Vaudeville," *Journal and Tribune* (Knoxville, TN), January 6, 1914, 11; "Suffragists Hurl Political Threat," *Boston Globe*, March 3, 1914, 1; Harris, *Dr. Mary Walker*, 247–48 (see page 250).

Robert Graves, "Of Dr. Mary E. Walker;" "Refused Hand of Pres. Arthur," *New Castle* (PA) *News*, March 28, 1914, 13 (see page 250).

Ida Husted Harper, ed., *History of Woman Suffrage, Volume 5, 1900–1920* (New York: National American Woman Suffrage Association, 1922), 438, https://babel.hathitrust.org/cgi/pt?id=njp.32101075729044&view=2up&seq=468, accessed July 12, 2019; "Suffragists and Antis See Wilson," *The Sun* (New York), December 15, 1915, 6 (see page 250).

"25,000 Get in Line for Parade of Suffragists in Face of a Biting Wind," *The Sun* (NY), October 24, 1915, 1; Mary Marshall, "Western Women Bring Cheer to District Suffragettes," *Washington Herald*, December 7, 1915, 10 (see page 251).

"Dr Mary Walker Tells President She Decries 'Silent Sentinel' Idea," *Boston Globe*, January 17, 1917, 3; " 'Suffs Are Simple,' Says Dr. Mary Walker," *Washington Herald*, January 29, 1917, 10 (see page 251).

Ida Husted Harper, "Answers Dr. Mary Walker," *Washington Herald*, February 4, 1917, 10 (see page 252).

"History," Congressional Medal of Honor Society, www.cmohs.org/medal-history.php, accessed August 19, 2019; Harris, *Dr. Mary Walker*, 251 (see page 252).

"An Act Granting an Increase of Pension to Mary E. Walker, July 7, 1898," Mary E. Walker file, RG 15, NARA; Dr. Mary E. Walker, MD, to [Department of the Interior, Bureau of Pensions], June 19, 1916; G. M. Saltzgaber to Dr. Mary E. Walker, June 26, 1916, In the Case of Mary Edwards Walker, RG 94, NARA (see page 252).

"Asks Kaiser to Confer," *Brooklyn* (NY) *Citizen*, April 8, 1917, 1 (see page 253).

"Mary Walker Ill," *Washington Herald*, May 5, 1917, 2; Harris, *Dr. Mary Walker*, 251 (see page 253).

EPILOGUE: THE MEDAL OF HONOR RESTORED

Bess Furman, "Portraits Honor Medical Women," *New York Times*, October 27, 1957, 84 (see page 255).

Judy Burke, "Slighted Civil War Doctor May Get Medal of Honor Back," *Northwest Arkansas Times* (Fayetteville, AR), May 23, 1976, 11; Edith P. Mayo to Mrs. Jack Wilson, March 6, 1974, In the Case of Mary Edwards Walker, RG 94, NARA; City of Oswego, New York, "Motions, Resolutions and Notices," April 26, 1976, In the Case of Mary Edwards Walker, RG 94, NARA (see page 257).

Army Board for Correction of Military Records, Transcript of Hearing, Case of Mary Edwards Walker, May 4, 1977, 16 (see page 257).

Army Board for Correction of Military Records, 16, 24 (see page 257).

"Move Afoot to Restore Medal to Mary Walker," *Courier News* (Blytheville, AR), June 29, 1977, 29; "Medal Restored to Historic Surgeon," *Pocono Record* (Stroudsburg, PA), June 11, 1977, 2; "Army Restoring Medal of Honor to Lady Surgeon," *Odessa* (TX) *American*, June 11, 1977, 2; Colonel J. F. Fahey to Navy and Old Army Branch, National Archives and Records Services, July 7, 1977, In the Case of Mary Edwards Walker, RG 94, NARA; "Medal of Honor Is Restored to Civil War Woman Doctor," *Washington Post*, June 11, 1977, n.p. (see page 258).

Lisa Tetrault, *The Myth of Seneca Falls: Memory and the Women's Suffrage Movement, 1848–1898* (Chapel Hill: University of North Carolina Press, 2014), 193–94; Jo Freeman, "The National Women's Conference in Houston, 1977," JoFreeman .com, www.jofreeman.com/photos/IWY1977.html, accessed August 22, 2019 (see page 258).

Tetrault, *The Myth of Seneca Falls*, 194; Freeman, "The National Women's Conference in Houston, 1977" (see page 259).

Marjorie J. Spruill, *Divided We Stand: The Battle Over Women's Rights and Family Values that Polarized American Politics* (New York: Bloomsbury, 2017), ch. 1 (see page 259).

INDEX

A

abolition, xii, 2, 3, 22, 23, 29, 33, 59, 60, 89, 94, 106, 146, 160, 167, 169, 171, 210, 214

Abzug, Bella, 258

"A Colony for New Women", 244

activists, women's rights, 30, 58, 106, 168, 170, 182, 196, 200, 201, 212, 225

Acton, Thomas, 173, 174

Act Prohibiting the Return of Slaves, 61

Addams, Jane, 248, 249

advocates, "pro-family," 259

advocates, women's rights, 4, 6, 28, 169, 185, 197

African Americans
  and unions, 198
  citizenship, 10, 106
  contraband workers, 55
  equal rights, 192
  freed slaves, 59, 67, 85
  ladies' aid societies, 3
  men's suffrage, 170, 171, 181, 184, 186, 190, 193, 196, 205, 217, 225
  military, 2, 82, 100, 128, 138
  slavery. *See* slavery
  suffrage, 169, 182, 184
  women's job training, 161
  women's suffrage, 171, 232

Alcott, Louisa May, 2, 3, 19

Alexander Jr., Clifford, 257

Alexander, George W., 126

allopathic medical schools, 33, 51, 167

allopathy, 7, 26, 32, 48, 111

American Anti-Slavery Society, 22, 80

American Civil Liberties Union, 256

American Equal Rights Association (AERA), 172, 182, 183, 184, 185, 189, 196

American Hydropathic Institute, 27

American Phrenological Journal, 51

American Red Cross, 257

American Revolution, 22, 23, 101, 185, 212

American Woman Suffrage Association (AWSA), 196, 197, 200, 202, 203, 207, 209, 210, 215, 225, 240, 241, 247

Ames, Daniel, 55

Ames, Mary Clemmer, 55

Amputation, 49, 50, 77, 114

Anderson, Mary, 212

Andrews, James, 166

Andrews Raiders, 166

Angelou, Maya, 259

Antebellum Period, vii, 21, 28, 32, 66

Antebellum Reform, 2, 3

Anthony, Susan B., xiii, 22, 30, 106, 171, 172, 182, 183, 184, 186, 188, 189, 190, 192, 193, 194, 195, 196, 197, 198, 199, 200, 201, 202, 203, 208, 209, 212, 213, 214, 215, 216, 217, 218, 219, 221, 222, 224, 225, 226, 227, 233, 235, 236, 240, 241, 243, 245, 246, 247, 248, 251

Antietam, 61, 62, 64, 65, 67, 69, 70, 74, 75, 84, 86, 87, 142

Antislavery, 9, 10, 20, 22, 23, 27, 29, 68, 158, 177

Aquia Creek, 16, 75, 82, 83, 84, 142

Armory Square Hospital, 89, 141, 142

Army of Northern Virginia, 69, 85, 86

Army of Tennessee, xi, 99, 123, 124, 135

Army of the Cumberland, viii, 98, 99, 111, 113, 135, 161

Army of the Ohio, ix, 53

ABOUT THE AUTHOR

THERESA KAMINSKI HOLDS A PhD IN HISTORY FROM THE UNIVERSITY of Illinois at Urbana-Champaign. For more than twenty-five years she worked as a history professor at a state university, where she taught courses on American women's history, feminism and women's rights, women and war, and historical writing and methodology. She is the author of a trilogy of nonfiction history books on American women in the Philippine Islands during World War II, the most recent of which is *Angels of the Underground: The American Women Who Resisted the Japanese in the Philippines in World War II*. She is currently completing the first full-length biography of America's favorite cowgirl, Dale Evans. Theresa lives with her husband in a small town outside of Madison, Wisconsin.